W9-BWG-880

NATION OF NATIONS

THE
ETHNIC
EXPERIENCE
AND THE
RACIAL
CRISIS

edited by
PETER I. ROSE
Smith College

Random House
New York

NATION OF NATIONS

THE ETHNIC EXPERIENCE AND THE RACIAL CRISIS

N 106

For Anne and Alfred

I am of old and young, of the foolish as much as the wise,
Regardless of others, ever regardful of others,
Maternal as well as paternal, a child as well as a man,
Stuff'd with the stuff that is coarse and stuff'd with the stuff
    that is fine,
One of the Nation of many nations, the smallest the same
    and the largest the same,
A Southerner soon as a Northerner, a planter nonchalant
    and hospitable down by the Oconee I live,
A Yankee bound my own way ready for trade, my joints
    the limberest joints on earth and the sternest joints on
    earth,
A Kentuckian walking the vale of the Elkhorn in my deer-
    skin leggings, a Louisianian or Georgian,
A boatman over lakes or bays or along coasts, a Hoosier,
    Badger, Buckeye;
At home on Kanadian snow-shoes or up in the bush, or
    with fishermen off Newfoundland,
At home in the fleet of ice-boats, sailing with the rest and
    tacking,
At home on the hills of Vermont or in the woods of Maine,
    or the Texan ranch,
Comrade of Californians, comrade of free North-West-
    erners, (loving their big proportions,)
Comrade of raftsmen and coalmen, comrade of all who
    shake hands and welcome to drink and meat,
A learner with the simplest, a teacher of the thoughtfullest,
A novice beginning yet experient of myriads of seasons,
Of every hue and caste am I, of every rank and religion,
A farmer, mechanic, artist, gentleman, sailor, quaker,
Prisoner, fancy-man, rowdy, lawyer, physician, priest.

I resist any thing better than my own diversity,
Breathe the air but leave plenty after me,
And am not stuck up, and am in my place.

(The moth and the fish-eggs are in their place,
The bright suns I see and the dark suns I cannot see are
    in their place,

The palpable is in its place and the impalpable is in its
    place.)

from "Song of Myself"
Leaves of Grass
Walt Whitman

EDITOR'S NOTE

"I'm just an Irish, Negro, Jewish, Italian, French and English,
Spanish, Russian, Chinese, Polish, Scotch, Hungarian, Litvak,
Swedish, Finnish, Canadian, Greek and Turk and Czech and
double Czech American."

from *Ballad for Americans* by John Latouche and
Earl Robinson*

This book is about the strains experienced by the various peoples who
comprise the American nation. It is a collection of essays and articles by
novelists and journalists, historians and sociologists, offering different
views, perspectives, and positions on several important areas of scholarly
and practical concern.

—Is America (or has it ever been) a melting pot? Or is the country more
aptly characterized by the metaphor of a seething cauldron?
—How similar are the experiences of colored minorities to those of the
white immigrants who came to these shores? Can we speak of both categories in the same terms or must new models be devised for assessing
black and brown and red history in contrast to white?
—What happens when people long oppressed begin to challenge the
system which, in many ways, has kept them in servitude? With whom
do they have to compete most directly? Who wins? Who loses?

These questions and many others are posed in the middle three sections
of this book. The reader is advised, however, to begin his study at the
beginning where, by way of prologue, ten vignettes are offered that set
the stage. These portraits include both fictional and autobiographical accounts by such authors as James Fenimore Cooper, Abraham Cahan,
James T. Farrell, Jerre Mangione, Richard Wright, and Piri Thomas.
Each describes (directly or through the words of his character) what it
meant to grow up in America—a promised land for some, a purgatory for
others, and, for still others . . . Babylon.

This volume contains two end notes, the sort that can best be under-

---

stood only *after* careful study of the issues raised in the three middle sections. Here Ralph Levine and James Baldwin portray some of the human consequences of the contemporary American racial crisis. Each has profound meaning for the current social scene.

Nation of Nations was conceived and designed as a companion to my book, *They and We,* originally published by Random House in 1964 and now being revised and enlarged.

Together, it is hoped, these two volumes will assist the American student-reader and his teacher to better understand the complex nature of racial and ethnic relations in the United States and the controversies that continue to concern social scientists, policy makers, and laymen alike. It is also my hope that these volumes will give foreign scholars an opportunity to gain some insight into the ethnic crosscurrents that flow (and long have flowed) in American society.

October 1971   Peter I. Rose

ACKNOWLEDGEMENTS

To the authors whose work is printed or reprinted here,

To my friends, Ted Caris, Arthur Strimling, and David Bartlett, who pressed me to do this volume as companion to *They and We*,

And, especially, to Lynne Farber of Random House,

My grateful thanks.

Peter I. Rose

South Wellfleet, Massachusetts

CONTENTS

Part Four
Competition and Conflict

Part Five
Ending Notes

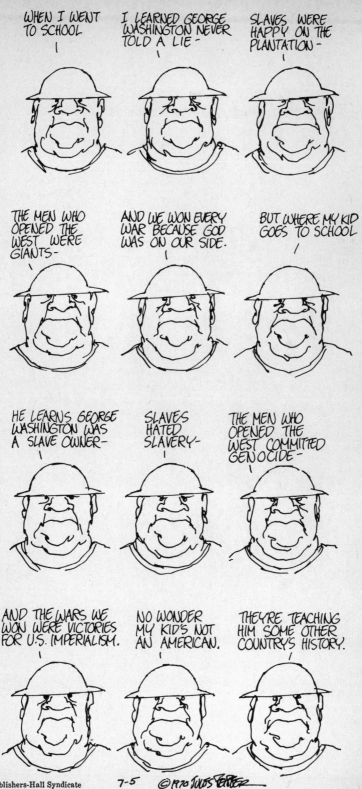

7-5 ©1970 Jules Feiffer

AMERICA, AMERICA ★★★
ECHOES FROM THE PAST

In which the voices of observers and
participants in the quest for a place in
America are heard through the pages of
autobiographies, novels, and essays
written in days gone by.

THE DEERSLAYER
James Fenimore Cooper

American individualism was a dominant literary theme
in the middle of the eighteenth century. James Fenimore
Cooper's character "Deerslayer" embodied the quint-
essential Emersonian figure—rugged and rational, concerned with the rights of man and particularly with man
in his natural state.

Here, in a brief selection from *The Deerslayer*, the hero
exchanges ideas on white men and others with his companion and offers his protoanthropological views on
cultural relativism. The dialogue also reflects certain
persisting concerns about who is to judge the deeds of
those who differ from oneself.

As they [Deerslayer and Hurry Harry] went paddling down the lake a hot
discussion was maintained concerning the respective merits of the pale-
faces and the red-skins. Hurry had all the prejudices and antipathies of a
white hunter, who generally regards the Indian as a sort of natural competitor, and not unfrequently as a natural enemy. As a matter of course, he
was loud, clamorous, dogmatical, and not very argumentative. Deerslayer,
on the other hand, manifested a very different temper; proving, by the
moderation of his language, the fairness of his views, and the simplicity of
his distinctions, that he possessed every disposition to hear reason, a strong,
innate desire to do justice, and an ingenuousness that was singularly in-
disposed to have recourse to sophisms to maintain an argument, or to
defend a prejudice. Still, he was not altogether free from the influence of
the latter feeling. This tyrant of the human mind, which rushes on its prey
through a thousand avenues, almost as soon as men begin to think and
feel, and which seldom relinquishes its iron sway until they cease to do
either, had made some impression on even the just propensities of this

individual, who probably offered in these particulars a fair specimen of what absence from bad example, the want of temptation to go wrong, and native good feeling, can render youth.

"You will allow, Deerslayer, that a Mingo is more than half devil," cried Hurry, following up the discussion with an animation that touched closely on ferocity, "though you want to over-persuade me that the Delaware tribe is pretty much made up of angels. Now I gainsay that proposal, consarning white men, even. All white men are not faultless, and therefore all Indians *can't* be faultless. And so your argument is out at the elbow in the start. But this is what I call reason. Here's three colors on 'arth: white, black, and red. White is the highest color, and therefore the best man; black comes next, and is put to live in the neighborhood of the white man, as tolerable, and fit to be made use of; and red comes last, which shows that those that made 'em never expected an Indian to be accounted as more than half human."

"God made all three alike, Hurry."

"Alike! Do you call a nigger like a white man, or me like an Indian?"

"You go off at half-cock, and don't hear me out. God made us all, white, black, and red; and, no doubt, had his own wise intentions in coloring us differently. Still, he made us, in the main, much the same in feelin's; though I'll not deny that he gave each race its gifts. A white man's gifts are christianized, while a red-skin's are more for the wilderness. Thus, it would be a great offence for a white man to scalp the dead; whereas it's a signal vartue in an Indian. Then ag'in, a white man cannot amboosh women and children in war, while a red-skin may. 'Tis *cruel* work, I'll allow; but for them it's *lawful* work; while for *us,* it would be grievous work."

"That depends on your inimy. As for scalping, or even skinning a savage, I look upon them pretty much the same as cutting off the ears of wolves for the bounty, or stripping a bear of its hide. And then you're out significantly, as to taking the poll of a red-skin in hand, seeing that the very Colony has offered a bounty for the job; all the same as it pays for wolves' ears and crows' heads."

"Ay, and a bad business it is, Hurry. Even the Indians themselves cry shame on it, seeing it's ag'in a white man's gifts. I do not pretend that all that white men do is properly christianized, and according to the lights given them, for then they would be what they *ought* to be; which we know they are not; but I will maintain that tradition, and use, and color, and laws, make such a difference in races as to amount to gifts. I do not deny that there are tribes among the Indians that are nat'rally pervarse and wicked, as there are nations among the whites. Now, I account the Mingos as belonging to the first, and the Frenchers, in the Canadas, to the last. In a state of lawful warfare, such as we have lately got into, it is a duty to keep down all compassionate feelin's, so far as life goes, ag'in either; but when it comes to scalps, it's a very different matter."

"Just hearken to reason, if you please, Deerslayer, and tell me if the Colony can make an onlawful law? Isn't an onlawful law more ag'in natur' than scalpin' a savage? A law can no more be onlawful, than truth can be a lie."

"That *sounds* reasonable; but it has a most onreasonable bearing, Hurry. Laws don't all come from the same quarter. God has given us his'n, and some come from the Colony, and others come from the King and Parliament. When the Colony's laws, or even the King's laws, run ag'in the laws of God, they get to be onlawful, and ought not to be obeyed. I hold to a white man's respecting white laws, so long as they do not cross the track of a law comin' from a higher authority; and for a red man to obey his own red-skin usages, under the same privilege. But 'tis useless talking, as each man will think for himself, and have his say agreeable to his thoughts."

THE EAST SIDE
Henry James

Henry James, American novelist and traveler, spent twenty years of his life, from 1883 to 1904, away from his native land. Between his departure and return the country had undergone profound changes, most noticeably, for James, in the quality of urban life. When he left it was English (or Anglo-American) in style and in sound. When he came home the modest polis had been transformed into a bustling metropolis, and homogeneity no longer marked the character of the social structure.
The old streets of the cities, particularly along the eastern seaboard, had become warrens of poor immigrants, polyglot centers that, to the newcomers, were way stations on the road to success. To others, like James, they became bewildering and unpleasant symptoms of the loss of a more pristine and familiar America.
James was especially moved and revulsed by the Jews he observed on the East Side. Here is his firsthand account of impressions gleaned from visiting that "outpost of Israel." The reader should note how similar some of his phraseology is to that of more recent writers who describe other ghetto dwellers—such as those who now call Harlem home.

New York really, I think, is all formidable foreground; or, if it be not, there is more than enough of this pressure of the present and the immediate to cut out the close sketcher's work for him. These things are a thick growth all round him, and when I recall the intensity of the material picture in the dense Yiddish quarter, for instance, I wonder at its not having forestalled, on my page, mere musings and, as they will doubtless be called, moonings. There abides with me, ineffaceably, the memory of a summer evening spent there by invitation of a high public functionary domiciled on the spot—to the extreme enhancement of the romantic interest his visitor found him foredoomed to inspire—who was to prove one of the most liberal of hosts and most luminous of guides. I can scarce help it if this brilliant personality, on that occasion the very medium itself through which the whole spectacle showed, so colours my impressions that if I speak, by intention, of the facts that played into them I may really but reflect the rich talk and the general privilege of the hour. That accident moreover must take its place simply as the highest value and the strongest note in the total show—so much did it testify to the quality of appealing, surrounding life. The sense of this quality was already strong in my drive, with a companion, through the long, warm June twilight, from a comparatively conventional neighbourhood; it was the sense, after all, of a great swarming, a swarming that had begun to thicken, infinitely, as soon as we had crossed to the East side and long before we had got to Rutgers Street. There is no swarming like that of Israel when once Israel has got a start, and the scene here bristled, at every step, with the signs and sounds, immitigable, unmistakable, of a Jewry that had burst all bounds. That it has burst all bounds in New York, almost any combination of figures or of objects taken at hazard sufficiently proclaims; but I remember how the rising waters, on this summer night, rose, to the imagination, even above the housetops and seemed to sound their murmur to the pale distant stars. It was as if we had been thus, in the crowded, hustled roadway, where multiplication, multiplication of everything, was the dominant note, at the bottom of some vast sallow aquarium in which innumerable fish, of over-developed proboscis, were to bump together, for ever, amid heaped spoils of the sea.

The children swarmed above all—here was multiplication with a vengeance; and the number of very old persons, of either sex, was almost equally remarkable; the very old persons being in equal vague occupation of the doorstep, pavement, curbstone, gutter, roadway, and every one alike using the street for overflow. As overflow, in the whole quarter, is the main fact of life—I was to learn later on that, with the exception of some shy corner of Asia, no district in the world known to the statistician has so many inhabitants to the yard—the scene hummed with the human presence beyond any I had ever faced in quest even of refreshment; producing part of the impression, moreover, no doubt, as a direct consequence of the intensity of the Jewish aspect. This, I think, makes the individual Jew more of a concentrated person, savingly possessed of everything that is in him, than any other human, noted at random—or is it simply, rather, that the unsurpassed strength of the race permits of the chopping into myriads of fine fragments without loss of race-quality? There are small strange animals, known to natural history, snakes or worms, I believe, who, when cut into pieces, wriggle away contentedly and live in the snippet as completely as in the whole. So the denizens of the New York Ghetto, heaped as thick as the splinters on the table of a glass-blower, had each, like the fine glass particle, his or her individual share of the whole hard glitter of Israel. This diffused intensity, as I have called it, causes any array of Jews to resemble (if I may be allowed another image) some long nocturnal street where every window in every house shows a maintained light. The advanced age of so many of the figures, the ubiquity of the children, carried out in fact this analogy; they were all there for race, and not, as it were, for reason: that excess of lurid meaning, in some of the old men's and old women's faces in particular, would have been absurd, in the conditions, as a really directed attention—it could only be the gathered past of Israel mechanically pushing through. The way, at the same time, this chapter of history did, all that evening, seem to push, was a matter that made the "ethnic" apparition again sit like a skeleton at the feast. It was fairly as if I could see the spectre grin while the talk of the hour gave me, across the board, facts and figures, chapter and verse, for the extent of the Hebrew conquest of New York. With a reverence for intellect, one should doubtless have drunk in tribute to an intellectual people; but I remember being at no time more conscious of that merely portentous element, in the aspects of American growth, which reduces to inanity any marked dismay quite as much as any high elation. The portent is one of too many—you always come back, as I have hinted, with your easier gasp, to *that:* it will be time enough to sigh or to shout when the relation of the particular appearance to all the other relations shall have cleared itself up. Phantasmagoric for me, accordingly, in a high degree, are the interesting hours I here glance at content to remain—setting in this respect, I recognize, an excellent example to all the rest of the New York phantasmagoria. Let me speak of the remainder only as phantasmagoric too, so that I may both the more kindly recall it and the sooner have done with it.

I have not done, however, with the impression of that large evening in the Ghetto; there was too much in the vision, and it has left too much the sense of a rare experience. For what did it all really come to but that one had seen with one's eyes the New Jerusalem on earth? What less than that could it all have been, in its far-spreading light and its celestial serenity of multiplication? There it was, there it is, and when I think of the dark, foul, stifling Ghettos of other remembered cities, I shall think by the same stroke of the city of redemption, and evoke in particular the rich Rutgers Street perspective—rich, so peculiarly, for the eye, in that complexity of fire-escapes with which each house-front bristles and which gives the whole vista so modernized and appointed a look. Omnipresent in the "poor" regions, this neat applied machinery has, for the stranger, a common side with the electric light and the telephone, suggests the distance achieved from the old Jerusalem. (These frontal iron ladders and platforms, by the way, so numerous throughout New York, strike more New York notes than can be parenthetically named—and among them perhaps most sharply the note of the ease with which, in the terrible town, on opportunity, "architecture" goes by the board; but the appearance to which they often most conduce is that of the spaciously organized cage for the nimbler class of animals in some great zoological garden. This general analogy is irresistible—it seems to offer, in each district, a little world of bars and perches and swings for human squirrels and monkeys. The very name of architecture perishes, for the fire-escapes look like abashed afterthoughts, staircases and communications forgotten in the construction; but the inhabitants lead, like the squirrels and monkeys, all the merrier life.) It was while I hung over the prospect from the windows of my friend, however, the presiding genius of the district, and it was while, at a later hour, I proceeded in his company, and in that of a trio of contributive fellow-pilgrims, from one "characteristic" place of public entertainment to another: it was during this rich climax, I say, that the city of redemption was least to be taken for anything less than it was. The windows, while we sat at meat, looked out on a swarming little square in which an ant-like population darted to and fro; the square consisted in part of a "district" public garden, or public lounge rather, one of those small backwaters or refuges, artfully economized for rest, here and there, in the very heart of the New York whirlpool, and which spoke louder than anything else of a Jerusalem disinfected. What spoke loudest, no doubt, was the great overtowering School which formed a main boundary and in the shadow of which we all comparatively crouched.

But the School must not lead me on just yet—so colossally has its presence still to loom for us; that presence which profits so, for predominance, in America, by the failure of concurrent and competitive presences, the failure of any others looming at all on the same scale save that of Business, those in particular of a visible Church, a visible State, a visible Society, a visible Past; those of the many visibilities, in short, that warmly cumber the ground in older countries. Yet it also spoke loud that my friend was quartered, for the interest of the thing (from his so interesting point of view), in a "tenement-house"; the New Jerusalem would so have triumphed, had it triumphed nowhere else, in the fact that this charming little structure *could* be ranged, on the wonderful little square, under that invidious head. On my asking to what latent vice it owed its stigma, I was asked in return if it didn't sufficiently pay for its name by harbouring some five-and-twenty families. But this, exactly, was the way it testified—this circumstance of the simultaneous enjoyment by five-and-twenty families, on "tenement" lines, of conditions so little sordid, so highly "evolved." I remember the evolved fire-proof staircase, a thing of scientific surfaces, impenetrable to the microbe, and above all plated, against side friction, with white marble of a goodly grain. The white marble was surely the New Jerusalem note, and we followed that note, up and down the district, the rest of the evening, through more happy changes than I may take time to count. What struck me in the flaring streets (over and beyond the every-where insistent, defiant, unhumorous, exotic face) was the blaze of the shops addressed to the New Jerusalem wants and the splendour with which these were taken for granted; the only thing indeed a little ambigu-ous was just this look of the trap too brilliantly, too candidly baited for the wary side of Israel itself. It is not *for* Israel, in general, that Israel so artfully shines—yet its being moved to do so, at last, in that luxurious style, might be precisely the grand side of the city of redemption. Who can ever tell, moreover, in any conditions and in presence of any apparent anomaly, what the genius of Israel may, or may not, really be "up to"?

The grateful way to take it all, at any rate, was with the sense of its coming back again to the inveterate rise, in the American air, of every value, and especially of the lower ones, those most subject to multiplica-tion; such a wealth of meaning did this keep appearing to pour into the value and function of the country at large. Importances are all strikingly shifted and reconstituted, in the United States, for the visitor attuned, from far back, to "European" importances; but I think of no other mo-ment of my total impression as so sharply working over my own benighted vision of them. The scale, in this light of the New Jerusalem, seemed completely rearranged; or, to put it more simply, the wants, the gratifica-tions, the aspirations of the "poor," as expressed in the shops (which were the shops of the "poor"), denoted a new style of poverty; and this new style of poverty, from street to street, stuck out of the possible purchasers, one's jostling fellow-pedestrians, and made them, to every man and woman, individual throbs in the larger harmony. One can speak only of what one has seen, and there were grosser elements of the sordid and the squalid that I doubtless never saw. That, with a good deal of observation and of curiosity, I should have failed of this, the country over, affected me as by itself something of an indication. To miss that part of the spectacle, or to know it only by its having so unfamiliar a pitch, was an indication that made up for a great many others. It is when this one in particular is forced home to you—this immense, vivid *general* lift of poverty and gen-eral appreciation of the living unit's paying property in himself—that the picture seems most to clear and the way to jubilation most to open. For it meets you there, at every turn, as the result most definitely attested. You are as constantly reminded, no doubt, that these rises in enjoyed value shrink and dwindle under the icy breath of Trusts and the weight of the new remorseless monopolies that operate as no madnesses of ancient per-sonal power thrilling us on the historic page ever operated; the living unit's property in himself becoming more and more merely such a prop-erty as may consist with a relation to properties overwhelmingly greater and that allow the asking of no questions and the making, for co-existence with them, of no conditions. But that, in the fortunate phrase, is another story, and will be altogether, evidently, a new and different drama. There is such a thing, in the United States, it is hence to be inferred, as freedom to grow up to be blighted, and it may be the only freedom in store for the smaller fry of future generations. If it is accordingly of the smaller fry I speak, and of how large they massed on that evening of endless admonitions, this will be because I caught them thus in their comparative humility and at an early stage of their American growth. The life-thread has, I suppose, to be of a certain thickness for the great shears of Fate to feel for it. Put it, at the worst, that the Ogres were to devour them, they were but the more certainly to fatten into food for the Ogres.

Their dream, at all events, as I noted it, was meanwhile sweet and undisguised—nowhere sweeter than in the half-dozen picked beer-houses and cafés in which our ingenuous *enquête,* that of my fellow-pilgrims and I, wound up. These establishments had each been selected for its playing off some facet of the jewel, and they wondrously testified, by their range and their individual colour, to the spread of that lustre. It was a pious rosary of which I should like to tell each bead, but I must let the general sense of the adventure serve. Our successive stations were in no case of the "seamy" order, an inquiry into seaminess having been unanimously pronounced futile, but each had its separate social connotation, and it was for the number and variety of these connotations, and their individual plenitude and prosperity, to set one thinking. Truly the Yiddish world was a vast world, with its own deeps and complexities, and what struck one above all was that it sat there at its cups (and in no instance vulgarly the worse for them) with a sublimity of good conscience that took away the breath, a protrusion of elbow never aggressive, but absolutely proof against jostling. It was the incurable man of letters under the skin of one of the party who gasped, I confess; for it was in the light of letters, that is in the light of our language as literature has hitherto known it, that one stared at this all-unconscious impudence of the agency of future ravage. The man of letters, in the United States, has his own difficulties to face and his own current to stem—for dealing with which his liveliest inspiration may be, I think, that they are still very much his own, even in an Americanized world, and that more than elsewhere they press him to intimate communion with his honour. For that honour, the honour that sits astride of the consecrated English tradition, to his mind, quite as old knighthood astride of its caparisoned charger, the dragon most rousing, over the land, the proper spirit of St. George, is just this immensity of the alien presence climbing higher and higher, climbing itself into the very light of publicity.

I scarce know why, but I saw it that evening as in some dim dawn of that promise to its own consciousness, and perhaps this was precisely what made it a little exasperating. Under the impression of the mere mob the question doesn't come up, but in these haunts of comparative civility we saw the mob sifted and strained, and the exasperation was the sharper, no doubt, because what the process had left most visible was just the various possibilities of the waiting spring of intelligence. Such elements consti-

tuted the germ of a "public," and it was impossible (possessed of a sensibil-
ity worth speaking of) to be exposed to them without feeling how new a
thing under the sun the resulting public would be. That was where one's
"lettered" anguish came in—in the turn of one's eye from face to face for
some betrayal of a prehensile hook for the linguistic tradition as one had
known it. Each warm lighted and supplied circle, each group of served
tables and smoked pipes and fostered decencies and unprecedented accents,
beneath the extravagant lamps, took on thus, for the brooding critic, a
likeness to that terrible modernized and civilized room in the Tower of
London, haunted by the shade of Guy Fawkes, which had more than once
formed part of the scene of the critic's taking tea there. In this chamber of
the present urbanities the wretched man had been stretched on the rack,
and the critic's ear (how else should it have been a critic's?) could still
always catch, in pauses of talk, the faint groan of his ghost. Just so the
East side cafés—and increasingly as their place in the scale was higher—
showed to my inner sense, beneath their bedizenment, as torture-rooms of
the living idiom; the piteous gasp of which at the portent of lacerations to
come could reach me in any drop of the surrounding Accent of the Future.
The accent of the very ultimate future, in the States, may be destined to
become the most beautiful on the globe and the very music of humanity
(here the "ethnic" synthesis shrouds itself thicker than ever); but whatever
we shall know it for, certainly, we shall not know it for English—in any
sense for which there is an existing literary measure.

THE CITIZEN
James Francis Dwyer

People came to America for many reasons. Some were forced to come; most left their homelands to enjoy the promise that was said to await them on these shores. During the seventeenth and eighteenth centuries, most who came were, as one writer put it, "English or African." With notable exceptions, this was the reality. But, beginning with the birth of the new nation, others came too. First from western Europe and Ireland; then, in the latter part of the nineteenth century, from southern and eastern Europe and Asia as well.

James Francis Dwyer tells of some of those latter immigrants who, fleeing the oppressive rigors of Russian society, set forth to realize what had become an almost universal dream. The story of Ivan Berloff begins during his citizenship ceremonies and consists of a series of flashbacks.

The President of the United States was speaking. His audience comprised two thousand foreign-born men who had just been admitted to citizenship. They listened intently, their faces, aglow with the light of a newborn patriotism, upturned to the calm, intellectual face of the first citizen of the country they now claimed as their own.

Here and there among the newly-made citizens were wives and children. The women were proud of their men. They looked at them from time to time, their faces showing pride and awe.

One little woman, sitting immediately in front of the President, held the hand of a big, muscular man and stroked it softly. The big man was looking at the speaker with great blue eyes that were the eyes of a dreamer.

The President's words came clear and distinct:

You were drawn across the ocean by some beckoning finger of hope, by some belief, by some vision of a new kind of justice, by some expectation of a better kind of life. You dreamed dreams of this country, and I hope you brought the dreams with you. A man enriches the country to which he brings dreams, and you who have brought them have enriched America.

The big man made a curious choking noise and his wife breathed a soft "Hush!" The giant was strangely affected.

The President continued:

No doubt you have been disappointed in some of us, but remember this, if we have grown at all poor in the ideal, you brought some of it with you. A man does not go out to seek the thing that is not in him. A man does not hope for the thing that he does not believe in, and if some of us have forgotten what America believed in, you at any rate imported in your own hearts a renewal of the belief. Each of you, I am sure, brought a dream, a glorious, shining dream, a dream worth more than gold or silver, and that is the reason that I, for one, make you welcome.

The big man's eyes were fixed. His wife shook him gently, but he did not heed her. He was looking through the presidential rostrum, through the big buildings behind it, looking out over leagues of space to a snow-swept village that huddled on an island in the Beresina, the swift-flowing tributary of the mighty Dnieper, an island that looked like a black bone stuck tight in the maw of the stream.

It was in the little village on the Beresina that the Dream came to Ivan Berloff, Big Ivan of the Bridge.

The Dream came in the spring. All great dreams come in the spring, and the Spring Maiden who brought Big Ivan's Dream was more than ordinarily beautiful. She swept up the Beresina, trailing wondrous draperies of vivid green. Her feet touched the snow-hardened ground, and armies of little white and blue flowers sprang up in her footsteps. Soft breezes escorted her, velvety breezes that carried the aromas of the far-off places from which they came, places far to the southward, and more distant towns beyond the Black Sea whose people were not under the sway of the Great Czar.

The father of Big Ivan, who had fought under Prince Menshikov at Alma fifty-five years before, hobbled out to see the sunbeams eat up the snow hummocks that hid in the shady places, and he told his son it was the most wonderful spring he had ever seen.

"The little breezes are hot and sweet," he said, sniffing hungrily with his face turned toward the south. "I know them, Ivan! I know them! They have the spice odor that I sniffed on the winds that came to us when we lay in the trenches at Balaklava. Praise God for the warmth!"

And that day the Dream came to Big Ivan as he plowed. It was a wonder dream. It sprang into his brain as he walked behind the plow, and for a few minutes he quivered as the big bridge quivers when the Beresina sends her ice squadrons to hammer the arches. It made his heart pound mightily, and his lips and throat became very dry.

Big Ivan stopped at the end of the furrow and tried to discover what had brought the Dream. Where had it come from? Why had it clutched him so suddenly? Was he the only man in the village to whom it had come?

Like his father, he sniffed the sweet-smelling breezes. He thrust his great hands into the sunbeams. He reached down and plucked one of a bunch of white flowers that had sprung up overnight. The Dream was born of the breezes and the sunshine and the spring flowers. It came from them and it had sprung into his mind because he was young and strong. He knew! It couldn't come to his father or Donkov, the tailor, or Poborino, the smith. They were old and weak, and Ivan's dream was one that called for youth and strength.

"Ay, for youth and strength," he muttered as he gripped the plow. "And I have it!"

That evening Big Ivan of the Bridge spoke to his wife, Anna, a little woman, who had a sweet face and a wealth of fair hair.

"Wife, we are going away from here," he said.

"Where are we going, Ivan?" she asked.

"Where do you think, Anna?" he said, looking down at her as she stood by his side.

"To Bobruisk," she murmured.

"No."

"Farther?"

"Ay, a long way farther."

Fear sprang into her soft eyes. Bobruisk was eighty-nine versts away, yet Ivan said they were going farther.

"We—we are not going to Minsk?" she cried.

"Ay, and beyond Minsk!"

"Ivan, tell me!" she gasped. "Tell me where we are going!"

"We are going to America."

"*To America?*"

"Yes, to America!"

Big Ivan of the Bridge lifted up his voice when he cried out the words "To America," and then a sudden fear sprang upon him as those words dashed through the little window out into the darkness of the village street. Was he mad? America was 8,000 versts away! It was far across the ocean, a place that was only a name to him, a place where he knew no one. He wondered in the strange little silence that followed his words if the crippled son of Poborino, the smith, had heard him. The cripple would jeer at him if the night wind had carried the words to his ear.

Anna remained staring at her big husband for a few minutes, then she sat down quietly at his side. There was a strange look in his big blue eyes, the look of a man to whom has come a vision, the look which came into the eyes of those shepherds of Judea long, long ago.

"What is it, Ivan?" she murmured softly, patting his big hand. "Tell me?"

And Big Ivan of the Bridge, slow of tongue, told of the Dream. To no one else would he have told it. Anna understood. She had a way of patting his hands and saying soft things when his tongue could not find words to express his thoughts.

Ivan told how the Dream had come to him as he plowed. He told her how it had sprung upon him, a wonderful dream born of the soft breezes, of the sunshine, of the sweet smell of the upturned sod and of his own strength. "It wouldn't come to weak men," he said, baring an arm that showed great snaky muscles rippling beneath the clear skin. "It is a dream that comes only to those who are strong and those who want—who want something that they haven't got." Then in a lower voice he said: "What is it that we want, Anna?"

The little wife looked out into the darkness with fear-filled eyes. There were spies even there in that little village on the Beresina, and it was dangerous to say words that might be construed into a reflection on the Government. But she answered Ivan. She stooped and whispered one word into his ear, and he slapped his thigh with his big hand.

"Ay," he cried. "This is what we want! You and I and millions like us want it, and over there, Anna, over there we will get it. It is the country where a muzhik is as good as a prince of the blood!"

Anna stood up, took a small earthenware jar from a side shelf, dusted it carefully and placed it upon the mantel. From a knotted cloth about her neck she took a ruble and dropped the coin into the jar. Big Ivan looked at her curiously.

"It is to make legs for your Dream," she explained. "It is many versts to America, and one rides on rubles."

"You are a good wife," he said. "I was afraid that you might laugh at me."

"It is a great dream," she murmured. "Come, we will go to sleep."

The Dream maddened Ivan during the days that followed. It pounded within his brain as he followed the plow. It bred a discontent that made him hate the little village, the swift-flowing Beresina and the gray stretches that ran toward Mogilev. He wanted to be moving, but Anna had said that one rode on rubles, and rubles were hard to find.

And in some mysterious way the village became aware of the secret. Donkov, the tailor, discovered it. Donkov lived in one-half of the cottage occupied by Ivan and Anna, and Donkov had long ears. The tailor spread the news, and Poborino, the smith, and Yanansk, the baker, would jeer at Ivan as he passed.

"When are you going to America?" they would ask.

"Soon," Ivan would answer.

"Take us with you!" they would cry in chorus.

"It is no place for cowards," Ivan would answer. "It is a long way, and only brave men can make the journey."

"Are you brave?" the baker screamed one day as he went by.

"I am brave enough to want liberty!" cried Ivan angrily. "I am brave enough to want———"

"Be careful! Be careful!" interrupted the smith. "A long tongue has given many a man a train journey that he never expected."

That night Ivan and Anna counted the rubles in the earthenware pot. The giant looked down at his wife with a gloomy face, but she smiled and patted his hand.

"It is slow work," he said.

"We must be patient," she answered. "You have the Dream."

"Ay," he said. "I have the Dream."

Through the hot, languorous summertime the Dream grew within the brain of Big Ivan. He saw visions in the smoky haze that hung above the Beresina. At times he would stand, hoe in hand, and look toward the west, the wonderful west into which the sun slipped down each evening like a coin dropped from the fingers of the dying day.

Autumn came, and the fretful whining winds that came down from the north chilled the Dream. The winds whispered of the coming of the Snow King, and the river grumbled as it listened. Big Ivan kept out of the way of Poborino, the smith, and Yanansk, the baker. The Dream was still with him, but autumn is a bad time for dreams.

Winter came, and the Dream weakened. It was only the earthenware pot that kept it alive, the pot into which the industrious Anna put every coin that could be spared. Often Big Ivan would stare at the pot as he sat beside the stove. The pot was the cord which kept the Dream alive.

"You are a good woman, Anna," Ivan would say again and again. "It was you who thought of saving the rubles."

"But it was you who dreamed," she would answer. "Wait for the spring, husband mine. Wait."

It was strange how the spring came to the Beresina that year. It sprang upon the flanks of winter before the Ice King had given the order to retreat into the fastnesses of the north. It swept up the river escorted by a million little breezes, and housewives opened their windows and peered out with surprise upon their faces. A wonderful guest had come to them and found them unprepared.

Big Ivan of the Bridge was fixing a fence in the meadow on the morning the Spring Maiden reached the village. For a little while he was not aware of her arrival. His mind was upon his work, but suddenly he discovered that he was hot, and he took off his overcoat. He turned to hang the coat upon a bush, then he sniffed the air, and a puzzled look came upon his face. He sniffed again, hurriedly, hungrily. He drew in great breaths of it, and his eyes shone with a strange light. It was wonderful air. It brought life to the Dream. It rose up within him, ten times more lusty than on the day it was born, and his limbs trembled as he drew in the hot, scented breezes that breed the *Wanderlust* and shorten the long trails of the world.

Big Ivan clutched his coat and ran to the little cottage. He burst through the door, startling Anna, who was busy with her housework.

"The Spring!" he cried. "*The Spring!*"

He took her arm and dragged her to the door. Standing together they sniffed the sweet breezes. In silence they listened to the song of the river. The Beresina had changed from a whining, fretful tune into a lilting, sweet song that would set the legs of lovers dancing. Anna pointed to a green bud on a bush beside the door.

"It came this minute," she murmured.

"Yes," said Ivan. "The little fairies brought it there to show us that spring has come to stay."

Together they turned and walked to the mantel. Big Ivan took up the earthenware pot, carried it to the table, and spilled its contents upon the well-scrubbed boards. He counted while Anna stood beside him, her fingers clutching his coarse blouse. It was a slow business, because Ivan's big blunt fingers were not used to such work, but it was over at last. He stacked the coins into neat piles, then he straightened himself and turned to the woman at his side.

"It is enough," he said quietly. "We will go at once. If it was not enough, we would have to go because the Dream is upon me and I hate this place."

"As you say," murmured Anna. "The wife of Littin, the butcher, will buy our chairs and our bed. I spoke to her yesterday."

Poborino, the smith; his crippled son; Yanansk, the baker; Dankov, the tailor, and a score of others were out upon the village street on the morning that Big Ivan and Anna set out. They were inclined to jeer at Ivan, but something upon the face of the giant made them afraid. Hand in hand the big man and his wife walked down the street, their faces turned toward Bobruisk, Ivan balancing upon his head a heavy trunk that no other man in the village could have lifted.

At the end of the street a stripling with bright eyes and yellow curls clutched the hand of Ivan and looked into his face.

"I know what is sending you," he cried.

"Ay, *you* know," said Ivan, looking into the eyes of the other.

"It came to me yesterday," murmured the stripling. "I got it from the breezes. They are free, so are the birds and the little clouds and the river. I wish I could go."

"Keep your dream," said Ivan softly. "Nurse it, for it is the dream of a man."

Anna, who was crying softly, touched the blouse of the boy. "At the back of our cottage, near the bush that bears the red berries, a pot is buried," she said. "Dig it up and take it home with you and when you have a kopeck drop it in. It is a good pot."

The stripling understood. He stooped and kissed the hand of Anna, and Big Ivan patted him upon the back. They were brother dreamers and they understood each other.

Boris Lugan has sung the song of the versts that eat up one's courage as well as the leather of one's shoes.

"Versts! Versts! Scores and scores of them!
Versts! Versts! A million or more of them!
Dust! Dust! And the devils who play in it,
Blinding us fools who forever must stay in it."

Big Ivan and Anna faced the long versts to Bobruisk, but they were not afraid of the dust devils. They had the Dream. It made their hearts light and took the weary feeling from their feet. They were on their way. America was a long, long journey, but they had started, and every verst they covered lessened the number that lay between them and the Promised Land.

"I am glad the boy spoke to us," said Anna.

"And I am glad," said Ivan. "Some day he will come and eat with us in America."

They came to Bobruisk. Holding hands, they walked into it late one afternoon. They were eighty-nine versts from the little village on the Beresina, but they were not afraid. The Dream spoke to Ivan, and his big hand held the hand of Anna. The railway ran through Bobruisk, and that evening they stood and looked at the shining rails that went out in the moonlight like silver tongs reaching out for a low-hanging star.

And they came face to face with the Terror that evening, the Terror that had helped the spring breezes and the sunshine to plant the Dream in the brain of Big Ivan.

They were walking down a dark side street when they saw a score of men and women creep from the door of a squat, unpainted building. The little group remained on the sidewalk for a minute as if uncertain about the way they should go, then from the corner of the street came a cry of "Police!" and the twenty pedestrians ran in different directions.

It was no false alarm. Mounted police charged down the dark thoroughfare swinging their swords as they rode at the scurrying men and women who raced for shelter. Big Ivan dragged Anna into a doorway, and toward their hiding place ran a young boy who, like themselves, had no connection with the group and who merely desired to get out of harm's way till the storm was over.

The boy was not quick enough to escape the charge. A trooper pursued him, overtook him before he reached the sidewalk, and knocked him down with a quick stroke given with the flat of his blade. His horse struck the boy with one of his hoofs as the lad stumbled on his face.

Big Ivan growled like an angry bear, and sprang from his hiding place. The trooper's horse had carried him on to the sidewalk, and Ivan seized the bridle and flung the animal on its haunches. The policeman leaned forward to strike at the giant, but Ivan of the Bridge gripped the left leg of the horseman and tore him from the saddle.

The horse galloped off, leaving its rider lying beside the moaning boy who was unlucky enough to be in a street where a score of students were holding a meeting.

Anna dragged Ivan back into the passageway. More police were charging down the street, and their position was a dangerous one.

"Ivan!" she cried, "Ivan! Remember the Dream! America, Ivan! *America!* Come this way! Quick!"

With strong hands she dragged him down the passage. It opened into a narrow lane, and, holding each other's hands, they hurried toward the place where they had taken lodgings. From far off came screams and hoarse orders, curses and the sound of galloping hoofs. The Terror was abroad.

Big Ivan spoke softly as they entered the little room they had taken. "He had a face like the boy to whom you gave the lucky pot," he said. "Did you notice it in the moonlight when the trooper struck him down?"

"Yes," she answered. "I saw."

They left Bobruisk next morning. They rode away on a great, puffing, snorting train that terrified Anna. The engineer turned a stopcock as they were passing the engine, and Anna screamed while Ivan nearly dropped the big trunk. The engineer grinned, but the giant looked up at him and the grin faded. Ivan of the Bridge was startled by the rush of hot steam, but he was afraid of no man.

The train went roaring by little villages and great pasture stretches. The real journey had begun. They began to love the powerful engine. It was eating up the versts at a tremendous rate. They looked at each other from time to time and smiled like two children.

They came to Minsk, the biggest town they had ever seen. They looked out from the car windows at the miles of wooden buildings, at the big church of St. Catharine, and the woolen mills. Minsk would have frightened them if they hadn't had the Dream. The farther they went from the little village on the Beresina the more courage the Dream gave to them.

On and on went the train, the wheels singing the song of the road. Fellow travelers asked them where they were going. "To America," Ivan would answer.

"To America?" they would cry. "May the little saints guide you. It is a long way, and you will be lonely."

"No, we shall not be lonely," Ivan would say.

"Ha! you are going with friends?"

"No, we have no friends, but we have something that keeps us from being lonely." And when Ivan would make that reply Anna would pat his hand and the questioner would wonder if it was a charm or a holy relic that the bright-eyed couple possessed.

They ran through Vilna, on through flat stretches of Courland to Libau, where they saw the sea. They sat and stared at it for a whole day, talking little but watching it with wide, wondering eyes. And they stared at the great ships that came rocking in from distant ports, their sides gray with the salt from the big combers which they had battled with.

No wonder this America of ours is big. We draw the brave ones from the old lands, the brave ones whose dreams are like the guiding sign that was given to the Israelites of old—a pillar of cloud by day, a pillar of fire by night.

The harbor master spoke to Ivan and Anna as they watched the restless waters.

"Where are you going, children?"

"To America," answered Ivan.

"A long way. Three ships bound for America went down last month."

"Our ship will not sink," said Ivan.

"Why?"

"Because I know it will not."

The harbor master looked at the strange blue eyes of the giant, and spoke softly. "You have the eyes of a man who sees things," he said. "There was a Norwegian sailor in the *White Queen,* who had eyes like yours, and he could see death."

"I see life!" said Ivan boldly. "A free life—"

"Hush!" said the harbor master. "Do not speak so loud." He walked swiftly away, but he dropped a ruble into Anna's hand as he passed her by. "For luck," he murmured. "May the little saints look after you on the big waters."

They boarded the ship, and the Dream gave them a courage that surprised them. There were others going aboard, and Ivan and Anna felt that those others were also persons who possessed dreams. She saw the dreams in their eyes. There were Slavs, Poles, Letts, Jews, and Livonians, all bound for the land where dreams come true. They were a little afraid—not two per cent of them had ever seen a ship before—yet their dreams gave them courage.

The emigrant ship was dragged from her pier by a grunting tug and went floundering down the Baltic Sea. Night came down, and the devils who, according to the Esthonian fishermen, live in the bottom of the Baltic, got their shoulders under the stern of the ship and tried to stand her on her head. They whipped up white combers that sprang on her flanks and tried to crush her, and the wind played a devil's lament in her rigging. Anna lay sick in the stuffy women's quarters, and Ivan could not get near her. But he sent her messages. He told her not to mind the sea devils, to think of the Dream, the Great Dream that would become real in the land to which they were bound. Ivan of the Bridge grew to full stature on that first night out from Libau. The battered old craft that carried him slouched before the waves that swept over her decks, but he was not afraid. Down among the million and one smells of the steerage he induced a thin-faced Livonian to play upon a mouth organ, and Big Ivan sang Paleer's "Song of Freedom" in a voice that drowned the creaking of the old vessel's timbers, and made the seasick ones forget their sickness. They sat up in their berths and joined in the chorus, their eyes shining brightly in the half gloom:

"Freedom for serf and for slave,
 Freedom for all men who crave
 Their right to be free
 And who hate to bend knee
 But to Him who this right to them gave."

It was well that these emigrants had dreams. They wanted them. The sea devils chased the lumbering steamer. They hung to her bows and pulled her for'ard deck under emerald-green rollers. They clung to her stern and hoisted her nose till Big Ivan thought that he could touch the door of heaven by standing on her blunt snout. Miserable, cold, ill, and sleepless, the emigrants crouched in their quarters, and to them Ivan and the thin-faced Livonian sang the "Song of Freedom."

The emigrant ship pounded through the Cattegat, swung southward through the Skagerrack and the bleak North Sea. But the storm pursued her. The big waves snarled and bit at her, and the captain and the chief officer consulted with each other. They decided to run into the Thames, and the harried steamer nosed her way in and anchored off Gravesend.

An examination was made, and the agents decided to transship the emigrants. They were taken to London and thence by train to Liverpool, and Ivan and Anna sat again side by side, holding hands and smiling at each other as the third-class emigrant train from Euston raced down through the green Midland counties to grimy Liverpool.

"You are not afraid?" Ivan would say to her each time she looked at him.

"It is a long way, but the Dream has given me much courage," she said.

"Today I spoke to a Lett whose brother works in New York City," said the giant. "Do you know how much money he earns each day?"

"How much?" she questioned.

"Three rubles, and he calls the policemen by their first names."

"You will earn five rubles, my Ivan," she murmured. "There is no one as strong as you."

Once again they were herded into the bowels of a big ship that steamed away through the fog banks of the Mersey out into the Irish Sea. There were more dreamers now, nine hundred of them, and Anna and Ivan were more comfortable. And these new emigrants, English, Irish, Scotch,

French, and German, knew much concerning America. Ivan was certain that he would earn at least three rubles a day. He was very strong.

On the deck he defeated all comers in a tug of war, and the captain of the ship came up to him and felt his muscles.

"The country that lets men like you get away from it is run badly," he said. "Why did you leave it?"

The interpreter translated what the captain said and through the interpreter Ivan answered.

"I had a Dream," he said, "a Dream of freedom."

"Good," cried the captain. "Why should a man with muscles like yours have his face ground into the dust?"

The soul of Big Ivan grew during those days. He felt himself a man, a man who was born upright to speak his thoughts without fear.

The ship rolled into Queenstown one bright morning, and Ivan and his nine hundred steerage companions crowded the for'ard deck. A boy in a rowboat threw a line to the deck, and after it had been fastened to a stanchion he came up hand over hand. The emigrants watched him curiously. An old woman sitting in the boat pulled off her shoes, sat in a loop of the rope, and lifted her hand as a signal to her son on deck.

"Hey, fellers," said the boy, "help me pull me muvver up. She wants to sell a few dozen apples, an' they won't let her up the gangway!"

Big Ivan didn't understand the words, but he guessed what the boy wanted. He made one of a half dozen who gripped the rope and started to pull the ancient apple-woman to the deck.

They had her halfway up the side when undersized third officer discovered what they were doing. He called to a steward and the steward sprang to obey.

"Turn a hose on her!" cried the officer. "Turn a hose on the old woman!"

The steward rushed for the hose. He ran with it to the side of the ship with the intention of squirting on the old woman, who was swinging in midair and exhorting the six men who were dragging her to the deck.

"Pull!" she cried. "Sure, I'll give every one of ye a rosy red apple an' me blessing with it."

The steward aimed the muzzle of the hose, and Big Ivan of the Bridge let go of the rope and sprang at him. The fist of the great Russian went out like a battering ram; it struck the steward between the eyes, and he dropped upon the deck. He lay like one dead, the muzzle of the hose wriggling from his limp hands.

The third officer and the interpreter rushed at Big Ivan, who stood erect, his hands clenched.

"Ask the big swine why he did it," roared the officer.

"Because he is a coward!" cried Ivan. "They wouldn't do that in America!"

"What does the big brute know about America?" cried the officer.

"Tell him I have dreamed of it," shouted Ivan. "Tell him it is in my Dream. Tell him I will kill him if he turns the water on this old woman."

The apple-seller was on deck then, and with the wisdom of the Celt she understood. She put her lean hand upon the great head of the Russian and blessed him in Gaelic. Ivan bowed before her, then as she offered him a rosy apple he led her toward Anna, a great Viking leading a withered old woman who walked with the grace of a duchess.

"Please don't touch him," she cried, turning to the officer. "We have been waiting for your ship for six hours, and we have only five dozen apples to sell. It's a great man he is. Sure he's as big as Finn MacCool."

Some one pulled the steward behind a ventilator and revived him by squirting him with water from the hose which he had tried to turn upon the old woman. The third officer slipped quietly away.

The Atlantic was kind to the ship that carried Ivan and Anna. Through sunny days they sat up on deck and watched the horizon. They wanted to be among those who would get the first glimpse of the wonderland.

They saw it on a morning with sunshine and soft wind. Standing together in the bow, they looked at the smear upon the horizon, and their eyes filled with tears. They forgot the long road to Bobruisk, the rocking journey to Libau, the mad buck-jumping boat in whose timbers the sea devils of the Baltic had bored holes. Everything unpleasant was forgotten, because the Dream filled them with a great happiness.

The inspectors at Ellis Island were interested in Ivan. They walked around him and prodded his muscles, and he smiled down upon them good-naturedly.

"A fine animal," said one. "Gee, he's a new white hope! Ask him can he fight?"

An interpreter put the question, and Ivan nodded. "I have fought," he said.

"Gee!" cried the inspector. "Ask him was it for purses or what?"

"For freedom," answered Ivan. "For freedom to stretch my legs and straighten my neck!"

Ivan and Anna left the Government ferryboat at the Battery. They started to walk uptown, making for the East Side, Ivan carrying the big trunk that no other man could lift.

It was a wonderful morning. The city was bathed in warm sunshine, and the well-dressed men and women who crowded the sidewalks made the two immigrants think that it was a festival day. Ivan and Anna stared at each other in amazement. They had never seen such dresses as those worn by the smiling women who passed them by; they had never seen such well-groomed men.

"It is a feast day for certain," said Anna.

"They are dressed like princes and princesses," murmured Ivan. "There are no poor here, Anna. None."

Like two simple children, they walked along the streets of the City of

Wonder. What a contrast it was to the gray, stupid towns where the Terror waited to spring upon the cowed people! In Bobruisk, Minsk, Vilna, and Libau the people were sullen and afraid. They walked in dread, but in the City of Wonder beside the glorious Hudson every person seemed happy and contented.

They lost their way, but they walked on, looking at the wonderful shop windows, the roaring elevated trains, and the huge skyscrapers. Hours afterward they found themselves in Fifth Avenue near Thirty-third Street, and there the miracle happened to the two Russian immigrants. It was a big miracle inasmuch as it proved the Dream a truth, a great truth.

Ivan and Anna attempted to cross the avenue, but they became confused in the snarl of traffic. They dodged backward and forward as the stream of automobiles swept by them. Anna screamed, and, in response to her scream, a traffic policeman, resplendent in a new uniform, rushed to her side. He took the arm of Anna and flung up a commanding hand. The charging autos halted. For five blocks north and south they jammed on the brakes when the unexpected interruption occurred, and Big Ivan gasped.

"Don't be flurried, little woman," said the cop. "Sure I can tame 'em by liftin' me hand."

Anna didn't understand what he said, but she knew it was something nice by the manner in which his Irish eyes smiled down upon her. And in front of the waiting automobiles he led her with the same care that he would give to a duchess, while Ivan, carrying the big trunk, followed them, wondering much. Ivan's mind went back to Bobruisk on the night the Terror was abroad.

The policeman led Anna to the sidewalk, patted Ivan good-naturedly upon the shoulder, and then with a sharp whistle unloosed the waiting stream of cars that had been held up so that two Russian immigrants could cross the avenue.

Big Ivan of the Bridge took the trunk from his head and put it on the ground. He reached out his arms and folded Anna in a great embrace. His eyes were wet.

"The Dream is true!" he cried. "Did you see, Anna? We are as good as they! This is the land where a muzhik is as good as a prince of the blood!"

The President was nearing the close of his address. Anna shook Ivan, and Ivan came out of the trance which the President's words had brought upon him. He sat up and listened intently:

We grow great by dreams. All big men are dreamers. They see things in the soft haze of a spring day or in the red fire of a long winter's evening. Some of us let those great dreams die, but others nourish and protect them, nurse them through bad days till they bring them to the sunshine and light which come always to those who sincerely hope that their dreams will come true.

The President finished. For a moment he stood looking down at the faces turned up to him, and Big Ivan of the Bridge thought that the President smiled at him. Ivan seized Anna's hand and held it tight.

"He knew of my Dream!" he cried. "He knew of it. Did you hear what he said about the dreams of a spring day?"

"Of course he knew," said Anna. "He is the wisest man in America, where there are many wise men. Ivan, you are a citizen now."

"And you are a citizen, Anna."

The band started to play "My Country, 'tis of Thee," and Ivan and Anna got to their feet. Standing side by side, holding hands, they joined in with the others who had found after long days of journeying the blessed land where dreams come true.

I DISCOVER AMERICA
Abraham Cahan

"A klug zu Columbus" (a curse on Columbus).
Many a voyager repeated these sentiments (in Polish,
Russian, Greek, Italian, Turkish, as well as Yiddish) as
he sat in steerage rolling with a creaking ship, listening
to the omnipresent rush of the sea, wondering what he
had committed himself to and why he had left home.
On reflection, of course, like Big Ivan Berloff he could
answer his own questions. But still he cursed.
While many an immigrant repeated "David Levinsky's"
odyssey to and in America, few writers have matched
the skill of Abraham Cahan in conveying the excitement
of the voyage or the bewilderment of settlements. The
two brief chapters that follow are classic portrayals.

Chapter I

Two weeks later I was one of the multitude of steerage passengers on
a Bremen steamship on my way to New York. Who can depict the feeling of desolation, homesickness, uncertainty, and anxiety with which an
emigrant makes his first voyage across the ocean? I proved to be a good
sailor, but the sea frightened me. The thumping of the engines was drum-
ming a ghastly accompaniment to the awesome whisper of the waves. I
felt in the embrace of a vast, uncanny force. And echoing through it all
were the heart-lashing words:

"Are you crazy? You forget your place, young man!"

When Columbus was crossing the Atlantic, on his first great voyage,
his men doubted whether they would ever reach land. So does many an

Pp. 85–102 from *The Rise of David Levinsky* by Abraham Cahan. Copyright 1917, 1945
by Abraham Cahan. Reprinted by permission of Harper & Row, Publishers, Inc.

American-bound emigrant to this day. Such, at least, was the feeling that was lurking in my heart while the Bremen steamer was carrying me to New York. Day after day passes and all you see about you is an unbroken waste of water, an unrelieved, a hopeless monotony of water. You know that a change will come, but this knowledge is confined to your brain. Your senses are skeptical.

In my devotions, which I performed three times a day, without counting a benediction before every meal and every drink of water, grace after every meal and a prayer before going to sleep, I would mentally plead for the safety of the ship and for a speedy sight of land. My scanty luggage included a pair of phylacteries and a plump little prayer-book, with the Book of Psalms at the end. The prayers I knew by heart, but I now often said psalms, in addition, particularly when the sea looked angry and the pitching or rolling was unusually violent. I would read all kinds of psalms, but my favorite among them was the 104th, generally referred to by our people as "Bless the Lord, O my soul," its opening words in the original Hebrew. It is a poem on the power and wisdom of God as manifested in the wonders of nature, some of its verses dealing with the sea. It is said by the faithful every Saturday afternoon during the fall and winter; so I could have recited it from memory; but I preferred to read it in my prayer-book. For it seemed as though the familiar words had changed their identity and meaning, especially those concerned with the sea. Their divine inspiration was now something visible and audible. It was not I who was reading them. It was as though the waves and the clouds, the whole far-flung scene of restlessness and mystery, were whispering to me:

"Thou who coverest thyself with light as with a garment, who stretchest out the heavens like a curtain: who layeth the beams of his chambers in the waters: who maketh the clouds his chariot: who walketh upon the wings of the wind. . . . So is this great and wide sea wherein are things creeping innumerable, both small and great beasts. There go the ships: there is that leviathan whom thou hast made to play therein. . . . ."

The relentless presence of Matilda in my mind worried me immeasurably, for to think of a woman who is a stranger to you is a sin, and so there was the danger of the vessel coming to grief on my account. And, as though to spite me, the closing verse of Psalm 104 reads, "Let the sinners be consumed out of the earth and let the wicked be no more." I strained every nerve to keep Matilda out of my thoughts, but without avail.

When the discoverers of America saw land at last they fell on their knees and a hymn of thanksgiving burst from their souls. The scene, which is one of the most thrilling in history, repeats itself in the heart of every immigrant as he comes in sight of the American shores. I am at a loss to convey the peculiar state of mind that the experience created in me.

When the ship reached Sandy Hook I was literally overcome with the beauty of the landscape.

The immigrant's arrival in his new home is like a second birth to him. Imagine a new-born babe in possession of a fully developed intellect. Would it ever forget its entry into the world? Neither does the immigrant ever forget his entry into a country which is, to him, a new world in the profoundest sense of the term and in which he expects to pass the rest of his life. I conjure up the gorgeousness of the spectacle as it appeared to me on that clear June morning: the magnificent verdure of Staten Island, the tender blue of sea and sky, the dignified bustle of passing craft —above all, those floating, squatting, multitudinously windowed palaces which I subsequently learned to call ferries. It was all so utterly unlike anything I had ever seen or dreamed of before. It unfolded itself like a divine revelation. I was in a trance or in something closely resembling one.

"This, then, is America!" I exclaimed, mutely. The notion of something enchanted which the name had always evoked in me now seemed fully borne out.

In my ecstasy I could not help thinking of Psalm 104, and, opening my little prayer-book, I glanced over those of its verses that speak of hills and rocks, of grass and trees and birds.

My transport of admiration, however, only added to my sense of help-lessness and awe. Here, on shipboard, I was sure of my shelter and food, at least. How was I going to procure my sustenance on those magic shores? I wished the remaining hour could be prolonged indefinitely.

Psalm 104 spoke reassuringly to me. It reminded me of the way God took care of man and beast: "Thou openest thine hand and they are filled with good." But then the very next verse warned me that "Thou hidest thy face, they are troubled: thou takest away their breath, they die." So I was praying God not to hide His face from me, but to open His hand to me; to remember that my mother had been murdered by Gentiles and that I was going to a strange land. When I reached the words, "I will sing unto the Lord as long as I live: I will sing praise to my God while I have my being," I uttered them in a fervent whisper.

My unhappy love never ceased to harrow me. The stern image of Matilda blended with the hostile glamour of America.

One of my fellow-passengers was a young Yiddish-speaking tailor named Gitelson. He was about twenty-four years old, yet his forelock was gray, just his forelock, the rest of his hair being a fine, glossy brown. His own cap had been blown into the sea and the one he had obtained from the steerage steward was too small for him, so that gray tuft of his was always out like a plume. We had not been acquainted more than a few hours, in fact, for he had been seasick throughout the voyage and this was the first day he had been up and about. But then I had seen him on the day of our sailing and subsequently, many times, as he wretchedly lay in his berth. He was literally in tatters. He clung to me like a lover, but we spoke very little. Our hearts were too full for words.

As I thus stood at the railing, prayer-book in hand, he took a look at the page. The most ignorant "man of the earth" among our people can read holy tongue (Hebrew), though he may not understand the meaning of the words. This was the case with Gitelson.

"Saying, 'Bless the Lord, O my soul'?" he asked, reverently. "Why this chapter of all others?"

"Because—Why, just listen." With which I took to translating the Hebrew text into Yiddish for him.

He listened with devout mien. I was not sure that he understood it even in his native tongue, but, whether he did or not, his beaming, wistful look and the deep sigh he emitted indicated that he was in a state similar to mine.

When I say that my first view of New York Bay struck me as something not of this earth it is not a mere figure of speech. I vividly recall the feeling, for example, with which I greeted the first cat I saw on American soil. It was on the Hoboken pier, while the steerage passengers were being marched to the ferry. A large, black, well-fed feline stood in a corner, eying the crowd of new-comers. The sight of it gave me a thrill of joy. "Look! there is a cat!" I said to Gitelson. And in my heart I added, "Just like those at home!" For the moment the little animal made America real to me. At the same time it seemed unreal itself. I was tempted to feel its fur to ascertain whether it was actually the kind of creature I took it for.

We were ferried over to Castle Garden. One of the things that caught my eye as I entered the vast rotunda was an iron staircase rising diagonally against one of the inner walls. A uniformed man, with some papers in his hands, ascended it with brisk, resounding step till he disappeared through a door not many inches from the ceiling. It may seem odd, but I can never think of my arrival in this country without hearing the ringing footfalls of this official and beholding the yellow eyes of the black cat which stared at us at the Hoboken pier.

The harsh manner of the immigration offiers was a grievous surprise to me. As contrasted with the officials of my despotic country, those of a republic had been portrayed in my mind as paragons of refinement and cordiality. My anticipations were rudely belied. "They are not a bit better than Cossacks," I remarked to Gitelson. But they neither looked nor spoke like Cossacks, so their gruff voices were part of the uncanny scheme of things that surrounded me. These unfriendly voices flavored all America with a spirit of icy inhospitality that sent a chill through my very soul.

The stringent immigration laws that were passed some years later had not yet come into existence. We had no difficulty in being admitted to the United States, and when I was I was loath to leave the Garden.

Many of the other immigrants were met by relatives, friends. There were cries of joy, tears, embraces, kisses. All of which intensified my sense of loneliness and dread of the New World. The agencies which two Jewish charity organizations now maintain at the Immigrant Station had not yet been established. Gitelson, who like myself had no friends in New York, never left my side. He was even more timid than I. It seemed as though he were holding on to me for dear life. This had the effect of putting me on my mettle.

"Cheer up, old man!" I said, with bravado. "America is not the place to be a ninny in. Come, pull yourself together."

In truth, I addressed these exhortations as much to myself as to him; and so far, at least, as I was concerned, my words had the desired effect.

I lead the way out of the big Immigrant Station. As we reached the park outside we were pounced down upon by two evil-looking men, representatives of boarding-houses for immigrants. They pulled us so roughly and their general appearance and manner were so uninviting that we struggled and protested until they let us go—not without some parting curses. Then I led the way across Battery Park and under the Elevated railway to State Street. A train hurtling and panting along overhead produced a bewildering, a daunting effect on me. The active life of the great strange city made me feel like one abandoned in the midst of a jungle. Where were we to go? What were we to do? But the presence of Gitelson continued to act as a spur on me. I mustered courage to approach a policeman, something I should never have been bold enough to do at home. As a matter of fact, I scarcely had an idea what his function was. To me he looked like some uniformed nobleman—an impression that in itself was enough to intimidate me. With his coat of blue cloth, starched linen collar, and white gloves, he reminded me of anything but the policemen of my town. I addressed him in Yiddish, making it as near an approach to German as I knew how, but my efforts were lost on him. He shook his head. With a witheringly dignified grimace he then pointed his club in the direction of Broadway and strutted off majestically.

"He's not better than a Cossack, either," was my verdict.

At this moment a voice hailed us in Yiddish. Facing about, we beheld a middle-aged man with huge, round, perpendicular nostrils and a huge, round, deep dimple in his chin that looked like a third nostril. Prosperity was written all over his smooth-shaven face and broad-shouldered, stocky figure. He was literally aglow with diamonds and self-satisfaction. But he was unmistakably one of our people. It was like coming across a human being in the jungle. Moreover, his very diamonds somehow told a tale of former want, of a time when he had landed, an impecunious immigrant like myself; and this made him a living source of encouragement to me.

"God Himself has sent you to us," I began, acting as the spokesman; but he gave no heed to me. His eyes were eagerly fixed on Gitelson and his tatters.

"You're a tailor, aren't you?" he questioned him.

My steerage companion nodded. "I'm a ladies' tailor, but I have worked on men's clothing, too," he said.

"A ladies' tailor?" the well-dressed stranger echoed, with ill-concealed delight. "Very well; come along. I have work for you."

That he should have been able to read Gitelson's trade in his face and figure scarcely surprised me. In my native place it seemed to be a matter of course that one could tell a tailor by his general appearance and walk. Besides, had I not divined the occupation of my fellow-passenger the moment I saw him on deck?

As I learned subsequently, the man who accosted us on State Street was a cloak contractor, and his presence in the neighborhood of Castle Garden was anything but a matter of chance. He came there quite often, in fact, his purpose being to angle for cheap labor among the newly arrived immigrants.

We paused near Bowling Green. The contractor and my fellow-passenger were absorbed in a conversation full of sartorial technicalities which were Greek to me, but which brought a gleam of joy into Gitelson's eye. My former companion seemed to have become oblivious of my existence.

As we resumed our walk up Broadway the bejeweled man turned to me. "And what was your occupation? You have no trade, have you?"

"I read Talmud," I said confusedly.

"I see, but that's no business in America," he declared. "Any relatives here?"

"No."

"Well, don't worry. You will be all right. If a fellow isn't lazy nor a fool he has no reason to be sorry he came to America. It'll be all right."

"All right" he said in English, and I conjectured what it meant from the context. In the course of the minute or two which he bestowed upon me he uttered it so many times that the phrase engraved itself upon my memory. It was the first bit of English I ever acquired.

The well-dressed, trim-looking crowds of lower Broadway impressed me as a multitude of counts, barons, princes. I was puzzled by their preoccupied faces and hurried step. It seemed to comport ill with their baronial dress and general high-born appearance.

In a vague way all this helped to confirm my conception of America as a unique country, unlike the rest of the world.

When we reached the General Post-Office, at the end of the Third Avenue surface line, our guide bade us stop. "Walk straight ahead," he said to me, waving his hand toward Park Row. "Just keep walking until you see a lot of Jewish people. It isn't far from here." With which he slipped a silver quarter into my hand and made Gitelson bid me good-by.

The two then boarded a big red horse-car.

I was left with a sickening sense of having been tricked, cast off, and abandoned. I stood watching the receding public vehicle, as though its scarlet hue were my last gleam of hope in the world. When it finally disappeared from view my heart sank within me. I may safely say that the half-hour that followed is one of the worst I experienced in all the thirty-odd years of my life in this country.

The big, round nostrils of the contractor and the gray forelock of my young steerage-fellow haunted my brain as hideous symbols of treachery.

With twenty-nine cents in my pocket (four cents was all that was left of the sum which I had received from Matilda and her mother) I set forth in the direction of East Broadway.

Chapter II

Ten minutes' walk brought me to the heart of the Jewish East Side. The streets swarmed with Yiddish-speaking immigrants. The sign-boards were in English and Yiddish, some of them in Russian. The scurry and hustle of the people were not merely overwhelmingly greater, both in volume and intensity, than in my native town. It was of another sort. The swing and step of the pedestrians, the voices and manner of the street peddlers, and a hundred and one other things seemed to testify to far more self-confidence and energy, to larger ambitions and wider scopes, than did the appearance of the crowds in my birthplace.

The great thing was that these people were better dressed than the inhabitants of my town. The poorest-looking man wore a hat (instead of a cap), a stiff collar and a necktie, and the poorest woman wore a hat or a bonnet.

The appearance of a newly arrived immigrant was still a novel spectacle on the East Side. Many of the passers-by paused to look at me with wistful smiles of curiosity.

"There goes a green one!" some of them exclaimed.

The sight of me obviously evoked reminiscences in them of the days when they had been "green ones" like myself. It was a second birth that they were witnessing, an experience which they had once gone through themselves and which was one of the greatest events in their lives.

"Green one" or "greenhorn" is one of the many English words and phrases which my mother-tongue has appropriated in England and America. Thanks to the many millions of letters that pass annually between the Jews of Russia and their relatives in the United States, a number of these words have by now come to be generally known among our people at home as well as here. In the eighties, however, one who had not visited any English-speaking country was utterly unfamiliar with them. And so I had never heard of "green one" before. Still, "green," in the sense of color, is Yiddish as well as English, so I understood the phrase at once, and as a contemptuous quizzical appellation for a newly arrived, inexperienced immigrant it stung me cruelly. As I went along I heard it again and again. Some of the passers-by would call me "greenhorn" in a tone of blighting gaiety, but these were an exception. For the most part it was

"green one" and in a spirit of sympathetic interest. It hurt me, all the
same. Even those glances that offered me a cordial welcome and good
wishes had something self-complacent and condescending in them. "Poor
fellow! he is a green one," these people seemed to say. "We are not, of
course. We are Americanized."

For my first meal in the New World I bought a three-cent wedge of
coarse rye bread, off a huge round loaf, on a stand on Essex Street. I was
too strict in my religious observances to eat it without first performing
ablutions and offering a brief prayer. So I approached a bewigged old
woman who stood in the doorway of a small grocery-store to let me wash
my hands and eat my meal in her place. She looked old-fashioned enough,
yet when she heard my request she said, with a laugh:

"You're a green one, I see."

"Suppose I am," I resented. "Do the yellow ones or black ones all eat
without washing? Can't a fellow be a good Jew in America?"

"Yes, of course he can, but—well, wait till you see for yourself."

However, she asked me to come in, gave me some water and an old
apron to serve me for a towel, and when I was ready to eat my bread she
placed a glass of milk before me, explaining that she was not going to
charge me for it.

"In America people are not foolish enough to be content with dry
bread," she said, sententiously.

While I ate she questioned me about my antecedents. I remember how
she impressed me as a strong, clever woman of few words as long as she
catechised me, and how disappointed I was when she began to talk of herself. The astute, knowing mien gradually faded out of her face and I had
before me a gushing, boastful old bore. My intention was to take a long
stroll, as much in the hope of coming upon some windfall as for the purpose of taking a look at the great American city. Many of the letters that
came from the United States to my birthplace before I sailed had contained a warning not to imagine that America was a "land of gold" and
that treasure might be had in the streets of New York for the picking. But
these warnings only had the effect of lending vividness to my image of an
American street as a thoroughfare strewn with nuggets of the precious
metal. Symbolically speaking, this was the idea one had of the "land of
Columbus." It was a continuation of the widespread effect produced by
stories of Cortes and Pizarro in the sixteenth century, confirmed by the
successes of some Russian emigrants of my time.

I asked the grocery-woman to let me leave my bundle with her, and,
after considerable hesitation, she allowed me to put it among some empty
barrels in her cellar.

I went wandering over the Ghetto. Instead of stumbling upon nuggets
of gold, I found signs of poverty. In one place I came across a poor family
who—as I learned upon inquiry—had been dispossessed for non-payment
of rent. A mother and her two little boys were watching their pile of furni-

ture and other household goods on the sidewalk while the passers-by were dropping coins into a saucer placed on one of the chairs to enable the family to move into new quarters.

What puzzled me was the nature of the furniture. For in my birthplace chairs and a couch like those I now saw on the sidewalk would be a sign of prosperity. But then anything was to be expected of a country where the poorest devil wore a hat and a starched collar.

I walked on.

The exclamation "A green one" or "A greenhorn" continued. If I did not hear it, I saw it in the eyes of the people who passed me.

When it grew dark and I was much in need of rest I had a street peddler direct me to a synagogue. I expected to spend the night there. What could have been more natural?

At the house of God I found a handful of men in prayer. It was a large, spacious room and the smallness of their number gave it an air of desolation. I joined in the devotions with great fervor. My soul was sobbing to Heaven to take care of me in the strange country.

The service over, several of the worshipers took up some Talmud folio or other holy book and proceeded to read them aloud in the familiar singsong. The strange surroundings suddenly began to look like home to me.

One of the readers, an elderly man with a pinched face and forked little beard, paused to look me over.

"A green one?" he asked, genially.

He told me that the synagogue was crowded on Saturdays, while on week-days people in America had no time to say their prayers at home, much less to visit a house of worship.

"It isn't Russia," he said, with a sigh. "Judaism has not much of a chance here."

When he heard that I intended to stay at the synagogue overnight he smiled ruefully.

"One does not sleep in an American synagogue," he said. "It is not Russia." Then, scanning me once more, he added, with an air of compassionate perplexity: "Where will you sleep, poor child? I wish I could take you to my house, but—well, America is not Russia. There is no pity here, no hospitality. My wife would raise a rumpus if I brought you along. I should never hear the last of it."

With a deep sigh and nodding his head plaintively he returned to his book, swaying back and forth. But he was apparently more interested in the subject he had broached. "When we were at home," he resumed, "she, too, was a different woman. She did not make life a burden to me as she does here. Have you no money at all?"

I showed him the quarter I had received from the cloak contractor.

"Poor fellow! Is that all you have? There are places where you can get a night's lodging for fifteen cents, but what are you going to do afterward? I am simply ashamed of myself."

" 'Hospitality,' " he quoted from the Talmud, " 'is one of the things which the giver enjoys in this world and the fruit of which he relishes in the world to come.' To think that I cannot offer a Talmudic scholar a night's rest! Alas! America has turned me into a mound of ashes."

"You were well off in Russia, weren't you?" I inquired, in astonishment. For, indeed, I had never heard of any but poor people emigrating to America.

"I used to spend my time reading Talmud at the synagogue," was his reply.

Many of his answers seemed to fit, not the question asked, but one which was expected to follow it. You might have thought him anxious to forestall your next query in order to save time and words, had it not been so difficult for him to keep his mouth shut.

"She," he said, referring to his wife, "had a nice little business. She sold feed for horses and she rejoiced in the thought that she was married to a man of learning. True, she has a tongue. That she always had, but over there it was not so bad. She has become a different woman here. Alas! America is a topsy-turvy country."

He went on to show how the New World turned things upside down, transforming an immigrant shoemaker into a man of substance, while a former man of leisure was forced to work in a factory here. In like manner, his wife had changed for the worse, for, lo and behold! instead of supporting him while he read Talmud, as she used to do at home, she persisted in sending him out to peddle. "America is not Russia," she said. "A man must make a living here." But, alas! it was too late to begin now! He had spent the better part of his life at his holy books and was fit for nothing else now. His wife, however, would take no excuse. He must peddle or be nagged to death. And if he ventured to slip into some synagogue of an afternoon and read a page or two he would be in danger of being caught red-handed, so to say, for, indeed, she often shadowed him to make sure that he did not play truant. Alas! America was not Russia.

A thought crossed my mind that if Reb Sender were here, he, too, might have to go peddling. Poor Reb Sender! The very image of him with a basket on his arm broke my heart. America did seem to be the most cruel place on earth.

"I am telling you all this that you may see why I can't invite you to my house," explained the peddler.

All I did see was that the poor man could not help unburdening his mind to the first listener that presented himself.

He pursued his tale of woe. He went on complaining of his own fate, quite forgetful of mine. Instead of continuing to listen, I fell to gazing around the synagogue more or less furtively. One of the readers attracted my special attention. He was a venerable-looking man with a face which, as I now recall it, reminds me of Thackeray. Only he had a finer head than the English novelist.

At last the henpecked man discovered my inattention and fell silent. A minute later his tongue was at work again.

"You are looking at that man over there, aren't you?" he asked.

"Who is he?"

"When the Lord of the World gives one good luck he gives one good looks as well."

"Why, is he rich?"

"His son-in-law is, but then his daughter cherishes him as she does the apple of her eye, and—well, when the Lord of the World wishes to give a man happiness he gives him good children, don't you know."

He rattled on, betraying his envy of the venerable-looking man in various ways and telling me all he knew about him—that he was a widower named Even, that he had been some years in America, and that his daughter furnished him all the money he needed and a good deal more, so that "he lived like a monarch." Even would not live in his daughter's house, however, because her kitchen was not conducted according to the laws of Moses, and everything else in it was too modern. So he roomed and boarded with pious strangers, visiting her far less frequently than she visited him and never eating at her table.

"He is a very proud man," my informant said. "One must not approach him otherwise than on tiptoe."

I threw a glance at Even. His dignified singsong seemed to confirm my interlocutor's characterization of him.

"Perhaps you will ask me how his son-in-law takes it all?" the voluble Talmudist went on. "Well, his daughter is a beautiful woman and well favored." The implication was that her husband was extremely fond of her and let her use his money freely. "They are awfully rich and they live like veritable Gentiles, which is a common disease among the Jews of America. But then she observes the commandment, 'Honor thy father.' That she does."

Again he tried to read his book and again the temptation to gossip was too much for him. He returned to Even's pride, dwelling with considerable venom upon his love of approbation and vanity. "May the Uppermost not punish me for my evil words, but to see him take his roll of bills out of his pocket and pay his contribution to the synagogue one would think he was some big merchant and not a poor devil sponging on his son-in-law."

A few minutes later he told me admiringly how Even often "loaned" him a half-dollar to enable him to do some reading at the house of God.

"I tell my virago of a wife I have sold fifty cents' worth of goods," he explained to me, sadly.

After a while the man with the Thackeray face closed his book, kissed it, and rose to go. On his way out he unceremoniously paused in front of me, a silver snuff-box in his left hand, and fell to scrutinizing me. He had the appearance of a well-paid rabbi of a large, prosperous town. "He is going to say, 'A green one,' " I prophesied to myself, all but shuddering at the prospect. And, sure enough, he did, but he took his time about it, which made the next minute seem a year to me. He took snuff with tantalizing deliberation. Next he sneezed with great zest and then he resumed sizing me up. The suspense was insupportable. Another second and I might have burst out, "For mercy's sake say 'A green one,' and let us be done with it." But at that moment he uttered it of his own accord:

"A green one, I see. Where from?" And grasping my hand he added in Hebrew, "Peace be to ye."

His first questions about me were obsequiously answered by the man with the forked beard, whereupon my attention was attracted by the fact that he addressed him by his Gentile name—that is, as "Mr. Even," and not by his Hebrew name, as he would have done in our birthplace. Surely America did not seem to be much of a God-fearing country.

When Mr. Even heard of my Talmud studies he questioned me about the tractates I had recently read and even challenged me to explain an apparent discrepancy in a certain passage, for the double purpose of testing my "Talmud brains" and flaunting his own. I acquitted myself creditably, it seemed, and I felt that I was making a good impression personally as well. Anyhow, he invited me to supper in a restaurant.

On our way there I told him of my mother's violent death, vaguely hoping that it would add to his interest in me. It did—even more than I had expected. To my pleasant surprise, he proved to be familiar with the incident. It appeared that because our section lay far outside the region of pogroms, or anti-Jewish riots, the killing of my mother by a Gentile mob had attracted considerable attention. I was thrilled to find myself in the lime-light of world-wide publicity. I almost felt like a hero.

"So you are her son?" he said, pausing to look me over, as though I had suddenly become a new man. "My poor orphan boy!"

He caused me to recount the incident in every detail. In doing so I made it as appallingly vivid as I knew how. He was so absorbed and moved that he repeatedly made me stop in the middle of the sidewalk so as to look me in the face as he listened.

"Oh, but you must be hungry," he suddenly interrupted me. "Come on."

Arrived at the restaurant, he ordered supper for me. Then he withdrew, commending me to the care of the proprietress until he should return.

He had no sooner shut the door behind him than she took to questioning me: Was I a relative of Mr. Even? If not, then why was he taking so much interest in me? She was a vivacious, well-fed young matron with cheeks of a flaming red and with the consciousness of business success all but spurting from her black eyes. From what she, assisted by one of the other customers present, told me about my benefactor I learned that his son-in-law was the owner of the tenement-house in which the restaurant was located, as well as of several other buildings. They also told me of the landlord's wife, of her devotion to her father, and of the latter's piety and dignity. It appeared, however, that in her filial reverence she would draw the line upon his desire not to spare the rod upon her children, which was really the chief reason why he was a stranger at her house.

I had been waiting about two hours and was growing uneasy, when Mr. Even came back, explaining that he had spent the time taking his own supper and finding lodgings for me.

He then took me to store after store, buying me a suit of clothes, a hat, some underclothes, handkerchiefs (the first white handkerchiefs I ever possessed), collars, shoes, and a necktie.

He spent a considerable sum on me. As we passed from block to block he kept saying, "Now you won't look green," or, "That will make you look American." At one point he added, "Not that you are a bad-looking fellow as it is, but then one must be presentable in America." At this he quoted from the Talmud an equivalent to the saying that one must do in Rome as the Romans do.

When all our purchases had been made he took me to a barber shop with bathrooms in the rear.

"Give him a hair-cut and a bath," he said to the proprietor. "Cut off his side-locks while you are at it. One may go without them and yet be a good Jew."

He disappeared again, but when I emerged from the bathroom I found him waiting for me. I stood before him, necktie and collar in hand, not knowing what to do with them, till he showed me how to put them on. "Don't worry, David," he consoled me. "When I came here I, too, had to learn these things." When he was through with the job he took me in front of a looking-glass. "Quite an American, isn't he?" he said to the barber, beamingly. "And a good-looking fellow, too."

When I took a look at the mirror I was bewildered. I scarcely recognized myself.

I was mentally parading my "modern" make-up before Matilda. A pang of yearning clutched my heart. It was a momentary feeling. For the rest, I was all in a flutter with embarrassment and a novel relish of existence. It was as though the hair-cut and the American clothes had changed my identity. The steamer, Gitelson, and the man who had snatched him up now appeared to be something of the remote past. The day had been so crowded with novel impressions that it seemed an age.

He took me to an apartment in a poor tenement-house and introduced me to a tall, bewhiskered, morose-looking, elderly man and a smiling woman of thirty-five, explaining that he had paid them in advance for a month's board and lodging. When he said, "This is Mr. Levinsky," I felt as though I was being promoted in rank as behooved my new appearance. "Mister" struck me as something like a title of nobility. It thrilled me. But somehow it seemed ridiculous, too. Indeed, it was some time before I could think of myself as a "Mister" without being tempted to laugh.

"And here is some cash for you," he said, handing me a five-dollar bill, and some silver, in addition. "And now you must shift for yourself. That's all I can do for you. Nor, indeed, would I do more if I could. A young man like you must learn to stand on his own legs. Understand? If you do well, come to see me. Understand?"

There was an eloquent pause which said that if I did not do well I was not to molest him. Then he added, aloud:

"There is only one thing I want you to promise me. Don't neglect your religion nor your Talmud. Do you promise that, David?"

I did. There was a note of fatherly tenderness in the way this utter stranger called me David. It reminded me of Reb Sender. I wanted to say something to express my gratitude, but I felt a lump in my throat.

He advised me to invest the five dollars in dry-goods and to take up peddling. Then, wishing me good luck, he left.

My landlady, who had listened to Mr. Even's parting words with pious nods and rapturous grins, remarked that one would vainly search the world for another man like him, and proceeded to make my bed on a lounge.

The room was a kitchen. The stove was a puzzle to me. I wondered whether it was really a stove.

"Is this used for heating?" I inquired.

"Yes, for heating and cooking," she explained, with smiling cordiality. And she added, with infinite superiority, "America has no use for those big tile ovens."

When I found myself alone in the room the feeling of desolation and uncertainty which had tormented me all day seized me once again.

I went to bed and began to say my bed-prayer. I did so mechanically. My mind did not attend to the words I was murmuring. Instead, it was saying to God: "Lord of the Universe, you have been good to me so far. I went out of that grocery-store in the hope of coming upon some good piece of luck and my hope was realized. Be good to me in the future as well. I shall be more pious than ever, I promise you, even if America is a godless country."

I was excruciatingly homesick. My heart went out to my poor dead mother. Then I reflected that it was my story of her death that had led Even to spend so much money on me. It seemed as if she were taking care of me from her grave. It seemed, too, as though she had died so that I might arouse sympathy and make a good start in America. I thought of her and of all Antomir, and my pangs of yearning for her were tinged with pangs of my unrequited love for Matilda.

HOME FROM THE WARS
John Steinbeck

Too often discussions of the American ethnic experience have an east coast bias. One forgets the Indians and Mexicans and Orientals for whom the west was home (and, for some, homeland). It is well to recognize that the ethnic mosaic that is America consists not only of the enclaves of Anglos and Irish and Italians and Jews and Blacks, but the reservations and the barrios as well.

This selection enables us to glimpse life in the California town of "Tortilla Flat," a fictional settlement conjured up in the mind of novelist John Steinbeck but that reflects the world of the west coast, circa 1918.

Danny, who would now be known as a Chicano, is home from the Great War. A small slice of his life comes alive in the following pages.

When Danny came home from the army he learned that he was an heir and an owner of property. The viejo, that is the grandfather, had died leaving Danny the two small houses on Tortilla Flat.

When Danny heard about it he was a little weighed down with the responsibility of ownership. Before he ever went to look at his property he bought a gallon of red wine and drank most of it himself. The weight of responsibility left him then, and his very worst nature came to the surface. He shouted, he broke a few chairs in a poolroom on Alvarado Street; he had two short but glorious fights. No one paid much attention to Danny.

At last his wavering bow-legs took him toward the wharf where, at this early hour in the morning, the Italian fishermen were walking down in rubber boots to go out to sea.

Race antipathy overcame Danny's good sense. He menaced the fishermen. "Sicilian bastards," he called them, and "Scum from the prison island," and "Dogs of dogs of dogs." He cried, *"Chinga tu madre, Piojo."* He thumbed his nose and made obscene gestures below his waist. The fishermen only grinned and shifted their oars and said, "Hello, Danny. When'd you get home? Come around to-night. We got new wine."

Danny was outraged. He screamed, *"Pon un condo a la cabeza."*

They called, "Good-by, Danny. See you to-night." And they climbed into their little boats and rowed out to the lampara launches and started their engines and chugged away.

Danny was insulted. He walked back up Alvarado Street, breaking windows as he went, and in the second block a policeman took him in hand. Danny's great respect for the law caused him to go quietly. If he had not just been discharged from the army after the victory over Germany, he would have been sentenced to six months. As it was, the judge gave him only thirty days.

And so for one month Danny sat on his cot in the Monterey city jail. Sometimes he drew obscene pictures on the walls, and sometimes he thought over his army career. Time hung heavy on Danny's hands there in his cell in the city jail. Now and then a drunk was put in for the night, but for the most part crime in Monterey was stagnant, and Danny was lonely. The bedbugs bothered him a little at first, but as they got used to the taste of him and he grew accustomed to their bites, they got along peacefully.

He started playing a satiric game. He caught a bedbug, squashed it against the wall, drew a circle around it with a pencil and named it "Mayor Clough." Then he caught others and named them after the City Council. In a little while he had one wall decorated with squashed bedbugs, each named for a local dignitary. He drew ears and tails on them, gave them big noses and mustaches. Tito Ralph, the jailer, was scandalized; but he made no complaint because Danny had not included either the justice of the peace who had sentenced him, nor any of the police force. He had a vast respect for the law.

One night when the jail was lonely, Tito Ralph came into Danny's cell bearing two bottles of wine. An hour later he went out for more wine, and Danny went with him. It was cheerless in the jail. They stayed at Torrelli's, where they bought the wine, until Torrelli threw them out. After that Danny went up among the pines and fell asleep, while Tito Ralph staggered back and reported his escape.

When the brilliant sun awakened Danny about noon, he determined to hide all day to escape pursuit. He ran and dodged behind bushes. He peered out of the undergrowth like a hunted fox. And, at evening, the rules having been satisfied, he came out and went about his business.

Danny's business was fairly direct. He went to the back door of a restaurant. "Got any old bread I can give my dog?" he asked the cook. And while that gullible man was wrapping up the food, Danny stole two slices of ham, four eggs, a lamb chop and a fly swatter.

"I will pay you sometime," he said.

"No need to pay for scraps. I throw them away if you don't take them."

Danny felt better about the theft then. If that was the way they felt, on the surface he was guiltless. He went back to Torrelli's, traded the four eggs, the lamb chop and the fly swatter for a water glass of grappa and retired toward the woods to cook his supper.

The night was dark and damp. The fog hung like limp gauze among the black pines that guard the landward limits of Monterey. Danny put his head down and hurried for the shelter of the woods. Ahead of him he made out another hurrying figure; and as he narrowed the distance, he recognized the scuttling walk of his old friend Pilon. Danny was a generous man, but he recalled that he had sold all his food except the two slices of ham and the bag of stale bread.

"I will pass Pilon by," he decided. "He walks like a man who is full of roast turkey and things like that."

Then suddenly Danny noticed that Pilon clutched his coat lovingly across his bosom.

"Ai, Pilon, *amigo!*" Danny cried.

Pilon scuttled on faster. Danny broke into a trot. "Pilon, my little friend! Where goest thou so fast?"

Pilon resigned himself to the inevitable and waited. Danny approached warily, but his tone was enthusiastic. "I looked for thee, dearest of little angelic friends, for see, I have here two great steaks from God's own pig, and a sack of sweet white bread. Share my bounty, Pilon, little dumpling."

Pilon shrugged his shoulders. "As you say," he muttered savagely. They walked on together into the woods. Pilon was puzzled. At length he stopped and faced his friend. "Danny," he asked sadly, "how knewest thou I had a bottle of brandy under my coat?"

"Brandy?" Danny cried. "Thou hast brandy? Perhaps it is for some sick old mother," he said naïvely. "Perhaps thou keepest it for Our Lord Jesus when He comes again. Who am I, thy friend, to judge the destination of this brandy? I am not even sure thou hast it. Besides I am not thirsty. I would not touch this brandy. Thou art welcome to this big roast of pork I have, but as for thy brandy, that is thine own."

Pilon answered him sternly. "Danny, I do not mind sharing my brandy with you, half and half. It is my duty to see you do not drink it all."

Danny dropped the subject then. "Here in the clearing I will cook this pig, and you will toast the sugar cakes in this bag here. Put thy brandy here, Pilon. It is better here, where we can see it, and each other."

They built a fire and broiled the ham and ate the stale bread. The brandy receded quickly down the bottle. After they had eaten, they huddled near the fire and sipped delicately at the bottle like effete bees. And the fog came down upon them and grayed their coats with moisture. The wind sighed sadly in the pines about them.

And after a time, a loneliness fell upon Danny and Pilon. Danny thought of his lost friends.

"Where is Arthur Morales?" Danny asked, turning his palms up and thrusting his arms forward. "Dead in France," he answered himself, turning the palms down and dropping his arms in despair. "Dead for his country. Dead in a foreign land. Strangers walk near his grave and they do not know Arthur Morales lies there." He raised his hands palms upward again. "Where is Pablo, that good man?"

"In jail," said Pilon. "Pablo stole a goose and hid in the brush; and that goose bit Pablo and Pablo cried out and so was caught. Now he lies in jail for six months."

Danny sighed and changed the subject, for he realized that he had prodigally used up the only acquaintance in any way fit for oratory. But the loneliness was still on him and demanded an outlet. "Here we sit," he began at last.

"—broken hearted," Pilon added rhythmically.

"No, this is not a poem," Danny said. "Here we sit, homeless. We gave our lives for our country, and now we have no roof over our head."

"We never did have," Pilon added helpfully.

Danny drank dreamily until Pilon touched his elbow and took the bottle. "That reminds me," Danny said, "of a story of a man who owned two whore houses—" His mouth dropped open. "Pilon!" he cried. "Pilon! my little fat duck of a baby friend. I had forgotten! I am an heir! I own two houses."

"Whore houses?" Pilon asked hopefully. "Thou art a drunken liar," he continued.

"No, Pilon. I tell the truth. The viejo died. I am the heir. I, the favorite grandson."

"Thou art the only grandson," said the realist, Pilon. "Where are these houses?"

"You know the viejo's house on Tortilla Flat, Pilon?"

"Here in Monterey?"

"Yes, here in Tortilla Flat."

"Are they any good, these houses?"

Danny sank back, exhausted with emotion. "I do not know. I forgot I owned them."

Pilon sat silent and absorbed. His face grew mournful. He threw a handful of pine needles on the fire, watched the flames climb frantically among them and die. For a long time he looked into Danny's face with deep anxiety, and then Pilon sighed noisily, and again he sighed. "Now it is over," he said sadly. "Now the great times are done. Thy friends will mourn, but nothing will come of their mourning."

Danny put down the bottle, and Pilon picked it up and set it in his own lap.

WHEN I GROW UP . . .
Jerre Mangione

Many of those who came to America in the late nineteenth and early twentieth century settled in the big port cities of New York, Philadelphia, Boston, and Baltimore. Some, however, pushed on. They moved to places where their "landsmen" or "paisanos" or "brothers" had found work and beckoned others to follow. Rochester, New York, was one such place. Center of the men's clothing industry, Rochester served as a magnet for many Jewish and Italian tailors.

Jerre Mangione writes about his people, first and second generation, the Sicilians of Rochester and their adjustment to life in the New World.

The lighthearted style should not mislead the reader. Mangione, through his characters, is saying something important about America and the American Dream, at least as seen through the eyes of the Amorosos of "Mount Allegro."

"When I grow up I want to be an American," Giustina said. We looked at our sister; it was something none of us had ever said.

"Me too," Maria echoed.

"Aw, you don't even know what an American is," Joe scoffed.

"I do so," Giustina said.

It was more than the rest of us knew.

The editor and publisher thank Jerre Mangione for permission to reprint "When I Grow Up . . .," from *Mount Allegro*, by Jerre Mangione. Originally published by Houghton Mifflin Company, 1943. Copyright 1942, 1952 by the author. All rights reserved by him.

"We're Americans right now," I said. "Miss Zimmerman says if you're born here you're an American."

"Aw, she's nuts," Joe said. He had no use for most teachers. "We're Italians. If y' don't believe me ask Pop."

But my father wasn't very helpful. "Your children will be *Americani*. But you, my son, are half-and-half. Now stop asking me questions. You should know those things from going to school. What do you learn in school, anyway?"

The world, my teacher insisted, was made up of all the colored spots on a globe. One of the purple spots was America, even though America wasn't purple when you looked at it. The orange spot was Italy. Never having been there, that wasn't so hard to believe. You never used this globe as a ball, even after Rosario Alfano gave you one as a birthday present. You just spun it, while some near-by grownup told you that Columbus discovered the world to be round.

You pretended to believe that because it was hard to argue with grownups and be polite at the same time, but you told yourself that any grownup who swallowed that must be nuts. It was confusing when your own father said it because you liked to think he was right about everything; but when your Uncle Sarafino said it, the uncle from Boston who promised to give you a dollar for eating some hot peppers raw, and then refused to give you the money, you were sure he was nuts and the world wasn't round.

Then one day one of your new teachers looked at you brightly and said you were Italian because your last name was Amoroso and that too was puzzling. You talked it over with some of the boys in the gang.

First with Tony Long, who was the leader. Tony said his father changed his name when he came to America because he got tired of spelling it out for a lot of dopes who didn't know how to spell. I showed Tony my globe and he pointed to a red spot on it and said that was where his mother and father came from. That's all he knew about it. Tony couldn't speak Polish and his mother hardly knew any American. He looked angry when she spoke to him in Polish in front of the other kids.

Then there was Abe Rappaport, who went to a synagogue every Saturday. Abe wore glasses and knew a lot. He said his parents came from Russia and pointed to a big gob of blue on the globe. It was close to Poland but Abe looked more like me than he did like Tony, who had blond hair. Abe was one of those who like to read and argue. We spent a whole day once asking each other, "How do you know I ain't God?" until the other guys said we were crazy.

The other boys in the gang claimed they were Americans even though their parents didn't know how to speak American well. When I showed them my globe and asked them to point to the country where their parents came from, they said they didn't know. They didn't care either.

I showed my globe to a guy who belonged to another gang. His name was Robert Di Nella and he had blond hair and blue eyes like Tony Long.

None of us liked him because he was always trying to boss us around, and we called him the Kaiser. He pointed to Italy on the globe, even though his mother didn't speak Italian the way mine did. Then he pointed to a tiny orange splash at the end of the Italian boot and called me a lousy *Siciliano*. I hit him on the jaw and, because he was taller and bigger, ran to safety with the globe tucked under my arm like a football.

This incident marked the beginning of a long and violent feud with the Kaiser. He ambushed me at every possible opportunity and preceded each attack by calling me a Sicilian. From the way he hissed the word at me, I soon realized that while being a Sicilian was a special distinction, it probably was not one that called for cheers and congratulations.

The Kaiser must have been descended from a Medici. He was a talented fiend and would lie in wait for me on Sunday mornings just as I was coming out of church. With my soul just whitewashed for the week, he could hardly have picked a better time to bully me. There I stood, without any of my gang around, hopelessly overflowing with peace and the religious ecstasy I had achieved by singing in tune with the rest of the choir boys.

As I saw the Kaiser waiting, his face ugly with a leer, the forces of good and evil would come to grips within me and before the good could be completely crushed, the Kaiser had already spat out his insults. In a lot behind the church, where we staged our battles, my conscience would make one last futile effort to persuade me to turn the other cheek, but by that time the Kaiser, quite unhampered by a conscience, had already landed the first blow and forced me to retaliate.

From anyone else the name *Siciliano* might not have been so insulting. From the Kaiser it rankled and assumed diabolical meaning, especially when he followed it up with such invectives as "blackmailer" and "murderer." For a time the boys in the gang used this propaganda against my brother and me whenever they became angry with us. As a result, Joe and I, who were usually at war with each other, began coming to one another's rescue when one of us was defending the honor of Sicilians and getting the worst of it.

By such teamwork we usually won our fights. But we soon learned that the odds were hopelessly against us. There were grownup Robert Di Nellas all around who were too big for us. There were also the newspapers, which delighted in featuring murder stories involving persons with foreign names. My father would read these accounts carefully, anxious to determine, first of all, if the killer was an Italian; if so, whether he hailed from Sicily. "It is bad enough for an Italian to commit a murder, but it is far worse when a Sicilian does," he would say.

In the event the murderer turned out to be a Sicilian, my father would solemnly announce that the criminal undoubtedly came from Carrapipi, a small town in Sicily which—according to my relatives—produced nothing but a population of potential thieves, blackmailers, and murderers. Few of them had ever seen Carrapipi, but the unpleasant experiences they had

had with some of its natives were enough to convince them that all Sicilians in the United States found guilty of serious crimes were born in Carrapipi.

My relatives developed a beautiful legend to substantiate this idea. The villain of the piece was a judge in Carrapipi who, in his zeal to save the state the expense of maintaining dangerous criminals in jail for many years, would send them to the United States instead of prison. His tactic was to pronounce a heavy sentence on finding a criminal guilty, and then inform him that a boat was leaving Palermo in a few days for New York. He would then blandly suggest that if the prisoner was found in Italy after the boat left, his sentence would be doubled.

"Naturally," my Uncle Nino explained whenever he told the story, "most of the criminals preferred to catch the boat. Going to America, where the streets were said to be lined with gold, certainly seemed more pleasant to them than spending their lives in jail. That pig of a judge, however patriotic his motives were, is undoubtedly to blame for the miserable reputation we Sicilians have in this unhappy land."

To call anyone *Carrapipanu,* whether or not he actually came from that town, was to insult him, for the name symbolized nearly everything that was villainous or ungracious. One of the most frequent charges made was that a native of Carrapipi could not even speak the Sicilian dialect properly. Instead of saying "Please come in," for instance, he would snarl the words—his tongue was likely to be as crooked as his soul—so that the invitation sounded like "Please do not come in."

For a long time I believed everything my relatives said about Carrapipi and imagined the town to be an island cut off from civilization and inhabited wholly by desperate characters whose chief ambition was to get to Rochester and prey on the Sicilians there. Joe and I went so far as to draw up careful plans for invading the place with powerful slingshots and rescuing our favorite movie queen from the clutches of the natives. It was a shock to discover a few years later that Carrapipi was a very short distance away from Girgenti, the city where most of my relatives were born, and that the people of Carrapipi considered the natives of Girgenti responsible for the bad reputation Sicilians had here. They had no legend to support their theory, but a nasty little couplet instead which they delighted in repeating every time Girgenti was mentioned:

> Girgenti
> Mal'agente

My feud with the Kaiser might have died a natural death if I had been able to disregard his name-calling, but already the thought that *Siciliano* implied something sinister had become implanted in me by dozens of small incidents and casual remarks.

Even before the Kaiser came along, my father had indicated that there might be some doubt about the good standing of Sicilians, by being on the defensive about them and by forbidding Joe and me to carry knives because of the unpleasant association they had in the public mind with Sicilians. He enforced this rule so thoroughly that we eventually came to accept it as though it were a self-imposed one. And although it prevented us from joining the Boy Scouts, it gave us great satisfaction to tell non-Sicilians who wanted to borrow a knife from us that we never carried one.

My father's edict came on the heels of an episode in our lives which was of such an unpleasant nature that Joe and I were ready to do anything, even accept his ruling, to prevent him from brooding over it too much. The incident involved Donna Maricchia, our Sicilian washerwoman, and her son, Angelo, and it had the effect of making my father worry as to whether or not knifing was a peculiarly Sicilian expedient which had been inherited by his sons from some vicious ancester he did not know about.

Donna Maricchia probably weighed less than ninety pounds, but she was an excellent washerwoman who attacked dirty clothes with the fury of a hellcat. Constantly angry with her husband or some of her eight children, she seemed to hoard her anger during the week, so that she could release it in a torrent of complaints and curses on the day she washed for us. With each curse she would give the clothes she held in her fists a savage twist, as though she actually had her husband or one of her children in her grasp. The electric washing machine, which eventually supplanted her, was less noisy and not nearly so dramatic.

Joe and I were her best audience because my mother was too busy making certain that Donna Maricchia did her work properly to care what she was saying. When it came to housework, my mother trusted no one, and stubbornly held to the notion that only she could make things clean. Donna Maricchia, who was almost stone deaf, politely pretended to understand my mother's elaborate instructions and then proceeded to do things her own way.

Donna Maricchia had grown up in a town that was only three or four miles from Realmonte, my mother's home town, but her pronunciation was harsher, and her stream of talk more rapid. Her deafness caused her to speak of the most casual matters in a roaring tone of voice. She was always mourning the death of some relative, here or abroad, and never wore anything but black. Joe and I, under the recent influence of some of Grimm's grimmer fairy tales, called her the Witch, and she figured in some of our more remarkable nightmares.

We were less afraid of her son Angelo. He accompanied his mother on all her washing expeditions because she did not trust him out of her sight. Angelo was chubby and a few years older than either of us. Although he would not permit us to play games with him at first, he taught us how to smoke and what to look for in girls and, of course, generally regarded us with contempt because, compared to him, we were such amateurs in worldly matters.

For a long time we hero-worshiped Angelo; then one day we saw his mother give him a wonderful whipping. Her slaps and his yelling could be heard in the next block. Since we had never been accorded such treatment by our parents, it made us feel quite superior to him. From then on, his attitude toward us improved, and it wasn't long before we were playing games with him on a footing that might have been regarded as equal if you didn't know how clever he was at cheating.

One Wednesday when Donna Maricchia had come to do the weekly wash, we quarreled fiercely with Angelo because we caught him trying to cheat us in a very obvious manner. One threat led to another, and in a few minutes we were both pummeling Angelo. As we tried to hold him down and extract from him the promise to "give up," he squirmed away and ran to a near-by rock pile. Picking up a large stone, he hurled it at Joe. It struck him just above the eye, making a deep gash which bled immediately and profusely. For a horrible moment I thought he had lost his eye, and I let out a screech that frightened Joe into screaming louder than ever. The screams were even heard by Donna Maricchia, who came running from the kitchen dripping with soapsuds. When she saw the blood, she threw up her hands in despair and sprinted toward Joe, invoking the names of her favorite saints as she ran.

Joe mistook her despair for violence and ran around her into the kitchen, where he locked the door. My mother was the only one who kept her head. She caught him in her arms and led him to the sink. As she washed and bandaged the wound, she talked to him quietly and soothingly until he stopped crying. But though the bleeding and tears had stopped, his feelings toward Angelo had developed to a state of determined violence.

"Mother," he said in a deadly calm voice, "please give me the kitchen knife. I'm going to get even with Angelo." The seriousness with which he made this unusual request, and the hate in his eyes, shocked my poor mother into tears. She seldom cried; when she did, she usually tried to hide her tears from us. Her unrestrained sobbing scared both of us, and we felt we had committed some terrible crime. Joe's mood changed completely and, as he begged her to stop crying, he himself burst into tears again. It was more than I could bear and I joined in too. When Donna Maricchia saw us through the kitchen window, the tears were running down both sides of her nose, and she was begging admittance, and forgiveness for her son. Angelo was nowhere in sight.

That evening there was a family council and it was decided that Donna Maricchia was never to bring Angelo with her again if she wanted to continue washing clothes for us.

The discussion centering around Joe's request for the kitchen knife presented problems that were more difficult to solve. My father gave us both a long lecture on the absurdity of seeking revenge, and blamed us as much as Angelo for the fight. That was to be expected, for he was always threatening to punish us if we got into fights and got the worst of them. He never carried out his threat, but if we came home with stories of fights we had lost, it was useless to expect any sympathy from him.

In this instance we could see that this fight worried him more than the others. First he wanted to know from Joe where he got the idea of knifing anyone. We were both too scared to attempt any explanation. Worried that we might be acquiring criminal habits from sources about which he did not know, my father persisted with his fiery cross-examination. Because I was the elder, I got the brunt of it, despite my protests that I was not the one who had asked for the knife. There was no relenting on my father's part. He was determined to get to the source of Joe's homicidal rage, but he was even more determined to learn why he had chosen a knife as the weapon. I think he would have felt much better if Joe had asked my mother for a revolver instead.

All through the questioning, Joe preserved the most golden of silences, while I sweated under the glare of my father's eyes. After a while I became panicky and threw caution to the winds. I said the first thing that came to my mind.

"What he was really looking for was a hatchet," I said brightly. My father frowned and looked interested. My brother gave me a look that meant he would try to beat me up the first chance he got.

My mother said, "What in the world do you mean?"

I didn't really know, but I found myself saying: "Well, our teacher told us that Washington used a hatchet to cut down a tree. But we don't have one. I mean we don't have a hatchet. I guess we have plenty of trees," I finished lamely.

This was all my father wanted to know. Unacquainted with either the cherry tree legend or its beautiful moral, he went into an oratorical rampage and delivered a blistering tirade against the American educational system, polishing it off with his inevitable conclusion that our teachers were "making pigs" of us. We knew no manners, we had no tact, and now, by the holy God and the sainted Devil, we were being taught to revenge ourselves on people we didn't like by scalping them with hatchets. *Porca miseria!* What kind of system was that, pray tell him? And why should he pay taxes for American school-teachers who were no better than murdering savages? Etc., etc. Under the fury of his castigation it would have been futile to talk to him about the father of our country. When he had exhausted himself and his repertoire of blasphemies, we all withdrew in respectful silence, quite convinced that school was a bad place for us. But the next morning my mother was screaming at us to get out of bed at once if we didn't want to be late again.

The incident had far-reaching consequences. It left Joe with a permanent scar over his eye, and it provided my father with a deep concern for the criminal tendencies of his sons as well as a new and lurid justification of his contempt for American schools. And, thanks to my mother's perspicacity, it deprived us of the joy of thrilling to the serial movie we used to follow on Saturday afternoons.

Dissatisfied with my father's analysis of the affair, my mother quizzed me further on the hatchet story. She was obviously relieved to learn that my father had misinterpreted it, and was thoroughly charmed with the full account of Washington and the cherry tree. Then she asked me what movies we had been seeing lately. I had barely begun to warm up to some of the exciting weekly episodes in the life of our favorite hero when she interrupted me, in the very middle of a scene where the hero has his back to the wall and the crooks are creeping up to him with knives in their teeth, and announced that we were not to attend the movies any longer on Saturday afternoons. Hereafter, if we must go to the movies it would be on Friday after supper in the company of my Uncle Luigi, who was a habitual movie-goer.

Life without our Saturday afternoon serial seemed rather dull to us for a while, but we soon began to find the adventures of Theda Bara, Mary Pickford, and William S. Hart just as alluring. I think my mother would have been disconcerted to know that there were just as many characters in those movies who won their arguments by the use of knives.

STUDS LONIGAN
James T. Farrell

Young Studs Lonigan sees himself as the emancipated
tough who no longer has to take it from those who tried
to bring him up to be a God-loving, nun-fearing Irish
American. His story, told in three volumes by James T.
Farrell, is both caricature and commentary on genera-
tional conflict in the 1930s. Each aspect is significant.
In the pages that follow Studs is introduced, as is his
father. The protagonist, cocky and proud (and seemingly free), is in many ways but a carbon of his old
man—though he is unaware of their similarities.

I

Studs Lonigan, on the verge of fifteen, and wearing his first suit of long
trousers, stood in the bathroom with a Sweet Caporal pasted in his mug.
His hands were jammed in his trouser pockets, and he sneered. He puffed,
drew the fag out of his mouth, inhaled and said to himself:

Well, I'm kissin' the old dump goodbye tonight.

Studs was a small, broad-shouldered lad. His face was wide and planed;
his hair was a light brown. His long nose was too large for his other features; almost a sheeny's nose. His lips were thick and wide, and they did
not seem at home on his otherwise frank and boyish face. He was always
twisting them into his familiar tough-guy sneers. He had blue eyes; his
mother rightly called them baby-blue eyes.

He took another drag and repeated to himself:

Well, I'm kissin' the old dump goodbye.

The old dump was St. Patrick's grammar school; and St. Patrick's meant

a number of things to Studs. It meant school, and school was a jailhouse
that might just as well have had barred windows. It meant the long, wide,
chalk-smelling room of the seventh- and eighth-grade boys, with its forty
or fifty squirming kids. It meant the second floor of the tan brick, undis-
tinguished parish building on Sixty-first Street that had swallowed so
much of Studs' life for the past eight years. It meant the black-garbed
Sisters of Providence, with their rattling beads, their swishing strides, and
the funny-looking wooden clappers they used, which made a dry snapping
sound and which hurt like anything when a guy got hit over the head with
one. It meant Sister Carmel, who used to teach fourth grade, but was dead
now; and who used to hit everybody with the edge of a ruler because she
knew they all called her the bearded lady. It meant Studs, twisting in his
seat, watching the sun come in the windows to show up the dust on the
floor, twisting and squirming, and letting his mind fly to all kinds of places
that were not like school. It meant Battleaxe Bertha talking and hearing
lessons, her thin, sunken-jawed face white as a ghost, and sometimes looking like a corpse. It meant Bertha yelling in that creaky old woman's voice
of hers. It meant Bertha trying to pound lessons down your throat, when
you weren't interested in them; church history and all about the Jews and
Moses, and Joseph, and Daniel in the lion's den, and Solomon who was
wiser than any man that ever lived, except Christ, and maybe the Popes,
who had the Holy Ghost to back up what they said; arithmetic, and square
and cube roots, and percentage that Studs had never been able to get
straight in his bean; catechism lessons . . . the ten commandments of God,
the six commandments of the church, the seven capital sins, and the seven
cardinal virtues and that lesson about the sixth commandment, which
didn't tell a guy anything at all about it and only had words that he'd
found in the dictionary like adultery which made him all the more curious; grammar with all its dry rules, and its sentences that had to be diagrammed and were never diagrammed right; spelling, and words like
apothecary that Studs still couldn't spell; Palmer method writing, that
was supposed to make you less tired and made you more tired, and the
exercises of shaking your arm before each lesson, and the round and round
(OOOOOOOOOOO)   and straight and straight ///////////// , and the
copy book, all smeared with ink, that he had gone through, doing exercise
after exercise on neat sheets of Palmer paper so that he could get a Palmer
method certificate that his old man kicked about paying for because he
thought it was graft; history lessons from the dull red history book, but
they wouldn't have been so bad if America had had more wars and if a
guy could talk and think about the battles without having to memorize
their dates, and the dates of when presidents were elected, and when
Fulton invented the steamboat, and Eli Whitney invented the cotton gin
or whatever in hell he did invent. School meant Bertha, and Bertha should
have been put away long ago, where she could kneel down and pray herself
to death, because she was old and crabby and always hauling off on some-

body; it was a miracle that a person as old as Bertha could sock as hard or holler as loud as she could; even Sister Bernadette Marie, who was the superior and taught the seventh and eighth grade girls in the next room, sometimes had to come in and ask Bertha to make less noise, because she couldn't teach with all the racket going on; but telling Bertha not to shout was like telling a bull that it had no right to see red. And smart guys, like Jim Clayburn, who did his homework every night, couldn't learn much from her. And school meant Dan and Bill Donoghue and Tubby and all the guys in his bunch, and you couldn't find a better gang of guys to pal with this side of Hell. And it meant going to mass in the barn-like church on the first floor, every morning in Lent, and to stations of the cross on Friday afternoons; stations of the cross were always too long unless Father Doneggan said them; and marching on Holy Thursday morning in church with a lily in your hand, and going to communion the third Sunday of every month at the eight o'clock mass with the boys' sodality. It meant goofy young Danny O'Neill, the dippy punk who couldn't be hurt or made cry, no matter how hard he was socked, because his head was made of hard stuff like iron and ivory and marble. It meant Vinc Curley, who had water on the brain, and the doctors must have taken his brains out, drowned and dead like a dead fish, that time they were supposed to have taken a quart of water from his oversized bean. The kids in Vinc's class said that Sister Cyrilla used to pound him on the bean with her clapper, and he'd sit there yelling he was going to tell his mother; and it was funny, and all the kids in the room laughed their guts out. They didn't have 'em as crazy as Vinc in Studs' class; but there was TB McCarthy, who was always getting his ears beat off, and being made to kneel up in front of the room, or to go in Sister Bernadette's room and sit with all the girls and let them laugh at him. And there was Reardon with horses' hoofs for feet. One day in geography in the fifth grade, Cyrilla called on Reardon and asked him what the British Isles consisted of. Reardon didn't know so Studs whispered to him to say iron, and Reardon said iron. Sister Cyrilla thought it was so funny she marked him right for the day's lesson. And St. Patrick's meant Weary Reilley, and Studs hated Weary. He didn't know whether or not he could lick Weary, and Weary was one tough customer, and the guys had been waiting for Studs and Weary to scrap ever since Weary had come to St. Patrick's in the third grade. Studs was a little leery about mixing it with Reilley . . . no, he wasn't . . . it was just . . . well, there was no use starting fights unless you had to . . . and he'd never backed out of a scrap with Weary Reilley or any other guy. And that time he had pasted Weary in the mush with an icy snowball, well, he hadn't backed out of a fight when Weary started getting sore. He had just not meant to hit Weary with it, and in saying so he had only told the truth.

St. Patrick's meant a lot of things. St. Patrick's meant . . . Lucy.

Lucy Scanlan would stand on the same stage with him in a few hours, and she would receive her diploma. She would wear a white dress, just like his sister Frances, and Weary's sister Fran, and she would receive her diploma. Everybody said that Fran Lonigan and Fran Reilley were the two prettiest girls in the class. Well, if you asked him, the prettiest girl in the class was black-bobbed-haired Lucy.

He got soft, and felt like he was all mud and mush inside; he held his hand over his heart, and told himself:

My Lucy!

He flicked some ashes in the sink, and said to himself:

Lucy, I love you!

Once when he had been in the sixth grade, he had walked home with Lucy. Now, he puffed his cigarette, and the sneer went off his face. He thought of the March day when he had walked home with her. He had walked home with her. All along Indiana Avenue, he had been liking her, wanting to kiss her. Now, he remembered that day as clearly as if it had just happened. He remembered it better than the day when he was just a punk and he had bashed the living moses out of that smoke who pulled a razor on him over in Carter Playground, and a gang of guys had carried him around on their shoulders, telling him what a great guy he was, and how, when he grew up, he would become the white hope of the world, and lick Jack Johnson for the heavyweight championship. He remembered the day with Lucy, and his memory of it was like having an awful thirst for a drink of clear cold water or a chocolate soda on a hot day. It had been a windy day in March, without any sun. The air had seemed black, and the sky blacker, and all the sun that day had been in his thoughts of her. He had had all kinds of goofy, dizzy feelings that he liked. They had walked home from school, along Indiana Avenue, he and Lucy. They hadn't spoken much, and they had stopped every little while to look at things. They had stopped at the corner of Sixtieth, and he had shown her the basement windows they had broken, just to get even with old Boushwah, the Hunkie janitor, because he always ran them off the grass when they goofed on their way home from school. And she had pretended that it was awful for guys to break windows, when he could see by the look in her eyes that she didn't at all think it so terrible. And they had walked on slow, pigeon-toed slow, slower, so that it would take them a long time to get home. He had carried her books, too, and they had talked about this and that, about the skating season that was just finished, and about the spelling match between the fifth- and sixth-grade boys and girls, where both of them had been spelled down at the first crack of the bat, and they had talked about just talk. When they came to the elevated structure near Fifty-ninth, he had shown her where they played shinny with tin cans, and she said it was a dangerous game, and you were liable to get your shins hurt. Then he had shown her where he had climbed up the girder to the top, just below the elevated tracks, and she had shivered because it was such a dangerous brave thing to do, and he had felt all proud, like a hero, or like Bronco Billy or Eddie Polo in the movies. They had walked home lazy, and he had carried her books, and wished he had the price to buy her candy or a soda, even if it was Lent, and they had stood before the gray brick two-story building where she lived, and he had wanted, as the devil wants souls, to kiss her, and he hadn't wanted to leave her because when he did he knew the day would get blacker, and he would feel like he did when he had been just out of his diapers and he used to be afraid of the night. There had been something about that day. He had gone on in school, wishing and wishing for another one like it to come along. And now he felt it all over again, the goofy, dizzy, flowing feelings it had given him.

He puffed, and told himself:

Well, it's so long to the old dump tonight!

He wanted to stand there, and think about Lucy, wondering if he would ever have days with her like that one, wondering how much he'd see of her after she went to high school. And he goddamned himself, because he was getting soft. He was Studs Lonigan, a guy who didn't have mushy feelings! He was a hard-boiled egg that they had left in the pot a couple of hours too long.

He took another drag of his cigarette.

He wanted that day back again.

He faced the mirror, and stuck the fag in the right-hand corner of his mouth. He looked tough and sneered. Then he let the cigarette hang from the left side. He studied himself with satisfaction. He placed the cigarette in the center of his puss, and put on a weak-kneed expression. He took the cigarette out of his mouth, daintily, barely holding it between his thumb and first finger, and he pretended that he was a grown-up mama's boy, smoking for the first time. He said to himself:

Jesus Christ!

He didn't know that he bowed his head when he muttered the Lord's name, just as Sister Cyrilla had always taught them to do. He took a vicious poke at the air, as if he were letting one fly at a mama's boy.

He stuck the fag back in his mouth and looked like Studs Lonigan was supposed to look. He lowered the lid on the toilet seat, and sat down to think. He puffed at his cigarette, and flicked the ashes in the sink.

He heard Frances talking:

"Get out of my way, Fritzie . . . Get out of my way . . . Please . . . And mother . . . Mother! MOTHER! . . . Will you come here, please . . . I told you the hem was not right on this dress . . . Now, mother, come here and look at the way my skirt hangs . . . If I ever appear on the stage with my skirt like this, I'll be disgraced . . . disgraced . . . Mother!"

He heard his old lady hurrying to Frances's room, saying:

"Yes, Frances darling; only you know I asked you not to call Loretta Fritzie . . . I'm coming, but I tell you, your dress is perfectly even all around. I told you so this afternoon when you tried it on with Mrs. Sankey here."

He could hear their voices as they jabbered away about her dress, but he didn't know what they were saying, and anyway, he didn't give two hoots in hell. Girls had loose screws in their beans. Well, girls like his sister anyway. Girls like Lucy, or Helen Shires, who was just like a guy, were exceptions. But there he was getting soft again. He said to himself:

I'm so tough that you know what happens? Well, bo, when I spit . . . rivers overflow . . . I'm so hard I chew nails . . . See, bo!

He took a last drag at his cigarette, tossed the butt down the toilet, and let the water run in the sink to wash the ashes down. He went to the door, and had his hand on the knob to open it when he noticed that the bathroom was filled with smoke. He opened the small window, and commenced waving his arms around, to drive the smoke out. But why in hell shouldn't they know? What did his graduating and his long jeans mean, then? He was older now, and he could do what he wanted. Now he was growing up. He didn't have to take orders any more, as he used to. He wasn't going to hide it any more, and he was going to tell the old man that he wasn't going to high school.

The bathroom was slow in clearing. He beat the air with his hands.

Frances rapped sharply on the door and asked him to get a move on.

He waved his arms around.

Frances was back in a moment.

"William, will you please . . . will you please . . . will you please hurry!" She rapped impatiently.

"All right. I'll be right out."

"Well, why don't you then? I have to hurry, I tell you. And I'm in the play tonight, and you're not. When you had your play last May, I didn't delay you like this, and I helped you learn your lines and everything, and now when I have to be there . . . William, *will you please hurry* . . . PLEASE! . . . oh, mother . . . Mother! Won't you come here and tell Studs to hurry up out of the bathroom?"

She furiously pounded on the door.

Studs was winded. He stopped trying to beat the smoke out. The smoke was still thick.

"All right, don't get . . . a . . . don't get so excited!"

He whewed, and wiped his forehead, as if there had been perspiration on it. That was a narrow escape. He'd almost told his sister not to get one on, and then there'd have been sixteen kinds of hell to pay around the house.

Whew!

You'da thought he wanted to stay in there, the way she was acting. Well, he was going to walk out and let 'em see the smoke, and when they blew their gobs off, he would tell them from now on he was his own boss, and he would smoke where and when he damn well pleased; and furthermore, he wasn't going to high school.

"William, will you please . . . please . . . *please* let me in . . . Mother, won't you please . . . please . . . OH, PLEASE, come here and make him get out. He's been in there a half-hour. He's reading. He's always mean and selfish like that . . . Mother, please . . . PLEASE!"

She banged on the door.

"Aw, I heard you," Studs said.

"Well, if you did, come on out!" she snapped.

He heard his mother coming up to the door, while Frances banged and shouted away. He took a towel . . . why didn't he think of it sooner? . . . and started flapping it around.

His mother said:

"William, won't you hurry now, like a good son? Frances has to go in there, and she has to finish dressing and be up there early because she's going to be in the play. Now, son, hurry!"

"All right. I can't help it. I'll be right out."

"Well, *please* do!" Frances said.

The mother commenced to tell Frances that William was going to let her right in; but Frances interrupted:

"But, mother, he's been in there almost an hour . . . He has no consideration for other people's rights . . . He's selfish and mean . . . and oh, mother, I got to go in there . . . and what will I do if I spoil my graduation dress on his account . . . make him, mother . . . and now I'm getting unnerved, and I'll never be able to act in the play."

The old lady persuaded. And she told Studs that she and his father couldn't go until they had all the children off, and they would be disgraced if they came late for the entertainment on the night their son and daughter graduated.

Frances banged on the door and yelled.

"Aw, don't get so darn crabby," Studs said to her while he fanned the air with his towel.

"See, mother! See! He says I'm insane just because I ask him to hurry after he's been in there all day. He's reading or smoking cigarettes . . . Please, make him hurry!" "Why, Frances, how dare you accuse him like that!" Mrs. Lonigan commenced to say.

Studs heard his sister dashing away, hollering to the old man to come and do something. He fanned vigorously, and his mother stood at the door urging.

II

Old man Lonigan, his feet planted on the back porch railing, sat tilted back in his chair enjoying his stogy. His red, well-fed-looking face was wrapped in a dreamy expression; and his innards made slight noises as they diligently furthered the process of digesting a juicy beefsteak. He puffed away, exuding burgher comfort, while from inside the kitchen came the rattle of dishes being washed. Now and then he heard Frances preparing for the evening.

He gazed, with reverie-lost eyes, over the gravel spread of Carter Playground, which was a few doors south of his own building. A six-o'clock sun was imperceptibly burning down over the scene. On the walk, in the shadow of and circling the low, rambling public school building, some noisy little girls, the size and age of his own Loretta, were playing hopscotch. Lonigan puffed at his cigar, ran his thick paw through his brown-gray hair, and watched the kids. He laughed when he heard one of the little girls shout that the others could go to hell. It was funny and they were tough little ones all right. It sounded damn funny. They must be poor little girls with fathers and mothers who didn't look after them or bring them up in the right home atmosphere; and if they were Catholic girls, they probably weren't sent to the sisters' school; parents ought to send their children to the sisters' school even if it did take some sacrifice; after all, it only cost a dollar a month, and even poor people could afford that when their children's education was at stake. He wouldn't have his Loretta using such rowdy language, and, of course, she wouldn't, because her mother had always taught her to be a little lady. His attention wandered to a boy, no older than his own Martin, but dirty and less well-cared-for, who, with the intent and dreamy seriousness of childhood, played on the ladders and slides which paralleled his own back fence. He watched the youngster scramble up, slide down, scramble up, slide down. It stirred in him a vague series of impulses, wishes and nostalgias. He puffed his stogy and watched. He said to himself:

Golly, it would be great to be a kid again!

He said to himself:

Yes, sir, it would be great to be a kid!

He tried to remember those ragged days when he was only a shaver and his old man was a pauperized greenhorn. Golly, them were the days! Often there had not been enough to eat in the house. Many's the winter day he and his brother had to stay home from school because they had no shoes. The old house, it was more like a barn or a shack than a home, was so cold they had to sleep in their clothes; sometimes in those zero Chicago winters his old man had slept in his overcoat. Golly, even with all that privation, them was the days. And now that they were over, there was something missing, something gone from a fellow's life. He'd give anything to live back a day of those times around Blue Island, and Archer Avenue. Old man Dooley always called it Archey Avenue, and Dooley was one comical turkey, funnier than anything you'd find in real life. And then those days when he was a young buck in Canaryville. And things were cheaper in them days. The boys that hung out at Kieley's saloon, and later around the saloon that Padney Flaherty ran, and Luke O'Toole's place on Halsted. Old Luke was some boy. Well, the Lord have mercy on his soul, and on the soul of old Padney Flaherty. Padney was a comical duck, good-hearted as they make them, but crabby. Was he a first-rate crab! And the jokes the boys played on him. They were always calling him names, pigpen Irish, shanty Irish, Padney, ain't you the kind of an Irishman that slept with the pigs back in the old country. Once they told him his house was on fire, and he'd dashed out of the saloon and down the street with a bucket of water in his hand. It was funny watching him go, a skinny little Irishman. And while he was gone, they had all helped themselves to free beers. He came back blazing mad, picked up a hatchet, called them all the choice swear words he could think of, and ran the whole gang out into the street. Then they'd all stood on the other corner, laughing. Yeh, them was the days! And when he was a kid, they would all get sacks, wagons, any old thing, and go over to the tracks. Spike Kennedy, Lord have mercy on his soul, he was bit by a mad dog and died, would get up on one of the cars and throw coal down like sixty, and they'd scramble for it. And many's the fight they'd have with the gangs from other streets. And many's the plunk in the cocoanut that Paddy Lonigan got. It's a wonder some of them weren't killed throwing lumps of coal and ragged rocks at each other like a band of wild Indians. To live some of those old days over again! Golly!

He took a meditative puff on his stogy, and informed himself that time was a funny thing. Old Man Time just walked along, and he didn't even blow a How-do-you-do through his whiskers. He just walked on past you. Things just change. Chicago was nothing like it used to be, when over around St. Ignatius Church and back of the yards were white men's neighborhoods, and Prairie Avenue was a tony street where all the swells lived, like Fields, who had a mansion at Nineteenth and Prairie, and Pullman at Eighteenth and Calumet, and Fairbanks and Potter Palmer and the niggers and whores had not roosted around Twenty-second Street, and Fifty-eighth Street was nothing but a wilderness, and on Sunday afternoons the boulevards were lined with carriages, and there were no automobiles, and living was dirt cheap, and people were friendlier and more neighborly than they now were, and there were high sidewalks, *and he and Mary were young.* Mary had been a pretty girl, too, and at picnics she had always won the prizes because she could run like a deer; and he remembered that first picnic he took her to, and she won a loving cup and gave it to him, and then they went off sparking, and he had gotten his first kiss, and they sat under a tree when it was hushed, like the earth was preparing for darkness, and he and Mary had looked at each other, and then he knew he had fallen, and he didn't give a damn. And the bicycle parties.

Daisy, Daisy, give me your answer true,
We won't have a stylish marriage,
We can't afford a carriage,

But you'll look sweet,
Upon the seat, of a bicycle built for two.

And that Sunday he had rented a buggy, even though it cut a terrible hole in his kick, and they had driven way out south. Who would have ever thought he and she would now be living in the same neighborhood they had driven into that Sunday, and that they would have their own home, and graduate their kids from it? Now, who would have thought it? And the time he had taken her to a dance at Hull House, and coming home he had almost gotten into a mixup with some soused mick because the fellow had started to get smartalecky, like he was a kike. Yes sir, them was the days. He hummed, trying first to strike the right tune to *Little Annie Rooney;* then the tune of *My Irish Molly 'O.* He sang to himself:

Dear old girl, the robin sings above you!
Dear old girl, it speaks of how I love you,
Dear old girl, it speaks of how I love you . . .

He couldn't remember the rest of the song, but it was a fine song. It described his Mary to a T. His . . . Dear Old Girl.

And the old gang. They were scattered now, to the very ends of the earth. Many of them were dead, like poor Paddy McCoy, Lord have mercy on his soul, whose ashes rested in a drunkard's grave at Potter's Field. Well, they were a fine gang, and many's the good man they drank under the table, but . . . well, most of them didn't turn out so well. There was Heinie Schmaltz, the boy with glue on his fingers, the original sticky-fingered kid. And poor Mrs. Schmaltz, Lord have mercy on her poor soul. God was merciful to take her away before she could know that her boy went up the road to Joliet on a ten-year jolt for burglary. The poor little woman, how she used to come around and tell of the things her Heinie found. She'd say, in her German dialect, My Heinie, he finds the grandest things. Vy, ony yesterday, I tell you, I tell you, he found a diamond ring, vy, can you himagine hit! And that time she and Mrs. McGoorty got to talking about which of their boys were the luckiest, and about the fine things my Heinie found, and the foine things my Mike is always pickin' up. Good souls they were. And there was Dinny Gorman, the fake silk-hat. When Dinny would tote himself by, they'd all haw-haw because he was like an old woman. He was too bright, if you please, to associate with ordinary fellows. Once a guy from New York came around, and he was damned if High-hat Dinny, who'd never been to the big burg, didn't sit down and try to tell this guy all about New York. Dinny had made a little dough, but he was, after all, only a shyster lawyer and a cheap politician. He had been made ward committeeman because he had licked everybody's boots. And there were his own brothers. Bill had run away to sea at seventeen and nobody had ever heard from him again. Jack, Lord have mercy on his soul, had always been a wild and foolish fellow, and man or devil couldn't persuade him not to join the colors for the war with Spain, and he'd been killed in Cuba, and it had nearly broken their mother's heart in two. Lord have mercy on his and her and the old man's souls. He'd been a fool, all right! Poor Jack! And Mike had run off and married a woman older than himself, and he was now in the east, and not doing so well, and his wife was an old crow, slobbering in a wheel chair. And Joe was a motorman. And Catherine, well, he hadn't even better think of her. Letting a traveling salesman get her like that, and expecting to come home with her fatherless baby; and then going out and becoming . . . a scarlet woman. His own sister, too! God! Nope, his family had not turned out so well. They hadn't had, none of them, the persistence that he had. He had stuck to his job and nearly killed himself working. But now he was reaping his rewards. It had been no soft job when he had started as a painter's apprentice, and there weren't strong unions then like there were now, and there was no eight-hour day, neither, and the pay was nothing. In them days, many's the good man that fell off a scaffold to die or become permanently injured. Well, Pat Lonigan had gone through the mill, and he had pulled himself up by his own bootstraps, and while he was not exactly sitting in the plush on Easy Street, he was a boss painter, and had his own business, and pretty soon maybe he'd even be worth a cool hundred thousand berries. But life was a funny thing, all right. It was like Mr. Dooley said, and he had never forgotten that remark, because Dooley, that is Finley Peter Dunne, was a real philosopher. Who'll tell what makes wan man a thief and another man a saint?

He took a long puff. He gazed out, and watched a group of kids, thirteen, fourteen, fifteen, boys like Bill, who sat in the gravel near the backstop close to the Michigan Avenue fence. What do kids talk about? He wondered, because a person's own childhood got so far away from him he forgot most of it, and sometimes it seemed as if he'd never been a kid himself, he forgot the way a kid felt, the thoughts of a kid. He sometimes wondered about Bill. Bill was a fine boy. You couldn't find a better one up on the graduating stage at St. Patrick's tonight, no more than you would see a finer girl than Frances. But sometimes he wondered just what Bill thought about.

He puffed. It was nice sitting there. He would like to sit there, and watch it slowly get dark, because when it was just getting dark things were quiet and soft-like, and a fellow liked to sit in all the quiet and well, just sit, and let any old thoughts go through his mind; just sit and dream, and realize that life was a funny thing, but that he'd fought his way up to a station where there weren't no real serious problems like poverty, and he sits there, and is comfortable and content and patient, because he knows that he has put his shoulder to the wheel, and he has been a good Catholic, and a good American, a good father, and a good husband. He just sits there with Mary, and smokes his cigar, and has his thoughts, and then, after it gets dark, he can send one of the kids for ice cream, or maybe sneak down to the saloon at Fifty-eighth and State and have a glass of beer. But there was many another evening for that, and tonight he'd have to go and see the kids get a good sendoff; otherwise he wouldn't be much of a father. When you're a father you got duties, and Patrick J. Lonigan well knew that.

While Lonigan's attention had been sunk inwards, the kids had all left the playground. Now he looked about, and the scene was swallowed in a hush, broken only by occasional automobiles and by the noise from the State Street cars that seemed to be more than a block away. Suddenly, he experienced, like an unexpected blow, a sharp fear of growing old and dying, and he knew a moment of terror. Then it slipped away, greased by the thickness of his content. Where in hell should he get the idea that he was getting so old? Sure, he was a little gray in the top story, and a little fat around the belly, but, well, the fat was a healthy fat, and there was lots of stuff left in the old boy. And he was not any fatter than old man O'Brien who owned the coal yards at Sixty-second and Wabash.

He puffed at his stogy and flicked the ashes over the railing. He thought about his own family. Bill would get himself some more education, and then learn the business, starting as a painter's apprentice, and when he got the hang of things and had worked on the job long enough, he would step in and run the works; and then the old man and Mary would take a trip to the old sod and see where John McCormack was born, take a squint at the Lakes of Killarney, kiss the blarney stone, and look up all his relatives. He sang to himself, so that no one would hear him:

Where the dear old Shannon's flowing,
Where the three-leaved shamrock grows,
Where my heart is I am going,
  To my little Irish Rose.
And the moment that I meet her,
With a hug and kiss I'll greet her,
For there's not a colleen sweeter,
  Where the River Shannon flows.

He glowed over the fact that his kids were springing up. Martin and Loretta were coming along faster than he could imagine. Frances was going to be a beautiful girl who'd attract some rich and sensible young fellow. He beat up a number of imaginary villains who would try to ruin her. He returned to the thought that his kids were growing up; and he rested in the assurance that they had all gotten the right start; they would turn out A No. 1.

Martin would be a lawyer or professional man of some kind; he might go into politics and become a senator or a . . . you never could tell what a lad with the blood of Paddy Lonigan in him might not become. And Loretta, he just didn't know what she'd be, but there was plenty of time for that. Anyway, there was going to be no hitches in the future of his kids. And the family would have to be moving soon. When he'd bought this building, Wabash Avenue had been a nice, decent, respectable street for a self-respecting man to live with his family. But now, well, the niggers and kikes were getting in, and they were dirty, and you didn't know but what, even in broad daylight, some nigger moron might be attacking his girls. He'd have to get away from the eight balls and tinhorn kikes. And when they got into a neighborhood property values went blooey. He'd sell and get out . . . and when he did, he was going to get a pretty penny on the sale.

He puffed away. A copy of the *Chicago Evening Journal* was lying at his side. It was the only decent paper in town; the rest were Republican. And he hated the *Questioner,* because it hadn't supported Joe O'Reilley, past grand master of Lonigan's Order of Christopher lodge, that time in 1912 when Joe had run for the Democratic nomination for State's Attorney. Lonigan believed it was the *Questioner* that had beaten Joe; he wouldn't have it in his house. He thought about the Christys, and decided he would have to be taking his fourth degree, and then at functions he could be all dolled up with a plume in his hat and a sword at his side that would be attached to a red band strung across his front. And then he'd get a soup-and-fish outfit and go to the dinners all rigged out so that his own family wouldn't know him. He wasn't a bad-looking guy, and he'd bet he could cut a swath all togged up in soup and fish. And when his two lads grew up, he was going to make good Christys out of them too. And he'd have to be attending meetings regularly. It might even help his business along, and it was only right that one Christy should help another one along. That was what fraternalism meant. He looked down at the paper and noticed the headlines announcing Wilson's nomination at St. Louis. There was a full-length photograph of long-faced Wilson; he was snapped in summery clothes, light shoes and trousers, a dark coat and a straw hat. He held an American flag on a pole about four feet long. Next to him in the photograph was the script of a declaration he had had drafted into the party platform, forecasting the glorious future of the American people and declaring inimical to their progress any movement that was favorable to a foreign government at the expense of the American Nation. The cut was worded, THE PRESIDENT AND THE FLAG.

Now, that was a coincidence. On the day that Bill and Frances were graduated, Woodrow Wilson was renominated for the presidency. It was a historic day, because Wilson was a great president, and he had kept us out of war. There might be something to coincidences after all. And then the paper carried an account of the day's doings at the Will Orpet trial; Orpet was the bastard who ruined a girl, and when she was in the family way, went and killed her rather than marry her like any decent man would have done. And the baseball scores. The White Sox had lost to Boston, two to one. They were only in fifth place with an average of five hundred, but things looked good and they might win the pennant anyway. Look at what the Boston Braves had done in 1914. The Sox would spend the last month home. He'd have to be going out and seeing the Sox again. He hadn't been to a game since 1911 when he'd seen Ping Bodie break up a seventeen-inning game with the Tigers. Good old Ping. He was back in the minors, but that was Comiskey's mistake. Cicotte and Faber were in form now, and that strengthened the team, and they had Zeb Terry at shortstop playing a whale of a game, with Joe Jackson on the club, and Weaver at third, playing bang-up ball and not making an error a game like he had playing shortstop, and Collins and Schalk, and a better pitching staff, they would get going like a house on fire, and he'd have to be stepping out and seeing them play regular. Well, he could read all about it, and about the food riots in Rotterdam, and the bloody battle in which the Germans had captured Vaux, afterwards. Now, he'd have to be going inside, putting on his tie, and going up with Mary and the kids for the doings. He sat there, comfortable, puffing away. Life was a good thing if you were Patrick J. Lonigan and had worked hard to win out in the grim battle, and God had been good to you. But then, he had earned the good things he had. Yes, sir, let God call him to the Heavenly throne this very minute, and he could look God square in the eye and say he had done his duty, and he had been, and was, a good father. They had given the kids a good home, fed and clothed them, set the right example for them, sent them to Catholic schools to be educated, seen that they performed their religious duties, hustled them off to confession regularly, given them money for the collection, never allowed them to miss mass, even in winter, let them play properly so they'd be healthy, given them money for good clean amusements like the movies because they were also educational, done everything a parent can do for a child.

He puffed his stogy and sat there. The sun was imperceptibly burning low. Old man Lonigan looked about. He puffed on his stogy, and his innards made their customary noises as they diligently furthered the digestive process.

Frances rushed up on him, and with excited little-girl madness she asked him to make William get out of the bathroom.

The old man rapped on the bathroom door and told Bill to hurry up.

"Father, he's just a mean old brute. He's been in there an hour. He's reading or smoking cigarettes."

"Why, Frances!" the mother said.

"No, I ain't."

"Bill, tell me . . . are you smoking?"

"Aw, she's all vacant upstairs."

"Why, that is no language for an educated Catholic boy to use," the mother said.

"Father, he's mean and selfish. He's a brute, a beast. He isn't fair, and he doesn't give anyone else the least bit of consideration. I'll be late. I can't go. You'll have to get my diplomas, and they'll have to let someone else act. I can't go. I can't go. He's made me all nervous and unstrung. I'm unstrung, and I can't act now. I can't. And I'm worried because I'm not sure if my dress is even or not and I have to *go* in there. Father, *please* make the brute come out," Frances said melodramatically.

"All right. I'll be right out. I can't help it," Studs said.

"Make him, father!"

"Goddamn it, Bill, hurry!"

"I will."

"He's always like this," Frances said.

"I ain't."

"Every time I'm in a hurry, he's getting in the way. He's selfish, and don't think of anyone but his dirty old self, and he always monopolizes the bathroom . . . he's an ole . . . goat," said Frances.

"Aw, shut up and go to hell," said Studs as he fanned the air.

"Why, William Lonigan! Father, did you hear him insult me, swear at me, like I was one of those roughnecks from Fifty-eighth Street I sometimes see him with?"

"Bill, come right out. I'll not have you cursing in this house. I'm boss here, and as long as I am, you will use gentlemanly language when you address your sister. Where do you learn to speak like that, you, with the education I've given you? You don't hear anyone around here speaking like that," said the old man.

"Aw, heck, she's always blowing off her bazoo," said Studs.

"William, I wish that you wouldn't use such language. After receiving such a fine education . . . I'm shocked," said the mother.

"He doesn't know any better. He couldn't be a gentleman if he tried to," Frances said.

"Now, Frances, don't add fuel to the fire," the mother said.

"All right. I'm coming right out. I couldn't help it. Only it gets me sore to hear her yelling her ears off like that, over nothin'."

"Well, it's a good thing I do. Someone ought to expose him, and tell him how mean and selfish and inconsiderate he is, and how he only thinks of himself."

"Now, children, this is your graduation night, and you know your graduation night ought to be one of the happiest of your lives," the mother said.

The smoke had cleared now, so Studs could take a chance. He marched out, leaving the bathroom in perfect order. Frances indignantly brushed by him, her head held proud.

Frances was a very pretty girl of thirteen. Her body had commenced to lose its awkwardness, and she had a trim little girlish figure. Her plain white graduation dress set her off well, with her dark hair and her blackish eyes. She looked older than Studs.

"William, you should be more considerate," the mother said, unheard.

"Bill, you're gettin' at the age where you should be more . . . more chivalrous toward the ladies," the old man said as he chewed away at the remains of his stogy.

"Yeah, but heck, the way she yells over nothing, and starts raisin' all kinds of Cain when there ain't no reason," he said.

Father and mother cautioned him on the use of the word ain't. It was not polite, or good diction.

"Bill, you have to put up with the ladies, and make allowances fer their . . . defugalties," the old man said pompously.

He nudged Studs, intimately, and slipped him a buck as a graduation present. Studs felt good over getting the buck, and went to his bedroom to put on the white tie he hated to wear, but had to. He looked at the tie, feeling uncomfortable. He looked out the window, and Goddamned the tie.

He heard his old man and his old lady speaking.

"Well, Mary, we got our children started now. We got Bill and Frances pretty near raised."

"Yes, Patrick, and I'm so happy, because it's been such a hard job, you know."

"Yeah, we done well by 'em, and paid their way, and now it won't be so hard as it was, and when we get 'em all raised, and brought up, and educated, we'll take a trip to Ireland. It will be our second honeymoon . . . And, Mary, you and I'll have to give more time to ourselves and spark about a little. This summer sure, we'll go out to Riverview Park and have a day of our own, like we planned for so long," he said.

"Yes, Patrick . . . And, Patrick, these little spats the children have, they're nothin' at all," she said.

"Nope. They happen in the best regulated families," the old man said; he laughed, as if he had cracked a good joke.

"And nobody can say we ain't done right by our children," he said. "They certainly can't."

"And we paid their way," he said.

"Yes . . . and Sister Bernadette Marie told me how fine a boy William was, and how grand a girl Frances is," Mrs. Lonigan said.

"Yeah!" the old man said.

Then the old lady started to talk about the high school they would send Studs to. Studs knew what was coming. She was going to suggest that he be sent to study for the priesthood. He got sore, and wanted to yell at her. But the old man dismissed the whole subject. He said they could decide later, adding:

"I got the money, and we can send the lad any place we want to."

"But here, you get your tie on and comb your hair. We have to go, Patrick . . . And, Martin, come here and let me see your fingernails and behind your ears. Did you wash your neck? That's a good boy. And your teeth? Open your mouth . . . Well, for once you are presentable . . . and

Loretta, is your dress on? Come here. Yes, you look like a little lady . . ."

She entered Stud's room, retied his tie, and recombed his hair, much to his discomfort, and made him go over his fingernails again; he felt as if they were trying to make a mollycoddle out of him. She pinned on the long class ribbons of golden yellow and silvery blue. He sat on the bed, waiting for them, thinking about all kinds of things.

Looking like Sunday, or as if they had just walked out of a dusty family album, the Lonigan family promenaded down Michigan Avenue. Studs and Frances marched first. Studs felt stiff; he told himself he must look like some queer egg or other. Frances marched along, proud and lady-like. She did not deign to glance at Studs, but she teased him in a voice so loud that all heard her. He walked along, looking straight ahead, his eyes vacant; he thought up all the curse words he could and silently flung them at her. Loretta and Martin followed. Loretta was carrying the beautiful bouquet of white roses and carnations that were for Frances, and she walked along imitating her sister. She even teased Martin with the same words that Frances was using. Martin had to be cautioned by his parents, because he did not suffer in sulky silence, as Studs did. Father and mother formed the rear guard; parental pride oozed from them like healthy perspiration; the lean mother looked frugal, even in the plain but expensive blue dress she had bought for the occasion. Passersby glanced at them a second time, and they smiled with satisfaction. The old man kept repeating that he hoped Father Gilhooley would give the kids a big send-off.

"Studs's got long pants on," Martin said, to escape the teasing of Fritzie. Fritzie giggled.

"Close your beak," Studs turned and said.

"Martin, how many times have I forbade you to call him that awful name . . . and William, don't talk like that to my baby . . . The two of you cutting up like that in public . . . I'm ashamed of you," the mother said.

"Now, cut it out," the old man said authoritatively.

"I ain't a baby," Martin said.

"I'm walking with the baby," Frances said.

The Lonigans promenaded along Michigan Avenue, looking like Sunday.

THE ETHICS OF LIVING JIM CROW
Richard Wright

"If you're white you're right; if you're brown hang aroun'; but if you're black brother, get back."
The litany has been repeated for several hundred years. Until quite recently staying back and learning to play prescribed roles was the fate of millions of Americans. According to Richard Wright, black people had to learn how to live as *Negroes,* as second-class citizens. Here, in an excerpt from his famous autobiography, Wright explains how it was done and indicates the painful course of internalizing the disgrace in which others placed and held him. The selection ends with a timely portend spoken through the voice of one of Wright's companions: "Lawd, man! Ef it wuzn't fer them polices 'n' them ol' lynch mobs, there wouldn't be nothin' but uproar down here!"
One is reminded of the prophetic poem of another great black writer, Langston Hughes, who wrote:

> Negroes
> Sweet and docile,
> Meek, humble, and kind:
> Beware the day
> They change their mind!*

I

My first lesson in how to live as a Negro came when I was quite small. We were living in Arkansas. Our house stood behind the railroad tracks. Its skimpy yard was paved with black cinders. Nothing green ever grew in that yard. The only touch of green we could see was far away, beyond the tracks, over where the white folks lived. But cinders were good enough for me, and I never missed the green growing things. And, anyhow, cinders were fine weapons. You could always have a nice hot war with huge black cinders. All you had to do was crouch behind the brick pillars of a house with your hands full of gritty ammunition. And the first woolly black head you saw pop out from behind another row of pillars was your target. You tried your very best to knock it off. It was great fun.

I never fully realized the appalling disadvantages of a cinder environment till one day the gang to which I belonged found itself engaged in a war with the white boys who lived beyond the tracks. As usual, we laid down our cinder barrage, thinking that this would wipe the white boys out. But they replied with a steady bombardment of broken bottles. We doubled our cinder barrage, but they hid behind trees, hedges, and the sloping embankments of their lawns. Having no such fortifications, we retreated to the brick pillars of our homes. During the retreat a broken milk bottle caught me behind the ear, opening a deep gash which bled profusely. The sight of blood pouring over my face completely demoralized our ranks. My fellow combatants left me standing paralyzed in the center of the yard, and scurried for their homes. A kind neighbor saw me and rushed me to a doctor, who took three stitches in my neck.

I sat brooding on my front steps, nursing my wound and waiting for my mother to come from work. I felt that a grave injustice had been done me. It was all right to throw cinders. The greatest harm a cinder could do was leave a bruise. But broken bottles were dangerous; they left you cut, bleeding, and helpless.

When night fell my mother came from the white folks' kitchen. I raced down the street to meet her. I could just feel in my bones that she would understand. I knew she would tell me exactly what to do next time. I grabbed her hand and babbled out the whole story. She examined my wound, then slapped me.

"How come yuh didn't hide?" she asked me. "How come yuh always fightin'?"

I was outraged, and bawled. Between sobs I told her that I didn't have any trees or hedges to hide behind. There wasn't a thing I could have used as a trench. And you couldn't throw very far when you were hiding behind the brick pillars of a house. She grabbed a barrel stave, dragged me home, stripped me naked, and beat me till I had a fever of one hundred and two. She would smack my rump with the stave and, while the skin was still smarting, impart to me gems of Jim Crow wisdom. I was never to throw cinders any more. I was never to fight any more wars. I was never, never, under any conditions, to fight white folks again. And they were absolutely right in clouting me with the broken milk bottle. Didn't I know she was working hard every day in the hot kitchens of the white folks to make money to take care of me? When was I ever going to learn to be a good boy? She couldn't be bothered with my fights. She finished by telling me that I ought to be thankful to God as long as I lived that they didn't kill me.

All that night I was delirious and could not sleep. Each time I closed my eyes I saw monstrous white faces suspended from the ceiling, leering at me.

From that time on the charm of my cinder yard was gone. The green trees, the trimmed hedges, the cropped lawns grew very meaningful, became a symbol. Even today, when I think of white folks, the hard, sharp outlines of white houses surrounded by trees, lawns, and hedges are present somewhere in the background of my mind. Through the years they grew into an overreaching symbol of fear.

It was a long time before I came in close contact with white folks again. We moved from Arkansas to Mississippi. Here we had the good fortune not to live behind the railroad tracks or close to white neighborhoods. We lived in the very heart of the local Black Belt. There were black churches and black preachers; there were black schools and black teachers, black groceries and black clerks. In fact, everything was so solidly black that for a long time I did not even think of white folks, save in remote and vague terms. But this could not last forever. As one grows older one eats more. One's clothing costs more. When I finished grammar school I had to go to work. My mother could no longer feed and clothe me on her cooking job.

There is but one place where a black boy who knows no trade can get a job. And that's where the houses and faces are white, where the trees, lawns, and hedges are green. My first job was with an optical company in Jackson, Mississippi. The morning I applied I stood straight and neat before the boss, answering all his questions with sharp yessirs and nosirs. I was very careful to pronounce my sirs distinctly, in order that he might know that I was polite, that I knew where I was, and that I knew he was a white man. I wanted that job badly.

He looked me over as though he were examining a prize poodle. He questioned me closely about my schooling, being particularly insistent about how much mathematics I had had. He seemed very pleased when I told him I had had two years of algebra.

"Boy, how would you like to try to learn something around here?" he asked me.

"I'd like it fine, sir," I said, happy. I had visions of "working my way up." Even Negroes have those visions.

"All right," he said. "Come on."

I followed him to the small factory.

"Pease," he said to a white man of about thirty-five, "this is Richard. He's going to work for us."

Pease looked at me and nodded.

I was then taken to a white boy of about seventeen.

"Morrie, this is Richard, who's going to work for us."

"Whut yuh sayin' there, boy!" Morrie boomed at me.

"Fine!" I answered.

The boss instructed these two to help me, teach me, give me jobs to do, and let me learn what I could in my spare time.

My wages were five dollars a week.

I worked hard, trying to please. For the first month I got along O. K. Both Pease and Morrie seemed to like me. But one thing was missing. And I kept thinking about it. I was not learning anything, and nobody was volunteering to help me. Thinking they had forgotten that I was to learn something about the mechanics of grinding lenses, I asked Morrie one day to tell me about the work. He grew red.

"Whut yuh tryin' t' do, nigger, git smart?" he asked.

"Naw, I ain' tryin' t' git smart," I said.

"Well, don't, if yuh know whut's good for yuh!"

I was puzzled. Maybe he just doesn't want to help me, I thought. I went to Pease.

"Say, are you crazy, you black bastard?" Pease asked me, his gray eyes growing hard.

I spoke out, reminding him that the boss had said I was to be given a chance to learn something.

"Nigger, you think you're white, don't you?"

"Naw sir!"

"Well, you're acting mighty like it!"

"But, Mr. Pease, the boss said—"

Pease shook his first in my face.

"This is a white man's work around here, and you better watch yourself!"

From then on they changed toward me. They said good morning no more. When I was just a bit slow in performing some duty, I was called a lazy black son-of-a-bitch.

Once I thought of reporting all this to the boss. But the mere idea of what would happen to me if Pease and Morrie should learn that I had "snitched" stopped me. And after all, the boss was a white man too. What was the use?

The climax came at noon one summer day. Pease called me to his workbench. To get to him I had to go between two narrow benches and stand with my back against a wall.

"Yes sir," I said.

"Richard, I want to ask you something," Pease began pleasantly, not looking up from his work.

"Yes sir," I said again.

Morrie came over, blocking the narrow passage between the benches. He folded his arms, staring at me solemnly.

I looked from one to the other, sensing that something was coming.

"Yes sir," I said for the third time.

Pease looked up and spoke very slowly.

"Richard, Mr. Morrie, here, tells me you called me Pease."

I stiffened. A void seemed to open up in me. I knew this was the showdown.

He meant that I had failed to call him Mr. Pease. I looked at Morrie. He was gripping a steel bar in his hands. I opened my mouth to speak, to protest, to assure Pease that I had never called him simply Pease and that I had never had any intentions of doing so, when Morrie grabbed me by the collar, ramming my head against the wall.

"Now, be careful, nigger!" snarled Morrie, baring his teeth. "I heard yuh call 'im Pease! 'N' if yuh say yuh didn't, yuh're callin' me a liar, see?" He waved the steel bar threateningly.

If I had said, "No sir, Mr. Pease, I never called you Pease," I would have been automatically calling Morrie a liar. And if I had said, "Yes sir, Mr. Pease, I called you Pease," I would have been pleading guilty to having uttered the worst insult that a Negro can utter to a Southern white man. I stood hesitating, trying to frame a neutral reply.

"Richard, I asked you a question!" said Pease. Anger was creeping into his voice.

"I don't remember calling you Pease, Mr. Pease," I said cautiously. "And if I did, I sure didn't mean—"

"You black son-of-a-bitch! You called me Pease, then!" he spat, slapping me till I bent sideways over a bench. Morrie was on top of me, demanding:

"Didn't yuh call 'im Pease? If yuh say yuh didn't, I'll rip yo' gut string loose with this bar, yuh black granny dodger! Yuh can't tell a white man a lie 'n' git erway with it, you black son-of-a-bitch!"

I wilted. I begged them not to bother me. I knew what they wanted. They wanted me to leave.

"I'll leave," I promised. "I'll leave right now."

They gave me a minute to get out of the factory. I was warned not to show up again or tell the boss.

I went.

When I told the folks at home what had happened, they called me a fool. They told me that I must never again attempt to exceed my boundaries. When you are working for white folks, they said, you got to "stay in your place" if you want to keep working.

II

My Jim Crow education continued on my next job, which was portering in a clothing store. One morning, while polishing brass out front, the boss and his twenty-year-old son got out of their car and half dragged and half kicked a Negro woman into the store. A policeman standing at the corner looked on, twirling his night stick. I watched out of the corner of my eye, never slackening the strokes of my chamois upon the brass. After a few minutes I heard shrill screams coming from the rear of the store. Later the woman stumbled out, bleeding, crying, and holding her stomach. When she reached the end of the block, the policeman grabbed her and accused her of being drunk. Silently I watched him throw her into a patrol wagon.

When I went to the rear of the store, the boss and his son were washing their hands at the sink. They were chuckling. The floor was bloody and strewn with wisps of hair and clothing. No doubt I must have appeared pretty shocked, for the boss slapped me reassuringly on the back.

"Boy, that's what we do to niggers when they don't want to pay their bills," he said, laughing.

His son looked at me and grinned.

"Here, have a cigarette," he said.

Not knowing what to do, I took it. He lit his and held the match for me. This was a gesture of kindness, indicating that even if they had beaten the poor old woman, they would not beat me if I knew enough to keep my mouth shut.

"Yes sir," I said, and asked no questions.

After they had gone, I sat on the edge of a packing box and stared at the bloody floor till the cigarette went out.

That day at noon, while eating in a hamburger joint, I told my fellow Negro porters what had happened. No one seemed surprised. One fellow, after swallowing a huge bite, turned to me and asked:

"Huh. Is tha' all they did t' her?"

"Yeah. Wasn't tha' enough?" I asked.

"Shucks! Man, she's a lucky bitch!" he said, burying his lips deep into a juicy hamburger. "Hell, it's a wonder they didn't lay her when they got through."

III

I was learning fast, but not quite fast enough. One day, while I was delivering packages in the suburbs, my bicycle tire was punctured. I walked along the hot, dusty road, sweating and leading my bicycle by the handle bars.

A car slowed at my side.

"What's the matter, boy?" a white man called.

I told him my bicycle was broken and I was walking back to town.

"That's too bad," he said. "Hop on the running board."

He stopped the car. I clutched hard at my bicycle with one hand and clung to the side of the car with the other.

"All set?"

"Yes sir," I answered. The car started.

It was full of young white men. They were drinking. I watched the flask pass from mouth to mouth.

"Wanna drink, boy?" one asked.

I laughed, the wind whipping my face. Instinctively obeying the freshly planted precepts of my mother, I said:

"Oh no!"

The words were hardly out of my mouth before I felt something hard and cold smash me between the eyes. It was an empty whisky bottle. I saw stars and fell backwards from the speeding car in the dust of the road, my feet becoming entangled in the steel spokes of my bicycle. The white men piled out and stood over me.

"Nigger, ain' yuh learned no better sense'n tha' yet?" asked the man who hit me. "Ain' yuh learned t' say *sir* t' a white man yet?"

Dazed, I pulled to my feet. My elbows and legs were bleeding. Fists doubled, the white man advanced, kicking my bicycle out of the way.

"Aw, leave the bastard alone. He's got enough," said one.

They stood looking at me. I rubbed my shins, trying to stop the flow of blood. No doubt they felt a sort of contemptuous pity, for one asked:

"Yuh wanna ride t' town now, nigger? Yuh reckon yuh know enough t' ride now?"

"I wanna walk," I said simply.

Maybe it sounded funny. They laughed.

"Well, walk, yuh black son-of-a-bitch!"

When they left they comforted me with:

"Nigger, yuh sho better be damn glad it wuz us yuh talked t' tha' way. Yuh're a lucky bastard, 'cause if yuh'd said tha' t' somebody else, yuh might've been a dead nigger now."

IV

Negroes who have lived South know the dread of being caught alone upon the streets in white neighborhoods after the sun has set. In such a simple situation as this the plight of the Negro in America is graphically symbolized. While white strangers may be in these neighborhoods trying to get home, they can pass unmolested. But the color of a Negro's skin makes him easily recognizable, makes him suspect, converts him into a defenseless target.

Late one Saturday night I made some deliveries in a white neighborhood. I was pedaling my bicycle back to the store as fast as I could, when a police car, swerving toward me, jammed me into the curbing.

"Get down and put up your hands!" the policemen ordered.

I did. They climbed out of the car, guns drawn, faces set, and advanced slowly.

"Keep still!" they ordered.

I reached my hands higher. They searched my pockets and packages. They seemed dissatisfied when they could find nothing incriminating. Finally one of them said:

"Boy, tell your boss not to send you out in white neighborhoods this time of night."

As usual, I said:

"Yes sir."

V

My next job was as hallboy in a hotel. Here my Jim Crow education broadened and deepened. When the bellboys were busy, I was often called to assist them. As many of the rooms in the hotel were occupied by prostitutes, I was constantly called to carry them liquor and cigarettes. These women were nude most of the time. They did not bother about clothing even for bellboys. When you went into their rooms, you were supposed to take their nakedness for granted, as though it startled you no more than a blue vase or a red rug. Your presence awoke in them no sense of shame, for you were not regarded as human. If they were alone, you could steal sidelong glimpses at them. But if they were receiving men, not a flicker of your eyelids must show. I remember one incident vividly. A new woman, a huge, snowy-skinned blonde, took a room on my floor. I was sent to wait upon her. She was in bed with a thickset man; both were nude and uncovered. She said she wanted some liquor and slid out of bed and waddled across the floor to get her money from a dresser drawer. I watched her.

"Nigger, what in hell you looking at?" the white man asked me, raising himself upon his elbows.

"Nothing," I answered, looking miles deep into the blank wall of the room.

"Keep your eyes where they belong, if you want to be healthy!"

"Yes sir," I said.

VI

One of the bellboys I knew in this hotel was keeping steady company with one of the Negro maids. Out of a clear sky the police descended upon his home and arrested him, accusing him of bastardy. The poor boy swore he had had no intimate relations with the girl. Nevertheless, they forced him to marry her. When the child arrived, it was found to be much lighter in complexion than either of the two supposedly legal parents. The white men around the hotel made a great joke of it. They spread the rumor that some white cow must have scared the poor girl while she was carrying the baby. If you were in their presence when this explanation was offered, you were supposed to laugh.

VII

One of the bellboys was caught in bed with a white prostitute. He was castrated and run out of town. Immediately after this all the bellboys and hallboys were called together and warned. We were given to understand that the boy who had been castrated was a "mighty, mighty lucky bastard." We were impressed with the fact that next time the management of the hotel would not be responsible for the lives of "trouble makin' niggers."

VIII

One night, just as I was about to go home, I met one of the Negro maids. She lived in my direction, and we fell in to walk part of the way home together. As we passed the white night watchman, he slapped the maid on her buttock. I turned around, amazed. The watchman looked at me with a long, hard, fixed-under stare. Suddenly he pulled his gun and asked:

"Nigger, don't yuh like it?"

I hesitated.

"I asked yuh don't yuh like it?" he said again, stepping forward.

"Yes sir," I mumbled.

"Talk like it, then!"

"Oh yes, sir!" I said with as much heartiness as I could muster.

Outside I walked ahead of the girl, ashamed to face her. She caught up with me and said:

"Don't be a fool; yuh couldn't help it!"

This watchman boasted of having killed two Negroes in self-defense.

Yet, in spite of all this, the life of the hotel ran with an amazing smoothness. It would have been impossible for a stranger to detect anything. The maids, the hallboys, and the bellboys were all smiles. They had to be.

IX

I had learned my Jim Crow lessons so thoroughly that I kept the hotel job till I left Jackson for Memphis. It so happened that while in Memphis I applied for a job at a branch of the optical company. I was hired. And for some reason, as long as I worked there, they never brought my past against me.

Here my Jim Crow education assumed quite a different form. It was no longer brutally cruel, but subtly cruel. Here I learned to lie, to steal, to dissemble. I learned to play that dual role which every Negro must play if he wants to eat and live.

For example, it was almost impossible to get a book to read. It was assumed that after a Negro had imbibed what scanty schooling the state furnished he had no further need for books. I was always borrowing books from men on the job. One day I mustered enough courage to ask one of the men to let me get books from the library in his name. Surprisingly, he consented. I cannot help but think that he consented because he was a Roman Catholic and felt a vague sympathy for Negroes, being himself an object of hatred. Armed with a library card, I obtained books in the following manner: I would write a note to the librarian, saying: "Please let this nigger boy have the following books." I would then sign it with the white man's name.

When I went to the library, I would stand at the desk, hat in hand, looking as unbookish as possible. When I received the books desired, I would take them home. If the books listed in the note happened to be out, I would sneak into the lobby and forge a new one. I never took any chances guessing with the white librarian about what the fictitious white man would want to read. No doubt if any of the white patrons had suspected that some of the volumes they enjoyed had been in the home of a Negro, they would not have tolerated it for an instant.

The factory force of the optical company in Memphis was much larger than that in Jackson, and more urbanized. At least they liked to talk and would engage the Negro help in conversation whenever possible. By this means I found that many subjects were taboo from the white man's point of view. Among the topics they did not like to discuss with Negroes were the following: American white women; the Ku Klux Klan; France, and how Negro soldiers fared while there; French women; Jack Johnson; the entire Northern part of the United States; the Civil War; Abraham Lincoln; U. S. Grant; General Sherman; Catholics; the Pope; Jews; the Republican party; slavery; social equality; Communism; Socialism; the Thirteenth and Fourteenth amendments to the Constitution; or any topic calling for positive knowledge or manly self-assertion on the part of the Negro. The most accepted topics were sex and religion.

There were many times when I had to exercise a great deal of ingenuity to keep out of trouble. It is a Southern custom that all men must take off their hats when they enter an elevator. And especially did this apply to us blacks with rigid force. One day I stepped into an elevator with my arms full of packages. I was forced to ride with my hat on. Two white men stared at me coldly. Then one of them very kindly lifted my hat and placed it upon my armful of packages. Now the most accepted response for a Negro to make under such circumstances is to look at the white man out of the corner of his eye and grin. To have said: "Thank you!" would have made the white man *think* that you *thought* you were receiving from him a personal service. For such an act I have seen Negroes take a blow in the mouth. Finding the first alternative distasteful and the second dangerous, I hit upon an acceptable course of action which fell safely between these two poles. I immediately—no sooner than my hat was lifted—pretended that my packages were about to spill and appeared deeply distressed with keeping them in my arms. In this fashion I evaded having to acknowledge his service and, in spite of adverse circumstances, salvaged a slender shred of personal pride.

How do Negroes feel about the way they have to live? How do they discuss it when alone among themselves? I think this question can be answered in a single sentence. A friend of mine who ran an elevator once told me:

"Lawd, man! Ef it wuzn't fer them polices 'n' them ol' lynch mobs, there wouldn't be nothin' but uproar down here!"

ON THE MARGIN
Kathleen Tamagawa

In the 1920s and 1930s sociologists such as Robert E. Park and Everett Stonequist wrote of the "marginal man . . . whom fate has condemned to live in two antagonistic cultures." In subsequent years many have debated whether members of ethnic groups in, say, the United States, are personally marginal or whether in their socialization—like that of David Levinsky or Studs Lonigan—they grow to become well adjusted members of a marginal culture.

True marginality, it is argued, is enjoyed or suffered only by those products of "mixed marriages" who are born into two social worlds and must find their own identity in the face of counter pulls and pressures. A classic case of personal marginality is that of Kathleen Tamagawa. In her autobiography she relates what it was like to be an Irish-Japanese American. Part of Miss Tamagawa's story is presented below.

The trouble with me is my ancestry. I really should not have been born. No, I am not illegitimate, but just an outlawed product of a legal marriage. Illegitimacy is often inconspicuous and easily concealed and sometime it is even paraded for purposes of publicity. My problem goes deeper than that, for no law can change, no later ceremony right it—the problem of ancestry will remain.

My parents came from two small islands on opposite sides of the Earth. My mother was "North of Ireland," my father is Japanese and I have faced

Taken from *Holy Prayers in a Horse's Ear* by Kathleen Tamagawa © 1932 by Kathleen Tamagawa Eldridge. Used by permission of Crown Publishers, Inc.

the traditions of two worlds, so to speak; an occidental and an oriental. Ireland and Japan! Even an instant's consideration of that combination will convey the thought that such a field of battle for life needs be a "scene of tragedy and intense gaiety."

My father came to America when he was a little boy of eleven. In those days when Japan was first opened, it was progressive for young Japan to accept gracefully and completely the new world. So father was sent here as a child to enter our Chicago public schools and study our strange barbaric customs.

He must have been a likeable chap for in my long and intimate dealings with him as a parent, he has always won my total admiration. It was in high school that he met my Uncle Frank, who became his best friend. Uncle Frank was not an ordinary person; in fact, none of the Adamses were ordinary.

Some one sent me a newspaper clipping just the other day headed, "The Adams Still Survive." Most of it spoke of the American branch but toward the end it said, "As a family they have been inclined to advocate unpopular causes, to speak out in meeting and sometimes to make themselves obnoxious. But no one has ever questioned their ability, their patriotism, their honesty of purpose, or their integrity of character." I can't resist the temptation to quote this, because it so typically describes my mother. I don't know whether she included my father among her early advocacy of unpopular causes, but when Uncle Frank brought him home she promptly fell in love with him.

Grandmother disapproved. She disapproved all over the map, so much so, in fact, that when her husband's sisters sent for one of the children to "finish" in Europe, at the time of my Grandfather's death, it was mother who was chosen. I'm sure my Grandmother must have recognized all the danger my father was to her daughter, who was a real Adams—"inclined to advocate unpopular causes, to speak out in meeting and to make themselves obnoxious." I can see her now, in that old Chicago house, settling that "outlandish affair of Kate's"—packing mother off to Europe to "get her senses."

My mother stayed six years in Europe, yet all the while answering father's missives. Perhaps words are nothing, nothing but pleasant little tinkling symbols blown upon white fields of blank paper, unless they might be judged by their effectiveness upon the reader. Father's words brought mother home from Europe, brought her home against the wishes of the Adams' aunts, of my inflexible Grandmother and her own better judgment, and were, in a way, responsible for my very being.

Her marriage to father was the result of so many causes that one might almost believe it to have been fate. Besides my father's love for her there was this lack of sympathy at home and her own desire for the extraordinary. Someone called her a woman with a "flair." She revelled in adventure and daring; after all she was the daughter of "Dare-Devil-Dick-

Adams," who had been arrested time and again for driving six horses tandem through the streets of Londonderry. Then, too, my father was very much in the position of an "unpopular cause."

They eloped.

For mother an elopement seems quite in season, but for my father it seems too fantastic to be true. Young men in Japan still marry according to the dictates of their family . . . and these two eloped in eighteen eighty something. For him to marry anyone of a different race was astonishing enough, for he came of good family, but for him to marry without his family's consent and against the wishes of hers is, indeed, inconceivable from a Japanese standpoint.

Grandmother was essentially cold, but when she heard the news, she simply froze. This blue white glacier in her soul remained intact, until I unconsciously began thawing it at the age of three. During the interim Kate's name was nonexistent in that household and woe to any reference to Japan. It was Uncle Frank who, making a trip east, went a little out of his way to see the banished Kate. He begged mother to forget, forgive and take father and me home to Chicago, to Grandmother. . . .

I don't know the exact details of the war which he must have fought with Grandmother on his return to Chicago, but the result was that my earliest memories are all of that rather grim household with its ultra polished floors and its slippery Turkish rugs.

It's well that tonsils and appendixes had not become the rage then, or I should undoubtedly have lost mine. Everything was "done," everything that could possibly improve me, but the thing they could not change and which I did not escape, was my heritage—the "Japanese." This thought-stimulating, imagination-firing label which inevitably leads to complications.

To the friends who visited us in those days, I felt myself to be a comicality, a toy. I was often spoken of as a "Japanese doll," or worse still as the "cute," little Japanese. My mother's guests found in me what Pierre Loti found in all Japan, "qui n'a pas l'air sérieux, qui fait l'effet d'une chose pour rire." I felt this more keenly than I understood it. I had never been to Japan; I was as innocent of any real knowledge of the Japanese as those who visited us, but whatever I did, of good or of bad, was sure to be because I was Japanese.

These mental pit-falls surprised me, and alienated me from all the rest of the world, even from old, fat Nan, the colored wash woman.

One lovely summer's afternoon when I was about six, I was down in the basement, where I spent much of my time. Our cat had had kittens and while Nan was busy with the family washing, I watched the antics of the sprawling kittens over their languid mother. Suddenly it occurred to me that the large collie dog across the street might also be interested in the new kittens. Mother was in the attic when she heard my voice in the side yard, "Come along Friskey, I want to show you our nice, new kittens . . ."

She rushed down three long flights of stairs only to find a revolving mass of cat and dog among the furnace pipes. Nan's wig had been snatched from her head in the mix-up and every movable article in the laundry room displaced.

"Oh, Mother," I cried, choking on my tears, "I didn't know they would do that!"

I shall never forget how funny Nan looked without her wig or how thought-inspiring her words. "Maybe cats and dogs don't have no fights in Japan, but they sure do in the U-u-nited States."

Strange, distant and delightful Japan, land of childhood dreams, where anything might be! But all of my encounters with this mythical Japan were not so fascinating. There was the dirty-faced boy who sat on the back fence calling, "Chink! Chink!" whenever I ventured into his presence in search of a playmate.

Hurrying back to my mother and weeping real tears brought small comfort for she only said, "Why didn't you tell him you were not a Chink?" She did not seem to understand my problem, for she never, even to her dying day, admitted that there was, or could be, a problem.

"But Mother," I parried, on that first occasion, "you told me never to contradict."

This sent the family into peals of mirth.

But I see it as an early tragedy, however funny, for what could I have told the young warrior on the back fence? That I was not a "Chink"—only a "Jap"? My childish instinct had but introduced me to the polite withdrawal, as one of the few possible responses to other people's little phantasms concerning me. True, I have long since reached the saturation point, and now frequently view with intense gaiety the mental gyrations of my critics.

At that time I was attending John Dewey's School of Education, but there I was the very conspicuous Japanese. This was exactly what they strove to avoid, but their constant reassurance made one doubt. There was Barr, a Mexican girl who came each day with her swarthy Mexican nurse, there was a Dutch boy with a peculiarly blurred accent, there was a French Miss whose dresses were always copied by sewing mothers, there was Aie Fujita, a real Japanese child, the consul's little girl and there were still a good majority of thorough Anglo-Saxons for contrast. Our teachers constantly reiterated that, "All nations are the same. Though the little Dutch boys wear wooden shoes and the little Chinese ladies pinch their feet and the little Eskimos wear fur boots, we are all the same, we are just alike. One human family." Dear teachers, kind, well meaning souls who so earnestly fought to blanket the word "human." But this little polyglot community of my early school days was "human" enough to make us feel our differences. We were a collection of freaks, of children with race contrasts or faddist mothers and we never doubted it for an instant! How many internationalists make this same mistake! Do they ever convince?

Every summer Mother and I made a pilgrimage to Forest Hall. The long summer months spent there brought me a fulfillment of love for America, which can never be broken. Slowly and secretly this country became my native land. Secretly, because at the time my mother had taught me to say, "Grandmother, Mother and Uncle Frank are British, but Father and I are Japanese," and to look forward to a time when I should find my real home in that remote, unknown Japan.

But the peace and security of these early days were all shattered and broken by the death of my Uncle Frank. My Grandmother for the only time in my remembrance of her, seemed crushed. But strangest of all my mother and father seemed to have lost something vital from their relationship. All the pleasant chatter and intimacy were gone. As for myself, I buried all of my happiest childhood in his grave. And then, one day, I was thirteen at the time, my mother announced that we were going to Japan as father was being sent out by the Corticelli Silk Company as a silk buyer.

I dreaded leaving my Grandmother, for I could not readjust myself so suddenly to the new order, and my cousins became doubly dear. Now that I was actually going, I lost my curiosity about Japan, I was not at all sure that I wanted to see Japan after all. I began to understand that what was for my mother a flaring adventure, and for my father a turning homeward, was for me only the tragedy of tearing away all my early roots of home and homeland.

My only consoling thought was that at last I would cease to be "une chose pour rire"—"the little Japanese"—a toy for the passing whim of the public mind. In other words I was at last to become ordinary, inconspicuous. I was to feel a oneness with a people. I should no longer be "different." It is only when one can understand my utter faith in my Orientalism, that one can glimpse the extent of my disappointment and disillusionment!

Disillusionment can be a comedy and a tragedy all rolled into one! I had believed that I was Japanese and that Japan was my home. Why should I have doubted this when no one had ever suggested otherwise, when everyone, in fact, had assured me that it was so?

Fear is said to be man's greatest emotion and with fear I greeted Japan. And with every step I took after alighting from our ship at Yokohama, my original fear increased. Nothing I had been taught, told or imagined was in the least like Japan and this much being true, what was I to expect? Such disillusionment gave me an uncertainty as to everything in the world. No kitten was ever put in a cage with wild cats with more instincts for self-preservation than I and to me Japan was even worse than wild cats— it was gargoyles and disenchantment.

In Chicago I had been merely conspicuous in what now appeared to have been a limited social group. In Yokohama I was something far worse than conspicuous, I was a regular show for the entire city! I was not even going to be able to walk down the street without a crowd forming. This was demolition of illusion with vengeance. My only alternative was not to care and this I could not quite do, for I was half Japanese.

"What does the word *ijin san* mean?" I asked at last of my father.

His look was full of sympathy as he answered quietly, "It means foreigner."

The facts were these—in America I was Japanese. In Japan I was an American. I had an Oriental father who wished to live like an Occidental and an Irish mother who wished to live like a Japanese. I had a series of eccentric traditions on my Western side and a thousand unknown, silent Tamagawas, buried in their own family cemetery on the other.

My mother's friends had thought of me as a decoration, or a gimcrack; and my father's friends now thought of me as a barbarism and a blemish. I had had an uncle in America who had played doll's store on the ironing board for my amusement, and I now had an uncle in Japan who sat on a cushion, in the mysterious dimness of an inner temple and "thought he was God"—Was this to be for my amusement also?

Somewhere in between all this, I existed. I was neither American, nor Irish, nor Japanese. I had no race, nationality or home. Everybody, who seriously considered me at all, immediately focused upon me an eye glued to a microscope or monocle. I was a curiosity, of that I was certain and I could see little concealment or delicacy in it all. What I wanted to know was whether I was a pleasing or an unpleasing curiosity, for I could not spend my life chasing other people's trains of thought and missing one train after another. That was annoying even to an Irish-Japanese of thirteen years.

There was something vitally wrong with the logic of the whole situation. I was as far from being what I now recognized as the "Japanese doll," as a monkey is from being a jelly fish. But on the other hand, could I be as completely crude and boorish as my father's friends evidently thought me? My thinking resulted in chaos. There were no answers to these questions. They were all perplexing whirlpools of thought to me, aged thirteen, and instead of becoming quiet lakes of reflections, some of them have become regular maelstroms, now that I am thirty-six. I began to see that people thought in groups, in societies, in nations and in whole races, and they all thought differently. The unaccepted, the unexpected, like myself, must remain forever outside of it all, but nature fortunately left such exceptions with a sense of humor.

I lived on in Japan and yet never as a Japanese would live, and I was Japanese and I was not Japanese. For no one who had even the most superficial knowledge of Japan considered that I was Japanese, and the Japanese themselves considered me as a foreigner, and yet was I a real American? Would I ever be completely anything? Or must I always be the exception? Unanswerable questions.

Meanwhile I grew up in the foreign community of Yokohama, and reached at last the leisurely years of 1910–12. I made my debut and was "popular" as all we girls bred in the foreign community were. It was an October evening in 1911 that I first met Frank Eldridge, "one of the boys from the American Consulate," at one of the most festive of consular parties. I fell in love with him immediately because I thought him divinely ordinary.

If there was one thing I longed for above all others at that point of my existence, it was the ordinary. To be simple—insignificant—and to melt inconspicuously into some environment—seemed to me worth the ambition of a lifetime. This was quite understandable for I had found my seat on the bucking bronco of internationalism, anything but restful . . . Try as I would I could never find the charm in being raceless, country-less, and now to all intents and purposes practically relativeless as well—though mother said it was charming and many agreed with her. Like the old song from the opera *Pinafore,* I "might have been a Roosian or a French or Turk or Proosian, or perhaps Itali-an." For by the time I was introduced to my prince of the proletariat, I had had the opportunity of dismissing a number of worldly and attractive men of different nationalities. But I had had my practical lessons in trying to be a native in two countries and I lacked any curiosity for a third splicing of my nationality.

We were married a year later. I was nineteen at the time and Frank was twenty-three. Of course, I was to find that the most actually extraordinary man of the lot was my husband. But I did not discover this until I was so firmly rooted in the character of the conservative Mrs. Eldridge, that I had forgotten I had even been considered, or had considered myself a freak, and from that safe viewpoint could even admire his unexpectedness.

In the spring of 1914 Frank sailed for America to enter private business. The plan was for me to stay on in Japan and await the success of his business affairs before following him and so it was not till the next spring that he sent for me.

There were many, many things that entered into my feeling about my homegoing. I wanted to go. I had never really loved Japan, though I had been deeply interested. Nevertheless the language, the habits, the Bushido had made a stranger of me; to Japan I was always a foreigner.

I sailed on the *S. S. China.* My destination in the United States was the South. That meant only a place "where Frank was" to me then, but it turned out to be a place where a lot of other people were as well.

To live in a small southern town, to do my own work and be Mrs. Eldridge,—a nice insignificant, every-day sort of person—was just what I had most wished to do. I had never discussed the matter with my husband. Needless to say I had not stressed the fact that I especially admired what I considered his "divine ordinariness" and it never occurred to me that he might have admired me for any of my unusualness. This I had always believed to be but an illusion in other people's minds. But Frank had been a whole year in that southern town and he had been enthusiastically expecting me for months. He met me filled with desire to present me to his new-found friends, and attentions were heaped upon me by everyone.

It is of these attentions which I wish to speak. They are the "prayers in the horse's ear." They came to me in that southern town and they come to me still from the majority of the people I meet. They surprise me. They seem to me to be vague utterances of a mystic Western philosophy, which my horse's ear refuses to understand. They are definite schools of thought with which people here in the United States make their friendly onslaughts upon me.

As a little girl when I went to Japan I had thought I was to be Japanese, but the Japanese themselves had gaped at me and decided differently. Now that I had returned to America, the problem was something complex and at first confusing to me in that quiet southern town.

People did a great deal more than gape at me. They had "ideas" about me, theories, preconceptions—*beliefs!*

One type thought of me as "cute." I remember once being taken to an Arts Club by one of these persons, and being introduced as the "little Japanese lady."

Then there are the people who insist that I am an Oriental and when I even meekly suggest that I have certain doubts on the subject, they assume the attitude that I am posing as an Occidental but that they are too clever and have discovered me. They usually end by getting very sentimental over Oriental art and religion and find in my reticence all sorts of mysterious and beautiful philosophies which I, being an Oriental, do not reveal.

There are the moderns who analyze my sentences as I talk, "Ah, now—that's your Irish," "Ah, now—that's your Japanese." These are usually the most annoying, for they consistently refuse to be human. They generally close their ears to what I am saying in their efforts to have me properly assorted and psychologically tabulated.

There are the anthropological hounds. They are not half bad, because in their intellectual peregrinations they have discovered that mixed races have existed since the world began. Their examinations are limited to the shape of my nose and the quality of my hair.

There are the dramatists who are interested in what they call my "racial pulls." What am I feeling? In America, do I long for Japan? In Japan do I long for America: Or do my feelings explode when they clash somewhere in the middle of the Pacific as they rush violently in both directions?

The educationalists (and not all of them are confined to the schools and colleges) have a keen desire to make something out of me. Meanwhile they consider me a sort of Oriental information bureau. "Are the Japanese becoming a Christian Nation?" "Is it true that the Chinese are more honest than the Japanese?"—and so on.

There are the people who are actually afraid of me. I am a menace!

I find them in all classes of society from the most charming of Californians to my colored scrub-woman, whom I found one night sitting on the front door-step.

"Lucy, what are you doing out here?"

"Oh, Miss Eldridge, I'se afeared. I never did like to work with them idols in the house nohow, and money ain't gwine to hire me to stay in thar after it gits dark."

Fortunately for the welfare of my soul, however, there is a great middle class who after they have discovered my heredity, do accept the "is" where they find it. They start by asking me, "Just when did you learn to eat with a knife and fork?" "How long did it take your feet to grow?" Then they urge me to "say something in Japanese so I can hear what it's like," and by that time they are feeling almost as foolish as they care to feel and begin to be human by "say, which do you think is better to lead from, a sneak or just follow the fourth-highest-of-your-longest-suit rule?"

Frank introduced me to all these varieties of thought in that southern town. After several months of their attention and consideration, I began to wonder seriously if I was actually as phenomenal as without doubt I was supposed to be.

My eldest son, Francis, was expected in July 1916. It was decided that I was to go to the hospital to receive him. At the time I was miserable and depressed. I was very happy with my husband but I had not found myself living the nice sequestered life I had pictured. Though I had been supplied with all the materials, a good husband, a small salary; a quiet town, life's most conventional domestic situation; a coming baby . . . and so far as I could see, it should have been the most ordinary of all American situations and I the most average and usual of all American girls—I was not!

As soon as I reached the hospital I was greeted by a young nurse who ushered me into the stifling hot little room where my son was to be born, and when I gave my name, she grinned a knowing assurance, "Oh, we all know *all* about you. We are all so interested."

I think most women feel when they enter the hospital on these occasions that they are victims of one of Nature's dreadful traps, but I suddenly felt as I looked at my neat uniformed attendant, that I was trapped by Humanity as well. I had not crawled into some impersonal hole wherein I could have my baby in peace. Instead, I had been heralded by Heaven alone what mysterious beliefs about me. Was I a Japanese doll, or a menace? Her sickly sweet smile informed me that in her case at least it was the Japanese doll.

After a while another nurse whisked into the room. She was cold and formal, but I soon felt that she too "knew all about me." She dismissed the first with a quiet stare and jammed a thermometer into my mouth with a do-or-die attitude that was provoking. To this one I was a menace, but at least I could hope to count on her impersonal service.

Then, a long animal-like cry shattered my thoughts.

"What's that?"

"That?" She dismissed it with a sniff. "One of those half-nigger girls in the ward. It is her first baby. She has been going on like that for hours. You can hear her all over the place every time the door is opened.

"Poor, poor thing. Can't something be done for her?"

"Oh, she's alright. These niggers make an awful 'to-do' about nothing."

"Oh—" the pain had wrenched my back. But I must not let this woman say that about me. I must be silent. This place wasn't a hospital. No. It was a sort of moral testing ground. Whatever happened I would be "decent." No one would ever say, "It's that Jap girl in room 31, making an awful 'to-do' about nothing."

Hour after hour the pains grew more terrible. But I was silent. With each new racking attack of horror I drew on every atom of my will power not to cry out, not to betray my mother, my father and husband who believed me to be decent.

The room, the doctor and the nurses all faded away from my sight into a blazing world of pain. Then suddenly as if suffering were only an asbestos curtain at the theatre, it lifted and I was conscious of the room and the people and my coral-colored son who was being held up by his heels and shaken by the doctor.

I must admit that just for a second or so I felt heroic. Everyone in the room seemed to be feeling that emotional relief that can but be called happiness. But all this feeling of ecstasy lasted for only five or ten minutes. It was the youngest nurse who smashed it all with, "Isn't the baby too cute! It's not often that the Stork brings us a little Japanese baby!"

Next morning the old nurse was as ungracious as ever. My heroism of the night before had not melted her.

I dared to question her, "Was there anything unusual about the birth?"

"No, absolutely normal."

That was something to be glad about. I could at least have an average birth to my credit. I was not unusual or extraordinary in that.

But half an hour later the younger nurse had destroyed my illusions.

"The doctor says it's a perfectly *marvelous* case. Of course these things have been known to be true in the Orient. But to have it happen right here in our own hospital!"

"What happened?"—"What is it?"

"A *painless* birth!"

Nineteen seventeen—the war, and we were off to Washington, Frank accepting the post of assistant Chief of the Far Eastern Division, Department of Commerce. In Washington I found that I was no longer an Adams or a Tamagawa,—I was Mrs. Eldridge. I baked and scrubbed and attended functions and played bridge with the other wives of the Department officials. Most of the other Department officials' wives were doing the same thing. I was not sequestered, nor even rooted, but, at least, I was ordinary.

I belonged completely and absolutely to this international group of roving diplomats and cruising Trade Commissioners and Attachés and their families. I felt and knew their esprit de corps and was one with them as I never have been one with any other group. These people were filled with too many other interests to bother about whether I was Japanese or not. Who-is-who and why was a far more interesting question than whether or not I was a little Japanese lady, or a menace.

The years went on in Washington, happy, satisfying years. Although our Washington friends still arrived and departed we ourselves had now begun to feel like old residents. In fact, never before had I felt such delusions of a rooted security. Day followed day without the tremor of a change—nothing seemed to indicate the slightest disturbance of my happily dull and calm existence . . .

And then, a shattering event took place on the other side of the world which was to vitally affect our lives—September first 1923, the great earthquake of Japan! This tremendous cataclysm changed the destinies of almost all those who had even the remotest connections over there, however far they were scattered over the world. It shook us out of our smugness of mind, scattered our peace, demolished our illusions of security. It brought Mother back to America, shaken in spirit, in faith and in her ability to "flair."

My mother's presence in our household made us face facts that might otherwise have been buried in our busy lives. When she came to us she brought Japan with her and renewed my own mental confusion regarding my ancestry without meaning to do so. In fact, her intention was just the opposite, to make me forget my Japanese. Her expressed position was that there was no problem in an Eurasian marriage and she retained her viewpoint until the day she died.

However, I do not approve of Eurasian marriages. I do not approve of international marriages. Because this world is full of uncertainties, confusions and insecurities for all of us. Occidental and Oriental alike are afraid to climb down from the psychological horses they are riding however many prayers our priests of philosophy, science, economy and travel may be muttering. We must stick to our horses or fall, because we have not yet learned to unhorse gracefully. I disapprove of Eurasian marriages because there are so few among the many in Europe, in Asia or in America who have the wit and ability or the moral and spiritual stamina and determination, or the keen, blind, deaf and dumb intellect that will allow them to drive their psychological horse in triumph to its goal.

And now with my mother gone and my father in Japan the problem of their marriage should have ended. But I now find that it has only just seriously begun, for the Japanese Government now tells me that I do not exist, that I never have existed, as far as they are concerned, because I was never registered as a Japanese. Here, then, is an official refusal to accept the "is" of the thing. Legally I am not and never was; therefore, I cannot be the lineal descendant of my parents or an inheritor of my mother's estate.

My lawyers say that I am "an ultimate, international, legal absurdity." As a citizen of Nowhere, I don't know whether it's better to be a born Oriental, or a born Occidental. I don't know whether Japan is the delightful fairyland of Lafcadio Hearn, or the dangerous yellow peril of the Californians. I don't know whether I have had the ideal home and the perfectly mated parents that my mother said I had, or whether I was the victim of one of the most horrible marital combinations ever perpetrated. I'm not even sure that I'm not the world's prize freak, though I believe myself to be addicted to the conventional life. Who can say whether it's better to dance on your heels with your toes turned in, or on your toes with your heels turned in?

Perhaps it's wise to be foolish and foolish to be wise. But it's safer, much safer, to ride a nice, still, conventional wooden horse secured to a merry-go-round than a wild, untrained and untamed international steed.

For, only the non-existent can stand on their feet in mid-Pacific!

PUERTO RICAN PARADISE
Piri Thomas

Sociologists use technical terms to label social processes. One such word is "assimilation." It refers to what
happens when the members of different ethnic groups
meet and the minority begins to adopt some of the
manners and mores of the dominant society.

In this selection from Piri Thomas' autobiography *Down
These Mean Streets*, the author shows the impact of
New York life and work on his Puerto Rican parents. His
father gets caught up (or, better stated, ground down)
in the constant pursuit of steady work in the cold city.
His mother longs for home, romanticizes the past, and
fills her children with stories of the warmth of her island
home.

Piri and his brothers and sisters listen but their attention
wanes. It is time for their favorite radio programs,
including "Jack Armstrong, the All-American Boy."

Poppa didn't talk to me the next day. Soon he didn't talk much to anyone.
He lost his night job—I forget why, and probably it was worth forgetting
—and went back on home relief. It was 1941, and the Great Hunger called
Depression was still down on Harlem.

But there was still the good old WPA. If a man was poor enough, he
could dig a ditch for the government. Now Poppa was poor enough again.

The weather turned cold one more time, and so did our apartment. In
the summer the cooped-up apartments in Harlem seem to catch all the
heat and improve on it. It's the same in the winter. The cold, plastered

From *Down These Mean Streets* by Piri Thomas. Copyright © 1961 by Piri Thomas.
Reprinted by permission of Alfred A. Knopf, Inc. and Barrie and Jenkins, Limited.

walls embrace that cold from outside and make it a part of the apartment, till you don't know whether it's better to freeze out in the snow or by the stove, where four jets, wide open, spout futile, blue-yellow flames. It's hard on the rats, too.

Snow was falling. "My *Cristo*," Momma said, "*qué frio*. Doesn't that landlord have any *corazón*? Why don't he give more heat?" I wondered how Pops was making out working a pick and shovel in that falling snow.

Momma picked up a hammer and began to beat the beat-up radiator that's copped a plea from so many beatings. Poor steam radiator, how could it give out heat when it was freezing itself? The hollow sounds Momma beat out of it brought echoes from other freezing people in the building. Everybody picked up the beat and it seemed a crazy, good idea. If everybody took turns beating on the radiators, everybody could keep warm from the exercise.

We drank hot cocoa and talked about summertime. Momma talked about Puerto Rico and how great it was, and how she'd like to go back one day, and how it was warm all the time there and no matter how poor you were over there, you could always live on green bananas, *bacalao*, and rice and beans. "*Dios mio*," she said, "I don't think I'll ever see my island again."

"Sure you will, Mommie," said Miriam, my kid sister. She was eleven. "Tell us, tell us all about Porto Rico."

"It's not Porto Rico, it's Puerto Rico," said Momma.

"Tell us, Moms," said nine-year-old James, "about Puerto Rico."

"Yeah, Mommie," said six-year-old José.

Even the baby, Paulie, smiled.

Moms copped that wet-eyed look and began to dream-talk about her *isla verde*, Moses' land of milk and honey.

"When I was a little girl," she said, "I remember the getting up in the morning and getting the water from the river and getting the wood for the fire and the quiet of the greenlands and the golden color of the morning sky, the grass wet from the *lluvia* . . . Ai, *Dios*, the *coquis* and the *pajaritos* making all the *música* . . ."

"Mommie, were you poor?" asked Miriam.

"*Si, muy pobre,* but very happy. I remember the hard work and the very little bit we had, but it was a good little bit. It counted very much. Sometimes when you have too much, the good gets lost within and you have to look very hard. But when you have a little, then the good does not have to be looked for so hard."

"Moms," I asked, "did everybody love each other—I mean, like if everybody was worth something, not like if some weren't important because they were poor—you know what I mean?"

"*Bueno hijo,* you have people everywhere who, because they have more, don't remember those who have very little. But in Puerto Rico those around you share *la pobreza* with you and they love you, because only poor people can understand poor people. I like *los Estados Unidos,* but it's sometimes a cold place to live—not because of the winter and the landlord not giving heat but because of the snow in the hearts of the people."

"Moms, didn't our people have any money or land?" I leaned forward, hoping to hear that my ancestors were noble princes born in Spain.

"Your grandmother and grandfather had a lot of land, but they lost that."

"How come, Moms?"

"Well, in those days there was nothing of what you call *contratos,* and when you bought or sold something, it was on your word and a hand-shake, and that's the way your *abuelos* bought their land and then lost it."

"Is that why we ain't got nuttin' now?" James asked pointedly.

"Oh, it—"

The door opened and put an end to the kitchen yak. It was Poppa coming home from work. He came into the kitchen and brought all the cold with him. Poor Poppa, he looked so lost in the clothes he had on. A jacket and coat, sweaters on top of sweaters, two pairs of long johns, two pairs of pants, two pairs of socks, and a woolen cap. And under all that he was cold. His eyes were cold; his ears were red with pain. He took off his gloves and his fingers were stiff with cold.

"*Cómo está?*" said Momma. "I will make you coffee."

Poppa said nothing. His eyes were running hot frozen tears. He worked his fingers and rubbed his ears, and the pain made him make faces. "Get me some snow, Piri," he said finally.

I ran to the window, opened it, and scraped all the snow on the sill into one big snowball and brought it to him. We all watched in frozen won-der as Poppa took that snow and rubbed it on his ears and hands.

"Gee, Pops, don't it hurt?" I asked.

"*Sí,* but it's good for it. It hurts a little first, but it's good for the frozen parts."

I wondered why.

"How was it today?" Momma asked.

"Cold. My God, ice cold."

Gee, I thought, *I'm sorry for you, Pops. You gotta suffer like this.*

"It was not always like this," my father said to the cold walls. "It's all the fault of the damn depression."

"Don't say 'damn,' " Momma said.

"Lola, I say 'damn' because that's what it is—*damn.*"

And Momma kept quiet. She knew it was "damn."

My father kept talking to the walls. Some of the words came out loud, others stayed inside. I caught the inside ones—the damn WPA, the damn depression, the damn home relief, the damn poorness, the damn cold, the damn crummy apartments, the damn look on his damn kids, living so damn damned and his not being able to do a damn thing about it.

And Momma looked at Poppa and at us and thought about her Puerto Rico and maybe being there where you didn't have to wear a lot of extra clothes and feel so full of damns, and how when she was a little girl all the green was wet from the *lluvias*.

And Poppa looking at Momma and us, thinking how did he get trapped and why did he love us so much that he dug in damn snow to give us a piece of chance? And why couldn't he make it from home, maybe, and keep running?

And Miriam, James, José, Paulie, and me just looking and thinking about snowballs and Puerto Rico and summertime in the street and whether we were gonna live like this forever and not know enough to be sorry for ourselves.

The kitchen all of a sudden felt warmer to me, like being all together made it like we wanted it to be. Poppa made it into the toilet and we could hear everything he did, and when he finished, the horsey gurgling of the flushed toilet told us he'd soon be out. I looked at the clock and it was time for "Jack Armstrong, the All-American Boy."

José, James, and I got some blankets and, like Indians, huddled around the radio digging the All-American Jack and his adventures, while Poppa ate dinner quietly. Poppa was funny about eating—like when he ate, nobody better bother him. When Poppa finished, he came into the living room and stood there looking at us. We smiled at him, and he stood there looking at us.

All of a sudden he yelled, "How many wanna play 'Major Bowes' Amateur Hour'?"

"Hoo-ray! Yeah, we wanna play," said José.

"Okay, first I'll make some taffy outta molasses, and the one who wins first prize gets first choice at the biggest piece, okay?"

"Yeah, hoo-ray, *chevere*."

Gee, Pops, you're great, I thought, *you're the swellest, the bestest Pops in the whole world, even though you don't understand us too good.*

When the candy was all ready, everybody went into the living room. Poppa came in with a broom and put an empty can over the stick. It became a microphone, just like on the radio.

"Pops, can I be Major Bowes?" I asked.

"Sure, Piri," and the floor was mine.

"Ladies and gentlemen," I announced, "tonight we present 'Major Bowes Amateur Hour,' and for our first number—"

"Wait a minute, son, let me get my ukelele," said Poppa. "We need music."

Everybody clapped their hands and Pops came back with his ukelele.

"The first con-tes-tant we got is Miss Miriam Thomas."

"Oh no, not me first, somebody else goes first," said Miriam, and she hid behind Momma.

"Let me! Let me!" said José.

Everybody clapped.

"What are you gonna sing, sir?" I asked.

"Tell the people his name," said Poppa.

"Oh yeah. Presenting Mr. José Thomas. And what are you gonna sing, sir?"

I handed José the broom with the can on top and sat back. He sang well and everybody clapped.

Everyone took a turn, and we all agreed that two-year-old Paulie's "gurgle, gurgle" was the best song, and Paulie got first choice at the candy. Everybody got candy and eats and thought how good it was to be together, and Moms thought that it was wonderful to have such a good time even if she wasn't in Puerto Rico where the grass was wet with *lluvia*. Poppa thought about how cold it was gonna be tomorrow, but then he remembered tomorrow was Sunday and he wouldn't have to work, and he said so and Momma said *"Sí,"* and the talk got around to Christmas and how maybe things would get better.

The next day the Japanese bombed Pearl Harbor.

"My God," said Poppa. "We're at war."

"Dios mío," said Momma.

I turned to James. "Can you beat that," I said.

"Yeah," he nodded. "What's it mean?"

"What's it mean?" I said. "You gotta ask, dopey? It means a rumble is on, and a big one, too."

I wondered if the war was gonna make things worse than they were for us. But it didn't. A few weeks later Poppa got a job in an airplane factory. "How about that?" he said happily. "Things are looking up for us."

Things *were* looking up for us, but it had taken a damn war to do it. A lousy rumble had to get called so we could start to live better. I thought, *How do you figure this crap out?*

I couldn't figure it out, and after a while I stopped thinking about it. Life in the streets didn't change much. The bitter cold was followed by the sticky heat; I played stickball, marbles, and Johnny-on-the-Pony, copped girls' drawers and blew pot. War or peace—what difference did it really make?

ON THOSE WHO CAME

In which the nature of the American
Nation is discussed, the paths to
assimilation are considered, and the
changes that occurred are introduced.

PEOPLE AND PLACE
Max Lerner

In the first section of this volume the reader is introduced to various Americans and their spokesmen from the insider's point of view. These personal accounts of the trials and tribulations of newcomers could be matched by countless others. Taken together, they would offer us a composite portrait of America and her variegated peoples.

In *America as a Civilization* Max Lerner offers us another perspective. Instead of recounting the experiences of one man or group he attempts to write about them all. His vision is macroscopic; his subject, the ethnic experience writ large.

Here, in a brief selection from the larger work, Lerner gives his views on the question of whether one can speak of *the* American, offering scaffolding on which one can begin to build a theory of assimilation.

1. Is There an American Stock?

Every traveler in the tropics comes away with an unforgettable sense of the pervasive jungle enclosing him. America's jungle is its ethnic environment of a myriad of peoples. In such a tropical luxuriance every ethnic type is present, everything grows fast and intertwines with everything else, anything is ethnically possible.

The best vantage points for observing the variety of American ethnic strains are on a subway in New York or a San Francisco street or at an Army induction center. Each is a broad channel through which the human material of America streams. Every people in Europe, most of the varied stocks of European and Asian Russia; peoples from Israel and the Arabs of the Middle East; peoples from China and Southeast Asia, from the Philippines, Hawaii, Australia, from the farthest reaches of India, from Liberia and Nigeria, from the Gold Coast and the Ivory Coast, from Kaffirland and the Witwatersrand, from every country in South and Central America, from every Caribbean island, from British and French Canada, from Greenland and Iceland—there is scarcely a stock on the ethnic map of the world that is not represented in America.

Let me make my use of terms clear. I use "stock" rather than "race," and "ethnic" rather than "racial," because in both cases I mean something in which race is only one ingredient. I have in mind a compound of influences from race, nationality, language, religion, region or sub-region—any recognizable strain which not only by its common descent but by its length of living on the same soil, under the same sky, and in the same community has formed a relatively stable biopsychological and cultural type.

Is any one of these ethnic stocks more "American" than the others? To say of someone that "he is of American stock" has come to mean that he is white, probably Protestant and of Anglo-Saxon descent, and that his forebears emigrated to America some generations back. But there is little of solace here for the distinction-hunters. In most civilizations the conquering stock has tried to set itself off on the one hand from the conquered natives, on the other from the newcomers who may want to get in on the power and the glory. In America this has been difficult on several scores: the natives were too few and were so ruthlessly stripped of land, home, and livelihood that the deed trailed little glory behind it. If "American stock" is to mean descent from those who were most immediately in on the kill, the leaders of the Great Predation, it would carry a guilt of which many would be gladly rid. The real conquest of America was not a military conquest, to deck out a boast that the strength of killers flows in one's blood: it was a conquest of forest and plain, of mountain and valley and river, of new technologies and new social forms; and in it every wave of immigrants took part. Although the largest single group came from the British Isles, there was no one stock that pre-empted the glory of settling America: even in the early decades of the Republic, there was a variety of stocks shaping the amalgam of "this new man, the American." Finally, the leveling force of the democratic idea has resulted in a crossbreeding and mingling of stocks which have made the task of the racial purist a hopeless one.

This effort to pre-empt the term "American" for a single strain out of many, and exclude from it all the others, is a familiar device in the technique of prescriptive prestige. Whatever meaning it may have in the case of a more inbred and homogeneous people, in America it is meaningless. Yet there are some who recoil from racism but regard the length of settlement as a crucial distinguishing mark. "Wouldn't European stocks which have been here longer," a friend writes me, "be more 'American' than the recent ones? Isn't a Lowell or a Roosevelt, for example, likely to be more 'American' than my Chinese laundryman's son?" By the test of time the most "American" stocks would be the American Indians, the descendants of the Pilgrims, and the descendants of the early Negro slaves—which is not exactly what was meant. The idea that European stocks are more "American" not by the fact of long settlement but by the fact of being European (West European, not Mediterranean or Slavic), is an idea easy to succumb to. Its strength derives from the fact that the English, Scottish, French Huguenot, and Dutch influences are interwoven with early American history. It is easier and more natural to think of a Lowell or Roosevelt as American than of a recent Chinese immigrant or a descendant of an early Indian or Negro family, but this is because the West Europeans have run the show in America since early times and have therefore made the rules and set the admission price. They feel more at home and have made others feel less at home.

Our thinking will be clearer if we say that there are three levels of meaning attached to "American": the links of family and stock with American history over time; the equal or unequal claims to rights and privileges under the law; the sense of commitment to American life. Only on the first level does the question of stock enter, however irrationally. On the second level there can be no discrimination between a Lowell or Roosevelt and the Chinese laundryman's son. On the third level the problem is one of individuals, not of stock: Americans belonging to the newer stocks may be as committed to the obligations and meanings of the American experience as the older ones, and many have enriched it greatly.

Yet in the world's most notable ethnic democracy there remains a hierarchy of prestige depending partly on stock—black, yellow, brown, and red at the bottom, white Protestant, West European on top, with the lines between the rest drawn partly in terms of closeness to Colonial descent, partly of geographic closeness to the British center of origin of the early settlements. A roughly chronological chart of the sequence of waves of immigration—English, Dutch, German, Scotch-Irish, French, Scandinavian, Irish, Mediterranean, Jewish, Balkan, Slavic, Mexican and Latin American, Filipino, Middle Eastern, Oriental—would correspond roughly to the descending scale of prestige in the ethnic hierarchy. The big divergences are that the Indians who came first, are not at the top but toward the bottom of the pyramid; and the Negroes, who were brought over early, are not near the top but at the very bottom. On the prestige chart of the ethnic hierarchy, one could superimpose a residence map showing which stocks are distributed in slum areas, in tolerable living quarters, in middle-class districts, in residential areas. Over that one could draw an occupational chart of the functions to which the ethnic groups have been more or less specialized.

This is fluid, but the correspondences are roughly there. Making allow-

ance for the constant breaking of the mold and the emergence of many
Negroes as doctors, lawyers, teachers, ministers, businessmen, it remains
true that in the South the Negroes have done and still do the heavy labor
in the fields, and everywhere the dirty jobs in the factories and on the
roads and wharves, in digging ditches and laying tracks and building tun-
nels, while their women are domestics. The Chinese, Filipinos, and Puerto
Ricans are also still specialized to do domestic and routine jobs. The
Mexicans (or "Spanish-speaking Americans") work at sweated labor in
the factories of the Southwest and as migratory workers on the farms of the
Southwest and California. The Poles, Czechs, Magyars, and Slovaks are
in the coal mines of Pennsylvania, West Virginia, and Illinois, in the steel
mills and at the open-hearth furnaces of Gary and Pittsburgh and Buffalo.
The Scandinavians are farmers in the Midwest and loggers in the lumber
camps. The Irish of the later immigration are policemen, saloonkeepers,
and bartenders in New York and Boston, but also day laborers and build-
ing-trades workers, transport workers, longshoremen. The Italians and the
Jews work in the garment trades of New York and the other Eastern
centers; the Italians are also barbers and shoeshine boys and musicians,
and they work the truck gardens in New Jersey and the vineyards of
California, as do the Japanese; while the Jews move from the sweatshops
into the small trades and the middlemen functions, and into medicine,
law, dentistry, teaching, and the entertainment world.

But in the fluid life of America, the specialization does not stick. Cutting across the ethnic occupation map is the fact that it is the new arrivals
of most stocks who do the menial and dirty work and drift to the periph-
eral occupations, while the earlier and resourceful ones break out of their
cultural molds, buy farms and houses, get university training, attain skills,
and move up to become members of the middle class. The epithets do
often stick—"Wop," "Dago," "Sheeny," "Kike," "Nigger," "Norske,"
"Mick," "Spick," "Polack," "Hunkie," "Bohunk," "Chink," "Jap," "wetback," "greaser"—betraying a class and xenophobe animus as well as a
racist one.

Sometimes, in overcompensation for this prevalent animus, one is
tempted to ask whether we can in fact distinguish stock from stock,
or whether there are not simply *individuals* in a rich and bewildering
variety?

It is true that the differences between the stocks are not clear-cut, that
one could find within one of them—say the Jews—wider differences of
physiognomy, height, bone structure, skull structure, temperament, than
between particular Jews on the one hand and particular Italians or Irish
or Portuguese or Syrians on the other. It is also true that ethnic differences
do not carry with them the differences of superiority or inferiority that the
racists ascribe to them. Although there are no supermen in America, there
are Americans who hunger for a cult of the blond Anglo-Saxon gods;
although there are no sub-men in America, there are whites who cling

to their color out of a panic sense of emptiness and who pant to assign Negroes or Puerto Ricans or Mexicans or Chinese to the category of inferior men. There are no Americans who belong to radically different branches of the human family, in the sense that their blood is of a different genus, or that some are closer to apes and others closer to gods, some born to work and others to lord it over them. There is not even an ethnically pure group in America (unless we speak of ethnic sub-pockets like the Hutterites from Russia who settled in South Dakota and have been almost completely endogamous) for at this point in history the chromosomes of any group contain also some genes from most of the others.

Yet it would be foolish to deny the reality of ethnic stocks in America and the differences between them. Those who came to America came from relatively stable ethnic groups. They brought with them obvious physical hereditary differences and habits of life that set them off from the others, and the social hostility they encountered often made them huddle together in more or less isolated ethnic communities. Many of them thus retained and even froze their sense of separateness, while others kept themselves open to every influence from other groups, including interbreeding. If we recognize that there is no stigma to membership in any one of the ethnic stocks of America the whole question of stock can be taken with realism and without passion.

The fact is that America is more than an agglomerate of individuals jumbled in hopeless confusion. America is a myriad of stocks, each with some identity maintained from the earliest to the latest migration. What gives America its biological richness is that it is a mingling of ethnic strains. What gives America its cultural richness is that it is a mingling of traditions and temperaments. Unless the stocks had brought an identity of their own, it would be meaningless to talk of their mingling. Unless those identities were changed and dissolved in the process, shaped and reshaped, caught up in the ever-flowing stream of the life of all of them together, it would be meaningless to talk of America.

Does the unlimited crossbreeding of ethnic stocks hurt or help the quality of American life? True, there are some valid objections to be raised against unlimited crossbreeding. In the process of mixture, the groups with the higher birth rate will predominate, biologically and culturally, and while a high birth rate may be one of the indices of vitality, the crucial question is that of the quality of the individuals and cultures which are crossed. There is, however, a double and contradictory line of reasoning in the "pure America" argument. One is that the more recent immigrants are clannish, refuse to intermarry, and should therefore be kept out. The other is that they will flood into the country and overwhelm and corrupt the "native" stock by the weight of numbers and birth rate and by interbreeding. One argument rests on the theory that they do not mix, the other on the theory that they mix all too much. I suspect that logic is less important here than emotion—the emotions of invidiousness, guilt, pride, and fear that dominate the thinking of the "pure America" group.

On biological grounds alone, if these emotions can be ruled out, the central argument for an exclusive concept of American stock is the argument that unlimited crossbreeding will mean the mongrelization of America. Even reputable writers seem to have been made panicky by the possible biological and cultural corruption of pure Anglo-Saxonism by the Negroes, Asians, Slavs, Jews, and Mediterranean peoples. If mongrelization has any meaning, it assumes a "pure" (but nonexistent) stock thinned out and corrupted by unlimited crossbreeding. The fear of mongrelization is the fear of strange blood and ways on the part of groups that believe their economic and social supremacy threatened by outsiders, and fix upon the racial invaders as the enemy.

This fear reaches nightmare proportions in the Southern states, where the governing group has sought to protect its "white supremacy" by a set of state miscegenation laws. States like Mississippi and Georgia, in a triumph of paranoia, enacted laws making any marriage felonious and void if it involves a white person and one with an "ascertainable trace" of African, West Indian, Asian Indian, or Mongolian blood. One of the wider aspects of the miscegenation laws, if they are regarded in terms of any rational threat of mongrelization, is that they are found in the North as well as the South, and that in eight of the states covered by them the Negroes against whom they are directed form less than 1 per cent of the population.

This is not to deny the reality of crossbreeding in America. But there can be no question of mongrelization because there is no norm of purity. Each ethnic strain, in the process of crossbreeding, "corrupts" the other; each dilutes and enriches the other. The fact is that crossbreeding is in itself neither good nor bad. Its chief effect is to increase variations at both ends of the curve of inherited traits: in other words, we may dilute the quality of what is transmitted as a result of the vast interchange of genes, but we may also get more geniuses on the top level. The range of potentials is widened in both directions. Everything depends, as I have said, on the individuals and cultures entering into the mixture. The characteristic ethnic quality of America is the outcome of the mingling of stocks and traditions on a scale unparalleled in history. Although some cultural historians maintain that the dilution of native stock is followed by cultural decadence, the example of the Italian city-states, Spain, Holland, Britain, and now Russia and India as well as America indicates that the most vigorous phase may come at the height of the mingling of many stocks. The greater danger lies in closing the gates.

No stock, once it has come to America, remains what it was. Each breeds away from type, both by the influence of the new physical environment and by the fact of intermingling. Every stock, by its migration, breaks with its past environment and enters a new one. Continued migration from one American region to another and mobility from one class and therefore one set of living standards to another continue the process of environmental reconditioning. How substantial the changes may be was shown in 1912 in the classic study by Franz Boas, *Changes in Bodily Form of Descendants of Immigrants.* Despite the prevailing view that skull measurements are an unchanging racial characteristic, Boas showed that the skull indices of the children of Jewish and Italian immigrants differed appreciably from those of the parents. This is environmental change away from ethnic type, whether due to diet, living standards, climate, or other factors in the natural and cultural environment. Boas was dealing with the physical factor that one would expect to be most resistant to change. What applied to skull changes would apply more easily to psychic and cultural changes; and what applied under the influence of environmental and standard-of-living change would apply more easily as the result of biological mixture.

I find a surprising misreading of Boas's meaning in Arnold Toynbee's *Study of History* (Vol. I, 220-1), which argues that Boas is, like his opponents, an adherent of race thinking. Boas writes that his study is suggestive "because it shows that not even those characteristics of a race which have proved to be most permanent in their old home remain the same under the new surroundings; and we are compelled to conclude that when these features of the body change, the whole bodily and mental make-up of the immigrants may change." Toynbee gathers from this "what is the fundamental postulate of all race theories: that is, the postulate that physical and psychical characteristics are correlated." But this is to miss the meaning of the phrase *"may* change," which carries with it an emphasis on the plasticity of *both* the cultural-psychic and the physical traits under environmental pressure. The whole point of racist thinking is that there is no such plasticity but that a given set of inherent physical traits of a superior or inferior caste carries with it a rigid set of psychic traits of a similarly superior or inferior caste. Boas proved the plasticity (although he felt it was a limited one) and rejected the moral hierarchy. The racists assert the moral hierarchy and reject the plasticity.

The process of plasticity has been described in Paul Engle's *America Remembers.*

> *The ancient features of the type were changed*
> *Under a different sun, in a clearer air*
> *That entered the lungs like wine, the swarthy face*
> *Paled, cheekbones lifted and narrowed, hair*
> *Straightened and faded, and the body moved*
> *With a lighter step, the toes springy, the eyes*
> *Eager as a bird's, and every man*
> *Had a coiled spring in his nerves that drove him*
> *In a restless fury of life.*
>
>   *The bloods mingled*
> *Madly* . . . . *(Who knows*

What strange multi-fathered child will come
Out of the nervous travail of these bloods
To fashion in a new world continent
A newer breed of men?)

Given conditions making for rapid change, the question thus put is the question of how far the plasticity of the American stock is likely to lead. Clearly, every ethnic stock in America, unless it is caught and isolated in some eddy of the American stream, is breeding away from type. But is it breeding toward a new form of its own type, where it will be more or less stabilized? Or is the process of change a continuing and cumulative one resulting in the emergence of an inclusive new ethnic type, like a loose sort of tent to cover the existing types which will survive yet be transformed?

The probabilities point to something less defined than either of these. We do not yet know what ethnic future lies ahead for America, since genetics is changing its insights and outlook so rapidly. Earnest Hooton, a physical anthropologist who liked to make bold forays into the future, predicted that "the stubby, bone-and-muscle Mr. Americas of today" are doomed to disappear or to be "reduced to the ranks of the institutionalized malefactors." They will be replaced (said Hooton) by a more "attenuated" body build, "taller and more gangling than ever, with big feet, horse faces, and deformed dental arches"; the women "less busty and buttocky than those of our generation." There are other guesses of the future stock, some of them less unattractive. But their common premise is that a new ethnic entity is forming which will carry with it the multiform freightage of all past generations, but in which there will also be some central cast of temperament, physique, and lineament that crops up more and more frequently.

This does not mean that the old stocks will disappear or that America will become ethnically uniform. The processes of heredity and their interplay with the physical and cultural environment are too complex to allow for uniformity. The gene variants of so heterogeneous a population as the American are fantastically large in number, and the potential directions of American stock are great. This is the first great instance in history where ethnic abundance has combined with so great a freedom in marriage, to produce an unimaginable ethnic future.

If then we ask again, "Is there an American stock?" the answer must be that there are many stocks in America—more than have ever been gathered together before within a national unit; that none of them, whatever its claims and arrogance, is more American than the others, and none, whatever its sense of inferiority, less American; that each is different from what it was in its area of ethnic origin—each touched and changed by the alchemy of the American environment, by the fact of living and mingling with all the others on the American continent. America has become a great biological and psychological laboratory, whose experiments may issue in undreamed-of results. In all the stocks there has been, whether obviously or subtly, a breeding away from type; there has also been, subtly rather than obviously, slowly, ever so slowly, and yet unmistakably, a breeding *toward* new types that have not yet emerged.

When they emerge they will be the creature of America, not America *their* creature. Yet as we watch the yeast working in the ever-re-created human material of America, can we doubt that the determiners of a not unimaginable American future are at work here? "There is but one victory that I know is sure," wrote Saint-Exupéry, "and that is the victory that is lodged in the energy of the seed." Given what we know about American stock, we must take this to mean the victory not of the seed's rigidity but of its plasticity.

2. The Immigrant Experience

For centuries the strength and richness of America have been swelled by the great tides of immigration from Europe, with the sources moving roughly from the British Isles to western Europe and the Scandinavian countries, to the Mediterranean countries, to the Slavic countries. In 1790 America had fewer than four million people, of whom three quarters of a million were Negroes: 82 per cent of the total white population was English. For the next forty years, until 1830, immigrants were slow in coming. In the 1830s the "Atlantic Migration" quickened, first with Irish countrymen, then with German farmers and artisans, and then with land-hungry Scandinavians. In the early 1880s came a greater wave of the "new" immigration—"new" in the double sense that they were no longer from western and northern Europe but from eastern and southern Europe, and that they were more likely to settle in the big cities and work in the mines and mills and factories than on the land.

A few figures tell a dramatic story. From 1800 to 1914 some fifty million people left Europe, of whom almost thirty-five million came to the United States. In the century and a half from 1800 to 1950 some forty million newcomers moved to the United States, 85 per cent of them from Europe, 11 per cent from other countries in the American hemisphere, 3 per cent from Asian countries, and 2 per cent from the rest of the world. In the single peak decade of 1904-1914, ten million came, and in the peak year of 1907 more than a million and a quarter.

As the convulsions of tyranny, war, and famine shook the world, and as the "opportunity line" thinned out in the Old World and grew bolder in the New, millions of people came spilling down the sluiceways to America, and an almost manic quality seemed to infect immigration. It was fed by the steamship companies, who sent out agents to recruit immigrants and depict the glories and grandeurs of the new star of the West; and it was aided by the increasing cheapness of transportation. But even without these stimulants the migration would have taken place.

America-as-magnet exercised a hypnotic force strong enough to draw millions to the shores of promise.

It was, in the main, the peasants who came, from Ireland, from Germany, from the Scandinavian countries, from Italy, from Russia and Poland, from the Balkans. There were many others who came from the cities too—artisans without jobs, ruined shopkeepers, political *émigrés*, intellectuals who had failed to make their way and who were to establish "Latin farms" (as they were called with gentle derision) in America. But mostly the families who came had lived on the land, and the land had been unable to sustain them. The plots were too small and the village community ways were too traditionally set to yield to the new agricultural techniques. Debt was a humiliating master to serve, and poverty a bleak companion. When famine began to nibble on the margins of your life, and your little plot of land was foreclosed and you found yourself dispossessed, you began to feel the narrowing confines of your village intolerable. Ridden by the weight of feudal and clerical tradition, with no hope left for yourself and no promise to hold out to your children, what was more natural than to surrender to the image of a country where land could still be had and a man could keep moving until he had found a challenge to his strength and boundless possibilities for his young? "The rich stay in Europe," De Crèvecoeur had written much earlier, "it is only the middling and the poor that emigrate."

There was always a bitter spell of waiting and enduring between dislocation from the old home and settlement in the new. There were the weary vigils at lodging houses along the wharves in the seaport cities of Europe until passage was arranged with some broker and the ship finally sailed. The steerage quarters, oversold through greed, were often cold, crowded, dirty, disease-ridden, rat-infested. In the darkness the long nights and days differed little from each other. Scanty provisions and bad water made scurvy, dysentery, and "ship's fever" lethal adversaries. When the ship arrived the immigrant found himself, dazed and bewildered, in a world with which his traditional peasant qualities could not cope. He had to get work immediately—work of any kind, at any pay, with whatever hours and conditions—in order to sustain life; he became thus a ready prey for exploiting employers, swindling fellow countrymen, greedy moneylenders. Sometimes he settled in the first big city he came to, huddling in a ghetto with his countrymen; sometimes he was able to push on into the interior and take up a piece of land or serve his apprenticeship as a "hired man"—again, usually, near others of his own ethnic stock. In both cases he needed first to convert his work and skill into capital: for years after his arrival, thus, he had to save and scrimp, living on almost nothing, so that he could get a real start in a store or restaurant or on a farm or as a small entrepreneur.

For years, perhaps for the rest of their lives, many of these immigrants were to remain (as Oscar Handlin has so movingly described in *The Up-*

rooted) alienated men—alienated from the culture they had left and from the one that had not yet wholly welcomed them and that they did not understand, and alienated finally from themselves. The old patterned ways of the village community, however galling, formed a path of stability, where a man knew what was expected of him. The new ways of the buzzing big American cities and the quickly growing farm villages were bewildering. The immigrant became an object, caught within forces over which he had no mastery, having to convert his strength on the market into dollars with which he could get what he needed for life.

The tight family of the peasant community or of the Jewish tradition was subjected to the strains and dislocations of the new society; often it was fatally split, although those that survived found that the ties of cohesiveness were strengthened by the fact of their members having to face together an alien world. Most tragic of all, the immigrants often found that their own children—adapting more easily to the new ways, caught up in the new rhythms, accepting the new life goals, and eager to merge themselves with the new environment—drifted away and became alienated from their parents. Perhaps in order to wipe out the cleavage between themselves and their new fellows, they saw their father and mother through the eyes of the "Americans" and came to think of them as outsiders and strangers—in short, as objects. The circle of alienation was completed.

The immigrant experience was thus somber and tragic. Yet it would be a mistake to see it thus without adding that it was also one of excitement and ferment. Millions of the immigrants, after giving their strength to the new country, died with a sense of failure and frustration. But many more millions survived their ordeal, became men of influence in their communities, and lived to see the fulfillment of the American promise in their own lives doubly fulfilled in the lives of their children. "Everything tended to regenerate them," De Crèvecoeur wrote of his fellow immigrants, "new laws, a new mode of living, a new social system; here they are become men: in Europe they were so many useless plants, wanting vegetable mold, and refreshing showers. They withered and were mowed down by want, hunger, and war; but now by the power of transplantation, like all other plants, they have taken root and flourished!" One doubts whether this lyric description, written at the end of the eighteenth century, would have been accepted as a faithful one a century later; yet it described a process which would have meaning for many through the whole course of the immigrant experience and even more meaning for the second and third generations, who reaped the harvest of the transplanting of their fathers without having had to suffer the ordeal.

Yet there was also something in the ordeal that enriched the immigrant and his new country. He may have deemed himself a failure in the old village and helpless on the crossing, and he may have begun to doubt his manliness after every defeat. But one thing that could never be stripped from him was the immediacy of his experience: whatever he had achieved had been due to himself and his own efforts. The experience of the immigrants recapitulated the early American pioneer hardships, in many ways on harder terms, since the difficulties they encountered were those of a jungle society rather than a jungle wilderness. It added a dimension of tragic depth which American life needed: even in its most tragic phases it furnished a ferment of vitality which re-created the American experience in every decade. There was much in the American mind that tended to become fixed and conformist. The immigrant experience hurled itself against this with insistent eagerness, kindling a warmth that thawed out much of the glacial rigidity. In recent years, with the gates almost closed, there have been fewer new immigrants to keep the regenerative process going.

The immigrants eventually found their place in the American economy, each new layer that came from below pushing up the earlier arrivals to the next stratum. But the economy also felt the impact of the immigration which provided a labor force for a rapidly expanding industrialism. Whatever one may say of the importance of American natural resources, the richest resource was man power: without the immigrants America could not have found quickly enough the man power to build the railroads, mine the coal, man the open-hearth steel furnaces, and run the machines. Moreover, while most of the immigrants were pushed into the unskilled, backbreaking jobs, enough of them were skilled—carrying over techniques from a European industrialism which had made an earlier start—so that the Great Migration was not only one of people but of talents, skills, and cultural traditions. The increase of immigration also meant more consumers as well as more producers. The new machines cut production costs and prices, yet the steadily mounting millions of consumers kept big profits flowing back into industry. And since the immigrants started on so little, their living standards kept steadily improving, and the home market grew not by arithmetical but by geometrical progression.

The immigrant's obsession with rising living standards was something he gave to American life as well as something he took from it. He was a man in a hurry, not only to make money but to show he had made it, not only to sow the crop of his labor and ingenuity but to reap the harvest of his success. The stories of the "self-made man" that caught the American imagination were in many cases the Horatio Alger rags-to-riches stories of immigrant boys who rose to the top of the heap. Their business methods were little different from the methods of the earlier Americans, but since they were so avid for results the legend grew that they were distinctively unscrupulous, and there was often a cleft between the world of "respectable" (i.e., "nativist") business and "immigrant" business. Certainly there was a febrile intensity about the immigrant that was part of his world of wonder: he was the small boy with his nose pressed against the shopwindow whose sweets were out of his reach unless he could come in with a fistful of coins. He was full of wonder at the miracles of science and mechanical inventions, at the headlong course of progress, at the dizzying peaks of wealth and power. He was full of a sense of promise and possibility which renewed the pioneer spark.

When the promise faltered and the possibility ran into the sands, he could express his bitterness through labor or radical movements which started as the protest of some ethnic stock and broadened out into a dissident splinter group or even a third-party movement. But the political impact of the immigrant was felt as much in the machine politics of the big city as in the dissenting politics of the Middle West. The boss politics of Boston, Philadelphia, New York, Chicago, St. Louis, was an interchange of the loyalties of the lonely immigrants, who needed a very personal kind of help in their encounters with jobs and the law, for the protection of the men who had become sophisticated and knew the power of the massed immigrant vote.

The first-generation immigrant, whether he was on a farm or in a big city, was likely to live out his life on the margin of the new society, and from there he sent coursing through much of the culture the current of his hope, his loneliness, his individuality. It was his son, the second-generation immigrant, who was lampooned by the novelists as one driven either to imitate or to outdo the "native Americans" at their own game. He was the Sammy of Budd Schulberg's *What Makes Sammy Run?* and the Harry Bogen of Jerome Weidman's *I Can Get It for You Wholesale.* He acted as if some "equalizer" had been built into him, driving him to excesses of energy or (as in cases less noted by the novelists) to excesses of protective coloration.

The third-generation immigrant was caught in a paradox. On the one hand the continuing pressures from the world of those whose ancestors were accepted as the nation's ancestors turned him toward stability and conformism, and thus further away from his links with the immigrant experience. On the other hand Marcus Hansen pointed out in a notable essay that "what the son wishes to forget the grandson wishes to remember," and that the third-generation immigrant, no longer ashamed of his cultural ancestry, has had the courage to embrace it. Both tendencies may be found in the grandchildren and great-grandchildren of the immigrant, struggling for mastery; but I am convinced that what Hansen noted will prove the stronger.

A great change came over American attitudes toward immigration after World War I and led to the racist discrimination of the quota legislation of 1921 and 1924. Actually the movement for restrictive legislation started before the turn of the century, almost with the start of the Great Wave of the new immigration. Every people is "ethnocentric," which is a way of saying it is the sun around which the earth and moon and stars revolve; and this is particularly true of the way the dominant group feels. The Americans of English descent—whether New England Yankees or transplanted Yankees in the Middle West—felt that their old dominance had been undercut by the hordes of strange new arrivals; nurtured in the democratic dogma, some of the best of them were deeply troubled and split in their emotions. The Southern whites, trying to keep the South "a white man's country" and therefore fearful of the Negroes who surrounded them, turned their fears into a more general suspicion of "foreigners." The reserve army of labor, which meant so much to the businessman because it gave him the human material for industrial expansion, seemed a threat to many labor leaders who feared the competition of cheap labor. Some of the intellectuals of the Progressive Era, anxious about the continuity of the native tradition, turned strongly anti-immigrant. Others were influenced by European theories of racial superiority and inferiority and found "scientific" buttressing for their purist fears about what Madison Grant called "the passing of the great race."

An alliance of Yankees, Southerners, trade-unionists, Progressive intellectuals, racist theorists, population purists, and professional xenophobes made headway in convincing the descendants of the earlier immigrants that the later immigration was dangerous and should be severely restricted. They scared them with images of criminality, radicalism, and Oriental cunning, with examples drawn from the Mafia and the Black Hand, from the Haymarket anarchists and the Jewish peddlers who became international bankers. They succeeded in frightening fearful Americans who thought the country of their fathers would be made unfit for their children by newcomers who sold themselves cheap, pulled down wage standards, read dangerous books, lived like pigs, and bred like rabbits.

Certainly there was a shift in the meaning of the whole immigrant experience, on the part of both the hosts and the newcomers. Writing in the 1880s, James Bryce noted that "the intellectual and moral atmosphere into which the settlers from Europe come has more power to assimilate them than their race qualities have to change it." He thus paid tribute to the transforming power of the American environment and defended the immigrant against the charge of being a corrupting serpent in an American Eden. Yet even as he wrote, a change was coming over the American scene. To be an immigrant in the earlier years was to be part of an experience in the making. You didn't feel unwanted or a misfit, nor did you have to feel ashamed of your cultural origin. But after the Civil War, with the triumph of industrialism, America became the country where miracles were in full swing and where entrance was an admission to the miracle-making. As an immigrant coming to something no longer experimental but already tested and created, you were suspect of trying to cash in on a good thing. As a combined entrance fee and expiation, you were crowded into slums, forced to do the dirty and poorly paid jobs, made to feel an outsider.

The "natives" began to ask how these gate-crashers dared be so different from them. "If a few million members of the Alpine, Mediterranean, and

Semitic races are poured among us," wrote the novelist Kenneth Roberts, "the result must inevitably be a hybrid race of people as worthless and futile as the good-for-nothing mongrels of Central America and south-eastern Europe." There were so many "mongrels" pouring in; they looked strange, swarmed everywhere, were too loud; they came from a Europe thick with revolutionary conspiracy to an America where the possessors were becoming insecure. Besides, there was always in the background the monstrous (and fascinating) sexual threat that the purity of America's blood would be polluted by miscegenation with the swarthy foreigners.

Thus the later phase of immigration corroded the generous energies of the earlier America. The Israel Zangwill vision of America as a "melting pot"—a crucible into which poured metals from every country while "the great alchemist melts and fuses them with his purging flame"—was greeted with enthusiasm, but it was a dangerous metaphor since it implied that all the immigrant strains must be purified by being assimilated with something more "American." In World War I the fear cropped up of the "hyphenated American" who was not being melted, fused, and purged rapidly enough. The "Red scare" that followed the war was directed against the foreign-born and, like the even more intense furor after World War II, it reinforced the whole agonizing doubt about the nature of American identity. Some Americans found in it a sadistic outlet for their aggression; many others fell prey to intellectual and emotional confusion. The quota formula embodied in the 1921 Immigration Act was thought up by a well-intentioned China missionary who saw in the quota system a way of merging the restrictions upon Oriental immigration with more general ones and thus in effect denying their existence. In the 1924 law the base year on which the quota for each country was fixed (the "national origins provision") was pushed back in order to minimize the number of Mediterranean and East European entries. It was hard for Europeans to fathom a democratic philosophy which admitted only 3,000 French and 5,000 Italians a year, as against roughly 25,000 Germans and 65,000 British.

Immigration restriction thus became deliberately discriminatory and racist, remaining thus through the McCarran-Walter Law of 1952 to the present day. "The "Golden Door" of Emma Lazarus was swung all but shut. Where, in 1900, 13 per cent of Americans were foreign-born, in 1950 only 7 per cent, in 1960 the percentage will be negligible. The irony of the exclusionist policy was that since it could not be applied to Puerto Rico (which was part of territorial America) the exclusionists had to tolerate the influx of Puerto Ricans, who were very different from their ideal type. If the purpose of immigration policy was to ensure a stable admittance of, say, 250,000 immigrants a year, this could have been achieved more rationally by setting that figure and admitting them either in the order of their application acceptance or in terms of whether they possessed the needed skills. The fight to relax the harshness of the immigration laws and their administration is still carried on but halfheartedly, as if no one believed any longer that the trend could be reversed, since (whatever the intellectuls may think) the anti-alien component in Congress and the constituencies is still strong.

Even before the door was closed the impact of the narrowing attitudes had made itself felt in the minds of the immigrants themselves. Having caught the fever of the rush to America, they were overeager and overtense. Everything in them was heightened: the love of freedom, the urge to "make good," the vulnerability to scorn, the anxiety to belong. The structure of the immigrant family was corroded, and the pride of belief in the traditions which had been brought across the seas was shaken.

The immigrant found himself caught between two ghettos. One was the outer ghetto of economic and social discrimination imposed upon him. The other was the inner ghetto which came from his feverish efforts to meet this assault either by wearing the badges and aping the ways of the new culture, thus rejecting his own family and ethnic tradition, or by an equal overemphasis on retreat within the shell of the old culture, taking the form of an ethnic chauvinism. There was thus a double process of overcompensation at work—that of an anxious assimilationism and that of a belligerent ethnic orthodoxy. In both cases it was a response to hostility and an expression of alienation. The success stories of individual immigrants do not belie this but rather confirm it. Most of the immigrant-boy-to-tycoon success stories are about men who found the transition from one culture to another too precipitous to be bridged without a single-minded effort that left its effects on the personality.

The "melting pot" phase of American thinking about the immigrants was happily short-lived. Today there are few serious writers and thinkers who do not see through the fallacy of viewing American culture as a kind of manufacturing process which stamps out cultural diversities and turns complex human material into a monolithic Great Stone Face. To be sure, the flow of new immigrants has become the merest trickle (since 1940 it has averaged not much over 100,000 a year), and the issue is therefore how the second and third and later generations are to guide their lives. Among the newer immigrant groups the current of thinking that has triumphed is the one set in motion by Randolph Bourne and Horace Kallen—the idea of a "cultural pluralism" in which the ethnic groups cherish their own traditions while refusing to isolate themselves from the larger culture.

The problem for the recent newcomers and their children, as indeed for all Americans, is to hold several cultures in organic suspension, weaving each in with the other in a process without which American society as we know it could not have been formed. The question is not whether the older traditions are to change; for change, with a measure of absorption, is inevitable. The real problem is to make certain that the pace of change is not destructively rapid and that it does not involve a flight from the rootedness of one's fathers which leaves the sons and grandsons with no base on which to make a transition. The difference is one of mood and value as well as tempo. It is the difference between *assimilation,* which is a one-way drive that attaches no value to what is left behind and marked for extinction, and *integration,* which is a two-way circuit, where the new national consciousness adds a new dimension to the older ethnic tradition, and the older tradition adds emotional depth and rootedness to the new cultural product.

THE GHETTOS
Oscar Handlin

The New World was imposing and, for many who came, life was harsh. But hard times were made more endurable because of an interdependence of fate. With ones kith and kin—whether from England or Germany, Ireland or Italy—one could find succor and needed solace.

As historian Oscar Handlin shows in this moving portrait, old ways were not transplanted but transmuted. Americanization moved forth apace as many compatriots and coreligionists worked out their own means of meeting the challenges of the new society, looking both forward and backward.

The place was important too. Settlement in America had snipped the continuity of the immigrants' work and ideas, of their religious life. It would also impose a new relationship to the world of space about them. In the Old Country setting, the physical scene had been integral with the existence of the men in it. Changes would have explosive repercussions.

In the United States, the newcomers pushed their roots into many different soils. Along the city's unyielding asphalt streets, beside the rutted roads of mill or mining towns, amidst the exciting prairie acres, they established the homes of the New World. But wherever the immigrants went, there was one common experience they shared: nowhere could they transplant the European village. Whatever the variations among environments in America, none was familiar. The pressure of that strangeness exerted a deep influence upon the character of resettlement, upon the usual forms of behavior, and upon the modes of communal action that emerged as the immigrants became Americans.

The old conditions of living could not survive in the new conditions of space. Ways long taken for granted in the village adjusted slowly and painfully to density of population in the cities, to disorder in the towns, and to distance on the farms. That adjustment was the means of creating the new communities within which these people would live.

★   ★   ★

Although the great mass of immigrants spent out their days in the great cities, there was always an unorganized quality to settlement in such places that left a permanent impress upon every fresh arrival. Chance was so large an element in the course of migration, it left little room for planning. The place of landing was less often the outcome of an intention held at the outset of the journey than of blind drift along the routes of trade or of a sudden halt due to the accidents of the voyage. Consequently the earliest concentrations of the foreign-born were in the chain of Atlantic seaports: Boston, Philadelphia, Baltimore, New Orleans, and most of all New York, the unrivaled mart of Europe's commerce with America. For the same reasons, later concentrations appeared at the inland termini, the points of exchange between rail and river or lake traffic—Cleveland, Chicago, Cincinnati, Pittsburgh, and St. Louis.

In all such places the newcomers pitched themselves in the midst of communities that were already growing rapidly and that were therefore already crowded. Between 1840 and 1870, for instance, the population of New York City mounted by fully 50 per cent every ten years; for every two people at the start of a decade, there were three at its end. (In all, the 312,000 residents of 1840 had become 3,437,000 in 1900.) Chicago's rise was even more precipitate; the 4000 inhabitants there in 1840 numbered 1,700,000 in 1900. Every ten-year interval saw two people struggling for the space formerly occupied by one.

These largest cities were representative of the rest. The natural increase through the excess of births over deaths, with the additional increase through the shift of native-born population from rural to urban areas, and with the further increase through overseas immigration, all contributed to the enormous growth of American municipalities. To house all the new city dwellers was a problem of staggering proportions. Facilities simply did not keep pace with the demand.

To house the immigrants was more difficult still. For these people had not the mobility to choose where they should live or the means to choose how. Existing on the tenuous income supplied by unskilled labor, they could not buy homes; nor could they lay out much in payment of rent. Their first thought in finding accommodations was that the cost be as little as possible. The result was they got as little as possible.

The willingness to accept a minimum of comfort and convenience did not, however, mean that such quarters would always be available. Under the first impact of immigration, the unprepared cities had not ready the housing immigrants could afford. The newcomers were driven to accept hand-me-downs, vacated places that could be converted to their service at a profit.

The immigrants find their first homes in quarters the old occupants no longer desire. As business grows, the commercial center of each city begins to blight the neighboring residential districts. The well-to-do are no longer willing to live in close proximity to the bustle of warehouses and offices; yet that same proximity sets a high value on real estate. To spend money on the repair or upkeep of houses in such areas is only wasteful; for they will soon be torn down to make way for commercial buildings. The simplest, most profitable use is to divide the old mansions into tiny lodgings. The rent on each unit will be low; but the aggregate of those sums will, without substantial investment or risk, return larger dividends than any other present use of the property.

Such accommodations have additional attractions for the immigrants. They are close to the familiar region of the docks and they are within walking distance of the places where labor is hired; precious carfare will be saved by living here. In every American city some such district of first settlement receives the newcomers.

Not that much is done to welcome them. The carpenters hammer shut connecting doors and build rude partitions up across the halls; middle-class homes thus become laborers'—only not one to a family, but shared among many. What's more, behind the original structures are grassy yards where children once had run about at play. There is to be no room for games now. Sheds and shanties, hurriedly thrown up, provide living space; and if a stable is there, so much the better: that too can be turned to account. In 1850 already in New York some seven thousand households are finding shelter in such rear buildings. By this time too ingenuity has uncovered still other resources: fifteen hundred cellars also do service as homes.

If these conversions are effected without much regard for the convenience of the ultimate occupants, they nevertheless have substantial advantages. The carpenter aims to do the job as expeditiously as possible; he has not the time to contrive the most thorough use of space; and waste square feet leave luxurious corners. There are limits to the potentialities for crowding in such quarters.

There were no such limits when enterprising contractors set to work devising edifices more suitable for the reception of these residents. As the population continued to grow, and the demand with it, perspicacious owners of real estate saw profit in the demolition of the old houses and the construction, between narrow alleys, of compact barracks that made complete use of every inch of earth.

Where once had been Mayor Delavall's orchard, Cherry Street in New York ran its few blocks to the East River shipyards. At Number 36, in 1853, stood Gotham Court, one of the better barrack buildings. Five stories in height, it stretched back one hundred and fifty feet from the street, between two tight alleys (one nine, the other seven feet wide). Onto the more spacious alley opened twelve doors through each of which passed the ten families that lived within, two to each floor in identical two-room apartments (one room, 9 × 14; one bedroom, 9 × 6). Here without interior plumbing or heat were the homes of five hundred people. Ten years later, there were some improvements: for the service of the community, a row of privies in the basement, flushed occasionally by Croton water. But by then there were more than eight hundred dwellers in the structure, which indeed continued in use till the very end of the century.

That these conditions were not then reckoned outlandish was shown in the model workmen's home put up by philanthropic New Yorkers at Elizabeth and Mott Street. Each suite in this six-story structure had three rooms; but the rooms were smaller (4 × 11, 8 × 7, and 8 × 7). There were gas lights in the halls; but the water closets were in sheds in the alleys. And well over half the rooms had no windows at all.

At the middle of the nineteenth century, these developments were still chaotic, dependent upon the fancy of the individual builder. But the pressure of rising demand and the pattern of property holding gradually shaped a common form for the tenement house. The older barracks still left waste space in alleys, halls, and stair wells; and they did not conform to the uniform city real-estate plot, twenty or twenty-five feet wide and one hundred feet deep. As the cost of land went up, builders were increasingly constrained to confine themselves to those rectangular blocks while pushing their edifices upward and eliminating the interstitial alleys.

Ultimately, the dumbbell tenement lined street after street, a most efficient structure that consumed almost the entire area of the real-estate plot. Attached to its neighbors on either side, it left vacant only a strip, perhaps ten feet deep, in the rear. On a floor space of approximately twenty by ninety feet, it was possible, within this pattern, to get four four-room apartments.

The feat was accomplished by narrowing the building at its middle so that it took on the shape of a dumbbell. The indentation was only two-and-a-half feet wide and varied in length from five to fifty feet; but, added to the similar indentations of the adjoining houses, it created on each side an airshaft five feet wide. In each apartment three of the rooms could present their windows to the shaft, draw from it air and light as well; only one chamber in each suite need face upon the street or rear yard. The stairs, halls, and common water closets were cramped into the narrow center of the building so that almost the whole of its surface was available for living quarters.

These structures were at least six stories in height, sometimes eight. At the most moderate reckoning, twenty-four to thirty-two families could be housed on this tiny space, or more realistically, anywhere from one hundred and fifty to two hundred human beings. It was not a long block that held ten such tenements on either side of the street, not an unusual block that was home for some four thousand people.

There were drastic social consequences to living under these dense conditions. The immigrants had left villages which counted their populations in scores. In the Old World a man's whole circle of acquaintances had not taken in as many individuals as lived along a single street here. By a tortuous course of adjustments, the newcomers worked out new modes of living in response to their environment. But the cost of those adjustments was paid out of the human energies of the residents and through the physical deterioration of the districts in which they lived.

The tenement flourished most extensively in New York, the greatest point of immigrant concentration. But it was also known in Boston and in the other Atlantic ports. In the interior cities it was less common; there land values were not so rigid and commercial installations not such barriers to the centrifugal spread of population. From the barracklike buildings of the area of first settlement, the immigrants could move out to smaller units where at least the problems of density were less oppressive. Little two-story cottages that held six families were characteristic of places like Buffalo. Elsewhere were wooden three- and four-floor structures that contained a dozen households. Even single homes were to be found, dilapidated shanties or jerry-built boxes low in rent. Yet internally these accommodations were not superior to those of the tenement. In one form or another, the available housing gave the districts to which the immigrants went the character of slums.

★   ★   ★

Well, they were not ones to choose, who had live in the thatched peasant huts of home. Nor was it unbearably offensive to reside in the least pleasant parts of the city, in Chicago over against the slaughterhouses, in Boston hemmed in by the docks and markets of the North End, in New York against the murky river traffic of the East Side. Such disadvantages they could survive. The hardship came in more subtle adjustments demanded of them.

Certainly the flats were small and overcrowded. In no room of the dumbbell tenement could you pace off more than eleven feet; and the reforming architects of 1900 still thought of chambers no larger than those of Gotham Court. In addition, the apartments shrank still further when shared by more than one family or when they sheltered lodgers, as did more than half those in New York at the end of the century. But that was not the worst of it.

Here is a woman. In the Old Country she had lived much of her life, done most of her work, outdoors. In America, the flat confines her. She divides up her domain by calico sheets hung on ropes, tries to make a place for her people and possessions. But there is no place and she has not room to turn about. It is true, everything is in poor repair, the rain comes through the ceilings, the wind blows dirt through the cracks in the wall. But she does not even know how to go about restoring order, establishing cleanliness. She breaks her back to exterminate the proliferating vermin. What does she get? A dozen lice behind the collar.

The very simplest tasks become complex and disorganizing. Every day there is a family to feed. Assume she knows how to shop, and can manage the unfamiliar coal stove or gas range. But what does one do with rubbish who has never known the meaning of waste? It is not really so important to walk down the long flight of narrow stairs each time there are some scraps to be disposed of. The windows offer an easier alternative. After all, the obnoxious wooden garbage boxes that adorn the littered fronts of the houses expose their contents unashamed through split sides and, rarely emptied, themselves becomes the nests of boldly foraging rodents.

The filthy streets are seldom cleaned; the municipality is not particularly solicitous of these, the poorest quarters of the city. The alleys are altogether passed by and the larger thoroughfares receive only occasionally the services of the scavenger. The inaccessible alleys and rear yards are never touched and, to be sure, are redolent of the fact. In the hot summer months the stench of rotting things will mark these places and the stained snow of winter will not conceal what lies beneath. Here and there an unwitting newcomer tries the disastrous experiment of keeping a goat, adds thereby to the distinctive flavor of his neighborhood.

It was the same in every other encounter with the new life. Conveniences not missed in the villages became sore necessities in the city; although often the immigrants did not know their lack till dear experience taught them. Of what value were sunlight and fresh air on the farm? But how measure their worth for those who lived in the three hundred and fifty thousand dark interior rooms of New York in 1900!

There was the rude matter of what Americans called sanitation. Some of the earliest buildings had had no privies at all; the residents had been expected to accommodate themselves elsewhere as best they could. Tenements from mid-century onward had generally water closets in the yards and alleys, no great comfort to the occupants of the fifth and sixth floors. The newest structures had two toilets to each floor; but these were open to the custom of all comers, charged to the care of none, and left to the neglect of all. If in winter the pipes froze in unheated hallways and the clogged contents overflowed, weeks would go by before some dilatory repairman set matters right. Months thereafter a telling odor hung along the narrow hallways.

What of it? The filth was inescapable. In these districts where the need was greatest, the sewerage systems were primitive and ineffectual. Open drains were long common; in Boston one such, for years, tumbled down the slope of Jacob's Ladder in the South Cove; and in Chicago the jocosely named Bubbly Creek wended its noisome way aboveground until well into the twentieth century.

With the water supply there had always been trouble at home too: poor wells, shallow, and inconveniently situated. The inconvenience here was not unexpected. Still it was a burden to carry full tubs and jugs from the taps in the alley up the steep stairs. Not till late was city water directly connected with the toilets; it was later still to reach the kitchen sink; and bathrooms had not yet put in an appearance in these quarters. Then, too, the consequences were more painful: city dirt was harder to scrub away, and there was no nearby creek. It could well be, as they came to say, that a man got a good bath only twice in his life: from midwife and undertaker.

All might yet be tolerable were not the confining dimensions of the flat so oppressive. The available space simply would not yield to all the demands made upon it. Where were the children to play if the fields were gone? Where were things to be stored or clothes to be hung? Beds or bedding consumed the bedroom; there was only one living room, and sink and stove left little free of that. The man in the evening, come home from work, found not a niche for rest; the tiny intervals of leisure were wasted for want of a place to spend them. Privacy now was more often sought for than in the Old Country where every person and every thing had its accustomed spot. Yet privacy now was difficult to achieve; there was no simple way of dividing space too small to share. Under pressure of the want, the constricted beings bowed to a sense of strain.

Disorganization affects particularly the life of the home. In these tiny rooms that now are all they call their home, many traditional activities wither and disappear. Not here will the friends be welcomed, festivals commemorated, children taught, and the family unite to share in the warmth of its security. Emptied of the meaning of these occurrences and often crowded with strange lodgers, home is just the feeding and sleeping place. All else moves to the outside.

The street becomes the great artery of life for the people of these districts. Sometimes, the boys and girls play in back in the narrow yards, looking up at the lines of drying clothes that spiderweb the sky above them. More often the crowded street itself is the more attractive playground. They run in games through the moving traffic, find fun in the appearance of some hopeful street musician, or regard with dejected envy the wares of the itinerant vendors of seasonal delicacies, the sweet shaved ice of summer, the steaming potatoes and chestnuts of fall and winter.

The adults too drift out, sit on the steps, flow over onto the sidewalks.

The women bring their work outdoors, the men at evening hang about, now and then talk. They begin to be neighborly, learn to be sensitive to each other. That is the good of it.

There is also the bad. The street in its strangeness is the evidence of the old home's disintegration. Why, the very aspect is forbidding: the dear sun never shines brightly, the still air between the high buildings is so saturated with stench it would take a dragon to hold out. These are all signs of the harshness of the physical environment, of the difficulties of living in these quarters, of the disintegration here of old ways. Those children in earnest play at the corner—who controls them, to what discipline are they subject? They do not do the things that children ought. No one does the things he ought. The place prevents it.

Almost resignedly, the immigrants witnessed in themselves a deterioration. All relationships became less binding, all behavior more dependent on individual whim. The result was a marked personal decline and a noticeable wavering of standards.

Some of the reactions to the new conditions of living were immediate, direct, and overt. The low level of health and the high incidence of disease were certain products of overcrowding. Residents of the tenements did not need the spotted maps of later students to tell them where tuberculosis hit, a terror of an illness that spread from victim to victim in the stifling rooms. If the cholera came, or smallpox, or diphtheria—and all did in their time—it was impossible to limit their decimating course. Little else by now remained communal; but contagion and infection these people could not help but share with each other.

The mortality rate was an indication of their helplessness against disease. The immigrants were men and women in the prime of life, yet they died more rapidly than the generality of Americans. Everywhere their life expectancy was lower; and, as might be anticipated, it was particularly infants who suffered. In one Chicago precinct at the end of the nineteenth century, three babies of every five born died before they reached their first birthday.

That, they might say, was sad, but in the nature of things. No act of will, no deed of commission or omission could stay the coming of death. The grim reaper, an old familiar fellow, had simply emigrated with them. But other consequences of living in these quarters confronted the newcomers with a choice or at least with the appearance of a choice. Under the disorganizing pressure of the present environment, men found it difficult, on the basis of past habits, to determine what their own roles should be. They could question neither the validity of the old values nor the exigencies of the new necessities. Having inherited the conceptions of their proper roles, they had been projected into a situation where every element conspired to force them into deviations. They yielded at the points of least resistance: not every one of them, but many, at one point or another. And those who withstood the pressure did so at the expense of continuous, exhausting strain.

What if a man were to think then (as some did) and say to himself: *Why shall I forever beat my head against this unyielding wall? There will be no end to my toil, and my labor gains me nothing. For what a life do I work. And did not the time in any case come of idleness, when not a crust was in the house and I must go cap in hand for help?* His whole being would at first have revolted at the indignity of the thought; in the peasant world the person who did not earn his own bread was not fully a man, lost thereby status and esteem in the eyes of the community. But what status had the laborer in America to lose, what esteem? Was it then such a reprehensible thing to get by without work?

They recalled as they thought of it that at home also there were some who had habitually lived at the expense of others. That had itself been not so terrible; and indeed the beggars had even a magical or religious quality. The humiliation had come from the circumstance that forced a man into alms seeking: from his improvidence, or lack of foresight, or dissolute character, or spendthrift habits. But in America, pauperism was not sought out; it came of itself to good and wicked alike. No blame could attach here to him who could not always earn a livelihood, who came to depend for his sustenance on the gifts of charity.

In what they had there was precious little to keep those weary of the effort from following the persuasive logic of this line of thought. Almost without self-pity and altogether without reproach, they surrendered to the institutions that maintained the dependent, or they abandoned their families, or they became not quite permanent clients of the relief agencies. If they were aged and infirm the choice was quicker made; if they were victims of accident or illness, quicker still; and if they were left widowed or fatherless, then the doubt hardly existed.

Suppose a man found the surrender to pauperism no solution, was unwilling to throw up the burden of his own maintenance; but thought about it and struggled with it. Every morning he would wake to face it, see through the big eyes of fear the oppressive problems of the day ahead. He could look through the narrow airshaft out at the blank wall of his own existence, regard despondently the symbols of a hopeless future. Loaded down with unbearable obligations, many sighed with him who admitted, *Were it not for my soul for which I am anxious, lest I lose it in eternity, I should have drowned myself.* Some, in that last extremity, found the charge of their own souls too heavy a responsibility.

Others yielded in a different way. They closed their eyes; and as the lids of delusion fell and blotted out the brass ugliness of the bed's footboard, they perceived in the sudden perceptions of madness visions of the utmost delight. The darkening walls fell away, revealed an undefined brightness through which they, yes they themselves, ran lightly and effortless, wrapped up in the enjoyment of some unimaginable pleasure.

Or, as on any other morning, you might come down in the chill pre-dawn, half awake on the stairs, counting the creak of your own treads, and turn, in hope of something today, onto the street that led to market or shop. Only there would be something peculiar this now in the shape of the shadows as you hurried from island to island around the flickering pillars of light. As your thoughts wandered their habitual way over yester-day's disappointments and the fears of tomorrow, you began to pick out the fall of following footsteps; round a corner and still they came; again; till, trotting heavily, you outdistanced them—that time. What if they should lie in secret wait, however; and what if among the jostling strangers who swept around you as you hastened onto the avenue were those already on to you? Who would hear your cry, or care? They eyed you with their hostile stares, condemning, pressed in upon you in seeming random movements. When you stopped against the tall board fence to take the dreadful blow, you knew at once that this was he, and struck and struck, till they pinned you down; and that was all, while the for-eign tongues murmured on above you.

The woman too found relief; so many dangers worried her. Today they would not survive, the man and the young ones perilously outside. He would lose the job or not bring home the pay. There would be not enough to eat and, sickening, no money for the doctor. She could no longer swallow her anxiety and rubbed the harder on the board, over and over, for the gray spots kept reappearing as she endlessly washed them out.

Psychopathic disorders and neuroses, they were all one to the admitting officers who kept the count of the insane. On their rolls the immigrants were disproportionately prominent.

There were other means of release, temporary of duration and there-fore more subject to control. It was thus possible, for a time, to dissolve in alcohol the least soluble of problems. After a day's effort to hammer happiness out of the unyielding American environment it was good, now and then, to go not to the narrow realities of home but to the convivial where through Europe the habit of imbibing was well known. There places where the glass played the main part. The setting could take a variety of forms: basement shops, combination kitchen-and-bars, little cafés, the Irish grocery of 1850, the German *Bierstube* of 1870, the Italian speakeasy of 1900 to which prohibition would later bring another cli-entele. But the end was the same, a temporary relaxation of tension. And the end was so clear that some could achieve it alone, in the fastness of their own rooms, with the solitary company of a bottle.

There were immigrants who came to America with the inclination to drunkenness already well established. In Ireland, whisky went farther than bread as a relief from hunger; in Norway, eighteen quarts of alco-hol were consumed for every person in the country each year; and else-were other newcomers who learned to know the consolations of a dram in the course of the crossing. A bit of grog was the regular prescription for seasickness; if it effected no cure, it dulled the misery.

It was that relief a man needed as much as the eyes in his head. Sometimes he drank away without thought what he had bathed in sweat to earn; but he gained in return an interval free of recollection or anticipation. In the good company, as his burdens lightened, he discovered in himself altogether unexpected but exhilarating powers, acquired daring and self-confidence beyond any sober hope. Well, and sometimes it would lead to a brawl, and the falling clubs of policemen, and the cold awakening of a cell; or, if not that, simply to the next day's throbbing reckoning of costs: what things the money might have bought! But there was none to point the finger of blame; and temptation came again and again. Not a few succumbed in every group of immigrants, though more in some groups than in others.

There was still another way of entering immediately into a realm of hope that shone in bright contrast to the visible dreariness about them. In that realm the evil dame, Chance, was transfigured into a luminous goddess; no longer as in real life did she strike down the lowly, but elevated them. Chance, here, ceased to deal out disaster; instead, conjured up the most heartwarming dreams.

Sometimes the men gambled among themselves, drew cards or lots for little stakes. There was a finger game Italians played, and among eastern Europeans a liking for pinochle. But these were sociable as much as gambling occasions, and had unpleasant disadvantages. The sum of little fortunes around the table hardly made a total worth the winning. One man's gain was another's loss; the joy of one, another's sorrow. Chance had not free rein; skill was as well involved, and the strain of calculation. Most of all, there was not the solitude in which the mind could drift away from time and place and rock itself in the comfort of hope.

Much preferable was some form of the lottery; the stakes were small, the rewards enormous; one might win, but none lost much; and chance was absolute. Lottery took many guises from the informal picks and chances of bar and shop to the highly organized enterprises city-wide in extension. Beneath was the attractiveness of an identical dream.

He can sit with a card, one of scores, in a club or saloon, check the squares, wait the call. Over and over and over again the little cage spins and no one knows when the little cage stops and a little ball hops and the number comes forth for the fortunate man. There's no telling—who knows? This may be when. The word's on his lips; let but chance give the sign and he will rise, *keno, lotto, bingo*; and all will be his.

She buys the slip from a policy man, who may be the corner grocer, the mailman, or anyone who in a daily round encounters a constant circle of people. Her number costs what she can spare, a dime, a nickel, just a penny. She chooses by what signs chance may give, a dream, an omen, a sudden intuition; and all day carries hope in her apron.

Did they really think to win who could not afford to lose? Yes, in a way they did, although they knew what odds were against them. But *why not* they? They would grant you that thousands lost for one who won, but could they surrender that one hope too? His hand that holds the card is soft and white, a hand that signs checks and gestures commands, the hand of a man who will drive to the comfort of a decent home. Her slip rests in the pocket of a gown, a gown that rustles leisurely as she walks with shining children up the steps. Indeed they have so often spent the money, and had the pleasure of dreaming it, it hardly mattered that they lost. At the price they paid, such dreams were cheap enough.

It was significant of such deviations—pauperism, insanity, intemperance, gambling—that they represented a yielding to the disorganizing pressure of the environment. These men did not step out of their roles as sober, industrious, thrifty breadwinners as a means of defying society, as a pure act of will. They deviated out of compulsion.

Where willful defiance of law was involved, the immigrants drew back. The rate of crime among the foreign-born was lower than among natives. There were frequent arrests for drunkenness; but those involved neither will nor, generally, crimes. And occasional petty thefts represented mostly a lack of clarity about property distinctions that had not applied at home. The peasant had recognized certain kinds of taking that were not robbery, by one member of a family from another, for instance, or of raw materials not the product of human labor, such as wood or game. The attempt to do the same in the United States led to trouble.

But the crime willfully planned and executed for gain rarely involved the immigrant. The lawbreakers often congregated in the districts in which the newcomers lived and sometimes recruited the American-born children, but not the immigrants themselves.

It was not hard to know what was going on, for after 1870 certainly these quarters were plunged into a regime of violence from which no one could escape. Organized gangs in alliance with the police terrorized whole territories. It was in the North End in Boston or down near the East Side in New York that their enterprises could most conveniently be planted: dance halls, saloons, gambling places, houses of prostitution, out of sight of the respectable citizens. The guardians of the law were unconcerned, beyond the need of recouping the investments paid out for their jobs. Already by 1900 Al Adams, the New York policy king, had a widespread network; and increasingly crime was removed from the area of free enterprise.

The sharpers and thugs found in the poor their readiest victims. Sometimes the boys at the corner would beat up a passer-by not so much for the handful of change they shook out of his pockets, but simply because his looks offended them, or for no reason at all. There'd be no thought of complaints; no one would listen and he who bore tales to the authorities would find the gangsters swift and merciless in retaliation. Death was never far from the door, why hasten its visit? In the New World, the immigrants feared to have recourse to the traditional peasant crimes of revenge, arson, and homicide. Here was too much risk, too great an exercise of the will.

The inability to use force was the crowning irony of the immigrants' disorganization; the fact that they were law-abiding was less the product of their own choice than of fear to make a choice. As in so many other ways, the constricting environment forced them into deviations from their proper roles. If only a small number actually plunged into pauperism, or insanity, or drunkenness, many more lived long on the verge. And more still lived under the tension of avoiding the plunge; you could tell it by their new habits, endless smoking and the intrusion of profane swearing into their conversation.

Without a doubt they wished also to escape from the physical environment itself. As the years went by they got to know that the city held also pleasant tree-shaded streets where yards and little gardens set the houses off from each other. To these green spaces the most daring hearts aspired.

After 1850, cheaper rapid-transit systems brought the suburbs closer to the heart of the city. On the street railway the trolley took the horse's place and was joined by subway and elevated lines. Through these channels, the laboring masses spilled out from the district of first settlement to the surrounding regions. Naturally, this was a selective process; those who had a modicum of well-being, who could afford the higher rents and transportation charges, moved most freely. The poorest were immobilized by their poverty.

Those who went gained by going, but not by any means all they hoped for. Somehow, what they touched turned to dross. The fine house they saw in their mind's vision across the bridge or over the ferry turned out in actuality to have been converted into narrow flats for several families. In the empty spaces, little cottages rose; and long rows of two- and three-story attached buildings shut off the sight of the trees. The trouble was, so many moved that these newer places began to repeat the experience of the area of first settlement.

Never mind, for a time at least it was better. There was room to keep a goat, a few chickens; the men could sit at ease in their own front rooms facing the friendly street, while the women visited through the sociable low windows. This was a home to which attachments could grow, a place where deviations were less likely to appear.

And if in time the pressure of mounting population brought here too the tenement, and the spreading slum engulfed this first refuge, then those who could launched upon a second remove. Then a third. Till at last the city was a patchwork of separated districts, the outlines of which were shaped by the transit facilities, by the quality of available housing, and by the prior occupancy of various groups of immigrants. Always in this winnowing process the poorest were left in the older sections; the ability to move outward went with prosperity. Unfortunately it was the outer regions that were the thinnest settled. Least capable of organizing their lives to the new environment, the great mass long clustered at the center.

On the farms, space was too ample, not too little. Emptiness, not over-crowding, was the disorganizing element; and for those whose habits of life were developed in the peasant village, the emptiness of the prairie farm was in its own way as troublesome as the crowding of the city slum.

Here they called them neighbors who lived two or three miles off. Here one could stand on the highest rise of land and see nowhere but in the one farmstead any sign of man's tenancy. Such distances were too great to permit easy adjustment by the newcomers.

The peculiar characteristics of the prairie where the distances were greatest tested the immigrants to the utmost. In the midst of the open places they came by wagon and confronted the problem of shelter. They would live in what they could themselves build, for there was no com-munity to help them; and certainly nothing was ready, awaiting their arrival. If they were fortunate, they found a nearby wood where the stove could rest and they could camp while the men chopped the logs for the cabin.

The cabin, no doubt, had its defects as a residence. It was small, per-haps twelve by fourteen feet in all; and above and below and about was mud, for the floor was as they found it and the spaces in the roof and walls were chinked with clay to keep the weather out.

But the people who settled into such quarters had only to compare situations with those who found no wood nearby, to count their own blessings. The cost of bringing timber in was at first prohibitive. If there were none on the spot, home would be of another material. Some would burrow dugouts into the slopes, return unknowingly to the life of the caves. Many cut the sun-baked surface of the earth, piled the sod in a double wall with dirt between, and in these huts spent a long period of trial.

Often years went by before such farmers advanced to the dignity of a frame house, with separate plastered rooms. There were first a barn and all the appurtenances of agriculture to be acquired. Meanwhile they got on in narrow quarters, felt the wind of winter through the cracks, heard the sides settle in the spring thaw, saw surprised snakes or gophers pene-trate the floor.

Under such circumstances, there was an additional depth to their help-lessness. No trees shielded them against the blast of winds. They were parched in the dry heat and they perished in the merciless blizzards. Hail and drought came and the clouds of grasshoppers that ate up their crops. On a limited monotonous diet the immigrants sickened, from the sudden shifts in climate the ague got them, from the prevalence of dirt, the itch. No doctors were near and home remedies or self-prescribed cures from bottles put a sad but decisive end to their misery. Alone in these distances they could expect no help.

That was the worst of it. The isolation which all immigrants sensed to some degree, on the farm was absolute; and not only on the prairie but everywhere. In the older Midwestern states, where the newcomers were not the first to settle, they found homes built and clearings made at their arrival; and soil and climate were not so hostile. Still, even there, they were detached, cut off from the company of other men. Each family was thrown in upon itself; every day the same faces round the same table and never the sight of outsiders. To have no familiarity of one's own age and sex was a hard deprivation.

They would think sometimes of the friendly village ways, of the common tasks lightened for being done in common; they would remember the cheering inn, and the road on which some reassuring known figure could always be seen. At such times, alone in the distance, helpless in their isolation, a vague and disturbing melancholia fell over them. It was easier for them when they added acres and when stocked barns and heavy wagonloads gave a sense of substance and achievement to their lives. Still, even then would come regrets for the disorganization wrought in their existence by the place. Insanity appeared among some; others sought solace in alcohol; and most continued to work, under strain, eager for relief.

They would probably have said that it was the mill town made the least demand upon them. This was not so large as a single city ward and here space was not at a premium; yet neither was there here the complete isolation of the farm. The immigrants' round of activities here fell into a unit the size of which they could comprehend.

What pressure there was came from the situation of such communities. Often a single company or at most a single industry supplied the employment for all the residents. Any man who came to work in the mine or factory was altogether dependent upon the sole hirer. He was not free to choose among jobs or to argue long about terms; he could only acquiesce or leave. In that sense, it was a condition of his membership in this community that he cut himself off from the world outside the town.

Confined within the immediate locality, the laborers discovered that there was plenty of space, but not plenty of housing. Despite the low density of population, the available quarters were so restricted there was serious overcrowding. As the workers arrived they found at first only the farm or village buildings, quickly converted to their use. The single men were likely to live in makeshift boardinghouses; those with families in cut-up portions of the old houses. Shortly either the company or individual investors threw up additional facilities. Into the surrounding farm land, narrow alleys were pushed, lined with three-story frame tenements or with tiny two-room cottages. The company which controlled all was hardly interesting in increasing the supply of housing to an unprofitable excess over demand; nor was it anxious to go to the expense of providing gas, water, and sewerage. The results matched those of the city slums.

Still, the open fields were not far off, and there was not the same total lack of space. The disorganizing effects of the environment were therefore probably less harsh, the deviations less pronounced. What strain there was, was the product of confinement in the town and of constricted housing.

To some degree, these factory town immigrants, like those who went to the cities and those who settled on farms, found the physical conditions of life in America hostile. Nowhere could they recapture the terms of village life; everywhere a difficult adjustment began with the disorganization of the individual, now grown uncertain as to his own proper role. Reorganization would involve first the creation of new means of social action within which the man alone could locate himself.

From the physical as from the religious experience with the New World, the immigrants had gained a deep consciousness of their separateness. It seemed sometimes as if there were only one street in the world, and only a single house on it, and nothing more—only walls and very few people, so that *I am in America and I do not even know whether it is America*. This street was apart as if a ghetto wall defined it. On other streets were other men, deeply different because they had not the burden of this adjustment to bear. This street and those did not run into each other; nor this farm into those. If the immigrants were to achieve the adjustment to their new environment, it had to be within the confines of the ghettos the environment created.

THE PROBLEM OF MINORITY GROUPS
Louis Wirth

The following essay was written during the last days of
World War II, a time when Nazism was being dealt its
death blows and a whole world was learning of its
atrocities against European minorities. It was also a
time of awakening. As the late Louis Wirth points out,
America, the land of minorities, was going to have to
do a better job understanding itself if it was to meet
the challenges of the future.
"The Problem of Minority Groups" quickly became a
classic work of definition and explication. And so it
remains. . . .

As the war approaches a climax and the nature of the peace becomes a
matter of public discussion the minorities question again moves into the
center of world attention. It is becoming clear that unless the problems
involved, especially on the continent of Europe, are more adequately
solved than they were upon the conclusion of the first World War, the
prospects for an enduring peace are slim. The influence which the United
States will exert in the solution of these problems abroad is contingent
upon the national conscience and policy toward minorities at home, for
it is unlikely that our leaders in their participation in making of the
peace will be able to advocate a more enlightened course for others than
we are able to pursue ourselves.

The minorities question in all parts of the world is coming to be more
and more indivisible as internal disturbances in any one country become

From *The Science of Man in the World Crisis* by Ralph Linton (ed.). Copyright 1948
by Columbia University Press. Reprinted with permission.

a threat to the peace of all and as the ideals and ideologies originating in one group are soon shared by others in remote corners of the earth. In this shrunken and interdependent world, social movements of all sorts assume a progressively universal character and recruit their supporters and adversaries among peoples near and far, irrespective of national boundaries. The implications of this trend are of special significance to the United States since, aside from its traditional championship of movements of liberation of oppressed peoples, virtually every minority group in the world has its representatives among our population. Our domestic and our foreign policies are thus closely bound up one with the other.

We may define a minority as a group of people who, because of their physical or cultural characteristics, are singled out from the others in the society in which they live for differential and unequal treatment, and who therefore regard themselves as objects of collective discrimination. The existence of a minority in a society implies the existence of a corresponding dominant group enjoying higher social status and greater privileges. Minority status carries with it the exclusion from full participation in the life of the society. Though not necessarily an alien group the minority is treated and regards itself as a people apart.

To understand the nature and significance of minorities it is necessary to take account of their objective as well as their subjective position. A minority must be distinguishable from the dominant group by physical or cultural marks. In the absence of such identifying characteristics it blends into the rest of the population in the course of time. Minorities objectively occupy a disadvantageous position in society. As contrasted with the dominant group they are debarred from certain opportunities— economic, social and political. These deprivations circumscribe the individual's freedom of choice and self-development. The members of minority groups are held in lower esteem and may even be objects of contempt, hatred, ridicule, and violence. They are generally socially isolated and frequently spatially segregated. Their subordinate position becomes manifest in their unequal access to educational opportunities and in their restricted scope of occupational and professional advancement. They are not as free as other members of society to join the voluntary associations that express their interests. They suffer from more than the ordinary amount of social and economic insecurity. Even as concerns public policy they are frequently singled out for special treatment; their property rights may be restricted; they may not enjoy the equal protection of the laws; they may be deprived of the right of suffrage and may be excluded from public office.

Aside from these objective characteristics by which they are distinguished from the dominant group and in large measure as a result of them, minorities tend to develop a set of attitudes, forms of behavior, and other subjective characteristics which tend further to set them apart. One cannot long discriminate against people without generating in them a sense of isolation and of persecution and without giving them a conception of themselves as more different from others than in fact they are. Whether, as a result of this differential treatment, the minority comes to suffer from a sense of its own inferiority or develops a feeling that it is unjustly treated—which may lead to a rebellious attitude—depends in part upon the length of time that its status has existed and in part upon the total social setting in which the differential treatment operates. Where a caste system has existed over many generations and is sanctioned by religious and other sentiments, the attitude of resignation is likely to be dominant over the spirit of rebellion. But in a secular society where class rather than caste pervades the stratification of people, and where the tradition of minority status is of recent origin, minorities, driven by a sense of frustration and unjustified subordination, are likely to refuse to accept their status and their deprivation without some effort to improve their lot.

When the sentiments and attitude of such a disadvantaged group become articulate, and when the members become conscious of their deprivations and conceive of themselves as persons having rights, and when they clamor for emancipation and equality, a minority becomes a political force to be reckoned with. To the individual members of such a group the most onerous circumstance under which they have to labor is that they are treated as members of a category, irrespective of their individual merits. Hence it is important to recognize that membership in a minority is involuntary; our own behavior is irrelevant. Many of us are identified with political, social, and intellectual groups which do not enjoy the favor of the dominant group in society, but as long as we are free to join and to leave such groups at will we do not by virtue of our membership in them belong to a minority. Since the racial stock from which we are descended is something over which we have perhaps least control and since racial marks are the most visible and permanent marks with which we are afflicted, racial minorities tend to be the most enduring minorities of all.

It should be noted further that a minority is not necessarily an alien group. Indeed, in many parts of the world it is the native peoples who constitute the minority, whereas the invaders, the conquerors, or the newcomers occupy the status of dominant groups. In the United States the indigenous Indians occupy the position of a minority. In Canada the earlier French settlers are a minority in relation to the more recent English migrants. In almost all colonial countries it is the "foreigners" who are dominant and the indigenous populations who are subordinate.

Nor should it be assumed that the concept is a statistical one. Although the size of the group may have some effect upon its status and upon its relationship to the dominant group, minorities are not to be judged in terms of numbers. The people whom we regard as a minority may actually, from a numerical standpoint, be a majority. Thus, there are many parts of the South in the United States where the Negroes are the over-whelming majority of the inhabitants but, nevertheless, are an unmis-takable minority in the sense that they are socially, politically, and economically subordinate.

It may even be true that a people may attain the status of a minority even though it does not become the object of disesteem, discrimination, and persecution. If it considers itself the object of such inferior treatment, an oppression psychosis may develop. If a group sets itself apart from others by a distinctive culture and perpetuates itself in this isolated con-dition long enough, the social distances between itself and others may grow so great as to lead to the accumulation of suspicion and noninter-course which will make it virtually impossible for members of these groups to carry on a truly collective life. Lack of intimate knowledge of and contact with others may in the course of time generate an incapacity for mutual understanding and appreciation which allows mental stereo-types to arise which the individual cannot escape. What matters, then, about minorities is not merely their objective position but the correspond-ing patterns of behavior they develop and the pictures they carry around in their heads of themselves and of others. While minorities more often than not stand in a relationship of conflict with the dominant group, it is their nonparticipation in the life of the larger society, or in certain aspects thereof, that more particularly marks them as a minority people and per-petuates their status as such.

It is easy enough to catalog the minority peoples in various parts of the world in accordance with a set of criteria such as race, national origin, language, religion, or other distinctive cultural traits. Thus it is possible to define the areas of the world where one or another racial, ethnic, linguistic, or religious group occupies a subordinate status with reference to some other group. In different parts of the world different groups are consigned to minority status. A given racial, ethnic, linguistic, or religious group may be dominant in one area and be the minority in another. Similar variations are found throughout history. Groups which in one epoch were dominant may in another be reduced to subordinate status. Because of the colonizing enterprises of some of the nation-states of West-ern Europe a large part of the rest of the world has been subordinated to their political rule, their economic control, and the technology and culture which the European settlers managed to superimpose upon the peoples and areas which they brought under their domain. On a world scale, therefore, there is an extraordinarily close association between the white Western Europeans as colonizers and conquerors and their status as dominant groups. Correspondingly, there is a close association between the nonwhite peoples of the world as the conquered and enslaved peoples and their status as minority groups. There are notable exceptions, how-ever, both in time and in space. In an earlier period of European history the yellow peoples of the East overran vast stretches of the European con-

tinent and for a time at least reduced the natives to inferior status. There
had been similar, though temporary, invasions of Europe from Africa in
the course of which Negroid groups became dominant over the white
Europeans. Similarly, the enterprise and military prowess of the Japanese
has led to the subjugation of vast stretches of the Orient beyond their
island empire which contain many areas and great populations of non-
Japanese stock, including European whites. On the whole, however, the
expansion of European civilization to the ends of the earth has been so
irresistible that from a racial standpoint, virtually the world over, the
whites constitute the dominant group and the colored peoples the minorities.

We are less concerned, however, in this analysis, with racial minorities
than with ethnic minorities, and hence it will be well to examine in some
detail the linguistic, religious, and national minorities within the white
group in Europe and in America. The existence of such groups in virtually every European and American country calls attention to the fact
that the modern nation-states into which we are accustomed to divide the
world and to which we are wont to ascribe a high degree of ethnic homogeneity are far from being as closely knit by intermarriage, in-breeding,
social intercourse, and freedom of opportunity for everyone as the stereotypes of national cultures appear to indicate.

In Europe and in America there are today vast differences between the
status of different ethnic groups from country to country and from region
to region. In pre-war Poland under the Czarist regime the Poles were a
distinct ethnic minority. When they gained their independence at the end
of the first World War, they lost their minority status but reduced their
Jewish fellow Poles to the status of a minority. As immigrants to the
United States the Poles again became themselves a minority. During the
brief period of Nazi domination the Sudeten Germans of Czechoslovakia
reveled in their position of dominance over the Czechs among whom they
had only recently been a minority. The European immigrants to the
United States from such dominantly Catholic countries as Italy and
Poland, for instance, find themselves reduced from a dominant to a minority group in the course of their immigration. It is not the specific characteristics, therefore, whether racial or ethnic, that mark a people as a
minority but the relationship of their group to some other group in the
society in which they live. The same characteristics may at one time and
under one set of circumstances serve as marks of dominant status and at
another time and under another set of circumstances symbolize identification with a minority.

It is much more important, therefore, to understand the nature and the
genesis of the relationship between dominant group and minority group
than it is to know the marks by the possession of which people are
identified as members of either. Once we know that almost any distinctive characteristics, whether it be the physical marks of race, or language,

religion, and culture, can serve as criteria of membership in a minority we will not be inclined to construct a typology of minorities upon the marks by which they are identified. A fruitful typology must rather be useful in delineating the kinds of relationships between minorities and dominant groups and on the kinds of behavior characteristically associated with these types of relationships.

An adequate typology of minorities must, therefore, take account of the general types of situations in which minorities find themselves and must seek to comprehend the *modus vivendi* that has grown up between the segments of those societies in which minority problems exist. There are a number of axes alongside of which the problems of minorities range themselves. Among these are: (1) the number and size of distinct minorities in the society in question; (2) the degree to which minority status involves friction with the dominant group or exclusion from participation in the common life of the society; (3) the nature of the social arrangement governing the relationship between minority and dominant group; and, (4) the goals toward which the minority and dominant groups are striving in quest of a new and more satisfactory equilibrium. A survey of historical and contemporary minority problems along these lines will probably not cover the whole range of minority problems and to that extent the typology will be partial. At the same time it should be understood that as long as the relations between minority and dominant group are fluid—and wherever they do not rest upon long-accepted and settled premises—any rigid typology will prove unsatisfactory. Conversely where the minority's relationship to the dominant group is definitely structuralized and embedded in the mores, laws, and institutions a typological approach may be highly rewarding.

The number of minorities that a country has appears to have a significant effect upon minority-dominant group relations. Where there is just one minority the attitudes of the dominant group are molded by the unique characteristics of that particular minority. This tends to bisect the country into two contending groups. This happens to be the case in Belgium where the Flemings and Walloons stand in relationship of dominant and minority group, respectively, to each other. The situation is quite different in the United States, where aside from the Negro, the Indian, and the Oriental, who constitute our leading racial minorities, we have many ethnic minorities, consisting of our European immigrant groups and their descendants and such religious minorities as Catholics, Jews, and Mormons in a predominantly Protestant country. A singular and unique minority must absorb all of the anxieties, frustrations, fears, and antipathies of the dominant group. But if dominant group attitudes are directed toward a number of minorities, some of these may escape relatively easily and often at the expense of the others. There is little doubt but that the Negro in the United States has become the principal shock absorber of the antiminority sentiment of the dominant whites. The

Negro in this country has been so clearly our leading minority that in comparison with his status the ethnic minorities have occupied a relatively dominant position. Indeed the attitude of the ethnic minorities toward the Negro differs little from the attitude of the long-established white Protestant settlers. Where there are several distinct minorities in a country the dominant group can allow itself the luxury of treating some of them generously and can at the same time entrench itself and secure its own dominance by playing one minority against another.

Similarly, the extent to which a minority differs from the dominant group conditions the relations between the two. Where the groups differ widely in race and culture and are thus easily distinguishable in appearance and behavior, the lines separating them tend to persist without much overt effort. Where the dominant group is the bearer of an advanced civilization and the subordinate group is without modern technology and is characterized by a folk culture, as is the case in colonial situations, the dominant group can maintain its superior position simply by manipulating the military and administrative machinery. Where, however, the respective groups are of the same racial stock but differ only as regards language, religion, or culture, the tension between them becomes more marked, and the attempts at domination of the minority become more evident. The segregation of minority groups may be relatively complete or only partial, and their debarment from rights and privileges may be negligible or severe. Much depends upon their relative numerical strength and the extent to which they are believed to constitute a threat to the existing order.

The nature of the social relationships existing between the dominants and the minorities comes closer than either of these factors to illuminating the problems that arise. When the relationship between the two groups is that of master and slave, of rulers and ruled, of exploiters and exploited, the conflicts that arise are those characteristic of situations of super- and subordination. They become essentially power relationships involving on the part of the dominant group resort to the sanctions of custom, law, and force, whenever persuasion, prestige, and the manipulation of economic controls do not suffice. Where the minority occupies the position of a caste the sanctions of religion and custom may be quite adequate, but in secular societies the perpetuation of a group in minority status requires the manipulation of public opinion and of economic and political power, and, if these fail, the resort to violence.

Thoroughgoing differences and incompatibilities between dominant and minority groups on *all* fronts—economic, political, social, and religious —or consistent and complete separation and exclusion of the minority from participation in the life of the larger society have tended toward more stable relationships between dominant and minority groups than similarity and compatibility on merely *some* points, and the mere segmental sharing of life on a few frontiers of contact. The granting of some political and civil rights to hitherto submerged groups has inevitably led to the claim for the full rights of citizenship and of equality of opportunity in other respects. Slavery as an institution in the Western World was moribund as soon as the religions of the white man invested the Negro with a soul.

While the above criteria might give us a basis for the classification of minorities, they do not come as close to the actual minority problems that plague the modern world as we can come by analyzing the major goals toward which the ideas, the sentiments, and the actions of minority groups are directed. Viewed in this way minorities may conveniently be typed into: (1) pluralistic; (2) assimilationist; (3) secessionist and (4) militant.

A pluralistic minority is one which seeks toleration for its differences on the part of the dominant group. Implicit in the quest for toleration of one's group differences is the conception that variant cultures can flourish peacefully side by side in the same society. Indeed, cultural pluralism has been held out as one of the necessary preconditions of a rich and dynamic civilization under conditions of freedom. It has been said in jest that "tolerance is the suspicion that the other fellow might be right."

Toleration requires that the dominant group shall feel sufficiently secure in its position to allow dissenters a certain leeway. Those in control must be convinced either that the issues at stake are not too vital, or else they must be so thoroughly imbued with the ideal of freedom that they do not wish to deny to others some of the liberties which they themselves enjoy. If there is a great gulf between their own status and that of the minority group, if there is a wide difference between the two groups in race or origin, the toleration of minorities may go as far as virtually to perpetuate several subsocieties within the larger society.

Even in the "sacred" society of medieval Europe dominated by the Church, there were long periods when heretics were tolerated, although at other times they faced the alternatives of conformity or extermination. The history of the Jews in medieval Europe offers ample evidence of the ability of a minority to survive even under minimum conditions of toleration. It should be noted, however, that at times the margin of safety was very narrow and that their ultimate survival was facilitated by the fact that they formed an alien cultural island within the larger Christian world and performed useful functions such as trade and commerce in which the creed of the dominant group would not allow its own members to engage. The coexistence of the Jews and Christians in the same countries often did not transcend the degree of mutuality characteristic of the symbiotic relations existing between different species of plants and animals occupying the same habitat but which are forced by their differential structure to live off one another. It involved a minimum of consensus.

The range of toleration which a pluralistic minority seeks may at first be quite narrow. As in the case of the Jews in medieval Europe, or the Protestants in dominantly Catholic countries, it may be confined to freedom to practice a dissenting religion. Or, as in the case of the ethnic minorities of Czarist Russia and the Austro-Hungarian empire of the Hapsburgs, it may take the form of the demand for the recognition of a language as the official medium of expression for the minority and the right to have it taught in their schools. While on the one hand the pluralistic minority craves the toleration of one or more of its cultural idiosyncrasies, on the other hand it resents and seeks protection against coerced absorption by the dominant group. Above all it wishes to maintain its cultural identity.

The nationalities of Europe, which in the nineteenth and early twentieth centuries embarked upon a course of achieving national independence, began their careers as pluralistic minorities bent merely upon attaining cultural autonomy. Some of these minorities had enjoyed national independence at an earlier period and merely wished to recover and preserve their cultural heritage. This was the case in Poland, for instance, which sought to recover from Czarist Russia a measure of religious and linguistic autonomy. Czech and Irish nationalism was initiated under similar historic circumstances.

It would be an error, however, to infer that the claims for cultural autonomy are generally pursued independently of other interests. Coupled with the demand, and often precedent to it there proceeds the struggle for economic and political equality or at least equalization of opportunity. Although the pluralistic minority does not wish to merge its total life with the larger society, it does demand for its members a greater measure of economic and political freedom if not outright civic equality. Ever since the revolutionary epoch of the late eighteenth century the economic and political enfranchisement of minorities has been regarded not merely as inherent in the "rights of man" but as the necessary instrument in the struggle for cultural emancipation. Freedom of choice in occupations, rights of landownership, entry into the civil service, access to the universities and the professions, freedom of speech, assembly, and publication, access to the ballot with a view to representation of minority voices in parliament and government—these and other full privileges of citizenship are the foundation upon which cultural freedom rests and the instruments through which it must be achieved and secured.

Throughout the period of awakening of dominant ethnic minorities in Europe in the nineteenth century and subsequently in all parts of the world the first stages of minority movements have been characterized by cultural renaissances. The primary emphasis in this stage of development has been upon accentuating the religious, linguistic, and cultural heritage of the group and driving to obtain recognition and toleration for these differences. This movement goes hand in hand with the clamor for economic and political equality. In the course of such movements what at first are marks of inferiority—a homely folk tongue, an alien religion, an obscure lore, and eccentric costume—are transformed into objects of pride and positive group values in which the intellectuals among the minority take an especially avid interest and the promotion of which becomes the road to their leadership and power. The aim of the pluralistic minority is achieved when it has succeeded in wresting from the dominant group the fullest measure of equality in all things economic and political and the right to be left alone in all things cultural. The atmosphere of liberalism in which pluralistic minorities developed has emerged since the Renaissance and has found expression in the movements for religious toleration at the end of the sixteenth century; it was further elaborated by the constitutional bills of rights wrested from absolute rulers in the course of the English, American and French revolutions, and found formal acceptance on a world scale in the minorities clauses of the treaties at the conclusion of the first World War. If the legal provisions of the minorities clauses have not been fully observed in practice, they have at least furnished a standard by which the relations between minorities and dominant groups may be more universally appraised by enlightened world opinion. If formal resolutions on such matters are valid as signs of the trend of opinion, the Catholic, Jewish and Protestant Declaration on World Peace, of October 7, 1943, may be adduced. On the Rights of Minorities this declaration says:

> National governments and international organizations must respect and guarantee the rights of ethnic, religious and cultural minorities to economic livelihood, to equal opportunity for educational and cultural development, and to political equality.

More important than such utterances however is the most advanced practice to be found among the nations of the world. Of these the practice of the Soviet Union with its minority peoples appears to be the outstanding example. There the recognition of pluralistic minorities has become the accepted national policy.

It should be recognized however that pluralistic minorities, like all structures expressive of dynamic social movements, are merely waystations on the road to further developments. They move on inexorably to other stages where correspondingly new types of social structures emerge. Unlike the pluralistic minority, which is content with toleration and the upper limit of whose aspiration is cultural autonomy, the assimilationist minority craves the fullest opportunity for participation in the life of the larger society with a view to uncoerced incorporation in that society. It seeks to lose itself in the larger whole by opening up to its members the greatest possibilities for their individual self-development. Rather than toleration and autonomy, which is the goal of the pluralistic minority, the assimilationist minority works toward complete acceptance by the dominant group and a merger with the larger society.

Whereas a pluralistic minority, in order to maintain its group integrity, will generally discourage intermarriage and intimate social intercourse with the dominant group, the assimilationist minority puts no such obstacles in the path of its members but looks upon the crossing of stocks as well as the blending of cultures as wholesome end products. Since assimilation is a two-way process, however, in which there is give and take, the mergence of an assimilationist minority rests upon a willingness of the dominant group to absorb and of the minority group to be absorbed. The ethnic differences that exist between the minority and the dominant group are not necessarily an obstacle to assimilation as long as the cultural traits of each group are not regarded as incompatible with those of the other and as long as their blending is desired by both. The "melting pot" philosophy in the United States which applied to the ethnic minorities but excluded the racial minorities, notably the Negro, in so far as it was actually followed, tended to develop both among immigrants and natives an atmosphere conducive to the emergence of a crescive American culture to which both the dominant and minority groups contributed their share. This new culture, which is still in the process of formation, comprises cultural elements derived from all the ethnic groups constituting the American people, but integrates them into a new blend.

The success with which such an experiment proceeds depends in part upon the relative numbers involved and the period of time over which the process extends. Although since the beginning of the nineteenth century the United States absorbed some 38 million immigrants from abroad, the influx was relatively gradual and the vast spaces and resources of the continent facilitated the settlement and absorption of the newcomers. America was a relatively young country, dominated by the spirit of the frontier and by a set of laws and social ideals strongly influenced by the humanistic, liberalistic doctrines of religious toleration and the rights of man. This, together with the great need for labor to exploit the vast resources of the continent, contributed to keeping American culture fluid and its people hospitable to the newcomers and the heritages they brought with them. No one group in the United States had so much power and pride of ancestry as to be able to assert itself as superior to all others.

Nevertheless as the immigrants came in great waves, and as the wide margin of economic opportunity shrank periodically, outbursts of intolerant and sometimes violent nativism and antialien feeling became manifest here too. As newer immigrant groups followed older waves the latest comers increasingly became the objects of prejudice and discrimination on the part of natives and older immigrants alike. Moreover, as the various ethnic groups concentrated in specific areas and in large urban colonies and thus conspicuously unfolded their old world cultural heritages, their life became virtually autonomous and hence, by isolating themselves, their contact with the broad stream of American culture was retarded. In addition, their very success in competing with native and older settlers in occupations, professions, and business provoked antipathies which found expression in intolerance movements and in the imposition of official and unofficial restrictions and handicaps.

Although the ethnic minorities in the United States suffer mainly from private prejudices rather than restrictive public policies, their path of assimilation is not without its serious obstacles. The distinctive cultures of the various ethnic groups are not merely assemblages of separable traits but historically welded wholes. Each immigrant group not only has its own language or dialect which serves as a barrier to intergroup communication and to the sharing of common ideas and ideals, but also its own religious, social, and even political institutions which tend to perpetuate group solidarity and to inhibit social intercourse with members of the "out" group. Moreover, each ethnic group in the United States, especially in the early period after its arrival, tends to occupy a characteristic niche in the economy which generates certain definite similarities among its members in occupation, standard of living, place of residence, and mode of life. On the basis of such likenesses within the group and differences without, stereotypes are built up and fixed attitudes arise which inhibit contact and develop social distances and prejudices. Overanxiety about being accepted sometimes results in a pattern of conduct among minorities that provokes a defense reaction on the part of the dominant group; these defense reactions may take the form of rebuffs which are likely to accentuate minority consciousness and thus retard assimilation.

No ethnic group is ever unanimous in all of its attitudes and actions, and minority groups are no exception. They, too, have their internal differentiations, their factions and ideological currents and movements. It should be understood, therefore, that the difference between a pluralistic and an assimilationist minority must be sought in the characteristic orientation and directing social movement of these groups. The Jews furnish an excellent illustration of a minority which especially in modern times has vacillated between these two types. When the "out" group was favorably disposed toward the Jews, assimilation proceeded apace, even in the face of occasional rebuffs and persistent discrimination. When the dominant group made entry of the Jews difficult, when intolerance movements became powerful and widespread, and when persecution came to be the order of the day, the Jews as a minority group generally withdrew into themselves and by virtue of being excluded became clannish. The most conspicuous example of this transformation is to be found in the shift in the attitude of the German Jews who—before the anti-Semitic wave climaxed by the Hitler epic—could have been correctly characterized as an assimilationist minority and whose optimum longing upon the advent of Hitler was for even a modicum of toleration. Among Jews in this country a similar differentiation is contemporaneously found. The older settlers and those who have climbed the economic and social scale seek on the whole full incorporation into the larger society and may truly be regarded as an assimilationist minority; but the later comers and those whose hopes have been frustrated by prejudice, those who through generations of persecution in the Old World retain a more orthodox ritual and a more isolated and self-sufficient community life, generally do not seek full cultural identification with American society at large. To be sure they aspire to full social and economic equality with the rest of the population but they seek to retain a degree of cultural autonomy.

There is little doubt that the world-wide crisis of the Jewish people precipitated by Fascism and its accompanying wave of racism and anti-Semitism has forged a new bond of solidarity among hitherto disparate sections of Jewry and has given impetus to a deep pessimism concerning the prospect of ultimate assimilation. But the eventual resumption of the assimilationist trend among the Jewish minorities in the Western World appears to have favorable prospects once Nazism has been defeated and the cult of racism to which it has given official sanction declines.

The secessionist minority represents a third distinct type. It repudiates assimilation on the one hand, and is not content with mere toleration or cultural autonomy on the other. The principal and ultimate objective of such a minority is to achieve political as well as cultural independence from the dominant group. If such a group has had statehood at an earlier period in its career, the demand for recognition of its national sovereignty may be based upon the cultivation among its members of the romantic sentiments associated—even if only in the imagination—with its former freedom, power, and glory. In such a case the minority's cultural monuments and survivals, its language, lore, literature, and ceremonial institutions, no matter how archaic or reminiscent of the epoch of the group's independence, are revivified and built up into moving symbols of national grandeur.

In this task the intellectuals among the minority group play a crucial role. They can find expression for their talents by recovering, disseminating, and inspiring pride in the group's history and civilization and by pleading its case before world public opinion. Having been rejected by the dominant group for higher positions of leadership, and often having been denied equal opportunity and full participation in the intellectual, social, economic and political life of the larger society, the intellectuals of such minorities tend to be particularly susceptible to a psychic malady bordering on an oppression psychosis. They find their compensation by plunging into the life of the smaller but more hospitable world of their minority.

The Irish, Czech, Polish, Lithuanian, Esthonian, Latvian and Finnish nationalistic movements culminating in the achievement of independent statehood at the end of the first World War were examples of secessionist minority groups. The case of the Jews may also be used to illustrate this type of minority. Zionism in its political, as distinguished from its cultural variety, has acquired considerable support as a result of the resurgence of organized anti-Semitic movements. The forced wholesale migration out of the countries practicing violent persecution and extermination has changed the conception of Palestine from a haven of refuge in which Jews are tolerated to a homeland to which Jews lay official claim.

The protest against the dominant group, however, does not always take the form of separatism and secessionism. It may, under certain circumstances express itself in movements to get out from under the yoke of a dominant group in order to join a group with whom there exists a closer historical and cultural affinity. This is particularly true of minorities located near national frontiers. Wars, and the accompanying repeated redefinitions of international boundaries rarely fail to do violence to the traditions and wishes of some of the populations of border territories. It is generally true that these marginal ethnic groups exhibit more fervid nationalistic feelings than those who have not been buffeted about by treaty-makers.

Secessionist minorities occupying border positions, moreover, generally can count upon the country with which they seek reunion for stimulation of minority consciousness. When France lost Alsace and Lorraine at the end of the Franco-Prussian war in 1871, the French culture of these "lost provinces" became the object of special interest on the part of Frenchmen in and out of these territories. And when these same provinces were lost to Germany at the end of the first World War, a similar propaganda wave on the German side was set in motion. When the Nazis came to power and embarked upon their imperialistic adventures they made the "reunion with the Fatherland" of such territories as the Saar, Alsace, Lorraine, Eupen-et-Malmédy; Sudetenland and the Danzig Corridor an object of frenzied agitation. By every means at their command they revived the flagging or dormant secessionist spirit among these ethnic groups. They created incidents wherever the slightest pretext existed to provoke violent outbreaks so as to elicit from the neighboring governments countermeasures that could be exploited for the purpose of creating a world opinion that the German minorities in these territories were suffering from extreme persecution and were anxiously waiting to be rescued by the armed might of the Fatherland.

The solidarity of modern states is always subject to the danger of the undermining influence of secessionist minorities, but it becomes particularly vulnerable if the minorities are allied with neighboring states which claim them as their own. Out of such situations have arisen many of the tensions which have provoked numerous wars in recent times.

There is a fourth type of minority which may be designated as militant. Its goal reaches far beyond toleration, assimilation, and even cultural and political autonomy. The militant minority has set domination over others as its goal. Far from suffering from feelings of inferiority, it is convinced of its own superiority and inspired by the lust for conquest. While the initial claims of minority movements are generally modest, like all accessions of power, they feed upon their own success and often culminate in delusions of grandeur.

Thus, for instance, the Sudeten Germans, aided and abetted by the Nazi propaganda, diplomatic, and military machine, made claims on the Czecho-Slovak republic which, if granted, would have reduced the Czechs to a minority in their own country. The story, let us hope it is legendary, of the slave who upon his emancipation immediately proceeded to buy himself a slave, suggests a perverse human tendency which applies to minorities as well. No imperialism is as ruthless as that of a relatively small upstart nation. Scarcely had Italy escaped the humiliation of utter defeat in the first World War when she embarked upon the acquisition of *Italia Irredenta* far beyond her own borders across the Adriatic. In recent times, the rise of the relatively obscure Prussian state to a position of dominance in Central Europe is illustrative of the dynamics of a militant minority in quest not merely of a secure basis of national existence but of empire. The none too generous treatment accorded by the newly emancipated Poles between the two World Wars to the Ukranian, White Russian, Lithuanian, Jewish, and other minorities allotted to the Polish state offers another case of the lack of moderation characteristic of militant minorities once they arrive at a position of power.

The problem of finding a suitable formula for self-government in India would probably have been solved long ago if the Hindu "majority," which considers itself a minority in relation to British imperial rule, could have been satisfied with an arrangement which stopped short of Hindu domination over Moslems. Similarly the problem of Palestine could be brought much nearer a sensible solution if certain elements among Jewish and Arab groups were less militant and did not threaten, in case either were given the opportunity, to reduce the other to the status of a minority.

The justification for singling out the four types of minorities described above for special delineation lies in the fact that each of them exhibits a characteristic set of collective goals among historical and contemporary minority groups and a corresponding set of motives activating the conduct of its members. These four types point to significant differences between actual minority movements. They may also be regarded as marking crucial successive stages in the life cycle of minorities generally.

The initial goal of an emerging minority group, as it becomes aware of its ethnic identity, is to seek toleration for its cultural differences. By virtue of this striving it constitutes a pluralistic minority. If sufficient toleration and autonomy is attained the pluralistic minority advances to the assimilationist stage, characterized by the desire for acceptance by and incorporation into the dominant group. Frustration of this desire for full participation is likely to produce (1) secessionist tendencies which may take the form either of the complete separation from the dominant group and the establishment of sovereign nationhood, or (2) the drive to become incorporated into another state with which there exists close cultural or historical identification. Progress in either of these directions may in turn lead to the goal of domination over others and the resort to militant methods of achieving that objective. If this goal is actually reached the group sheds the distinctive characteristics of a minority.

It should be emphasized, of course, that this typology of minorities is a theoretical construct, rather than a description of actually existing groups. We should not expect to find any one of these types to occur in pure form either in history or in the present. All minorities contain within themselves tendencies and movements in which we can discern the characteristic features of one or more of these types. Using such a typology as a tool we are in a better position to analyze the empirical problems of minority situations and to evaluate the proposed programs for their solution.

The basic fact accounting for the emergence of minorities is the lack of congruence between political and ethnic groups. Political boundaries are definite and almost always arbitrary. Cultural and ethnic areas are more difficult to delineate. Political areas can be gerrymandered, whereas cultural areas are the product of growth. Virtually every contest of power between nations, whether around the diplomatic conference table or on the battlefield, is followed by some redrawing of boundaries, leaving cultural pockets enveloped islandlike by an alien sea. Even in the absence of territorial revisions, the indeterminate fringes along the frontiers, where marginal groups are interspersed, tend to be chronic danger spots of ethnic friction.

A second factor causing minority groups to arise lies in the fact that culture and people are seldom coterminous. Every living culture must be carried by some people. But culture consists of many elements which may be carried in varying combinations by diverse groups of people. Thus, for instance, a group of people who speak the same language, have the same religion and have an ancient common cultural heritage, are capable of more effective collective action than a similar group with the same religion but different language, or the same language but an otherwise different cultural heritage. It is sufficient for the formation of minorities if merely a few of the ethnic characteristics that give them distinctiveness coincide, especially if these include such elements as language or religion. But if a group should by accident of history and geography find itself united on a great range of cultural characteristics and fairly densely concentrated in a compact area so that the contrast between its status and that of its neighbors stands out sharply, the emergence of that group as a minority is almost inevitable.

The genesis of minorities must therefore be sought in the fact that territory, political authority, people, and culture only rarely coincide. Since the disintegration of tribal society the human stocks occupying virtually every area of the world have become progressively diversified. Through the rise of the modern state the parochial principalities of earlier ages have disintegrated and heterogeneous groupings of people and diverse areas have been consolidated into vast political domains. Through conquest and migration formerly compact groups have become dispersed and split up among different political entities. Through modern transportation, communication, commerce and technology the surviving folk cultures are being increasingly drawn into the vortex of world civilization. There still remain, in various parts of the world, some relatively limited islands of homogeneity and stability in a sea of conglomerate and swiftly moving heterogeneity, but on the whole the civilizing process is leveling them. Minority problems are symptomatic of this profound world-wide transition.

In the long perspective of centuries, therefore, one might expect minority problems to solve themselves. But for the time being they are in need of the best solution we can invent if we would live in peace and promote human progress. Anyone who dispassionately surveys the background of the first and second World Wars cannot fail to see that minority questions have played a considerable part in their genesis. Unless these questions are more adequately solved in the next peace than they were in the last we shall, by that failure, contribute to an eventual new world conflagration; for in the future even more than in the past these problems will take on cosmic scope, no matter how local their origin. This is not to assert that minority problems are the major causes of international conflict, but merely that in the absence of effective world organization to regulate the play of interdependent economic, social, political, and military forces, these problems will continue to produce frictions and to furnish pretexts that may again lead to war.

In modern times, besides the technological and social changes that have profoundly affected the nature and significance of minority problems, there have been set afoot certain ideological forces which bear even more directly upon them. Of these, nationalism, the democratic ideology as applied to persons and groups, and secularism and science seem the most relevant.

The nineteenth century, which as often been called "the age of nationalism," saw the birth of a series of movements of national awakening, liberation, and consolidation resulting in the formation of modern Italy and Germany. It also saw the rapid development of modern empires and the crystallization of such movements as Pan-Slavism and Pan-Germanism, which became formidable threats to a state system based upon the balance of power. The lesser ethnic groups which were involuntarily enveloped by the nascent nations were frustrated and retarded in realizing their national aspirations. There were thus kindled seething movements of unrest which threatend the stability of the newly established states and the peace of the world. Minorities, especially those of the secessionist and militant variety, are in large part by-products of the ideology of nationalism, whose fundamental tenet it was that every people ought to have its own state but which failed to take full cognizance of the fact that political and ethnic lines do not always neatly coincide.

The forces of democracy and of nationalism were closely allied throughout most of the nineteenth century. The coalescence of these two ideologies became the principal weapon of the nationalities which were aspiring to independence at the peace discussions following the first World War. At Versailles the principle of national self-determination was invoked. It was construed to mean the right of every nation to form an independent state. But the conception of "nation" was far from clear and failed to take account of the many lesser ethnic and cultural groups which were not far enough advanced in the life-cycle of minorities to be considered eligible for nationhood and hence statehood. Versailles heard the articulate voices of the secessionist and militant minorities of the time, but failed to hear the softer whispering and petulant pleading of the pluralistic and assimilationist minorities who were put at the mercy of the former without more protection than the pious enunciation of high principles of toleration and nondiscrimination.

Woodrow Wilson, in insisting upon the right of self-determination before America's entrance into the war, said: "Every people has the right to choose the sovereignty under which they shall live."[1] When he came to interpret this principle under the Fourteen Points, however, he associated the concept of self-determination not with the freely expressed will of the people but with the criteria of nationality. In the drafting of the peace settlement, as E. H. Carr puts it, "it was assumed without more ado that nationality and self-determination meant the same thing and that, if a man had the objective distinguishing marks of a Pole or a Southern Slav, he wanted to be a citizen of a Polish or Southern Slav state."[2] The peace settlements had as one of their principal objectives the solution of the minorities questions and no doubt did assuage the legitimate claims of a number of oppressed peoples; at the same time they raised a number of new minority problems which hitherto had been either nonexistent or dormant.

The problems and the very existence of minorities rest upon the recognition of the rights of peoples, notably the right of self-determination. Ever since the revolutionary era of the late eighteenth century the liberation of oppressed peoples has been a cause which has enlisted the support of liberal thinkers. Though some of its advocates thought of this principle —which was implicit in the democratic ideology—as a step toward cosmopolitanism, its immediate effect was to intensify nationalism. The general principle of the Versailles treaty in effect proclaimed that any group belonging to a minority, whether ethnic, cultural, or religious, was entitled to equal protection and opportunity with others. This principle was easier to proclaim than to put into practice, especially among some of the newly created states comprising former minorities. Having gained their freedom, these militant minorities not infrequently reduced their fellow nationals with different ethnic characteristics to a state of barely tolerated minorities, and sometimes even made them objects of violent persecution.

In retrospect one of the great shortcomings in the application of the democratic principle under the treaty of Versailles was the emphasis upon groups rather than individuals. Unless the right of self-determination is applied not merely to nations or ethnic groups but also to the individual men and women comprising the nation or ethnic group, it can easily degenerate into license to suppress others. If in the coming peace the arrangement for setting up new states and redefining the territories of old ones does not provide a personal bill of rights for all inhabitants and for the protection of the rights of citizenship by an international authority, one of the most tragic lessons of the last peace will have been lost.

Even such an international guarantee of a universal bill of rights will probably prove insufficient to prevent the development of new minorities and the persistence of existing ones. Ethnic, linguistic, and religious differences will continue to divide people, and the prejudices that go with them cannot suddenly be wiped out by fiat. But whereas personal prejudices and antipathies can probably be expected to yield only to the tedious process of education and assimilation, collective programs and policies can be altered considerably in advance of the time when they have unanimous group consent. Law and public policy can go far toward minimizing the adverse effect even of personal prejudices. Moreover, it is for their public policies that we can and must hold states responsible.

The strategy for equalizing the opportunities of minorities has in the past been based upon the doctrine of the rights of man, which presumably applied to majority and minority alike. Only recently, however, has it been recognized that the subordination of minority ethnic groups and racial groups results in great cost to the whole society. From a military point of view it is undesirable because it weakens national loyalties and solidarity. The stunting of minority development reacts unfavorably upon the entire economy. As long as minorities suffer from discrimination and the denial of civil liberties the dominant group also is not free.

Another ideological factor that has appeared upon the modern scene and has left its impact upon the minorities problem is secularism. The secular trend in the modern world, which manifests itself in the spread of rationalism, science, and the general skepticism toward ideas and beliefs inherited from the past, has already made substantial inroads on parochial cults, on the divine right of some to rule, and on superstitions concerning the innate inferiority of racial and ethnic groups. It promises even greater progress in the future. Rigid caste systems, supported by sacred sanctions, are fast disintegrating. The separation of church and state has advanced to a point where a state religion is already regarded in most countries as intolerable. Even a "holy war" is almost inconceivable in modern times. With the spread of the ideal of equality of opportunity for all men there has come in most countries of the West a greater access for the masses of men, irrespective of race, ethnic affiliation, religion, or even economic status, to educational and cultural possibilities. The findings and methods of science may consequently find greater acceptance. The symbol of "the common man," despite the ridicule to which it has been subjected in some quarters seems to be on the way to making its influence felt the world over.

From anthropological studies of the last half century we should have gained a recognition of the inapplicability of the concept "race" as applied to the hybrid stocks comprising the European and American peoples. It is not race but culture—that is, linguistic, religious, economic, and social habits and attitudes, institutions, and values—that mark these peoples off from one another. And if science has demonstrated anything, it has shown conclusively that these traits are subject to human intervention, that they can be changed. The possibility of the ultimate assimilability of ethnic groups is thus beyond doubt.

It is coming to be recognized, moreover, that varying religious beliefs and cultural traits need not be a threat to national solidarity and are not necessarily disruptive of national loyalty. The private life of the individual is considered to an ever greater degree inviolable. What is required of the individual and of minority groups is that there be an adjustment to the social order and not necessarily that there be complete assimilation. Isolation of the minority from the body politic and social, on whatever ground it may be based and by whatever means enforced is increasingly regarded as the road to the perpetuation and accentuation of previously existing differences and as contrary to civilized public policy.

Until recently the United States in her policy toward her ethnic as distinguished from her racial minorities was regarded as the great experimental proving ground where minority problems either did not become acute or were being solved satisfactorily. Millions of our immigrants wanted to become Americans. Consequently we assumed that ours was the pattern after which other peoples would, if they could, model themselves. We had a further favorable fact to commend us in that we had a body of traditions and of fundamental laws expressive of the most liberal thought of mankind. Despite occasional relapses and despite the great contrast between the enlightened treatment we accorded our ethnic minorities and the backward policy we followed in the case of the Negro, the Indian, and the Oriental, it could still be said that the United States was in the forefront of the nations of the world in the treatment of minorities.

In recent years, however, world attention has been shifting to Russia's attempt to deal with her minorities. The Russian experiment is regarded by many as not only at least as enlightened as our own, but as much more relevant to the minority problems of Europe and the backward regions of the world. It is generally agreed among students of the problem that the Soviet nationalities and minorities policy represents one of the most outstanding achievements of the revolution and the period of reconstruction and that it holds great promise for the settlement of minority problems in the coming peace.

Inheriting as it did from the Czarist regime a tradition of deliberate hampering of industrialization, restricting the use of native languages and discouraging and suppressing the free development of the cultural life of its many and highly varied minorities, the Soviet Government under Lenin's leadership and with Stalin as Commissar for Nationalities, proceeded immediately after the Bolshevik revolution to inaugurate a policy which accords with the best scientific knowledge and the most enlightened moral principles. The achievement of the Soviet Union is all the more remarkable when it is considered that besides having to undo the accumulated effects of decades of cruelty, stupidity, and national chauvinism, the new state had to work against aggressive secessionist groups as well as mutual hostility and suspicion among her many minorities and armed external intervention and civil war.

The Declaration of the Rights of Peoples of Russia issued by the new government on November 15, 1917, one week after the Bolshevik revolution, over the signatures of Lenin and Stalin proclaimed the following principles: (1) Equality and sovereignty for the peoples of Russia; (2) The right of the peoples of Russia to self-determination to the point of separation from the state and creation of a new independent government; (3) Abolition of national and religious privileges; (4) Free development of national minorities and ethnographic groups inhabiting the territory of Russia.[3] This declaration became the guiding principle for later constitutional provisions and public policy. The policy followed was not improvised in the course of the revolutionary crisis. It had been well thought out. Writing in 1913 concerning the minorities situation in the Caucasus, Stalin expressed himself as follows:

> The national problem in the Caucasus can be solved *only by drawing the backward nations and peoples into the common stream of a higher culture.* . . . Regional autonomy in the Caucasus is acceptable because it draws the backward nations into the common cultural development; it helps to cast off the shell of isolation peculiar to small nationalities, it impels them forward and facilitates access to the benefits of higher culture; whereas national cultural autonomy acts in a diametrically opposite direction because it shuts up the nations within their old shells, chains them to the lower rungs of cultural development and prevents them from rising to the higher rungs of culture.[4]
>
> A minority is discontented not because there is no national union, but because it does not enjoy liberty of conscience, liberty of movement, etc. Give it these liberties and it will cease to be discontented. Thus *national equality in all forms (language, schools, etc.) is an essential element* in the solution of the national problem. A state law based on complete democracy in the country is required, prohibiting all national privileges without exception and all kinds of disabilities and restrictions on the rights of national minorities.[5]

After thirteen years experience with this policy, he wrote in 1930:

> The national cultures must be permitted to develop and expand and reveal all their potential qualities, in order to create the conditions necessary for their fusion into a single, common culture with a single, common language.[6]

When it is remembered that in 1941 the Soviet Union had books published in ninety languages to meet the linguistic variations of its peoples, the implications of the above principle becomes obvious.

The provisions in the Soviet Constitution of 1936 might be cited as the final official indication of Russian minority policy. It reads:

> Equality of rights of citizens of the U.S.S.R. irrespective of their nationality or race, in all spheres of economic, state, cultural, social and political life is an indefeasible law. Any direct or indirect restriction of the rights, or conversely any establishment of direct or indirect privileges for citizens on account of their race or nationality, as well as any advocacy of racial or national exclusiveness or hatred and contempt is punishable by law.[7]

Besides the experience of the United States and the Soviet Union, there are other indications in recent times of minority policies which point to a brighter prospect. The peaceful dissolution of the personal union between Norway and Sweden in 1905 furnished an example of a successful separatist solution, which, however, is not likely to be followed widely. Once the rights of persons as persons are recognized and respected by the state, once security and opportunity for all is guaranteed so that no group has to invent a scapegoat, once people are no longer regarded as objects of exploitation, the foundation will have been laid for a solution of the minorities problem if not for the disappearance of minorities altogether. Meanwhile it will be wise in the forthcoming peace settlements to recognize the importance in the drawing of national boundaries of the distribution of ethnic groups and to be prepared for the transference of people to more congenial states in case ethnic boundaries must be violated. The fairly satisfactory exchange of Turkish, Bulgar, and Greek populations after the Graeco-Turkish war of 1919–23 offers a valuable precedent, and the enlightened policy announced by the Czecho-Slovak Government with reference to the Sudeten Germans promises an equally humane, realistic solution. In the light of these events, the minority question can no longer be considered insoluble.[8]

NOTES

1. Woodrow Wilson: *Public Papers of Woodrow Wilson*, Vol. II: *The New Democracy* (New York, 1927), p. 187.
2. Edward Hulett Carr, *Conditions of Peace* (New World, 1943), p. 44.
3. Bernhard J. Stern, "Soviet Policy on National Minorities," *American Sociological Review*, IX (1944), 231.
4. Joseph Stalin, *Marxism and the National and Colonial Question* (New York, 1934), pp. 49–50. (Quoted from Stern, *op. cit.*, p. 231.)

5. *Ibid.*, pp. 58–59. (Quoted from Stern, *op. cit.*, p. 231.)
6. *Ibid.*, p. 235.
7. Stern, *op. cit.*, p. 235.
8. For a more detailed treatment of the problems in the United States see Louis Wirth, "The Present Position of Minorities in the United States" (University of Pennsylvania Bicentennial Conference on Political Science and Sociology), pp. 137–56.

AMERICAN IDEALS AND THE AMERICAN CONSCIENCE
Gunnar Myrdal

The best known and most widely quoted study of the
Negro in America is Gunnar Myrdal's monumental *An
American Dilemma*. With the sponsorship of the Car-
negie Corporation and the assistance of many black
and white American sociologists—including Arnold
Rose, Richard Sterner, Charles S. Johnson, Myrdal, a
Swedish economist, attempted a definitive analysis of
the black man's plight and position in this society. His
major thesis, written in 1944 and presented here, argued that Americans (white Americans) articulated a
creed of equality while practicing discrimination. In
time their recognition of such inconsistency and attendant guilt would lead to many positive changes.
Myrdal believed that integration was desirable and
possible and that social scientists should say so.

"Lip-Service"

The conflict in the American concept of law and order is only one side
of the "moral overstrain" of the nation. America believes in and aspires
to something much higher than its plane of actual life. The subordinate
position of Negroes is perhaps the most glaring conflict in the American
conscience and the greatest unsolved task for American democracy. But
it is by no means the only one. Donald Young complains:

In our more introspective moments, nearly all of us Americans will admit that our government contains imperfections and anachronisms. We who have been born and brought up under the evils of gang rule, graft, political incompetence, inadequate representation, and some of the other weaknesses of democracy, American plan, have developed mental calluses and are no longer sensitive to them.[1]

The *popular* explanation of the disparity in America between ideals and actual behavior is that Americans do not have the slightest intention of living up to the ideals which they talk about and put into their Constitution and laws. Many Americans are accustomed to talk loosely and disparagingly about adherence to the American Creed as "lip-service" and even "hypocrisy." Foreigners are even more prone to make such a characterization.

This explanation is too superficial. To begin with, the true hypocrite sins in secret; he conceals his faults. The American, on the contrary, is strongly and sincerely "against sin," even, and not least, his own sins. He investigates his faults, puts them on record, and shouts them from the housetops, adding the most severe recriminations against himself, including the accusation of hypocrisy. If all the world is well informed about the political corruption, organized crime, and faltering system of justice in America, it is primarily not due to its malice but to American publicity about its own imperfections. America's handling of the Negro problem has been criticized most emphatically by white Americans since long before the Revolution, and the criticism has steadily gone on and will not stop until America has completely reformed itself.

Bryce observed: "They know, and are content that all the world should know, the worst as well as the best of themselves. They have a boundless faith in free inquiry and full discussion. They admit the possibility of any number of temporary errors and delusions."[2] The present author remembers, from his first visit to this country as an inexperienced social scientist at the end of the 'twenties, how confused he often felt when Americans in all walks of life were trustingly asking him to tell them what was "wrong with this country." It is true that this open-mindedness, particularly against the outside world, may have decreased considerably since then on account of the depression, and that the present War might work in the same direction, though this is not certain; and it is true also that the opposite tendency always had its strong representation in America. But, by and large, America has been and will remain, in all probability, a society which is eager to indulge in self-scrutiny and to welcome criticism.

This American eagerness to get on record one's sins and their causes is illustrated in the often quoted letter by Patrick Henry (1772), where he confessed that he had slaves because he was "drawn along by the general inconvenience of living here without them."

I will not, I cannot, justify it. However culpable my conduct, I will so far pay my devoir to virtue as to own the excellence and rectitude of her precepts, and lament my want of conformity to them.[3]

American rationalism and moralism spoke through Patrick Henry. America as a nation is like its courageous and eloquent son of the Revolution. It is continuously paying its *devoir* to virtue; it is repeating its allegiance to the full American Creed by lamenting its want of conformity to it. The strength and security of the nation helped this puritan tradition to continue. No weak nation anxious for its future could ever have done it. Americans believe in their own ability and in progress. They are at bottom moral optimists.

In a great nation there is, of course, division of labor. Some Americans do most of the sinning, but most do some of it. Some specialize in muckraking, preaching, and lamentation; but there is a little of the muckraker and preacher in all Americans. On the other hand, superficially viewed, Americans often appear cynical. Their social science has lately developed along a deterministic track of amoralistic nonconcernedness; but this is itself easily seen to be a moralistic reaction. As a matter of fact, this young nation is the least cynical of all nations. It is not hypocritical in the usual sense of the word, but labors persistently with its moral problems. It is taking its Creed very seriously indeed, and this is the reason why the ideals are not only continuously discussed but also represent a social force—why they receive more than "lip-service" in the collective life of the nation. The cultural unity of the nation is this common sharing in both the consciousness of sins and the devotion to high ideals.

Americans accuse themselves, and are accused by others, of being materialists. But they are equally extreme in the other direction. Sometimes an American feels moved to put the matter right, as Josiah Royce did when he explained:

When foreigners accuse us of extraordinary love for gain, and of practical materialism, they fail to see how largely we are a nation of idealists. Yet that we are such a nation is something constantly brought to the attention of those whose calling requires them to observe any of the tendencies prevalent in our recent intellectual life in America.[4]

The American problem would, indeed, have an entirely different prognosis if this fact were forgotten.

Value Premises in *An American Dilemma*

For the study of a national problem which cuts so sharply through the whole body politic as does the Negro problem, no other set of valuations could serve as adequately as the norm for an incisive formulation of our value premises as can the American Creed. No other norm could compete in authority over people's minds. "The American democratic faith is a pattern of ideals providing standards of value with which the accomplishments of realistic democracy may be judged," observes an author surveying the historical trends of American thinking.[5]

And there is no doubt that these ideals are active realities. The student of American history must be professionally near-sighted or blinded by a doctrinal belief in a materialistic determinism if he fails to see the significance of tracing how the Creed is gradually realizing itself. *The American Creed is itself one of the dominant "social trends."* "Call it a dream or call it vision," says John Dewey, "it has been interwoven in a tradition that has had an immense effect upon American life."[6] Or, to quote a distinguished Negro thinker, the late Kelly Miller:

> In this country political, social and economic conditions gravitate toward equality. We may continue to expect thunderstorms in the political firmament so long as there exists inequality of political temperature in the atmosphere of the two regions. Neither Massachusetts nor Mississippi will rest satisfied until there is an equality of political condition in both States. . . . Democratic institutions can no more tolerate a double political status than two standards of ethics or discrepant units of weight and measure.[7]

But apart from trends, the American Creed represents the national conscience. The Negro is a "problem" to the average American partly because of a palpable conflict between the status actually awarded him and those ideals.

The American Creed, just because it is a living reality in a developing democracy, is not a fixed and clear-cut dogma. It is still growing. During the Revolutionary epoch the interests of statesmen and philosophers and of the general public were focused on the more formal aspects of freedom, equality and justice. After a long period of material expansion but not rapid spiritual growth, the American Creed is in this generation again in a formative stage. It is now discovering its ideals in the social and economic sphere and in the realm of international organization.

While this is going on, there are great disparities in opinions even on fundamentals in these new fields of valuation—as there were during the Revolution concerning the ideals which then became crystallized. Some Americans see in trade unions a denial of the rights to human liberty; others see in the unions an expression of the common man's right to reach for greater equality and freedom. Some Americans want to tax property and nationalize public utilities in order to defend equality of opportunity for the masses of the people and to preserve their liberties; others see in such attempts an assault upon American principles of liberty. In the international field American ideals in recent decades and even today seem divided and rambling in the wide space of the triangle marked by the three points: absolute isolationism, an organized world democracy, and American world imperialism.

These great disparities of opinion would, in any other social problem, considerably increase the technical difficulties of utilizing the Creed as a set of specified and definite value premises for research. When in later chapters we face the task of defining our value premises specifically, we shall find that this is not the case in the Negro problem. The Creed is expressive and definite in practically all respects of importance for the Negro problem. Most of the value premises with which we shall be concerned have actually been incorporated for a long time in the national Constitution and in the constitutions and laws of the several states.

The deeper reason for the technical simplicity of the value aspect of the Negro problem is this: From the point of view of the American Creed the status accorded the Negro in America represents nothing more and nothing less than a century-long lag of public morals. In principle the Negro problem was settled long ago; in practice the solution is not effectuated. The Negro in America has not yet been given the elemental civil and political rights of formal democracy, including a fair opportunity to earn his living, upon which a general accord was already won when the American Creed was first taking form. And this anachronism constitutes the contemporary "problem" both to Negroes and to whites.

If those rights were respected, many other pressing social problems would, of course, still remain. Many Negroes would, together with many whites, belong to groups which would invoke the old ideals of equality and liberty in demanding more effective protection for their social and economic opportunities. But there would no longer be a *Negro* problem. This does not mean that the Negro problem is an easy problem to solve. It is a tremendous task for theoretical research to find out why the Negro's status is what it is. In its unsolved form it further interwines with all other social problems. It is simple only in the technical sense that in America the value premises—if they are conceived to be the ideals of the American Creed— are extraordinarily specific and definite.

Finally, in order to avoid possible misunderstandings, it should be explained that we have called this Creed "American" in the sense that it is adhered to by the Americans. This is the only matter which interests us in this book, which is focused upon the Negro problem as part of American life and American politics. But this Creed is, of course, no American monopoly. With minor variations, some of which, however, are not without importance, the American Creed is the common democratic creed. "American ideals" are just humane ideals as they have matured in our common Western civilization upon the foundation of Christianity and pre-Christian legalism and under the influence of the economic, scientific, and political development over a number of centuries. The American Creed is older and wider than America itself.

NOTES

1. Donald R. Young, *American Minority Peoples* (1932), p. 224.
2. Bryce, *op. cit.,* Vol. 2, p. 371.

3. Quoted from Guion G. Johnson, *op. cit.*, p. 93.
4. *Race Questions, Provincialism and other American Problems* (1908), p. 111.
5. Gabriel, *op. cit.*, p. 418.
6. *Freedom and Culture* (1939), p. 55. Dewey is here referring to the theory of human freedom that was developed in the writings of the philosophers of the American Revolution, particularly in Jefferson's writings.
7. *Out of the House of Bondage* (1914) pp. 134–135.

AMERICA'S RACE PARADOX
Nathan Glazer

Nathan Glazer argues that the plight of black Americans is improving and that, like other ethnic groups, they will find their place within the broad mosaic that is this nation of many nations.
While aware of the oversimplified analogies that lump members of colored minority groups with whites of immigrant stock, Glazer warns against using the colonial imagery of, say, Frantz Fanon, to describe a situation that he feels is inaccurately labeled as such. His critique of the position of several writers whose views are offered in the succeeding part of this volume is particularly noteworthy.
As we shall see, the debate continues.

Something very strange is happening in the racial crisis in the United States. On the one hand, the concrete situation of Negro Americans is changing rapidly for the better. This is not only true when we look at economic measures of all kinds (although we all know that these are an inadequate measure of group progress, and that a people that feels oppressed will never be satisfied by the argument "you never had it so good"); but it is also true that things are better when we look at measures of political participation and power. It is even true when we look at the critical area of police behaviour and police attitudes. There is no question that police in city after city are becoming more careful in how they address Negro Americans, more restrained in the use of force, of fire-arms. The history of the riots alone, from 1964, demonstrates that.

But on the other hand, the political attitudes of Negroes have become

From *Encounter*, October 1968. Reprinted by permission.

more extreme and more desperate. The riots are called "rebellions," and hardly any Negro leader today bothers to deplore them. Militant groups become larger, and their language and demands more shocking. Cultural nationalism flourishes—and I think most people think that is good—but political separatism becomes an ever more popular demand, and hardly anyone can consider that without thinking again. (We all know what may happen when a country begins to break up. Look at Nigeria.)

This is an incredible dilemma for social policy. For the fact is that most of us—black and white, liberals and conservatives, socialists and free enterprisers—believe (1) that political and social attitudes reflect the concrete economic and social and political situation of people; (2) that we can affect those attitudes by changing the concrete conditions; and (3) that when things get better people become more satisfied, less violent, the society becomes more stable. When concrete conditions improve and political attitudes become at the same time more extreme and violent, we can resort to two explanations.

There is the well-known "revolution of rising expectations," and the ease with which expectations can outstrip concrete positive changes. And there is the theory of Alexis de Tocqueville, developed in his study of the French Revolution, that the improvement of conditions increases the desire for greater change and for revolutionary change, because people themselves feel stronger and more potent. Both of these processes are undoubtedly taking place, but one's attitude to them must depend on one's attitude to American society. If one looks upon American society as Tocqueville and the French people looked upon their Old Régime, that is, as a conservative, sclerotic, repressive, irrational, and selfish régime which prevented the free development of the people, then one of course will accept favourably the rise of extreme opinion, and look forward to the crash of the American Old Régime. But if one sees American society and state as fundamentally democratic, as capable of change, as responsive to people's wishes—then one will be deeply concerned whether this society and state can survive. That expectations should rise is good—that they should rise so fast that no policy of any type carried out by anybody can satisfy them, is bad. That people should feel potent and powerful and free to express their resentments and anger is encouraging—that that resentment and anger should serve to overthrow a system that works, that is capable of satisfying their needs and hopes, is deplorable.

A rapid rate of social change has improved the condition of Negro Americans and has gone some way to closing gaps between the condition of Negro and white Americans, but it has not only *not* moderated the rise of extremism and violence—it has been accompanied by it. At some point one must expect improvement and change to moderate extremism and violence, despite the revolution of rising expectations and the Tocquevillean hypothesis. If there is such a point, it is clear we are not only not arriving at it: we are getting further and further away from it.

There is, of course, another possible explanation of what is happening: that Negro Americans are no longer interested in Integration or even in educational, economic, and political advance within the American social system. They have begun to see themselves as "a subject people" and, as in the case of every such people, only independent political existence can satisfy them. This, in any case, is the direction that militant Negro demands have now begun to take. And if most Negro Americans follow the militant leaders, then all the political skill, ingenuity, and creativity the American nation possesses will be necessary to keep it from being torn apart.

First, let me briefly document the fact that things *are* getting better. We must do this because so many liberal and progressive shapers of opinion, and the vast flock that follows them, are convinced (and *insist*) that the concrete situation of Negro Americans has *not* changed, or has indeed got worse. Sadly enough, social scientists, who should know the facts best, are often among the worst offenders. The writer of that fine study of Negro street-corner men, *Tally's Corner,* for example, states casually that "the number of the poor and their problems have grown steadily since World War II. . . ." Social scientists who contend that the economic situation of Negroes is getting worse will point to the rising *absolute* gap between Negro and white incomes and ignore the fact that Negro incomes have come closer to white incomes as a *percentage* of white incomes. By this logic, if we come to a fortunate time when white median incomes are $10,000 and non-white median incomes are $8,000, it could be argued that Negroes are "worse off" than when whites made $5,000 and Negroes $3,500!

In October 1967, the Bureau of Labor Statistics and the Bureau of the Census put out a compendium of statistics on the *Social and Economic Conditions of Negroes in the United States.* Here are some of the major findings:

Income: In 1966, 23% of non-white families had incomes of more than $7,000, against 53% of white families. Ten years before, using dollars of the same value, only 9% of the non-white families had incomes at this level, against 31% of white families.

If we look at the U.S. outside the South, where the Negro situation on all measures is worst, we find in 1966 38% of non-white families with income above $7,000, against 59% of white families at that level.

Occupation: Between 1960 and 1966, the number of non-whites in the better-paying and more secure occupational categories increased faster than whites: a 50% increase for non-whites in professional, technical and managerial work, against a 13% increase for whites; a 48% increase in clerical occupations, against a 19% increase for whites; a 32% increase in sales workers, against a 7% increase for whites; a 45% increase in craftsmen and foremen, against a 10% increase for whites. And during the same time, the proportions of non-whites working as private household workers and labourers dropped.

Education: In 1960 there was a 1.9 years gap in median years of school completed between non-white and white males 25 to 29; by 1966, there was only a .5 years gap.

In 1960, 36% of non-white males 25 to 29 had completed high school, against 63% of white males; by 1966, 53% of non-white males had completed high school, against 73% of white males.

In 1960, 3.9% of Negro males 25 to 34 had completed college, against 15.7% of white males; in 1966, 7.4% of Negro males had completed college, against 17.9% of white males—a 90% increase among non-white college graduates, against a 14% increase in white college graduates.

Housing: Between 1960 and 1966, there was a 25% drop in the number of substandard housing units occupied by non-whites (from 2,263,000 to 1,691,000 units), and a 44% increase in the number of standard units occupied by non-whites—from 2,881,000 to 4,135,000 units.

If we look at political participation—voting, offices held, in effect, political power—we find an equally striking increase. Thus, Negro voter registration in the South increased from 2,164,000 in March 1964 to 3,072,000 in May 1968, while Negro population remained stable. The National Commission on Civil Disorders surveyed twenty cities to find out the extent of Negro political representation. The cities averaged 16% in Negro population; 10% in proportion of elected Negro political representatives. We have to interpret such a figure in the light of the fact that Negroes of voting age are generally a smaller proportion of the total Negro population in most cities than whites of voting age of the white population, since Negroes in cities have a higher proportion of young families and children, whites a higher proportion of the aged.

Even on that sorest point of black-white relations, the police, the Kerner Commission reports progress in one significant respect: there are now substantial numbers of Negroes on many city police forces—Washington 21%, Philadelphia 20, Chicago 17, St. Louis 11, Hartford 11, Newark 10, Atlanta 10, Cleveland 7, New York 5, Detroit 5.

These are simply overall measures. When one considers the large number of programmes devoted to getting Negroes into colleges, into graduate and professional schools, into various corporations, to raise their grades in the Federal Civil Service, to moderate police attitudes—and when one considers the incentives to do all these things to be found in riot and threat of riot, boycott and threat of boycott, one cannot help conclude that the situation of Negroes is changing . . . for "the better."

To be sure, all the figures I have quoted can be disputed. Thus, 14% of

Negro males as against only 2% of white males (we have recently become aware) never get counted by the census; and if they were counted, they would undoubtedly depress the Negro figures on income, education, occupation, housing. But as against this, it must be pointed out that we have probably not been counting similar proportions of Negro males of working age in earlier censuses; so the change from one census to another represents real change.

It can be argued that the quality of jobs held by Negroes, even if they are in white-collar and skilled labour categories, is worse than that held by whites; and this too is true. But the changes over time are real, and the quality of jobs has certainly not on the whole decreased. Indeed, it has probably improved. Less Negro professionals today are preachers, more are engineers.

It can be argued that the improvement in the economic and educational and housing condition of the Negro is largely an effect of their migration from the South, and from small town and rural areas, to the North and West, and to big cities; if we were to look at Negroes in the North and West alone, we would not find such marked changes. But the statistics show improvement in every section.

It has been argued that while these overall measures of improvement truly reflect improvement for the Negro middle classes and stable working classes, the lower working classes have relatively declined, and have shown no progress. But an unpublished analysis of income statistics by Dr. Albert Wohlstetter (of the University of Chicago) reveals that the *lower* Negro income groups have improved their position relatively to white low-income groups more in recent years than the Negro upper-income groups have improved their position relative to white upper-income groups. In other words, the gap between poor Negroes and poor whites in terms of income is narrower now than in the 1950s. At the same time it is true that other social indicators—*e.g.,* the proportion of broken families and of illegitimacy—continue to reveal worsening conditions.

Finally, one may argue that much of the advance to which I have pointed has taken place since the Viet Nam War expanded in 1965, just as the previous economic advances of the Negro took place during the Korean War, and came to an end when that war came to an end. Between the wars there was relative decline and stagnation.

There is much truth in these last two arguments with the gross statistics of recent improvement. But it is also true that the advances made during wars have not been fully wiped out in the past—it is rather that the rate of change has not kept up. By now the build-up of Negro political power and of national programmes and commitments that guarantee advance is so great and the scale of the advances that have taken place in recent years is so massive, that I cannot believe they will not continue after the war —if, that is, there is not a radical change in the political situation to reverse the social and economic trends of the last eight years.

More striking, however, than the advance itself is the fact that on the basis of our present social statistics we can not single out the Negro as a group in the United States which suffers unique deprivation, *i.e.*, as compared to other ethnic and racial groups which suffer from the effects of poor education, depressed rural backgrounds, and recent migration to urban areas. There has been a division among American social scientists as to how to view Negro Americans in the context of the ethnic and racial history of the United States. One tendency is to emphasize everything that is "unique"—and a great deal is unique: the manner of their arrival (by force, and in chains); the conditions under which they lived for two hundred years (slavery); the conditions under which they have lived for the last hundred years (legal inferiority in a good part of the country); finally, the special role of the Negro Americans in American imagination and in culture (as central participants in shaping it, and as the subjects of some of its major themes). But it is also possible to see Negro Americans as part of a sequence of ethnic and racial groups that have moved into American society and become a part of it.

A new illusion is now abroad in the land. It asserts that all white ethnic groups have rapidly moved into American society, achieving respectable levels of income, good conditions of living, and political power. All racially distinct groups, suffering from the racism of American society, have been held back; and the Negro American, suffering from the special character of chattel slavery, is furthest back. The truth is nothing like this. Some white ethnic groups—such as the Jews—have shown a rapid economic mobility. Others have been much slower to achieve economically. One of these economically-backward white ethnic groups, the Irish, has been politically gifted, and members of the group are to be found disproportionately among elected officials of every level and in almost every part of the country. Others, such as Italians and Poles, have done poorly both economically *and* politically. Some racially distinct groups—such as the Japanese—have done remarkably well in education and occupation. Most others have done badly.

The range in experience is enormous, and the cause of this difference is not only degree of discrimination and prejudice, though that is an important factor. Equally important is a whole range of elements we vaguely group under the term "culture"—attitudes and behaviour in connection with School, Work, Family. (These have their origin in history and it may well be that the discrimination and prejudice of the past creates the cultural attributes of the present.) Nor is it true that these grossly different patterns of achievement among different groups are to be found in the U.S.A. alone. They are to be found wherever different ethnic and racial groups live together, whether it is Malays, Chinese, and Indians in Malaya, or Indians and Africans in Kenya, or Chinese and Indonesians in Indonesia, or Maharashtrians and Gujaratis and South Indians in Bombay, *etc.* Indeed, it is often the case that when a group is politically favoured in terms of educational and job opportunities—*e.g.*, the Malays in Malaya—these powerful cultural factors prevent the group from taking full advantage of these opportunities; and they remain at a lower educational and economic level. The Negro situation is rather more complex than the gross simplification of having "started at the bottom and staying there." By some measures, the Puerto Ricans do worse in New York, and the Mexican Americans do worse in the South-west. One can indeed contend that the Negro is worst off of the major ethnic and racial groups in this country, but not that much worse off to explain by itself the special quality of despair and hysteria, and the tone of impending violence and doom that now dominates much Negro political discourse.

But of course we must add another factor to the equation: America's obligation as a nation to improve the position of Negroes is much greater than the obligation to groups that emigrated voluntarily. The Negro is aware of this obligation and responsibility, and so the inferiority of his position becomes far more grating than it would be in the case of ordinary immigrants.

The fact is that, regardless of the details of the actual economic and social position of the Negro, an increasingly large part of twenty-two million Negro Americans believes that Americans are "racists," insist on "keeping the Negro down," and will never allow equality, and that the only solution will be some form of separate political existence. One indicator as to how far we have moved is in the use of words. Consider, for example, "genocide." Last February, Stokely Carmichael spoke to a Negro audience in Oakland and felt he had to justify the use of "genocide" to describe the dangers facing Negroes:

> . . . we are not talking about politics tonight, we're not talking about economics tonight. we're talking about the survival of a race of people. . . . Many of us feel—many of our generation feel—that they are getting ready to commit genocide against us. Now many people say that's a horrible thing to say about anybody. But if it's a horrible thing to say, then we should do as Brother Malcolm said, we should examine history.

We have moved far in the course of a year. A leader of the SCLC says "genocide" is a danger. James Baldwin (in the June 2 Book Review section of the *New York Times*) asserts "white America appears to be seriously considering the possibilities of mass extermination." By now even moderate leaders use the term genocide, and feel they have to use it to appeal to young militants and to show they are not "Uncle Toms." By now, of course, white men who want to demonstrate their sympathy for Negroes will not demur from the use of the term; thus, Eliot Fremont-Smith, reviewing John Hersey's *The Algiers Motel Incident* in the *New York Times,* writes that the book, "shows America to be deeply—and unknowingly to most of its citizens—genocidal."

The public opinion polls report fantastically rapid changes of attitude among Negro Americans. A Louis Harris poll conducted *before* the Martin Luther King assassination reported on a measure of "alienation," and concluded that the numbers of Negroes "alienated" had risen from 34% in 1966 to 56% in 1968. The items measuring alienation included: *"Few people really understand how it is to live like I live"* (those agreeing rose from 32 to 66%); *"People running the country don't really care what happens to people like ourselves"* (those agreeing rose from 32 to 52%). The very same poll reports that 73% of the respondents agreed there has been "more racial progress" in recent years than there had been previously.

So the paradox exists in the very consciousness of Negro Americans. They agree there has been more progress, but also feel ignored, stepped upon, and remote from their society. (Whites do too, but in much lesser degree.) The changes in these general attitudes reported by the Harris poll are particularly striking because they are the sort of general question measuring malaise that one would not expect to vary much over time (*viz.*, "Are you happy?"); and yet they have changed rapidly. I speak of attitudes and the use of words. More striking are the realities of action— the riots since 1964, the general expectation of guerrilla warfare, the rise of the so-called Black Panthers in California and elsewhere and their amazing ability to seize the imagination of the Ghetto youth with a programme calling for armed resistance to the police, community control of the ghetto, freeing of black prisoners, and the ultimate hope for some type of national, separate, political existence for blacks.

There are three positions now current as to what to do about this strange impasse: social improvement and increasing extremism. One is that we must put down extremism, strengthen the police, create riot control forces. A second is that we must increase the rate of material advance more swiftly—eventually it must lead to a harmonious nation. A third is that social improvement is no longer the issue—separate political power and existence for Negro Americans is the only reality that will satisfy.

I think the majority of white Americans reject the first alternative as any full response to the crisis, though certainly most believe the maintenance of civil order must be part of any response.

The second position is the one for which the Kerner Commission has written a brief in its report, and most liberal Americans are likely to accept it. It is almost the only thesis one can put forward if one's conviction is that, on the whole, American society has been a success, that a major sign of its success is that it has incorporated and will continue to incorporate many diverse groups, and that it can handle the complex and frightening problems of an advanced technological society rather better than the varied assortment of Communist authoritarian states or vague utopias that is the rhetorical hope of the New Left. And yet the liberal position—and we can take the Kerner Commission report as expressing it best—has one basic difficulty.

It is that we have *already* carried out and are carrying out social programmes at an ever-increasing scale without, as we have seen, any movement towards the reward of "a united and peaceful nation." Take the figures of the Kerner Commission itself:

> Federal expenditures for manpower development and training have increased from less than $60 million in 1963 to $1.6 billion in 1968. The President has proposed a further increase, $2.1 billion in 1969 . . . to provide work experience, training, and supportive services for 1.3 million men and women . . . [which happens to be more than twice the number of non-white unemployed].
>
> Federal expenditures for education, training and related services have increased from $4.7 billion in fiscal 1964 to $12.3 billion in fiscal 1969.
>
> Direct Federal expenditures for housing and community development have increased from $600 million in fiscal 1964 to nearly $3 billion in fiscal 1969.

There have been similarly heavy increases in health and welfare expenditures. All these figures are reported in order to criticise the build-up of expenditures as "not rapid enough" and to demand "far more money" in these and other areas. I am left with an uneasy feeling. If these rates of expansion reported by the Kerner Commission have taken place at the same time as the spread of urban riots and political extremism, is it not questionable whether further expansion will stem them? I am *for* the expansion of these programmes because they are the major means we have for achieving equality in occupations, education, housing, *etc.* But I do not think we can count on them to moderate attitudes—for political attitudes and development have a life of their own, and are not simple reflections of economic and social conditions.

There is no question in my mind that the demand for "Black Separatism" will not be easily moderated by new social programmes. Accordingly, we must face up to the demand for separatism in its own terms.

Here one must note that "separatism" seems to mean many different things. Some of them appear to me to be valuable and healthy, both for Negroes and for American society: the emphasis on positive identification with the group, "Black Power" in its sense of greater political impact and representation of Negroes; "Black Capitalism"; "Black history" and art. The chief difficulty presented by Black Separatism arises in the demands for territorial autonomy and "extra-territoriality." These have now been presented in many forms: a group of states to become a black nation; black enclaves in the cities, with certain rights and powers; special legal rights for blacks, as in the "Free Huey" demand and its argument that white judges and juries cannot try blacks (even though there are blacks among them). There is no question that American political leaders (and the great majority of the American people) will resist the demand for territorial autonomy and extra-territoriality. One war has been fought to preserve the Union, and the sense of what all Americans gain from a united nation, and what they might lose from a divided one, is strong enough to ensure that these demands will continue to be resisted. Nor is it clear that any substantial part of Negro Americans at present agrees with the Separatists. But their dynamism is frightening, and they are powerfully supported, in my view, not by the realities of the Negro condition and the hopes they offer of improving it, but by powerful ideologies. In particular, it is the new ideology that Negroes in America are "a Colonial People" and require freedom from colonial status.

If the demand for territorial independence succeeds in capturing the minds of Negro Americans, it will be because blacks and whites have not truly understood the relationship between the varying groups that make up American society. Many, in both groups, see the society as far more monolithic and homogeneous than it has ever been. I am afraid that whites will be moved to fight to retain something that has never existed in this country, and the blacks will fight because they have not been convinced of the enormous scope for group diversity the society provides.

Almost every ethnic and racial group that has settled in this country has been "nationalistic" and "separatist," and the laws have permitted a level of separatism for many groups that has not yet been quite reached by American Negroes. Many groups have harboured and supported with money (and sometimes with armed volunteers) nationalist leaders interested in freeing or revolutionising their homelands, even when this was a matter of great embarrassment to the U.S.A. Most groups have maintained schools in their own tongue. Most groups have tried desperately to maintain the original home language, religion, and ethnic customs among their children in America. There has been one limit set on the free development of ethnic and racial groups in this country—territorial autonomy. But short of that, subtle and complex adjustments were made to accommodate a wide variety of differences.

The history of the gross prejudice and discrimination which almost all immigrant and racial groups have faced is well known; but we tend to be less aware of these "American adjustments" to accommodate a mixed population of different ethnic and racial groups. Thus, we have developed a pattern of political recognition, through the parties, in which groups of any substantial number get represented, through appointive and elective office. This system has worked well, without any laws requiring quotas, or specifications of "how much" and "what kind." There has been a pattern of economic integration in which groups have developed bases of economic independence. (Undoubtedly the general freedom this country has given to economic enterprises has aided this development.) Unfortunately, the ability to create such an independent economic base is now considerably limited by, among other things, the host of state and social licensing and regulatory requirements, trade union requirements, federal tax and accounting procedures, all of which today make it much harder for the less literate and sophisticated to become successful in business. We have allowed full freedom to religious organisation, and under the protection of religious organisation a wide range of cultural, social, political activities is carried on. We have given freedom to the creation of independent schools. All this has occurred even though a young patchwork nation has had the difficult task of fashioning a single national identity.

Compared with most countries that have tried to create themselves out of a mixed population, there has been a certain genius in the American style of confronting this problem. The principle has been: no formal recognition of the ethnic and racial groups, but every informal recognition of their right and desire to self-development, assimilation or integration at their own chosen rate, to an independent economic base, independent social, religious, and political institutions, and political recognition as part of a united country. The principle has often been broken: laws have been erected against certain groups—most massively in the case of Negroes, but also in the case of American Indians and Orientals; and we have often restricted the free and spontaneous development of various groups through movements of "Americanisation" and forced patriotism. But the most massive and inhumane breaks in these principles have in the end been recognised as "un-American," and wrong: slavery for the Negroes; "separate but equal" facilities for Negroes; public discrimination against Negroes; separate schools for the Chinese; land laws restricting the right of purchase by Japanese; the forced relocation of the Japanese and their loss of property; the immigration laws establishing quotas for peoples and races; attempts of states to ban private schooling. All these have in the end been overcome by courts and legislatures, and the basic principle—no public recognition of race or ethnicity; every private consideration of its reality and meaningfulness—has, in the end, prevailed.

Undoubtedly, to argue that the Negroes, who stand at the very heart of American civilisation as a cruelly harmed people, can be (and, indeed, have been in large measure) incorporated into this pattern, will appear to many an act of Pollyanna-ish refusal to face up to evil in American society. Professor Robert Blauner (of the University of California at Berkeley) has argued forcefully that there are certain "colonised" peoples in the United States who do not fit the ethnic pattern I have described; and these are the Negroes, the American Indians, and the Mexican Americans. According to this thesis, the ethnic pattern that permitted a self-regulated rate of integration into American life prevailed only for the European immigrant groups; and to a much more modest degree, it prevails for the Chinese and Japanese. But there was a different pattern for those peoples who were conquered or brought here as slaves. They have been "colonised," made inferior to the "settlers" in every part of life (political, economic, social, cultural), deprived of their power and "manhood"; and for them only the colonial pattern of rebellion, resistance, and forceful overthrow of settler dominance is meaningful. Thus Frantz Fanon's passionate argument for the significance of violence against the settlers in recreating the colonised as a people (in his *Wretched of the Earth*) speaks to American Negroes as it speaks to the colonised everywhere.

If Professor Blauner is right, then all that remains for us "non-colonised," as settlers, is to figure out how, when the colonised are so scattered among the settlers, we may give them the independence that will make them whole—or, if we refuse, wait for them to take it, or destroy the Union in the effort.

But I think he is wrong, and for one basic reason: whatever the relevance of the "colonisation hypothesis" to the past—when the Negroes lived as agricultural workers in the South, the Mexican Americans in villages in the Southwest, the American Indians on the reservation—it is scarcely relevant today when three-quarters of American Negroes have moved to cities to become not only workers and servants but skilled workers, foremen, civil servants, professionals, white-collar workers of all types; when (at a slower rate) the same thing is happening to Mexican Americans; and when even Indians can free themselves from any politically inferior status by giving up the reservation and moving to the city (as more and more are doing). These moves are voluntary—or if involuntary to some extent, no more so than the migration of many other groups escaping political persecution and economic misery. They lead to the creation of a voluntary community of self-help institutions. They lead to a largely self-regulated rate at which group cultural patterns are given up and new ones adopted. It is all quite comparable to what happened to the European immigrant groups. Statistics which show the wide range of outcomes that we find in all groups, whether European immigrant, racial immigrant, or the so-called "colonised," are strong evidence for the similarity.

Undoubtedly all these groups still face prejudice and discrimination; but this still does not make the "colonial" analogy fit. Prejudice and discrimination, it seems, are endemic wherever different groups socially interact. Are the Algerian workers of the slum settlements around Paris now "colonised"? Are the Spanish and Turkish immigrant workers of Europe "colonised"? Or are they not, rather, immigrant workers facing the prejudice and discrimination and inferior living conditions strangers so often do? Nor are prejudice and discrimination insuperable obstacles to economic advancement and political power. If we were to have to wait for "the end of prejudice and discrimination" before we could say the Negro was truly a part of American society, we would have to wait forever. The issue is: what is the *level* of prejudice and discrimination, how is it formulated in *harmful policies,* what *official assistance* does it get, and to what extent (on the other hand) *does the state act against its private manifestations.* If we apply these tests, I believe, we will find that the "colonial analogy" as applied to the American Negro is meaningless. For there has been a steady decline in all forms of expressed prejudice against Negroes, as indicated in public opinion polls and in everyday behaviour, and there has been stronger and stronger state action, outside the South (and even in some parts of the South) against manifestations of prejudice. Even the recent riots (as far as we can tell from the evidence) have led to no increase in prejudice or white antagonism.

The "colonial pattern" makes sense if one of two conditions prevails: there is a *legal* inferiority of the colonised, in which the settlers are given greater rights and prerogatives; or, even if there is a *formal* equality, in fact only tiny proportions of the colonised can reach high status in society. But this is not true of the Negro Americans, nor will it be true shortly of the Mexican Americans, and, if they so choose, of American Indians. The fact is that instead of keeping these groups out of privileged status most public policy and the programmes of most large private U.S. institutions is to bring them in larger and larger numbers into privileged status. What else is the meaning of the work of the Federal civil service in continually upgrading minority employees, of the colleges in recruiting them beyond the numbers that could normally qualify, of the various corporation programmes for training minority group executives and franchise holders? The scale of some of this is much too small; but the point is that its aim is to speed up a process of incorporating these groups into the mixed American society, rather than slowing it down.

The issue of whether Negro Americans are "colonised" or not is not to be settled by arguments between professors: it will be settled by Negro Americans themselves. If they view themselves as colonised, as suffering unbearable repression, as prevented from leading that degree of national and separate existence that they wish within the present prevailing American pattern, then they will do everything to break that pattern; and it will be up to all Americans to decide whether the awful suffering of wars of national unity is to be preferred to the dangers of separatism. No one who has thought deeply about the American Civil War (or what is happening in Nigeria now) will be able to give a pat answer to this question.

The issue, I think, is not yet settled, despite the extravagance of Negro militant rhetoric. Three factors still argue against the victory of the "colonial analogy" among Negroes.

1. The substantial numbers of Negroes who *are* integrated into American society—the civil servants, the white-collar workers, the union members, the political party members, the elected and appointed officials. They are truly in a tragic situation, and no one can say whether they will choose to identify with those who insist on seeing them as "colonised," or whether they will argue for integration into American life, along the pattern that I have described.

2. The second is the possibility that moderate and available social change can still pacify the militants. While making large separatist demands, they would perhaps be satisfied with more jobs, better jobs, more

Negro appointed and elected officials, better schools, better housing, a more integrated and respectful police force, and that degree of separate institutional identity and control which the American pattern can tolerate. Certainly we have done too little in all these areas; but we have done a good deal, and we must do more, hoping that in effect the separatists are not really as intransigent as they sound.

3. The enormous difficulty of any territorial solution to the demand for separatism, and the difficulty of devising any alternative.

But there are indeed factors which argue for the success of the "colonial analogy" and the victory of separatism.

One is the enormous impact on Negro experience of past and present experience in the South, where Negroes were held captive and colonised indeed, and where there still remains the most unrelenting and sophisticated resistance to Negro equality in whole states and in large sections of the population. The colonial imagery of the South has been transported to East and West and to the great cities which are largely free of colonialism. There it struggles against the immigrant analogy—and, on the whole, it is losing. They shout, "We are still slaves" and "We want freedom" in the North, where the issue is neither slavery nor freedom.

The second is our failure to adopt rapidly enough new approaches to achieving effective equality for the Negro. While the immigrant analogy is still, to my mind, in large measure valid, it is not fully valid. Negro business must be created, subsidised, sustained, advised; job programmes must become better and more meaningful; the colleges must learn new techniques for incorporating large numbers of minority students, and the urban schools must undergo a transformation (though its nature is hard to define) in becoming effective with minority students. But all this is enormously demanding, so demanding indeed that we may not succeed. Mayor Lindsay, speaking to businessmen in New York—and he was perhaps the dominant liberal member of the Kerner Commission—has described what businessmen must do to make the hard-core unemployed effective:

> You've got to literally adopt this kind of employee, be responsible for his total condition 24 hours a day, seven days a week. . . . Adopt their families, a piece of the block where they live, a chunk of the city and its future. Know where they live, their economic condition, how their children are, whether there's a police problem, what the neighbourhood pressures are. If it's a woman, you have to know whether there's a male in the house and what her problems are. . . .
>
> The businessman who does hire the hard-core unemployed is going to be confronted with absenteeism, poor working habits, deficiencies in reading and writing, negative attitudes. . . .

If this is truly what businessmen and perhaps teachers must do effectively to employ or educate a substantial part of the minority population, we may simply not have the required degree of compassion, commitment, and capacity to succeed.

The third is the inability of both black and white to comprehend the character of the American pattern of group incorporation which has already had so many successes. On the white side, there is widespread fear of Negro separatism and Negro power, and it is a fear which, as I have suggested, fails to understand that every group has gone through (and some have retained) a substantial degree of separatism, and all have demanded (and many have obtained) political representation in appointive and elective office, and control over pieces of the political action. As long as the nation does not succumb to a society of rigid compartments and fixed quotas and reserved seats, Americans can go some distance in meeting separatist demands. If suburban towns can have their own school systems and police forces, then, to my mind, there is no good reason why certain parts of the larger city should not have separate school systems and police forces. In any case, when the authority of teachers and the police have been destroyed—and they have been, in large measure, destroyed in the ghetto areas—there is no alternative to some pragmatic adjustment, to the creation of new social forms.

On the black side—and here blacks are joined of course by many whites, both liberal and progressive—there is an equal failure to comprehend the relationships of groups to the larger American society. There is a failure to understand that even while prejudice and discrimination exist, groups and individuals can achieve their ends and a satisfying and respected place in the American social structure. There is a failure to understand that groups vary in their cultural characteristics and in the area and character of their achievements, and that the owlish insistence on some total equality of representation is to deny the significance of special achievements and characteristics. There will come a time when the special gifts of Negro Americans may mean massive representation in politics, or in the arts, even if today it tends to mean over-representation only in such areas as professional sport. But the special character of American group life—its acceptance of individual merit and capacity and its calculated arrangements for group character and pride—should not be destroyed by a demand for fixed quotas and their incorporation into legal and semi-legal arrangements.

After all, I believe, there is a failure to understand, on the part of black militants and their too-complaisant white allies, that there *is* an American society with a tremendous power to incorporate and make part of itself new groups, to their advantage and not to the advantage of the larger society, and that this is not a *white* society. I find nothing so sad as hearing universities denounced as white racist enclaves, corporations denounced as white racist enterprises, the government denounced as a white racist establishment. A hundred years ago, it could have been easily said these were all "English institutions," and yet Germans and Irish became part of them. Fifty years ago it could have been said these were all "Christian institutions," and yet Jews became part of them. Today, it is contended that they are white institutions—and yet this too is not true. They will become and remain white institutions only if Negro Americans insist on some total separateness as a nation, only if they decide that the American pattern of group life cannot include them.

THE DECLINE OF THE WASP
Peter Schrag

This essay might better have been titled "The Rise and
Fall of the WASP" for here, in a few short pages,
Peter Schrag indicates the cultural hegemony of white
Anglo-Saxon Protestants which until recently held sway.
Never truly an ethnic group or a sociological minority
(in Louis Wirth's sense of the term), WASPs were to become both. The challenge came from the "Jews and
Negroes, Catholics and immigrants" of the left, right,
and center. Put bluntly, the Old Establishment has lost
its grip and is now clinging by its fingers to a world it
used to know—and rule.

For most of us who were born before World War II, America was a place
to be discovered; it was imperfect, perhaps—needed some reform, some
shaping up—but it did not need to be reinvented. It was all given, like
a genetic code, waiting to unfold. We all wanted to learn the style, the
proper accent, agreed on its validity, and while our interpretations and our
heroes varied, they were all cut from the same stock. Cowboys, pioneers,
athletes, entrepreneurs, men of letters: whatever we were offered we took
pretty much as our own. Whether we were small-town boys or the children
of urban immigrants, we shared an eagerness to become apprentices in the
great open democracy, were ready to join up, wanting only to be accepted
according to the terms that history and tradition had already established.
It never occurred to us to think otherwise.

What held that world together was not just a belief in some standard-
ized version of textbook Americanism, a catalogue of accepted values, but
a particular class of people and institutions that we identified with our

From *Harper's*, April 1970. Reprinted by permission of the author.

vision of the country. The people were white and Protestant; the institutions were English; American culture was WASP. We paid lip service to the melting pot, but if, for instance, one's grandmother asked, "Is it good for the Jews?" there wasn't any question in her mind about who was running the country. The critics, the novelists, the poets, the social theorists, the men who articulated and analyzed American ideas, who governed our institutions, who embodied what we were or hoped to be—nearly all of them were WASPs: Hemingway, Fitzgerald, Eliot, MacLeish, Sandburg, Lewis, Steinbeck, Dewey, Santayana, the Jameses, Beard, Parrington, Edmund Wilson, Van Wyck Brooks, Lester Frank Ward, Oliver Wendell Holmes; *The Saturday Evening Post* under George Horace Lorimer (with covers by Norman Rockwell); *The Atlantic* under Edward Weeks; *Harper's* in the days of Frederick Lewis Allen—to name only a few, and only from the twentieth century. Of all the major figures discussed by Henry Steele Commager in *The American Mind,* not one is a Jew, a Catholic, or a Negro. The American mind was the WASP mind.

We grew up with them; they surrounded us: they were the heroes of the history we studied and of the fantasy life we sought in those Monday-through-Friday radio serials. Even Hollywood, after all the creation of Jewish producers, never did much for pluralism. The stars were often ethnics—show business and sports constituting two major avenues for "outsiders" to make it into the mainstream—but their names and the roles they played rarely, if ever, acknowledged the existence of anything beyond that mainstream. The Hyman Kaplans were lovable jerks, immigrant Sambos; Rochester said, "Yassuh, Mr. Benny" (did we realize that Benny was a Jew?) and anything beginning with Mike, Pat, or Abie was set up for a laugh. Hollywood's Jews sold the American dream strictly in WASP terms.

They—the WASPs—never thought of themselves as anything but Americans, nor did it occur to others to label them as anything special until, about twenty-five years ago, their influence began to decline and they started to lose their cultural initiative and preeminence. There were, to be sure, regional distinctions, but whatever was "American" was WASP. Indeed, there was no "other"—was, that is, no domestic base of social commentary, no voice except their voice, for the discussion of "American" problems. The ethnics had their place and their strong loyalties, but insofar as that place was *American* it was defined by WASPs. We could distinguish Jews, Irishmen, Italians, Catholics, Poles, Negroes, Indians, Mexican-Americans, Japanese-Americans, but not WASPs. When WASPs were alienated it was because, as in the case of Henry Adams, the country had moved away from them, not because, as with the others, they regarded themselves as alien in heritage or tradition. (Southerners who had lost their war and their innocence were—in that respect—alien, ethnically WASPs but also in some sense unwilling immigrants; they were among the first to be out of place in their own country.) For most WASPs, their complaints were proprietary. That is, the old place was going down because the tenants weren't keeping it up properly. They were the landlords of our culture, and their values, with rare exceptions, were those that defined it: hard work, perseverance, self-reliance, puritanism, the missionary spirit, and the abstract rule of law.

They are, of course, still with us—in corporations and clubs, in foundations and universities, in government and the military, maintaining the interlocking directorates that make sociologists salivate and that give the Establishment its ugly name: the Power Structure, the Military-Industrial Complex; the rulers of America. But while they still hold power, they hold it with less assurance and with less legitimacy than at any time in history. They are hanging on, men living off their cultural capital, but rarely able or willing to create more. One can almost define their domains by locating the people and institutions that are chronically on the defensive: university presidents and trustees; the large foundations; the corporations; government; the military. They grew great as initiators and entrepreneurs. They invented the country, its culture and its values; they shaped the institutions and organizations. Then they drew the institutions around themselves, moved to the suburbs, and became org-men.

Who and what has replaced them, then, in the invention and production of our culture? Jews and Negroes, Catholics and immigrants. "Of the Americans who have come into notice during the past fifty years as poets, as novelists, as critics, as painters, as sculptors, and in the minor arts," wrote Henry Mencken in 1924, "less than half bear Anglo-Saxon names. . . . So in the sciences, so in the higher reaches of engineering and technology. . . ." Mencken's declaration was premature then; it is an understatement now: Mailer and Roth; Malamud and Bellow; Ellison and Baldwin; Edward Teller and Robert Oppenheimer and Wernher von Braun; Ralph Nader and Cesar Chavez; Noam Chomsky and Allen Ginsberg; John Rock and Jonas Salk; Paul Goodman and Herbert Marcuse; Bruno Bettelheim and Erik Erikson; Eldridge Cleaver and Malcolm X and Martin Luther King. The 1969 Pulitzer Prize for nonfiction was divided between a Jew from Brooklyn (Mailer) and a French immigrant (René Dubos); the Pulitzer Prize for fiction was awarded to an American Indian (Scott Momaday). The spokesmen of American literature and culture tend increasingly to represent the pluralistic residues of a melting pot that—for better or worse—never worked as well as some Americans had hoped. It is not simply that many of the major postwar journals of criticism—*Commentary, The New York Review of Books, The New American Review*—are edited by Jews, or that *Time* is edited by a Jewish refugee from Hitler, or that *The Saturday Evening Post* is dead, or that the function of radical muckraking was revitalized by *Ramparts,* originally established as a Catholic magazine, or that William Buckley, a Catholic, is the most articulate conservative in America; we do, after all, still have WASP writers and journals—*Foreign Affairs,* for example, and *The Atlantic* (not to mention

Life or *Reader's Digest*). It is, rather, that the style, ideas, traumas, perplexities, and passions tend to reflect other backgrounds and interests, and that the integrative capabilities of the WASP style have plunged into precipitous decline. The cultural issues of the 1960s enjoying the greatest cachet were not only ethnic and pluralistic, but also disintegrative—Alienation, the Identity Crisis, Black Power, Doing Your Own Thing, Dropping Out, the White Negro—and it seemed that any kind of material was acceptable as long as it was distinguishable from the old WASP mainstream: the life of the black ghetto, rock music and long hair and pot, Hindu gurus and Zen philosophers, Cuban guerrillas and Catholic radicals, black hustlers and Jewish anarchists. (The first thing I learned, coming from Brooklyn to Amherst in 1949 was that you didn't say "Bullshit" when you disagreed with someone, even your roommate. You said "Yes, but . . ." Now bullshit is back in style.) For the young, the chief villainy of the age is to be uptight, and who seems to them more uptight than WASPs, or the Jews and Irishmen trying to be like them? The 1960s was the decade of gaps—missile gaps, credibility gaps, generation gaps—when we became, in many respects, a nation of outsiders, a country in which the mainstream, however mythic, lost its compelling energy and its magnetic attraction. Now that the New Frontier and the Great Society have failed (not only as programs but as verbal rituals) so, at least for the moment, has the possibility of integration and, with it, traditional Americanism. The Average Man has become the Silent Majority. Both of these, of course, are merely convenient political fiction, but the change in labels points to a far deeper crisis of belief.

It is not that WASPs lack power and representation—or numbers—but that the once-unquestioned assumptions on which that power was based have begun to lose their hold. The foundation of WASP dominance in national politics and culture rested on the supposition that WASPdom was the true America, no subculture or special group. Now WASPs are beset by the need to enforce allegiance to something that their very place in power is supposed to take for granted. The problem is then compounded: government can become increasingly gray, trying to represent (or not to offend) "all the people," or it can begin to act as the voice of a distinctive group (the Forgotten Man, the Silent Majority)—in other words, to represent the majority as if it were a minority. (There is a third alternative, which I'll discuss later.) Nixon, characteristically, is trying to do both. When he was first elected in 1968 he brought to Washington a Cabinet of nonentities selected, it seemed, to illustrate the fix we were in: Winton Blount, Clifford Hardin, Maurice Stans, Walter Hickel, the old Agnew. (The exceptions—neither was then a regular Cabinet member—were Daniel Patrick Moynihan, an Irishman, and Henry Kissinger, a Central European immigrant.) They were men without visible personality, class, or place. Something of the same was true in Washington under Eisenhower, but then the Eisenhower atmosphere was tempered by an older lingering sense of independence, of region, a sense—finally—of principle. John Foster Dulles may have been a dangerous moralist, a stubborn Puritan, but he was not plastic. Nixon brought with him no John McCloy, no John Gardner, no Nelson Rockefeller (let alone a George C. Marshall or a Henry Stimson from an even earlier era of WASP assertion) nor does he carry Eisenhower's aura of small-town decency. (Eisenhower's men, like Nixon's, were or are institutional men, but many of them came from a tradition of "service" in which the social purposes of institutions tended to be more important than the problems of management.) We now have a government of "low profiles," gray men who represent no identifiable place, no region, no program. The security of the historic WASP position made regional roots and styles attractive; you weren't just an American but an American from a specific place, with a personality, with foibles and prejudices and attitudes. You didn't have to prove you were a WASP. But where is Nixon from? In what accent does he speak? What is his style, what are his convictions, even his hobbies? Nixon's campaign, his public conduct, and his tastes reflect not only the corporate-organization-man residue of WASPishness; they also symbolize the new insecurity of the mainstream culture.

There are advantages in all this: gray men are not crusaders; they don't speak about massive retaliation or final solutions (or, on the other hand, to be sure, the Great Society). But they are likely to regard any sort of noise as offensive and possibly dangerous. For a moment this afforded us some fun (Spiro Who?), but then Nixon, through the offices of Agnew and Mitchell, turned this quality of his Administration into a serious matter. The noise (of students, of Black Power, of protest) was, and is, scaring them. And for the first time in history—certainly for the first time since the 1920s—the majority has begun to act like a minority, like an ethnic group. The powerful are paranoid about the weak. (And needless to say, many ethnic groups are acting more like ethnic groups than they have at any time since the melting pot was pronounced a success.) This is what makes Agnew potentially more dangerous than Joe McCarthy. McCarthy's quarrels, finally, were those of an outsider attacking the Establishment, and the Establishment, which was still running the country, despite a bad case of nerves, ultimately put him down. But Agnew, Mitchell, and Nixon *are* the government, and among their most important targets are people who have no money, little organization, and access to nothing except the streets. The threat represented by Nixon's targets is not that of a foreign power, but that of a culture or cultures at odds with the mainstream. Inquisitions and witch-hunts generally mark the end, or the beginning of the end, of an age.

One of the major attributes of the WASP idiom was its self-confidence in its own Americanism. In following the ethic of the small town, in trying to make it, the WASP was operating in a system designed by his people, operated by his people, and responsive to his people. He wasn't trying to stand somebody else's ground or beat somebody else's game. But what is there for a nation that is urban (or suburban), in which the majority has (presumably) already made it, and where size and technology are rendering much of the system impersonal and unresponsive? It is no longer possible for anyone to control the country (or the world) as we once believed we could. With the exception of the balanced ticket (in politics or employment) we have no urban ethic. And so somewhere the self-confidence froze: what in the national spirit and imagery was expansive became conservative and restrictive, enterprise turned to management, ebullience to caution. Most of all, it tended to become dull. One of the most graphic illustrations of these differences in spirit is to be found in a book by John McPhee, *Levels of the Game,* an account of a tennis match between the Negro Arthur Ashe (then the highest-ranking American) and the WASP Clark Graebner (Shaker Heights suburban, churchy, the son of a dentist). Graebner speaks:

> I've never been a flashy stylist, like Arthur. I'm a fundamentalist. Arthur is a bachelor. I am married and a conservative. I'm interested in business, in the market, in children's clothes. It affects the way you play the game. He's not a steady player. He's a wristy slapper. Sometimes he doesn't even know where the ball is going. . . . I've never seen Arthur really discipline himself. He plays the game with the lackadaisical, haphazard mannerisms of a liberal. He's an underprivileged type who worked his way up. . . . There is something about him that is swashbuckling, loose. He plays the way he thinks. My style is playmaking—consistent, percentage tennis—and his style is shotmaking.

Ashe speaks:

> There is not much variety in Clark's game. It is steady, accurate, and conservative. He makes few errors. He plays stiff, compact Republican tennis.

Blacks, of course, can be disciplined grubbers as much as anyone else, and WASPs certainly never used to lack for swashbuckling types—soldiers, tycoons, ball players, frontiersmen, outlaws. Ashe, obviously, had to grub a lot harder than any white man to break into the big time, or to become a player at all, but he now manages his games with an aristocratic flair, not with what seems to be bourgeois lack of grace. But Graebner's description is otherwise right: he plays percentage tennis, Ashe takes chances. WASPs have learned to live by percentages "steady" (as Ashe says), "accurate, stiff, compact." A little uptight. In taking risks there is more to lose than to gain.

A lot of people, needless to say, have only barely made it, or haven't made it at all: prominent among them Negroes, Puerto Ricans, Poles, Irishmen, Italians, and a good number of underclass WASPs.

For them the decline in confidence tends to be traumatic. At the very moment that they are persuaded, or forced to believe, that the system will work for them—that they can make it, that their children must go to college, and all the rest—the signals from headquarters become confused and indistinct, and the rules seem to change. The children of the affluent march in the streets; long hair and at least the outward signals of sexual freedom are acceptable; hard work, stoicism, and perseverance aren't the ultimate values; individual initiative is not sufficient; the schools are "in trouble." The cultural colonies, forced by "modernization" (the super-market, urban renewal, automated equipment, Vatican II) to abandon their own styles of life—the hierarchical family, ward politics, closed unions, old neighborhoods, religion, language, food—become witnesses to behavior indicating that the (perhaps mythic) mainstream has begun to stagnate, that a lot of people no longer believe in it, or no longer believe in the old ways of getting there. Those on the move upward and outward have, in other words, no attractive place to go. Which is to say that the underclass tenants have discovered the neglect of the landlord.

Blacks are alienated because they have been kept out of the running. The white ethnics are frustrated because public attention, in defiance of the rhetoric of individual initiative and equality, has gone to blacks. (And because affluent WASPs, who had discriminated against all minorities, are trying to shift the burden of blame on the white underclass.) All of them, sensing the decline of WASP self-confidence and leadership, are left with choices among law and order (meaning militant normalcy, the old ethic), a return to their own cultural and political resources, or exotic combina-tions of the two. Following the lead, and to their eyes, success, of Black Power and Black Studies, a lot of minorities are trying to redevelop or to invent some exactly corresponding form of ethnic consciousness for them-selves. Most of the whites, however, are or in the end will be content to cheer on the cops. For the first time we have Polish vigilantes and a Hebrew posse (the Jewish Defense League). Blacks and honkies, talking like frontiersmen, are buying guns. If the old WASP ethic was the ethic of making it, it isn't surprising that the most militant contemporary expo-nents of that ethic—those inclined to take its legends of force and action literally—should be among people outside the system trying to break in.

A measure of the decline of the WASP style—perhaps the best measure we have—is the conquest of space. From Lindbergh to NASA (or from Jack Armstrong to Neil Armstrong), from the man who was still a conqueror trusting his own bets and his own skills, and therefore an underdog (no dry runs, no simulators, no mission control) to the org-man, programmed and computerized to the last $24-billion step and the last televised state-ment, betting his life on the competence and devotion of anonymous technicians: courageous yes, underdog never. A symbol of modern man, to be sure (what if the trains stop or the electricity fails, what if the water becomes polluted and poisonous?), but also a sign of the decline of the great old WASP virtues of self-reliance, initiative, irreverence. Lindbergh was free enterprise; Apollo was the work of a crowd. No ape could have flown the *Spirit of St. Louis* from New York to Paris. But we could have sent an ape to the moon. Or a robot. With a fake flag artificially distended for a dead place where there is no wind.

It was a WASP enterprise all the way. Is it possible to conceive of NASA sending a Negro, a Jew—or a woman? Muhammed Ali perhaps? Joe Namath? Norman Mailer (who wanted to go)? Can one conceive of an astronaut who does not fit absolutely congruously into the background, like Muzak in a supermarket or Spiro Agnew at a picnic of Legionnaires? Can one conceive of an astronaut's wife living in a Jewish section of the Bronx, or expressing an opinion critical of the Vietnam war, or not taking the children to church on Sunday, or having a career of her own? Was it not inevitable that one of the wives would get down on her knees in front of the television set to pray for a safe reentry? (One can imagine, in that setting, that Walter Cronkite *is* God.) Can one expect Richard Nixon not to say that the mission was the greatest thing since the Creation—or Billy Graham not to suggest, in reply, that perhaps the Resurrection was more important?

What made the moonshot interesting was its unbelievably bad taste, the taste of a cultural style that has lost its juice: suburbs and corporation offices, network television and the electric toothbrush, airline pilots and airline hostesses, "the whole mechanical consolidation of force," as Henry Adams wrote in the *Education,* "which ruthlessly stamped out the life of the class into which Adams was born, but created monopolies capable of controlling the new energies that America adored." Clearly space travel is technologically impossible except as a collective enterprise. But that is precisely the point. There is no role for the American (*i.e.* WASP) hero. Heroes presumably defy great odds alone. Gary Cooper has been replaced by Dustin Hoffman.

You ask yourself: Does the Establishment live? And the answer, clearly, is Yes. And yet it does not live in the style to which it was accustomed. Ever since the development of large bureaucracies and tenure systems there has been a tendency among outside intellectuals to overestimate the influence of elites. Not that corporations and institutions are going out of style (and they may, in case of a recession, regain some of their allure to the ambitious because they offer security), but that they have become so large, so stiff, and so beset by critics and complexity as to have lost considerable influence and all the romance of their former connection to success. (In Nixon's Republican party there are disparaging references to "The Eastern Establishment" which suggest that there might now be more than one—meaning, of course, that there is none at all.) Here is Francis T. P. Plimpton, the former Deputy U.S. Ambassador to the U.N., and one of the finest representatives of the old style of WASP culture in America. A gentleman, a man of parts. From *Who's Who in America* (1964-1965):

PLIMPTON, Francis T. P., diplomat; b. N.Y.C., N.Y., Dec. 7, 1900; s. George Arthur and Frances Taylor (Pearsons) P.; grad. Phillips Exeter Acad., 1917; A.B., magna cum laude, Amherst Coll., 1922: LL.B., Harvard University, 1925; LL.D., Colby College, 1960; married Pauline Ames, June 4, 1926; children— George Ames, Francis T. P., Jr., Oakes Ames, Sarah Gay. Admitted to bar, 1926; asso. with Root, Clark, Buckner & Ballantine. N.Y. City, 1925-32, in charge of Paris office, 1930-31; gen. solicitor, Reconstruction Finance Corp., Washington, D.C., 1932-33; partner Debevoise, Plimpton & McLean, N.Y.C., and predecessor firms 1933-61; dep. U.S. rep. to UN with rank ambassador E. and P., 1961—. Trustee U.S. Trust Co. of N.Y., Bowery Savs. Bank. Mem. U.S. delegation UN 15th-17th gen. assemblies. Trustee Tchrs. Ins. and Annuity Assn. (pres. trustees of stock), Coll. Retirement Equities Fund Corp., Amherst Coll., Barnard Coll. (vice chmn. bd.), Phillips Exeter Acad. (chmn. bd.), Union Theol. Sem., Athens Coll. (Greece), Lingnan U. (China), Dir. Philharmonic-Symphony Soc. N.Y., Roosevelt Hosp., Am.-Italy Soc., Fellow Am. Bar Found.; mem. Am., N.Y. State bar assns., Am. Law Inst., Bar Assn. City N.Y., Fgn. Policy Assn. . . .

The style is responsible, worldly involvement, directing institutions which nourished and arbitrated the culture; schools, universities, hospitals, the Council on Foreign Relations, the United Nations, the Church Peace Union, the missionary college in China, the Philharmonic. They were good institutions all, and many of them still do their good works, but with the possible exception of the federal courts, most of them are no longer sanctified as sources of social and cultural initiative, or even as mediators of conflict. There must have been a time when it was fun to be a university trustee.

The interest and action tend to come from others. George Plimpton, the son of Francis T. P. and probably the best-known WASP dealer in living culture, operates like a Paris salonist among Interesting People (Capote, Mailer, the Kennedys), writing brilliantly of his amateur involvement in The Real Stuff: fighting Archie Moore, playing quarterback for the Detroit Lions, pitching to the Yankees. (All sports are now saturated with ethnics.) It is a new role for the children of privilege. Is there a redeeming social utility in this work? Had Plimpton been Jewish he might have played *schlemiel* in a jockstrap, but as an upper-class WASP perhaps all he can do is represent the man whose dreams of command have turned to fantasy and whose greatest moments of glory come from watching other people do something well. A WASP playing honkie and nigger to find out how it feels to be upward bound. Does the aspiring WASP hero have a choice other than that between Apollo and *Paper Lion*?

The enervation of WASP culture may derive, more than anything, from a loss of place. The geographic and psychic worlds of the old mainstream become less distinct, but certain special neighborhoods, even if they are a generation away, survive as regions of the mind. The sense of place: Salem and Boston and Concord; Zenith and Winesburg; Yoknapatawpha County. It produced people with accents and fashions and biases—personalities—that they carried around as overtly as parasols and walking sticks. And because they knew who they were, they were quite willing to be eccentric and crazy. Now much of that material is gone. The black ghetto still remains as a real place, and so does the memory, if not the fact, of South Boston, of Brooklyn, of rural Mississippi and small-town Texas. But how much of a sense of place can grow in a bedroom suburb? What is the inner sense of Bronxville or Winnetka?

Because WASPs regarded themselves as the proprietors of history and the managers of destiny, there was a double displacement. While they were losing their regions they also began to lose their special role as the intrinsic Americans. When we discovered that the country and the world were no longer easily manageable—when we lost our innocence—it was the WASP role which was most affected. No matter how enthusiastically the ethnics waved the flag, they had always been partial outsiders. (Or perhaps better to say that they enjoyed dual citizenship.) In any case, their culture never depended on the assurance that they were running the show. They were tenants, had learned to survive as minorities. Obviously this produced problems, but it also created the tensions and identities of which modern literature (for example) is made. And these conditions of tenancy haven't yet been destroyed, may, indeed, have been strengthened through the mass media, which have nationalized isolated pockets of minority culture. Moreover, the media help create new minorities, new constituencies: students, for example, and women. What kids or blacks do in one town is now immediately communicated to others. Normalcy doesn't make good television, happenings do. The greatest effect of the melting pot, ironically, may not have been on immigrants and minorities, but on the mainstream.

The vacuum left by the old arbiters of the single standard—Establishment intellectuals, literary critics, English professors, museum directors, and all the rest—has produced a sort of cultural prison break. And not only by ethnics, by blacks and Indians, or by kids, but by a lot of others, including all sorts of WASPs themselves, who behave as if they have been waiting for this freedom all their lives. That a lot of what results from this new breakout is bad (and who, these days, can get away with saying that?), and that a lot will be transitory is hardly surprising. In a decade hundreds of thousands of "creative" people proclaimed themselves artists and poets, a million amateurs entered the culture biz, and God knows how many gurus, cultists, swamis, and T-group trainers hung out their shingles. No one could expect most of them to be good, or perhaps even to be serious. The wildcatters are working new territory and a lot are going to go bust. But for the moment they're thriving: the Stones and the Beatles, the groups and groupies, Polish Power and Black Studies, liberation schools and free universities, Norman Mailer's ego and Alexander Portnoy's mother, *The Graduate* and *Alice's Restaurant,* rebellious nuns and protesting priests, *Rat* and *Screw* and a hundred other underground papers, mixed-media shows and the Living Theater, bookstores of the occult, Tarot cards and freaks and hipsters, miniskirts and maxi coats, beads and joss sticks . . . all coexisting (barely, uneasily) with Lyndon Johnson's cornpone, Norman Vincent Peale's sermons, *I Love Lucy, Reader's Digest,* and Apollo 12. If the 1960s produced the beginning of any sort of renaissance, its characteristic instruments are the hand-held movie camera, the electric guitar, and the mimeograph machine, and if its efforts survive in nothing else, they will undoubtedly be remembered by the greatest outpouring of poster art in all history: peace doves and protest proclamations, the face of John Lennon, the pregnant Girl Scout over the motto "Be Prepared," and the pregnant black woman over the 1968 campaign slogan, "Nixon's The One." This is a counter culture—not high, not low or middle—but eclectic.

Until recently, when encouter groups, public therapy, and other psychic ceremonies became fashionable, reason had been more or less successfully keeping the dark night of the soul within the hidden closets of the mind. And WASPs were the most reasonable people of all. There were, obviously, advantages in that. Most people, I suspect, prefer dispassionate men for airplane pilots, surgeons, and commanders of nuclear-armed strategic bombers. Moreover, we may have survived the last twenty-five years precisely because we kept hot men from taking charge. But their style didn't do much for cultural enrichment. Now everything that a graying, nervous civilization kept jammed in those closets is coming out, whether it deserves to or not: sex in all forms, feelings, emotions, self-revelation, and forms of religion and ritual long condemned as superstition. "Honesty" replaces stoicism, and "love," however understood, overwhelms "work." It may well be that the kids are mining McLuhan's non-linear culture, that print and cool reason (and WASPs) will go under together. So far there is no way of knowing. What is certain is that the old media—books, newspapers, magazines—can no longer claim a monopoly on urgent cultural articulation, and that people who work the new territories have moved a long way from the old mainstream.

WASPs seem to have been crippled by their own sanity. They have become too levelheaded. Having confused their particular social order with the Immutability of Things (and with their own welfare), they have defaulted on their birthright of cussedness and irreverence. "This took courage, this took prudence, this took stoutheartedness," thinks Arthur Winner, Jr., James Gould Cozzens' hero, at the end of *By Love Possessed.* (He has just covered up—to his and Cozzens' satisfaction—some $200,000 worth of ledger-de-main perpetrated by one of his partners.) "In this life we cannot have everything for ourselves we might like to have. . . . Victory is not in reaching certainties or solving mysteries; victory is making do with uncertainties, in supporting mysteries." WASPs are willing to be "sick"—meaning that they can have their neuroses and their "reason" too— but never crazy. People who are willing to be crazy are almost invariably

Something Else. We no longer have, or seem to have the possibility of having, a figure like Bertrand Russell; we no longer even have an Everett Dirksen or a John L. Lewis.

WASP crimes these days are invariably dull—price fixing, antitrust capers, tax fraud—which is why we are so fascinated by Jimmy Hoffa, Roy Cohn, and the Mafia, why we need the Mafia, would have to invent it were we ever to suspect (as has Daniel Bell) that it doesn't really exist.

Beyond the formal institutions of business and government—the banks, the corporations, the State Department, and Congress—the unique provinces of WASP domination tend to be conservative (in the pure sense) and mediating. WASPs, I think, still regard themselves as the principal heirs of an estate in which the streams flowed clear, the air was clean, and the language pure. In the growing number of conservation societies, and in their almost exclusive dominion over libraries, dictionary-making, and (surprising as it may seem to those familiar with only the current "celebrities" in the profession) the teaching of English, they are trying to preserve some of that estate. But as "the environment" becomes a national issue, they are going to lose ground (you should pardon the pun) even as conservationists. There are going to be new men—technicians, population planners, engineers—who will move in on the Audubon Society, the Sierra Club, and the Izaak Walton League. The urban environment (John Lindsay vs. the New York legislature and Nelson Rockefeller) will demand parity with the environment of Daniel Boone and the bald eagle. On some issues urban and rural conservationists can make common cause, but on others (mass transit, housing, street cleaning, and garbage collection) they cannot.

But it would be unfortunate, perhaps even fatal, if the WASP's mediating function (through courts and other institutions) were also to be seriously eroded. It is inconceivable that America could ever be integrated on ethnic terms. Can one imagine this country as essentially Negro or Italian or Polish; or believe that the Republican party would nominate anyone named Spiro Agnopopoulos for Vice President; or visualize a trial in which the defendant is white and all the other participants—judge, jurors, lawyers, witnesses—are black? (It did, in fact, happen—in the preliminary proceedings against the Klansmen charged with plotting to murder Charles Evers, the black mayor of Fayette, Mississippi—but it may never happen again.) For if the minorities no longer accept the new style of the mainstream, they are even further from accepting each other. And somebody is going to have to help keep them from tearing each other apart: cops and kids, blacks and blue-collar whites, freaks and squares. Robert Kennedy, I think, recognized this need before he was killed (significantly by a crazy ethnic resenting Kennedy's sympathy with other ethnics). This is also what made the reelection of John Lindsay possible—and significant. The Jews and Negroes of New York may have distrusted him, but they trusted the Italians even less.

Even mediation, however, is no longer feasible on the old standard rigid WASP terms. For the first time, any sort of settlement among competing group interests is going to have to do more than pay lip service to minorities and to the pluralism of styles, beliefs, and cultures. The various commissions on violence and urban riots struggled with that problem but couldn't see beyond their assumptions to the logical conclusion. America is not on the verge of becoming two separate societies, one rich and white, the other poor and black. It is becoming, in all its dreams and anxieties, a nation of outsiders for whom no single style or ethic remains possible. The Constitutional prohibition against an established state religion was adopted because the Jeffersonians understood the destructive consequences of imposing a single set of cultural beliefs beyond the guarantees of freedom and due process.

The Establishment in America has, in part, lost its grip because it devoted itself too much to the management of its game, rather than to the necessary objective of making it possible for everyone to play his own. Minorities—cultural, ethnic, even minorities of one—are fighting over the wreckage of the WASP-abandoned cities and the WASP-forsaken culture. If the WASP Establishment is to act as umpire in this contest—and if we are not to become a police state—it will have to recognize the legitimacy of the contenders. One of the reasons that growing up in America is absurd and chaotic is that the current version of Americanization—what the school people call socializing children—has lost its appeal. We will now have to devise ways of recognizing and assessing the alternatives. The mainstream is running thin.

THREE

WHITE IMMIGRANTS
AND COLORED MINORITIES

In which the question of the similarities
of and differences between various American
ethnic and racial groups are considered.

THE NEGRO TODAY IS LIKE THE IMMIGRANT OF YESTERDAY
Irving Kristol

Irving Kristol feels that the newcomers to the city today
are repeating many aspects of the earlier story of migration and settlement. While acknowledging differences
between the plight of different minorities, Kristol feels
that these are too often exaggerated.
He is particularly concerned about the singular stress on
the "pathology" of Black Americans. Others agree with
the view but not its interpretations.

Let us suppose that, a century ago, Harvard had been host to a conference
on "the crisis in our cities." Let us suppose further that there were
sociologists in those times (sociologists such as we know them today, I
mean) and city planners and professors of social work and directors of
institutes of mental health and foundation executives—and that these as-
sembled scholars were asked to compose a description of the urban conditions in the United States. They would have been at no loss for words;
and their description would have gone something like this:

"Our cities are suffering a twofold crisis. First, there is the critical problem arising from the sheer pressure of numbers upon the amenities of
civilized life. Our air becomes ever more foul from the activities—both
at work and at play—of this large number; our water is shockingly polluted; our schools are overcrowded; our recreational facilities vandalized;
transportation itself, within the city, requires ever more heroic efforts.

"As if this were not enough, there is this second phenomenon to observe: our cities are being inundated *by people who are themselves problems.* These are immigrants—Irish, mainly—who are more often than not

illiterate and who are peculiarly unable to cope with the complexities of urban life. Their family life is disorderly; alcoholism is rampant among them; they have a fearfully high rate of crime and delinquency; not only do they live in slums, but they create slums wherever they live; they are bankrupting the resources of both public and private charities; they are converting our cities into vast cesspools of shame, horror and despair; they are—" And so on and so forth.

Any American of the nineteen-sixties could complete this bleak catalogue without overly exerting himself: it is the identical catalogue that any such conference today would come up with.

Now, it is important to realize that the scholars of a hundred years ago would have been telling the truth. Because we surmounted the particular crisis they endured, we would be inclined to think their concern bordered on hysteria, and that they unduly exaggerated the evils around them. They did nothing of the sort—I say "did" because, while this conference is hypothetical, the urban crisis was real enough at that time. We sneer gently at the agitation of years ago as representing a lack of imagination on the part of "The Brahmins"—the "old Americans"—and as testifying to a fear of historical change combined with an overrefined distaste for plebeian realities. We think of Henry James lamenting his "sense of dispossession"; and we do not think too flatteringly of him for doing so. But the question might be asked: are we not all Brahmins now?

I am not saying that the problems of American cities today are identical with, or even perfectly parallel with, those of yesteryear. Such identities do not exist in history; and all historical parallels are, in the nature of things, less than perfect. But I do think it important that we keep American urban history always in mind, lest we be carried away by a hysteria all our own.

Just how close we are to such a hysteria may be discovered by directing to ourselves the question: *how much of a disaster would it be if some of our major cities were to become preponderantly Negro?* I rather doubt we would answer this question candidly, but I am sure we would find the prospect disturbing—just as disturbing, probably, as the 19th-century "proper" Bostonian found the fact of his city becoming preponderantly Irish. *His* disaster happened to him; our disaster is still only imminent. I do believe that there is a sense in which we can properly speak of such transformations as "disasters"; but I also believe that it takes an impoverished historical imagination to see them *only* as disasters.

No one acquainted with the historical record can fairly doubt that American cities such as Boston and New York were much nicer places to live in before the immigrant mobs from Western Europe descended upon them in the eighteen-thirties and forties. Our conventional history textbooks—sensitive to the feelings (and to the political power) of yesterday's immigrants, who are by now very important people—tend to pass over this point in silence. They concentrate, instead, on the sufferings and privations of the immigrants, the ways in which they were discriminated against by older settlers, the fortitude they displayed in adverse circumstances, and the heroism of so many of them in coping with this adversity.

That is all true enough, and fair enough. Still, though it may not be advisable for our textbooks to make the point, it would be helpful to all of us if we could somehow do justice to the feelings of the older urban settlers. While chauvinism and xenophobia and gross self-interest certainly affected their attitudes, it is also true that their complaints and indignation had a quite objective basis. The fact is that American cities in the early decades of the 19th century seemed to have relatively few of those "urban problems" which were a traditional feature of the older cities of Europe, and which we now tend to regard as inherent in the urban experience itself.

There is no difficulty in explaining why this should have been the case. It had to do with no peculiar American virtues or unique American "genius." The reason there was no "urban crisis" is that the kinds of people who create an urban crisis simply didn't live in those cities. There was no urban "proletariat" to speak of—the comparatively high standard of living, the existence of free land, the constant creation of "new towns" out West, the general shortage of labor, the traditional mobility of the average American, and the religion of the "self-reliance" that most Americans subscribed to: all this made it impossible for the condition of the urban working classes in New York or Boston or Philadelphia to resemble that of the working classes of London or Manchester or Glasgow.

Even more important: there was no dispossessed *rural* proletariat whom the cities had to absorb—the rise of commerce and industry in this country, as contrasted with their rise in Europe, was not connected with the displacement of masses of people from country to city. American cities, in those early decades of the 19th century, grew larger, wealthier, and more populous; *but on the whole they performed no assimilatory role*—unlike the older cities of Europe, or the American cities subsequently.

All this changed, of course, with the arrival of European immigrants —heterogeneous in religion, language and customs, with few skills and no money—who settled in the larger seaboard cities. Instead of assimilating individually to American life, they challenged the city to assimilate them en masse. Despite the "melting pot" myth that later developed, it was a challenge that the American city did not meet with either grace or efficiency. The main reactions were resentment and anxiety and anger. Public order, public health, public education and public life were all thrown into disarray—and who can blame the older citizens for disliking these consequences? The transformation of the American city was a very real and very personal disaster for most of them. It destroyed their accustomed amenities, disrupted their neighborhoods, and quite ruthlessly interrupted their pursuit of happiness. Many of them began to move into what was then suburbia.

Well, that urban crisis was overcome, if ever so slowly. Not many people now think this would be a better country had those immigrants never come; their contributions to American life have been too notable, their indispensability for our American civilization is too obvious. And today it is the children and grandchildren of those immigrants who, faced with the mass movement of a rural Negro proletariat into "their" cities, echo all the old American laments and complaints.

They, too, have good reason—their discomfort and distress are not at all imaginary, despite what many liberal sociologists seem to think. (It is one thing to say abstractly that the great American city is, and has been for more than a century now, a social mechanism for the assimilation of "foreign" elements into American society. It is quite another thing for a concrete individual to try to live out a decent life in this "social mechanism.") But it does help to see this discomfort and this distress in historical perspective. And in such a perspective, the key question—often implicitly answered, less often explicitly asked—is: will we be able, decades from now, to look back upon our present "urban crisis" as but another, perhaps the final, stage in the "assimilation" of a new "immigrant" group, or is this crisis an unprecedented event that requires unprecedented and drastic social action?

★　★　★

That the American Negro is different from previous "immigrant" groups is clear enough. (I use quotation marks because there is patently something ironical in referring to Negroes as immigrants, when most of them are technically very old Americans indeed. Nevertheless, I think it is accurate enough, if one has in mind movement, not to America, but to the city; and I shall henceforth refer to them as immigrants, simply.) The color of his skin provokes all sorts of ancient racial fears and prejudices; and he lacks a point of "national origin" that could provide him with an authentic subculture of his own—one on which he could rely for psychological and economic assistance in face of the adversary posture of American civilization toward him.

The very special problems of the American Negro have been the subject of a literature so copious and so insistent that it is surely unnecessary to do more than refer to it. What I should like to emphasize, instead, is the danger we are in of *reducing* the Negro to his problematic qualities.

Underlying practically all of the controversies about the American city today there lies the question: can the Negro be expected to follow the path of previous immigrant groups or is his a special "pathological" case? This word "pathological" turns up with such surprising frequency in sociological literature today—on slums, on poverty, on education—that one might suspect a racist slur, were it not for the fact that those who use it most freely clearly intend to incite the authorities to corrective action by presenting the Negro's condition in the most dramatic terms.

Indeed, there has developed an entire rhetoric of liberal and melioristic slander that makes rational discussion of "the Negro problem" exceedingly difficult. Anyone who dares to suggest that the Negro population of the United States is not in an extreme psychiatric and sociological condition must be prepared for accusations of imperceptiveness, hardheartedness, and even soullessness. And when it is a Negro who occasionally demurs from this description, he runs the risk of being contemptuously dismissed as an "Uncle Tom."

From my own experience as a book publisher, I think I can say confidently that if a Negro writer today submits a manuscript in which dope addiction, brutality and bestiality feature prominently, he has an excellent chance of seeing it published, and of having it respectfully reviewed as a "candid" account of the way Negroes live now; whereas, if a Negro writer were to describe with compassion the trials and anxieties of a *middle-class* Negro family, no one would be interested in the slightest—middle-class families are all alike, and no one wants to read about Negroes who could just as well be white.

It is worth lingering on this last point for a moment—precisely because this unrelieved emphasis on the hellishness of the Negro condition reminds us, paradoxically, of the literature of previous immigrant groups. No one can doubt that, of all immigrants, it is the Jews who have been most successful in exploiting the possibilities that America offered them. Yet if one examines the literature that American Jews created about themselves, in the years 1880-1930, one discovers that it was a literature of heartbreak and misery. All during this period, we now know, the Jews were improving their condition and equipping themselves for full participation in American life.

There is not much trace of this process in the Jewish novels and stories of the period. This is not to be taken as a deficiency of the literature: it is never literature's job to tell the whole sociological truth—the literary imagination is "creative" exactly because it transcends mere social description and analysis. But it does serve to remind us that such a book as Claude Brown's "Manchild in the Promised Land," powerful and affecting as it is, cannot be taken to represent a definitive statement of the facts of Negro life in America—any more than one could take Michael Gold's "Jews Without Money," written in 1929, as a definitive statement of the facts of Jewish life in America.

Every year, tens of thousands of Negroes are moving out of poverty, and thousands more are moving into the middle class, both in terms of income and status of employment. Moreover, the rate of such movement is noticeably accelerating every year. More than half of Negro families in the North have incomes greater than $5,000 a year; and, over the nation, the proportion of Negroes living in dilapidated housing has been cut in half during the past decade.

These people exist and their numbers are increasing—just as the number of poor is decreasing: approximately one-half-million Negroes per year are moving above the poverty line. It is similarly worth noting that there are now something like a half-million Negroes in *each* of the following occupational categories: (a) professional and technical, (b) clerical, and (c) skilled workers and foremen. The total is about equal to that of Negro blue-collar factory operatives, and will soon be substantially larger.

But all this receives little attention from our writers and sociologists, both of whom are concerned with the more dramatic, and less innocently bourgeois, phenomena of Negro life. This is to be expected of the writers; it is less expected of sociologists, and the antibourgeois inclination of so much of current American sociology would itself seem to be an appropriate subject for sociological exploration.

The fact, incidentally, that so much of our indignant attention is centered on the northern urban Negro—who is, by any statistical yardstick, far better off than his Southern rural or smalltown counterpart—is in itself reassuring, since it follows a familiar historical pattern. In England and France, in the 19th century, the movement of the rural proletariat to the cities was accompanied by an increase in their standard of living, and a vast literature devoted to their urban miseries. These miseries were genuine enough—and it might even be conjectured that there is something qualitatively worse about urban poverty than about rural poverty, even where the latter is quantitatively greater. But, in the absence of a corresponding literature about the life of the rural poor, one can too easily see, in this process of urbanization, nothing but mass degradation, instead of a movement toward individual improvement—which, in retrospect, one can perceive it was. Obviously, it is absurd to expect the average Negro immigrant to the American city to have such a historical perspective on himself—he would have to cease being human and become some kind of sociological monster to contemplate his situation in this detached and impersonal way. But one does wish that those who are professionally concerned with our Negro urban problem, while not losing their capacity for indignation or their passion for reform, could avail themselves of such a longer view. After all, that presumably is what their professional training was for.

One could also wish that these same scholars were less convinced a priori of the uniqueness of the Negro's problem and more willing to think in terms of American precedents. A casual survey of the experiences of the first two generations of Irish immigration can be instructive in this respect. There is hardly a single item in the catalogue of Negro "disorganization," personal and social, that was not first applied—and that was not first applicable—to the Irish. "The Dangerous Classes of New York" was the title of a book published in 1872; it referred primarily to the Irish. Ten years later, Theodore Roosevelt confided to his diary that the average Irishman was "a low, venal, corrupt and unintelligent brute."

Alcoholism wreaked far greater havoc among the immigrant Irish than all drugs and stimulants do today among the Negroes. The "matrifocal family"—with the male head intermittently or permanently absent—was not at all uncommon among the Irish. Most of the Irish slums were far filthier than they need have been—and, if we are to believe contemporary reports, were not less filthy than the worst Negro slum today—because the inhabitants were unfamiliar with, and indifferent to, that individual and communal self-discipline which is indispensable to the preservation of civilized amenities in an urban setting. (We easily forget that our extensive public services rely, to a degree not usually recognized, upon rather sophisticated individual cooperation: for garbage to be collected efficiently, it must first be neatly deposited in garbage cans.)

It is one of the ironies of this matter that some of the very improvements in the life of the urban Negro are taken to represent the more problematic aspects of his condition. Everyone, for instance, is terribly concerned about the spread of Negro slums, both in the central city and, for some time now, in our suburbs. Why? The answer has been provided by Raymond Vernon in his excellent little book "The Myth and Reality of Our Urban Problems":

"As long as the slum was contained in a small congested mass within the old center of the city, most of the middle-income and upper-income inhabitants of the urban area could live out their lives without being acutely aware of its existence. As the slum dweller has taken to less dense living, however, the manifestations of his existence have not been quite so easy to suppress."

It will doubtless come as a surprise to most people that the density of habitation in the urban Negro slum today is less than it used to be—and is *considerably* less than it was for the Irish, Italian and Jewish immigrants when *they* lived in slums. Nevertheless, this is indisputably the case. (There is one slum area, on the Lower East Side of New York, where the Negro population is *one-third* of what the population was when this same area was a white slum 50 years ago.)

The population of the slum ghettos in our central cities is steadily decreasing, as the Negroes use their improved incomes to acquire more dwelling space per capita. To be sure, this means that poor Negroes now spread out more, that their slums and poor neighborhoods are more extensive, that they impinge far more powerfully upon the white neighborhoods than used to be the case. The whites, in turn, become highly agitated, as they discover that the problems of the slums and its inhabitants are now becoming their problems too, and can no longer be blandly ignored. Things *look* worse, and are *felt to be* worse, precisely because they have been getting better. This is one of the most banal of all sociological phenomena—but even sociology itself is being constantly caught off guard when confronted by it.

Another such ironic instance is the by-now famous "cycle of dependency." This ghost now insistently haunts all discussions of Negro poverty, and is invoked by all the authorities of the land, from the highest to the lowest. We are constantly being told, and are provided with figures to prove it, that not only do poor Negroes tend to beget poor Negroes—this tendency is true for whites as well, and does not astonish—but that poor Negroes on public welfare tend to beget poor Negroes who also end up as recipients of public welfare. Public policy, we are told, must—at whatever cost—aim at breaking this "vicious cycle" of dependency, if the Negro is ever to be truly integrated into American society and American life.

What we are *not* told, and what few seem even to realize, is that this "vicious cycle" is itself largely created by public policy—and that, indeed, so far from this being a vicious cycle, it is a function of humanitarianism. The point is really quite simple and, once made, exceedingly obvious: *the more money we spend on public welfare, and the easier we make it for people to qualify for public welfare, the more people we can expect to find on welfare.* Moreover, since—as we have noted—the children of poor people are always and everywhere more likely to end up as poor than the children of rich people (not *as* poor as their parents, of course, but poor by new and more elevated standards of poverty), it follows that dependency on welfare may easily flow from one generation to the next.

I have discovered, to my cost, that one must be very cautious in making this point, and I should therefore like to emphasize that I am *not* calling for a reduction in welfare expenditures, or for more restrictive qualifications for welfare. On the contrary, I believe that in most parts of the country such expenditures are niggardly and the qualifications idiotically rigid. I also believe that, everywhere in our affluent society, the poor and the distressed get too little money with too much fuss. We can afford to be more generous and—as a matter of both equity and morality—should be more generous. But what I do *not* think makes any sense is for us simultaneously to give more money to more poor people—and then to get terribly excited when they take it!

Does the "cycle of dependency" come down to much more than this? I doubt it. If anything like our present welfare system had been in existence 50 years ago, or 100 years ago, this same "cycle of dependency" would have been a striking feature of the Italian and Irish immigrant communities. In those days, however, the ideology of "self-reliance" was far more powerful than the ideology of "social welfare." In effect, American society coerced poor people into working at any kind of jobs that were available, at any rate of pay, in whatever disagreeable conditions. American society did this in easy conscience because Americans then thought it was "good" for poor people to experience the discipline of work, no matter how nasty.

We have changed our views on this matter, and I should say for the better. But if we hadn't changed our views, we would not be witnessing, or worrying about the "cycle of dependency." All of those women who now, as heads of households, get welfare and Aid-to-Dependent Children grants, would be forced to go into domestic labor—of which there is a great and growing shortage—or to take in washing and mending at home, as they used to. Our more humane welfare policies have liberated them from this necessity. It is this liberation that is the true meaning of the "cycle of dependency."

It is, to be sure, a frightening thought that generation after generation of a whole segment of society will be cut off from the mainstream of American life, by virtue of their status as welfare clients. But just how valid is such a projection? Robert Hunter, in his book, "Poverty," written in 1904, was already concerned about the "procreative" power of poverty, over the generations. His concern turned out to be baseless—will ours be less so?

After all, the basic premise of our welfare ideology is that people's moral fiber, their yearning for self-improvement and economic advancement, is not sapped by a more generous system of social welfare. We assume that most of those who receive welfare would prefer not to, and that once they are qualified to join the labor force, and once the labor force is ready to receive them, they will happily remove themselves from the welfare rolls. If this assumption is false, the very essence of the welfare state will be called into question. I happen to believe that the assumption is not false. And that is why I regard the vision of self-perpetuating and self-generating dependency as spectral rather than sociological.

★   ★   ★

To say that the problems of Negro migration into our large cities have relevant precedents in American history is not to assert that these immigrants do not face unique and peculiar dilemmas of their own. The fact that their "ethnicity" is racial rather than cultural, and the corollary fact that racial prejudice seems more deeply rooted than cultural prejudice, are certainly not to be minimized. It is not likely, for instance, that an increase in social acceptance—holding out the prospect of a substantial degree of intermarriage—will keep pace with an improvement in the Negro's social and economic status.

Even here, however, one cannot be sure: the whole world gets a little less bemused by skin color every day, as the new nations of Asia and Africa shed the colonial stigma; and many young people are militantly colorblind. In any case, unless one really believes in inherent and significant race differences, which I do not, then this question of social acceptance does not appear to be so terribly important for the visible future.

What is important is that, if anti-Negro prejudice is more powerful than, say, anti-Irish prejudice ever was, it is also true that public policy today is far, far more powerfully anti-discriminatory than it ever was.

The Negro migrants to the city start under a more onerous handicap than their predecessors—but they are receiving much more assistance than their predecessors. It is impossible to strike any kind of precise equation out of these opposed elements; but my own feeling is that they are not too far from balancing each other.

Another problem, one which is receiving a considerable amount of controversial attention, is that of the Negro family: specifically, the fact that the Negro father so often—at least relative to the white population—refuses to assume a permanent position as head of household, while the Negro mother so often (again relative to the white population) will have a large number of children by different and transient "husbands." The Moynihan Report dramatically focused on this issue. Anyone who has taken the trouble to read Daniel Moynihan's study of the United States Negro family cannot fail to be impressed by the truth of his claim that this unstable family situation makes it particularly difficult for the urban Negro both to cope with the disadvantages of his condition and to exploit the possibilities for advancement that do exist. Nevertheless, this problem, too, must be kept in perspective. Without going too deeply into a subject whose ramifications are endless—involving, as they do, the entire sociology of family life and the whole history of the Negro race—the following points can be made:

(1) We tend to compare the Negro urban family today with the white suburban family of today, rather than with the white urban family of yesteryear. Family life among the raw urban proletariat of 19th-century America, as in 19th-century Britain, showed many of the "pathological" features we now associate with the Negro family. Statistics on broken homes and illegitimacy are impossible to come by for the earlier times. But anyone familiar with the urban literature of that period cannot but be impressed by the commonplace phenomenon of Mrs. Jones or Mrs. O'Hara raising her brood while Mr. Jones and Mr. O'Hara have vanished from the scene.

(2) Having said this, one must also say that it does seem to be the case that the Negro family—not only in the United States, but in Canada, the West Indies and Latin America as well—is a less stable and less permanent unit than the "bourgeois" white family, as the latter has developed over the past four centuries. But it is not at all certain that this instability will persist indefinitely: there is no more passionately "bourgeois" a group than the middle-class Negro family in the United States today. And even if it should persist, to one degree or another, there is no reason I can see why American society cannot quite easily cope with it. Working mothers are not exactly a rare occurrence these days; and a comprehensive network of crèches and nursery schools should be able to provide the children with a decent home-away-from-home during the working hours.

(3) The evidence clearly suggests that the major problem of the Negro family is, quite simply, that there are too many children. Three-quarters

of the poor children in the United States today are in families of five or more children. If the average Negro family size were no larger than the white's, Negro per capita income would soar, a large section of the Negro proletariat would automatically move above the poverty line, and the question of the fatherless Negro family would become less significant.

A mother who has one or even two young dependents can manage, given a decent program of social assistance; the larger the family, the closer her situation approaches the impossible. The availability of birth-control information, and growing familiarity with birth-control techniques, should eventually work their effects. ("Eventually" is the operative word here: our experience with poor and highly reproductive people all over the world demonstrates that the deliberate control of family size is not something that can be achieved in a single generation.) In the more immediate future, a program of family allowances could certainly be helpful.

But all this is, if not beside the point, then all around the point. We can legitimately worry about the Negro's capacity to achieve full inclusion in American society only after our society has seriously tried to include him. And we have consistently shirked this task. The real tragedy of the American Negro today is not that he is poor, or black, but that he is a late-comer—he confronts a settled and highly organized society whose assimilatory powers have markedly declined over the past decades. The fact that the urban Negro is poor is less important than the fact that he is poor in an affluent society. This has both subjective and objective consequences.

Subjectively, it means that the poor urban Negro feels himself at odds with the entire society, in a way that was not true 50 years ago. He was then much worse off than he is today—but he was then also surrounded by lots of poor whites who were obviously not much better off. Misery loves company, as we know; and when misery has its company, it is far more tolerable. The lonely misery of the poor Negro in our society today takes a tremendous psychological toll, and it can so exacerbate his sensibilities as to hinder him from taking advantage of the modest opportunities to improve his status that do present themselves.

When Bayard Rustin writes—and I am quoting literally—that "to want a Cadillac is not un-American; to push a cart in the garment center is," he is writing absolute nonsense. Pushing a cart in the garment center is the traditional point of departure for pushing one's way into the garment industry—and, at the very least, it has always been thought to offer advantages over hanging around a street corner and perhaps "pushing" less innocent items than ladies' wear. But one can easily understand how, in view of the isolation of the Negro and his poverty, such nonsense can be persuasively demoralizing to those Negroes who listen.

But I myself suspect that fewer Negroes listen to "their" spokesmen (or should it be their "spokesmen"?) than is commonly assumed. We have convincing opinion-poll data to the effect that the overwhelming majority of American Negroes look to the future with confidence and hope, and that they feel they have been making real progress since the end of World War II. Even on specific, highly controversial issues there is a marked divergence between what Negro leaders say and what the average Negro thinks.

School integration, for instance, is one such issue. Despite the fact that this matter has been so urgently pressed by the civil-rights movements, all public-opinion polls show that a clear majority of Negroes—in the city's ghettos and out—think the quality of education in their neighborhood schools is a more important issue than the racial integration of these schools.

One could presumably infer from this that the mass of the Negroes are lagging in their "social consciousness." I think the more accurate inference is that the mass of Negroes are more rational in their thinking, and less affected by demagogic slogans, than their spokesmen. After all, it is a fact—and one which becomes more certain with every passing year—that, simply as a consequence of demographic forces now at work, the great majority of school children in our central cities are going to be Negro, and that there just aren't going to be enough white school children around to integrate. To be sure, one could bus white children in from the suburbs, or Negro children out to the suburbs. But this is political fantasy; and, interestingly enough, the majority of Negro parents who have been polled on this question are indifferent to or opposed to both kinds of busing.

In short, then, while the lonely poverty of the Negro in our affluent society renders his situation more difficult, it does not place him beyond the reach of intelligent social policy. There may be—there doubtless are— some unhappy few who, not seeing a Cadillac in their future, will decide this future is beyond redeeming. One cannot help but sympathize with their resentment and their resignation—it is unquestionably better to have a Cadillac than not to have one. But one is also glad they constitute, as they clearly do, a tiny minority. And even if and when they picket, or riot, they are still a tiny minority.

But will social policy achieve its potentialities? Here we run up against an "objective" consequence of the affluent society that is infinitely depressing. For this society is constantly in the process of so organizing itself as to exclude those who, like the Negroes, are poor, uneducated, and without previous ownership of a monopoly in any craft or trade. I am not referring to the process of "automation" which—as the report of the President's commission on this subject pointed out—has not yet had any observable effect on the labor market. I do mean the process of "pseudo-professionalization," which has received very little critical attention but whose consequences are notably pernicious.

We are all familiar with the way in which, over these past years, plumbers have become "sanitary engineers" and elevator operators have become "transportation specialists." One does not begrudge these men their fancy titles—we are all allowed our harmless vanities. Only it's not really so harmless as it seems. For this change in nomenclature is the superficial expression of a basic restrictionist attitude that is remorselessly permeating the whole society. The majority of the population that has secured its position in this society seems determined to make it ever more difficult for others to gain new entry.

A superb example is provided by the New York City civil service, which now establishes formal educational requirements for jobs—firemen, maintenance men, mechanics' helpers, etc.—where none were required 10 years ago. The jobs themselves have not changed; even the official descriptions of tasks, duties, and skills have not been revised; but the barriers have gone up.

This sort of thing is happening all over, with the enthusiastic cooperation of unions and management. There is no economic sense to it, or economic justification. Sociologically, of course, it is easy to understand—it is a reflection of that protectionist-guild state of mind that comes with a society's advancing years: everyone and everything seeks to "establish" itself. One would be content to go along with this trend, for the peace of mind it seems to provide—were it not for the fact that, in present circumstances, it threatens to *dis*establish, more or less permanently, a not insignificant proportion of America's Negroes.

Our social policy is *not* to provide suitable jobs for the Negroes; it is to provide suitable Negroes for the jobs. We have undertaken to reeducate, rehabilitate, retrain, readjust, recompense and re-just-about-everything-else the American Negro. Faced with the choice between modifying our occupational structure and transforming the people who seek a place in it, we have chosen the latter.

A nice instance of this choice can be found in the present activities of the U. S. Post Office. It is generally agreed that our postal service is in a sorry state, with only one mail delivery a day to noncommercial residences. To revert to a twice-daily delivery in our cities—one doesn't have to be even middle-aged to remember when this was the practice—would demand something like 60,000 new employees. These, in turn, would require little else than a minimum of literacy to be able to do the job—and if even this minimum were found to be an obstacle, a brief apprenticeship could be used to teach them what they needed to know.

This proposal had a short life in Washington. It was rejected in favor of (a) spending money trying to automate the postal system, and (b) spending money on the Job Corps, on elaborate programs of vocational training, and so on. Meanwhile, over the last three years the nonwhite proportion of postal workers has declined by a couple of percentage points.

This episode evoked no comment or protest from Negro spokesmen, civil rights leaders or warriors against poverty. They, too, seem more interested in ultimate Cadillacs than in actual mailbags. If asked about the matter, they would have doubtless dismissed it—as one did to me— with a few clipped words about the pointlessness of placing people in "dead-end" jobs. To which one can only reply that most people, even in our affluent society, end up in "dead-end" jobs of one kind or another; and that, for most *poor* people, "social mobility" is something that happens to their children, not to themselves. It goes without saying that it is preferable to have the unemployed or underemployed become engineers instead of postmen. But to try to enforce such a preference, as a matter of social policy, is utopian to the point of silliness.

Behind all this is a more fundamental choice: to put the emphasis on the elimination of relative *inequality* between Negro and white, rather than on the mere improvement, in absolute terms, of the Negro's condition. That the elimination of such relative inequality is a worthwhile goal, needs no saying; and all of those programs directed toward this end are highly meritorious. But the goal is a distant one, depending as it so largely does on equality of educational experience. And progress toward this goal is not likely to be at a steady and uniform pace; it will proceed through sharp and intermittent spurts, separated by long periods during which nothing seems to be happening. (The experience of the Japanese- Americans is illustrative of this point.)

In contrast, *poverty* can be abolished within the next decade—if we concentrate on the task. Right now, one of every four Negroes in their early twenties has not gone beyond the eighth grade; over half have not completed high school. These people exist; the formative years of their lives are passed beyond recall; it is cruel and demagogic to offer them an impossible "second chance"—while blithely refusing to offer them a realistic first chance.

We go around in a circle which, while one can hardly call it vicious, is nevertheless decidedly odd. We begin by prissily categorizing the Negroes as "pathological," we end by proclaiming vast and dubious programs for their instant conversion to middle-class values and upper-middle class status. Within this circle, the majority of our urban and suburban Negroes—these latter, incidentally, rapidly growing in numbers—are making substantial progress in their own way, at their own tempo, and largely by virtue of their own efforts.

In comparison with previous waves of immigration to the great cities, they are "making out" not badly at all. They need, and are entitled to, assistance from the white society that has made them—almost our oldest settlers—into new immigrants. But the first step toward effective help would seem to be a change in white attitudes. Until now, we have spent an enormous amount of energy and money trying to assimilate Negroes into "our" cities. Is it not time we tried helping them to assimilate into "their" cities?

THE UNITED STATES IS A "HERRENVOLK" DEMOCRACY
Pierre van den Berghe

Quite obviously Pierre van den Berghe disagrees with Irving Kristol's assessment of the comparison of white immigrants and Negroes. Van den Berghe is concerned with the persistence of Eurocentric models of the American experience, especially those that fail to recognize the different character of black and white history. One reason for this failure, he says, is that many scholars —and many others too—ignore the depth and consequences of institutionalized racism in the United States. Van den Berghe's historical summary differs in tone and temper from the glowing celebrations of "The American Experiment." To van den Berghe, in this country the word "democracy" must be qualified. He suggests the German adjective "Herrenvolk," for here, he feels, there is and has been freedom and opportunity for whites but not for those who are "colored"—whether black or brown or red.

Historiography might be defined as a new secularized way of creating a country's national mythology. This chapter takes issue with a long tradition of ethnocentrism and racism in the study of United States history. My central thesis is that, with the early development and later florescence of racism in the United States, this republic has been, since its birth and until World War II, a *Herrenvolk* democracy".[1]

The American "Revolution" was in fact a movement of political eman-

From *Race and Racism* by Pierre van den Berghe. Copyright © 1967 by John Wiley & Sons, Inc. Reprinted by permission of the publisher.

cipation by a section of the white settlers against control from England. That many of its leaders had been exposed to the French Enlightenment and used the rhetoric of freedom has led to the "official" interpretation of the American Revolution as a democratic, equalitarian, and libertarian movement similar to that of the French Revolution. Although a few idealists like John Quincy Adams interpreted the Declaration of Independence literally to apply to all people, and though a few more like Jefferson were perturbed by the contradiction between the libertarian rhetoric and the practice of slavery, to most whites of the time "people" meant "whites." The Constitution was a conservative document, a compact between the northern bourgeoisie and the southern slave-owning aristocracy. The economic life of the infant republic was so heavily dependent on slavery and the slave trade that most whites in the North as well as in the South regarded abolitionism as irresponsible and mischievous radicalism, much in the same way that their descendants later anathematized Socialism and Communism.

The Negro was defined as a subhuman, disfranchised part of the polity, as a special form of chattel, assessed at three fifths of a man by Constitutional compromise between South and North. The Indian groups with which the settlers clashed on the ever-expanding frontier were first treated as alien nations who could be either enemies or allies against competing European powers; later as a nuisance and an impediment to white expansion which had to be exterminated or pushed back; still later, as shiftless beggars and irresponsible wards of the republic; and only belatedly as fellow citizens. We may find ironic symbolism in the fact that the hallowed bell, which was to "Proclaim Liberty throughout all the land unto all the inhabitants thereof," cracked during its testing in 1752, was recast, cracked once more in 1835, and has remained in that condition ever since. Perhaps it was the bell's way of saying "I cannot tell a lie."

Myrdal's main theme is that one of the most important forces for change in American race relations is the guilt or at least discomfort of most members of the dominant group over the discrepancy between the "American Creed" and the treatment of the Negro.[2] Whatever the situation may have been during the last two or three decades, and notwithstanding some soul-searching by a few genteel slave-owning intellectuals like Jefferson and Madison in the late eighteenth and early nineteenth centuries, there is little evidence of an "American Dilemma" during most of the nineteenth century and the first third of the twentieth century. The democratic, egalitarian, and libertarian ideals were reconciled with slavery and genocide by restricting the definition of humanity to whites. Thus Chief Justice Roger Brooke Taney concluded in his famous Dred Scott decision of 1857 that he had no ground to assert that Negroes were not "beings of an inferior order . . . so far inferior that they had no rights which the white man was bound to respect." Abraham Lincoln who, contrary to all evidence, has been immortalized as the "Great Emancipator," was offended when he was accused of abolitionism and emphatically declared in 1858 during the Lincoln-Douglas debates:

"I am not, nor ever have been in favor of bringing about in any way the social and political equality of the white and black races; I am not, nor ever have been, in favor of making voters or jurors of Negros, nor qualifying them to hold office . . . I will say in addition to this that there is a physical difference between the white and black races which I believe will ever forbid the two races living together on terms of social and political equality. And in as much as they cannot so live, while they do remain together, there must be the position of superior and inferior, and I as much as any other man am in favor of having the superior position assigned to the white race."

Through a revealing twist of mind the Pennsylvania-born James Buchanan eloquently defended slavery on grounds of the people's freedom of self-determination and of the sacredness of private property and the Constitution. Even a man of Jefferson's intellectual stature made numerous racist statements concerning Negroes, though he wavered between racism and environmentalism.[3]

Apart from American Indians, and later a number of nonwhite immigrants such as Mexicans, Puerto Ricans, Chinese and Japanese, United States society has been divided into two major racial castes—Negroes and whites. Negroes have been defined traditionally as all persons with any black African ancestry who cannot "pass" as whites. In the *ante bellum* period the most common form of contact between whites and Negroes, indeed that which molded the entire pattern of race relations, took place on the slave plantations of the Black Belt of the South. Slavery was not restricted to the southern states; it existed on a smaller scale outside the South until the Civil War. (The 1860 Census lists 18 slaves in the northeastern region and 29 in the West. The Middle Atlantic states had slave holdings numbering in the tens of thousands until the 1820s when New York abolished slavery.) Similarly, not all Negroes were slaves, but the vast majority was. In 1860 on the eve of the Civil War, some 4.44 millions in a total population of 31.44 millions were Negroes, and only some 488,000 were free. Some 47 per cent of the free Negroes lived outside the South. Some of the slaves worked in cities as craftsmen or domestic servants; but the plantation based on the monoculture, first of tobacco in Virginia and later of cotton throughout the Black Belt, was the involuntary home of the mass of Negro Americans.

The slavery regime of the South, although much harsher than that of Brazil, showed a great many structural characteristics in common with it.[4] The plantation was largely an autonomous microcosm in which masters and slaves lived in close symbiosis. The slave owners constituted for the most part a feudal, land-owning aristocracy that dominated both the economic and the political life of the South, and indeed to a considerable extent of the nation. (Ten of the sixteen presidents elected before the Civil War were born in the South and as many were slave owners.) Slave

Table 1   United States Population by Race (1790–1960)

YEAR	PER CENT WHITE	PER CENT NEGRO	PER CENT OTHER NONWHITE	TOTAL IN THOUSANDS
1790	80.73	19.27	N.A.	3,929
1800	81.22	18.88	N.A.	5,308
1810	80.97	19.03	N.A.	7,240
1820	81.61	18.39	N.A.	9,638
1830	81.90	18.10	N.A.	12,866
1840	83.16	16.84	N.A.	17,069
1850	84.31	15.69	N.A.	23,192
1860	85.62	14.13	0.25	31,443
1870	87.11	12.66	0.23	38,558
1880	86.54	13.12	0.34	50,156
1890	87.53	11.90	0.57	62,948
1900	87.92	11.62	0.46	75,995
1910	88.86	10.69	0.45	91,972
1920	89.70	9.90	0.40	105,710
1930	89.82	9.69	0.49	122,775
1940	89.78	9.77	0.45	131,669
1950	89.55	9.98	0.47	150,697
1960	88.58	10.52	0.90*	179,323

* Includes Alaska and Hawaii.

owners comprised only a small minority of the white population; in 1860 there were around 350,000 slave owners, that is, about 1.3 per cent of the country's whites. The high and steadily rising value of slaves (by the end of the slavery era, a healthy young man was worth around $2000) limited slave ownership to the wealthy.

The small world of the plantation was rigidly stratified. An elaborate etiquette of race relations regulated interaction between master and slave. Slaves were expected to behave submissively through self-deprecatory gestures and speech, the frequent use of terms of respect toward whites, self-debasing clowning, and general fulfillment of their role expectation as incompetent and backward grown-up children. Conversely, masters addressed slaves familiarly by their first names, sometimes preceded by the term "uncle" or "aunt" with old family retainers. The owner's family lived in the big house in close physical proximity with the slave "elite" of house servants (chambermaids, cooks, butlers, coachmen, and nursemaids). Whites and Negroes grew up and played together as children; white infants were breast-fed and raised by black "mammies"; adolescent boys often had their first sexual experience with a slave and usually continued to have Negro concubines throughout their sexually active lifetimes. Miscegenation in the form of concubinage between white men and Negro women was accepted and was quite frequent, particularly between house slaves and their masters. Intermarriage was outlawed in most states and sexual relations between white women and Negro men were strongly condemned, but the other form of concubinage was an aspect of the general exploitation that was inherent in slavery.

The mass of unskilled field hands who were at the bottom of the slave hierarchy did not have as close contact with their owners as the house slaves. They lived in the slave barracks and rarely entered the big house; they interacted mostly with the plantation overseers who were often recruited from the poor white class of small farmers. Most of the few free Negroes who lived in the South were craftsmen or domestic servants, and their economic status, though higher than that of most field hands, was not substantially different from that of house slaves. Politically and legally, they were subjected to numerous disabilities in the North as well as the South.[5]

Stereotypes of whites concerning Negroes conformed to the paternalistic model of race relations. Negroes were regarded as immature, irresponsible, unintelligent, physically strong, happy-go-lucky, musically gifted, grown-up children. They were treated at best like a "stern but just" father would deal with backward children, at worst like special and expensive species of livestock whose labor was to be exploited for the greatest economic gain. Although, of course, slave owners were by nature neither more nor less depraved than any other human group, the United States variety of chattel slavery was one of the harshest in the world. Both church and state did little to interfere with the arbitrary power of the master over his human property, short of homicide. Not only did the slave have little legal recourse and standing but also the law buttressed slavery and successfully hindered emancipation by such devices as requiring the master to post a bond when manumitting a slave. Far from increasing over time, the proportion of free Negroes steadily declined from 18.8 per cent of the total Negro population in 1820 to 11.0 per cent in 1860. Most religious denominations sought Biblical rationalizations for the "peculiar institution" and did little to encourage baptism and marriage of slaves. Stable family life among slaves was impossible; even common law unions were frequently broken up by separate sale of partners; children above infancy were often separated from their mothers; and Negro women were constantly at the sexual disposal of their masters and their overseers. Even a century after emancipation the disruptive heritage of slavery in the most basic of all social groups, the nuclear family, is still profoundly felt and results in high illegitimacy rates and what Frazier called the "matrifocal" family.[6]

Not unexpectedly there were a number of slave revolts, of which the most notorious was the Nat Turner Rebellion of 1831. All of them, however, were quite limited and localized in scope and never came close to being successful, even temporarily. The constant fear by southern whites of a general slave uprising in the United States was certainly out of proportion with the actual danger, although the successful Haitian example lent some basis of plausibility to the fear. In fact, however, American slavery was such a shattering and dehumanizing institution that the Negroes were far too atomized and too geographically isolated on the various plantations for concerted collective action.

In addition, slavery brought about the virtually complete deculturation of Afro-Americans. Even though Negroes constituted up to 20 per cent of the population in the early days of the republic, they left hardly a trace of African culture on American soil. The wide variety of ethnic groups from which Afro-Americans came, the trauma of the "Middle Passage," the months spent in transit in slave depots, the dispersion and intermixture with whites and American-born slaves, and the destruction of family life were among the main factors contributive to the rapid cultural assimilation of Negroes with the dominant group. Along with this process of deculturation and acculturation, Negro slaves adopted to a large degree the values and attitudes of the whites to the extent of internalizing the feeling of their own social and "racial" inferiority. This "brain-washing" was so successful that many Negroes came to accept their status as inescapable and in some cases even developed feelings of affection and loyalty toward their masters.

Even today, a century after the abolition of slavery, self-deprecation, collective inferiority feelings, emulation of white standards and values, and compensatory phenomena are still evident among some Negro Americans.[7] To cite but one illustration, vast sums are spent by Negroes on hair-straighteners, skin-bleachers, and other cosmetics to make them resemble the dominant group more closely. (Consciously, the motivation is seldom that they want to look white, but rather that they have so profoundly internalized the esthetic biases of the dominant group that they identify straight hair and light skin with "beauty." Thus what is narcissism for the whites becomes ego-destroying self-hatred for Negroes.) There is little question that the ruthlessness and the thorough cultural disruption of United States slavery robbed a great many slaves of their self-respect, and hence that the social system of the ante-bellum South rested not only on coercion but also to a great measure on the sullen consent or acquiescence that accompanies conditions of extreme degradation.[8] Chattel slavery was, of course, dehumanizing not only for the Negroes but also for the whites.

A greater amount of blatantly racist and partisan literature has probably been written about the Civil War and the Reconstruction era than about any other period in American history.[9] Nevertheless, a number of the contentions made in accounts sympathetic to the Confederacy are closer to the truth than the quasi-official version which resulted from the *ex post facto* prettifying process of "liberal" historians. Although the long-standing conflict over the *extension* of slavery was important in bringing about the Civil War, the latter was obviously not fought to free the slaves. The Emancipation Proclamation of 1863 was largely a tactical maneuver issued in spite of Lincoln's considerable misgivings and a result of considerable pressure from Union Army generals who felt that it would deal the Confederacy a serious blow. Interestingly, it was carefully designed not to emancipate, in fact, a single slave; it excluded not only the slave-owning border states who fought on the Union side but also those districts of the Confederacy under Union Army occupation. Thus the Proclamation applied only to those areas in which it patently could not be enforced.

The Reconstruction period (which lasted until 1877 if one takes the "Compromise" and the withdrawal of Federal military occupation from the last of the former Confederate states as the criterion) was the closest the United States came to a social revolution. True enough, much of the program of the Radical Republicans was motivated more by a desire to smash the power of the old Bourbon aristocracy of the South than by pro-Negro considerations. The most that can be said is that Reconstruction was a complex mixture of vindictiveness, opportunism, and humanitarianism, and that racism was fully as prevalent in the North as in the South, even among "liberals." But the motivations of the Radicals are in the last analysis of little relevance; the fact is that the short-range accomplishments of Reconstruction were considerable. The economic basis of the old southern aristocracy was destroyed; slavery was abolished; a (segregated) school system was established to educate the freedmen; a number of freedmen were given land; within a few years Negroes were given the right to vote, both *de jure* and *de facto*, and were elected to important positions in state and federal governments. Between 1869 and 1876 two Negro senators and fourteen representatives were elected to the United States Congress, a record which has not since been equaled. By 1870 the Freedmen's Bureau had established more than 4200 schools with some 9300 teachers and 247,000 pupils.[10]

In short, Reconstruction shook the very foundations of the old South and for a period threw it in truly revolutionary turmoil. A century later we are painfully trying to recapture the gains achieved temporarily during Reconstruction, and we are still falling short of them in the political sphere. Why then did Reconstruction eventually fail, and how did the counter-revolution succeed in re-establishing white supremacy on a new basis in the South? Reconstruction failed largely because it was a "revolution from the top," directed by a segment of the dominant group (the Radical Republicans with the help of the Federal Army), with little active support and push from the masses of the freedmen. Obviously, this is not to imply that most Negroes did not welcome the demise of slavery and that significant numbers of individual Negroes did not play important, indeed distinguished, roles in the various Reconstruction regimes of the South. Du Bois has conclusively shown that a number of Negroes were not passive recipients of the blessings of Reconstruction but active participants in it. It remains true, however, that Negroes were "junior partners" in the revolution and that the mass of Negroes was too atomized, politically untrained, and unorganized to constitute an independent political force in the South.

The aftermath of the Civil War marked an abrupt change from a paternalistic to a competitive type of race relations, partly as a result of the disruption which followed the defeat of the Confederacy and partly as a consequence of wider and more profound transformations which affected the entire country. The old agrarian, feudal world of the slave plantation was destroyed, and with it the traditional master-servant model of race relations. Freed Negroes migrated in great numbers to the cities of the South, and to a lesser extent outside the South, and entered for the first time in direct competition on the labor market with the poor white farmers of the South and the urban white working class of both the North and the South.

Several trends, which began to manifest themselves on a large scale at the time of the Civil War or just before, made the second half of the nineteenth century the most dynamic period in United States history and exacerbated racial competition. The two years preceding the mid-century marked the beginning of two momentous events and the end of a third one. The California gold rush was the final phase of the territorial expansion of the United States by a process of land encroachment and frontier wars between white settlers and a number of small Indian groups. It took several more decades to beat the last remnants of the indigenous population into total submission and to reduce the last Indian lands to the status of human zoos for the amusement of tourists and the delight of anthropologists. However, by 1850 the Pacific Ocean had become the western frontier of the United States. The war of conquest against Mexico marked the beginning of the United States as the great imperialist power in the Western Hemisphere and almost gave the United States its present continental frontiers. Finally, the Irish potato famine triggered off the mass immigration of Europeans in response to the rising demand for industrial labor. Through European immigration the nonwhite population was gradually reduced to 10 per cent of the total.

The immediate pre-Civil War era also marked the massive development of heavy iron and steel industry, and of railway transportation, and the early phase in the growth of monopoly capitalism. The United States was in the process of becoming the first major non-European industrial power. Indeed, the Civil War was the first major conflict in the world in which warfare itself could be described as largely industrialized. Rapid urbanization, the mushrooming of working class slums, high unemployment, massive internal migration, and all the disruptive forces and conflicts of early capitalism contributed to the complete change in patterns of race relations and to a steadily rising tide of racial, ethnic, and religious bigotry.

Ideologically, the last third of the nineteenth century was characterized by a syndrome of *laissez-faire* capitalism in the economic sphere, of jingoism and imperialism in foreign relations, and of racial and ethnic intolerance in the domestic social sphere. The writings of Theodore Roosevelt and of other American racists like Madison Grant and Charles Carrol epitomize this era which could be termed the Gold Age of Racism. Social Darwinism and economic liberalism were fused to rationalize the survival of the wealthiest in the industrial jungle and to give racism the accolade of Science.[11] Negroes were not the sole victims, of course. Anti-Oriental agitation was rampant on the West Coast; anti-Semitism and anti-Catholic pogroms swept the large cities of the East; the Know-Nothings rivaled in xenophobia and ethnocentrism with the Ku Klux Klan,[12] but Negroes, being the largest and most visible group, bore the brunt of the new competitive form of prejudice that was flourishing.

More specifically, as the old system of agrarian paternalism was breaking down, new forms of oppression and exploitation were being developed to keep the Negro "in his place," and to maintain white supremacy. A number of paternalistic remnants such as the ante-bellum racial etiquette still linger on in the rural Black Belt.[13] However, starting in 1865, a new phase of race relations began, and new white attitudes toward Negroes developed. The sterotype of the "happy singing slave" gave way to that of the "uppity," "insolent," "pushy" Negro who did not know his place, who was out to compete with the white workers and to rape white women. Anti-Negro prejudice became heavily laden with sexuality; the already complex mythology of Negro sexual potency and eroticism and of the purity of the white woman was developed further; phobia of miscegenation grew; and interracial concubinage between white men and Negro women became more clandestine, more commercialized, and probably less fertile as well as less common.[14]

In the economic sphere slavery gave way to share-cropping and debt peonage. After an initial exodus to the towns, many freedmen had to return to the land to find a basis of subsistence. The plantation owners broke up their lands into small plots to be cultivated by individual tenants. The slave barracks near the big house gave way to a pattern of dispersed wooden shacks. Money lending, or rather the loan of food, seeds, tools, and other necessities to be charged at arbitrary prices against the value of the tenant's share of the crop, became an economic substitute for slavery. Through perpetual indebtedness, the tenant farmer was nearly as securely tied to the land and to his landlord as he was under slavery.

More important yet were the political and social aspects of the counter-revolution that followed Reconstruction. Interestingly, this counter-revolution did not set in immediately after the withdrawal of Federal troops. As shown by C. Vann Woodward, it did not gain momentum until about 1890, because in the interim period the old aristocracy attempted to maintain its power in southern states by manipulating the Negro vote against the poor whites.[15] With the demise of these Bourbon regimes and the rise of *Herrenvolk* democracy in the South, a whole set of new mechanisms for the repression of Negroes was instituted. Among the first measures were a number of state laws aimed at nullifying the effect of the Fifteenth Amendment. Since Negroes could not be deprived of the right to vote on grounds of race, a whole battery of literacy and educational tests, poll taxes, "white primaries," and "grandfather clauses" was developed to achieve the same result. In a few years the overwhelming mass of Southern Negroes had lost its franchise rights and was not to begin regaining them until after World War II. Indeed, we have yet fully to regain the achievements of Reconstruction in Negro voting and representation.

Disfranchisement was, however, only one prong of the trident used to put the Negro back "in his place." The second one was "Jim Crow," as physical segregation by race became known in the South. Segregation was, of course, not entirely new in the South; but what there was of it before the Civil War was the ecological and geographical expression of the distribution of slaves (in the Black Belt and in the *upper* class districts of old southern towns) rather than a mechanism of white domination. In fact, such ante-bellum segregation as existed was more along class than along racial lines. The mass of Negroes had little contact with the mass of whites, but the house servants lived in close symbiosis with their masters. There was little racial segregation for its own sake. Indeed, the elaborate mechanisms of *social* distance which existed under slavery left status inequality unthreatened, hence made segregation "unnecessary."

In spite of hygienic and moral rationalizations for Jim Crow after Reconstruction, whites, and particularly southern whites, continued to accept intimate contact with Negroes, provided it clearly took place in a situation of unequal status (e.g., between employer and employee, or master and servant). However, the abolition of slavery, rapid urbanization and industrialization, great geographical mobility, and other dynamic factors undermined the old mechanisms of caste distance and the entire fabric of paternalistic subordination of the Negro. The diffuse, intimate, noncompetitive, complementary, asymmetrical, particularistic, holistic roles that characterized Negro-white interaction were replaced by segmental, impersonal, competitive, and potentially symmetrical and universalistic relationships. The white farmers and workers (both indigenous and immigrant) were suddenly threatened by equal status contact with the mass of Negroes. To forestall this possibility and to replace the increasingly inappropriate and obsolete mechanisms of social distance which had regulated the interaction of the Bourbon aristocracy with their slaves, racial segregation was increasingly resorted to as a second line of defense for maintaining white supremacy.

Segregation was no longer simply an ecological correlate of the economic and social class system, but a calculated, invidious device of racial subordination. The monoracial urban ghetto with its set of duplicatory institutions (churches, schools, theaters, shops, professional services) became a socially and economically self-contained microcosm and replaced the biracial plantation or the urban mansion with its backyard servant quarters. Structurally, roles and institutions, which had hitherto been characterized by racial *complementarity* (e.g., in the division of labor), became increasingly *duplicatory*. Next to the dominant structure of the "white world" a subordinate but parallel Negro *Lumpenstruktur* developed, complete with its make-believe pseudo-bourgeoisie, its powerless pseudo-elite, and its debutante balls.[16] Racial segregation, to which the Supreme Court soon gave its blessing in its famous "separate but equal" doctrine propounded in the Plessy versus Ferguson decision of 1896, became a consuming monomania of whites. In the South, it was enforced through a multitude of laws and customs providing for separate and unequal (or nonexistent for Negroes) facilities in virtually every sphere of life. It became a punishable offense against the laws or the mores for whites and Negroes to travel, eat, defecate, wait, be buried, make love, play, relax, and even speak together, except in the stereotyped context of master and servant interaction. In the North, segregation was to a greater extent extra-legal, and outside the monolithic ghettoes with their separate institutional structure, it took a less blatantly visible form, but it was only slightly less rigid.

The third prong of the counter-revolutionary trident was the development of new terrorist tactics to supplement the other mechanisms of racial subordination. Secret organizations such as the Ku Klux Klan resorted to intimidation, brutality, and murder as their major means for keeping Negroes and "nigger-lovers" in their place, but so did spontaneous groups of unorganized private citizens as well as the police, which, in the South, has traditionally played the role of uniformed vigilantes in the service of the dominant whites. The most notorious and extreme form of terrorism was lynching, but other tactics were also used such as beatings, cross-burnings, masked night rides through Negro districts, verbal threats, hate rallies, public humiliations, and random discharging of shotguns in windows.

Lynching is difficult to define, because at the limit it can become synonymous with homicide. Here we shall define it as illegal homicide committed by one or more persons who are not regarded by most members of the dominant group in the local community as criminals, and whose intention is not only to punish the victim (who may, in fact, be known to be innocent of any crime) but also to exercise social control when the legal machinery is regarded as inadequate. In this sense, lynching existed before the Civil War, but it was overwhelmingly an act of whites against whites in attempting to control frontier lawlessness, where legal machinery was either absent or ineffective. After the Civil War, lynching assumed a different character. It became a racial phenomenon:

most victims were Negroes and most criminals were whites; it was no longer a device to control banditry in an anarchistic frontier, but rather a terrorist technique to maintain white supremacy in settled communities with an established legal order.

Two different subtypes of racial lynching can be distinguished. The "mob" or "proletarian" lynching assumed the character of a highly ritualized mass orgy of sadism which included torture, burning, castration, and the carving of "souvenirs" from the victim's clothing or body. Often the victim was not guilty of any crime or guilty simply of a breach of etiquette. In contrast to "mob" lynching, "Bourbon" lynching was engaged in by a few pillars of the community who, having made some attempt to ascertain the guilt of the victim, killed him expeditiously, usually by shooting and without publicity. During the decade after the Civil War alone an estimated 3500 Negroes were lynched. With the advent of the twentieth century there was a fairly steady decline in the incidence of lynchings, but, contrary to frequent statements, lynchings have not disappeared, except through a bit of semantic prestidigitation. Recent murders of civil rights workers are curiously not referred to as lynchings, perhaps to salvage the propaganda myth that lynching belongs to the past.

World War I marked the first indications of new changes in race relations. As a response to demand for labor and industrial expansion in the North, Negro emigration from the South accelerated, thereby scattering the nonwhite minority more and more widely over the nation and correspondingly reducing the Negro percentage in the South. In 1910, 89 per cent of the Negroes lived in the South and 30 per cent of the Southern population were Negroes. By 1930 these percentages had dropped to 79 and 25 per cent (see Table 4.2). Negro migration was also a process of

Table 2   Negro Population of the United States (1900–1960)

YEAR	PERCENTAGE OF NEGROES LIVING IN SOUTH	NEGRO PERCENTAGE OF SOUTHERN POPULATION
1900	89.69	32.31
1910	89.04	29.77
1920	84.18	26.90
1930	78.73	24.73
1940	76.99	23.77
1950	67.98	21.66
1960	60.92	20.91

increasing urbanization in both the South and the non-South. In summary, the Negro population left the rural Black Belt to populate the widely dispersed urban ghettoes of large metropolitan centers where they displaced as unskilled workers the European immigrants. World War I also exposed hundreds of thousands of Negro soldiers to conditions outside the South and overseas, and "uppity" returning veterans aroused mounting hostility from whites after the war, as shown by a wave of race riots and a temporary rise in the number of lynchings.

By the 1930s a few judicial decisions began to nibble at the edifice of racial segregation, and both the Great Depression and the New Deal policies exercised a certain leveling effect between poor whites and poor Negroes. Migration outside the South continued, if only in search of non-discriminatory relief. However, it took World War II to unleash forces powerful enough to undermine the racial status quo. Negro migration to the large industrial centers of the North, the Great Lakes, and as far as the West Coast greatly accelerated during the war and continued thereafter. By 1960 only 61 per cent of Negroes were living in the South and only 21 per cent of the southern population were Negro (see Table 4.2). More servicemen than ever before fought and lived abroad, albeit in a Jim Crow army, and came in contact with societies in which racial bigotry did not exist. The strong incentive not to waste manpower motivated the establishment of Fair Employment Practices Commissions and opened up new occupational opportunities for Negroes. Racism, of course, was far from dead, as shown by the wartime internment of United States citizens of Japanese descent condoned by Franklin D. Roosevelt.

The major landmarks of the history of postwar desegregation, such as the 1948 integration of the Armed Forces, the 1954 Supreme Court decision on the integration of public schools, and the Montgomery bus boycott, are too well known to need reiterating here.[17] Suffice it to say that the amount of progress realized to date warrants neither the optimism nor the complacency which, until the last three or four years, was fashionable among "liberal" intellectuals and social scientists. The objective situation has improved, to be sure, but the change is impressive only by conservative standards.

Recent developments seem to highlight two points. First, with the "revolution of rising expectations" on the part of Negro Americans, the gap between reality and aspirations has increased in spite of progress; consequently, the level of racial conflict, of frustration, and of alienation has risen in the past few years. The present situation is probably more explosive than ever before. Second, the real progress which has been made in the past seven years is the result of mass militancy and of the adoption of unconventional methods of protest such as passive resistance and civil disobedience by the oppressed minorities, rather than of magnanimity and benevolence from the Federal government or the dominant group at large.

Yet, can one speak of a "Negro revolution"? The answer is clearly "no," or at least "not yet." All the major civil rights groups (N.A.A.C.P., Urban League, C.O.R.E., Student Non-Violent Coordinating Committee, Southern Christian Leadership Conference) are reform movements in the sense that, far from questioning the underlying values and premises of

American society, they seek legitimacy in the American Creed and Christian ethics and plead for a change of practices in line with the dominant group ideology.[18] These movements have so far done little more than call the bluff of nearly 200 years of democratic rhetoric in the face of actual exploitation and oppression. If anything, the very respectability of civil rights as a protest cause probably deflects the attention of many people from many more fundamental problems such as the creative use of leisure, automation, the distribution of social rewards, the oligarchic exercise of power, militarism, and the ownership and control of means of production.

Many well-meaning American "liberals" mistakingly regard racism as the underlying cause of most evils in their society, instead of viewing it as but a fairly superficial symptom of much more widespread and basic problems. (Thus racial discrimination in housing is almost impossible to abolish effectively under a system that allows unlimited individual ownership of real estate and private control of the housing market.) Many "liberals" see a panacea in "whitewashing" their black fellow countrymen; they conceive of the struggle for the abolition of racial discrimination as a process of "bourgeoisification" of America.

Broadly speaking, ideological and political developments in the United States can take, it seems to me, two directions. Indeed, the present civil rights conflict has simultaneously activated and exacerbated both of these tendencies. On the one hand, there can be a generalized political radicalization of American society along socialist or "new left" lines, with the clear realization that race is an epiphenomenon devoid of intrinsic significance and that present conflicts and problems transcend race. (The "Great Society" program seems a timid attempt to graft some aspects of new left ideology onto old-fashioned liberalism, but the radical left is still very much a voice in the wilderness.)

The other alternative, of course, is militant black separatism, such as cropped up in both religious and secular versions. For demographic if for no other reasons black separatism does not have much of a long-range future, but its potential for short-range chaos is impressive.

Pluralism and even separatism can be viable policy alternatives if a group meets certain conditions of relative size, geographical concentration, economic self-sufficiency, and cultural distinctiveness and autonomy. Beyond the specific stigma of skin pigmentation and its numerous social and psychological consequences, Negro Americans have virtually nothing more in common than they do with any other Americans; and stigmatization itself, of course, is far from being a Negro monopoly. Surely a stigma can never be the basis of a program; it can at best become a slogan. It is easy enough to understand how the folly of white segregation generates the counterfolly of black separatism, but the prospect is not very appealing. The United States is now in the ironic situation of seeing integration ideology change camps as the country painfully gropes toward a resolution of social conflicts. Let us hope that the integrationists are not going to be defined as the next generation of Uncle Toms.

NOTES

1. For a recent statement that is generally congruent with my own position see Eli Ginzberg and Alfred S. Eichner, *The Troublesome Presence*. See also Thomas F. Gossett, *Race, The History of an Idea in America*.
2. Gunnar Myrdal, *An American Dilemma*.
3. In an unpublished study of racial attitudes of American Presidents, I found that, with the exception of the two Adamses and Garfield, all presidents openly expressed racial prejudice in and out of office until the 1950s. Some like Jackson and Theodore Roosevelt were even virulent bigots, although most of them simply reflected majority attitudes. The only president to emerge as distinctly antiracist and fully "modern" in his outlook on race was John Quincy Adams.
4. For sociological and historical accounts of slavery see Kenneth M. Stampp, *The Peculiar Institution;* Frederick L. Olmsted, *The Slave States;* Stanley M. Elkins, *Slavery;* Ulrich B. Phillips, *Life and Labor in the Old South;* and John Hope Franklin, *From Slavery to Freedom*.
5. Leon F. Litwack documents the status of free Negroes outside the South in his book *North of Slavery*.
6. E. Franklin Frazier, *The Negro in the United States,* and *The Negro Family in the United States*.
7. In his polemical book *Black Bourgeoisie,* E. Franklin Frazier bitterly attacked these traits among the Negro middle class.
8. The Nazi concentration camps provide us with more recent examples of similar phenomena. European colonial regimes in Africa also present some similarities but in a much milder form, because in Africa the Europeans seldom succeeded in destroying indigenous cultures (except among the Hottentots in the Western Cape). See my article "Racialism and Assimilation in Africa and the Americas."
9. Notable exceptions are W. E. B. Du Bois' *Black Reconstruction,* and more recently C. Vann Woodward, *The Strange Career of Jim Crow*.
10. W. E. B. Du Bois, *op. cit.,* p. 648.
11. Thomas F. Gossett, *Race, The History of an Idea in America*.
12. For accounts of ethnic prejudice see Oscar Handlin, *Race and Nationality in American Life;* and Gustavus Myers, *History of Bigotry in the United States*.
13. Cf. John Dollard, *Caste and Class in a Southern Town;* Allison Davis, B. B. Gardner, and M. R. Gardner, *Deep South;* Bertram W. Doyle, *The Etiquette of Race Relations in the South;* and Charles S. Johnson, *Shadow of the Plantation*.
14. One of the best psychoanalytic interpretations of race relations in the South can be found in Lillian Smith, *Killers of the Dream*.
15. Cf. *The Strange Career of Jim Crow*.
16. Frazier's *Black Bourgeoisie* remains the classic statement of this phenomenon.
17. Among over a score of recent surveys and accounts of recent race relations

research and of the desegregation process, see Milton M. Gordon, *Assimilation in American Life;* Thomas F. Pettigrew, *A Profile of the Negro American;* Peter I. Rose, *They and We;* Charles E. Silberman, *Crisis in Black and White;* James W. Vander Zanden, *American Minority Relations;* and J. Milton Yinger, *A Minority Group in American Society.* The results of a large-scale and recent study of United States race relations are reported in Robin Williams, *Strangers Next Door.*

18. The recent evolution of the SNCC under the leadership of Stokely Carmichael represents a partial departure from the ideological premises of the dominant group.

COMPARING THE IMMIGRANT AND NEGRO EXPERIENCE
Kerner Commission

The evidence suggests that conditions of life in the racial ghetto are not the same as those of an earlier period. The difference, according to the National Advisory Committee on Civil Disorders (the Kerner Commission), has to do with the fact that for immigrants the ghetto was often a gateway while for blacks (and others) it is a trap from which they have had great difficulty escaping. The summary cited below gives ample credence to Tom Wicker's preface to the entire *Report,* a preface in which he refers to America as one "nation, divided."

Here we address a fundamental question that many white Americans are asking today: why has the Negro been unable to escape from poverty and the ghetto like the European immigrants?

The Maturing Economy

The changing nature of the American economy is one major reason. When the European immigrants were arriving in large numbers, America was becoming an urban-industrial society. To build its major cities and industries, America needed great pools of unskilled labor. The immigrants provided the labor, gained an economic foothold, and thereby enabled their children and grandchildren to move up to skilled, white collar, and professional employment.

Since World War II, especially, America's urban-industrial society has matured; unskilled labor is far less essential than before, and blue-collar jobs of all kinds are decreasing in number and importance as a source of new employment. The Negroes who migrated to the great urban centers lacked the skills essential to the new economy; and the schools of the ghetto have been unable to provide the education that can qualify them for decent jobs. The Negro migrant, unlike the immigrant, found little opportunity in the city; he had arrived too late, and the unskilled labor he had to offer was no longer needed.

The Disability of Race

Racial discrimination is undoubtedly the second major reason why the Negro has been unable to escape from poverty. The structure of discrimination has persistently narrowed his opportunities and restricted his prospects. Well before the high tide of immigration from overseas, Negroes were already relegated to the poorly paid, low status occupations. Had it not been for racial discrimination, the North might well have recruited Southern Negroes after the Civil War to provide the labor for building the burgeoning urban-industrial economy. Instead, Northern employers looked to Europe for their sources of unskilled labor. Upon the arrival of the immigrants, the Negroes were dislodged from the few urban occupations they had dominated. Not until World War II were Negroes generally hired for industrial jobs, and by that time the decline in the need for unskilled labor had already begun. European immigrants, too, suffered from discrimination, but never was it so pervasive as the prejudice against color in America, which has formed a bar to advancement, unlike any other.

Entry into the Political System

Political opportunities also played an important role in enabling the European immigrants to escape from poverty. The immigrants settled for the most part in rapidly growing cities that had powerful and expanding political machines, which gave them economic advantages in exchange for political support. The political machines were decentralized; and ward-level grievance machinery, as well as personal representation, enabled the immigrant to make his voice heard and his power felt. Since the local political organizations exercised considerable influence over public building in the cities, they provided employment in construction jobs for their immigrant voters. Ethnic groups often dominated one or more of the municipal services—police and fire protection, sanitation, and even public education.

By the time the Negroes arrived, the situation had altered dramatically. The great wave of public building had virtually come to an end; reform groups were beginning to attack the political machines; the machines were no longer so powerful or so well equipped to provide jobs and other favors.

Although the political machines retained their hold over the areas settled by Negroes, the scarcity of patronage jobs made them unwilling to share with the Negroes the political positions they had created in these neighborhoods. For example, Harlem was dominated by white politicians for many years after it had become a Negro ghetto; even today, New York's Lower East Side, which is now predominantly Puerto Rican, is strongly influenced by politicians of the older immigrant groups.

This pattern exists in many other American cities. Negroes are still underrepresented in city councils and in most city agencies.

Segregation played a role here too. The immigrants and their descendants felt threatened by the arrival of the Negro and prevented a Negro-immigrant coalition that might have saved the old political machines. Reform groups, nominally more liberal on the race issue, were often dominated by businessmen and middle-class city residents who usually opposed coalition with any low-income group, white or black.

Cultural Factors

Cultural factors also made it easier for the immigrants to escape from poverty. They came to America from much poorer societies, with a low standard of living, and they came at a time when job aspirations were low. When most jobs in the American economy were unskilled, they sensed little deprivation in being forced to take the dirty and poorly paid jobs. Moreover, their families were large, and many breadwinners, some of whom never married, contributed to the total family income. As a result, family units managed to live even from the lowest paid jobs and still put some money aside for savings or investment, for example, to purchase a house or tenement, or to open a store or factory. Since the immigrants spoke little English and had their own ethnic culture, they needed stores to supply them with ethnic foods and other services. Since their family structures were patriarchal, men found satisfactions in family life that helped compensate for the bad jobs they had to take and the hard work they had to endure.

Negroes came to the city under quite different circumstances. Generally relegated to jobs that others would not take, they were paid too little to be able to put money in savings for new enterprises. Since they spoke English, they had no need for their own stores; besides, the areas they occupied were already filled with stores. In addition, Negroes lacked the extended family characteristic of certain European groups—each household usually had only one or two breadwinners. Moreover, Negro men had fewer cultural incentives to work in a dirty job for the sake of the family. As a result of slavery and of long periods of male unemployment afterwards, the Negro family structure had become matriarchal; the man played a secondary and marginal role in his family. For many Negro men, then, there were few of the cultural and psychological rewards of family life. A marginal figure in the family, particularly when unemployed, Negro men were often rejected by their wives or often abandoned their homes because they felt themselves useless to their families.

Although most Negro men worked as hard as the immigrants to support their families, their rewards were less. The jobs did not pay enough to enable them to support their families, for prices and living standards had risen since the immigrants had come, and the entrepreneurial opportunities that had allowed some immigrants to become independent, even rich, had vanished. Above all, Negroes suffered from segregation, which denied them access to the good jobs and the right unions, and which deprived them of the opportunity to buy real estate or obtain business loans or move out of the ghetto and bring up their children in middle-class neighborhoods. Immigrants were able to leave their ghettos as soon as they had the money; segregation has denied Negroes the opportunity to live elsewhere.

The Vital Element of Time

Finally, nostalgia makes it easy to exaggerate the ease of escape of the white immigrants from the ghettos. When the immigrants were immersed in poverty, they too lived in slums, and these neighborhoods exhibited fearfully high rates of alcoholism, desertion, illegitimacy, and the other pathologies associated with poverty. Just as some Negro men desert their families when they are unemployed and their wives can get jobs, so did the men of other ethnic groups, even though time and affluence has clouded white memories of the past.

Today, whites tend to exaggerate how well and how quickly they escaped from poverty, and contrast their experience with poverty-stricken Negroes. The fact is, among many of the Southern and Eastern Europeans who came to America in the last great wave of immigration, those who came already urbanized were the first to escape from poverty. The others who came to America from rural backgrounds, as Negroes did, are only now, after three generations, in the final stages of escaping from poverty. Until the last 10 years or so, most of these were employed in blue-collar jobs, and only a small proportion of their children were able or willing to attend college. In other words, only the third, and in many cases, only the fourth generation has been able to achieve the kind of middle-class income and status that allows it to send its children to college. Because of favorable economic and political conditions, these ethnic groups were able to escape from lower-class status to working class and lower middle-class status, but it has taken them three generations.

Negroes have been concentrated in the city for only two generations, and they have been there under much less favorable conditions. Moreover, their escape from poverty has been blocked in part by the resistance of the European ethnic groups; they have been unable to enter some unions and to move into some neighborhoods outside the ghetto because descendants of the European immigrants who control these unions and neighborhoods have not yet abandoned them for middle-class occupations and areas.

Even so, some Negroes have escaped poverty, and they have done so in only two generations; their success is less visible than that of the immigrants in many cases, for residential segregation has forced them to remain in the ghetto. Still, the proportion of nonwhites employed in white-collar, technical, and professional jobs has risen from 10.2 percent in 1950 to 20.8 percent in 1966, and the proportion attending college has risen an equal amount. Indeed, the development of a small but steadily increasing Negro middle class while the greater part of the Negro population is stagnating economically is creating a growing gap between Negro haves and have-nots.

This gap, as well as the awareness of its existence by those left behind, undoubtedly adds to the feelings of desperation and anger which breed civil disorders. Low-income Negroes realize that segregation and lack of job opportunities have made it possible for only a small proportion of all Negroes to escape poverty and the summer disorders are at least in part a protest against being left behind and left out.

The immigrant who labored long hours at hard and often menial work had the hope of a better future, if not for himself then for his children. This was the promise of the "American dream"—the society offered to all a future that was open-ended; with hard work and perseverance, a man and his family could in time achieve not only material well-being but "position" and status.

For the Negro family in the urban ghetto, there is a different vision— the future seems to lead only to a dead-end.

What the American economy of the late 19th and early 20th century was able to do to help the European immigrants escape from poverty is now largely impossible. New methods of escape must be found for the majority of today's poor.

COLONIALISM: THE CASE OF THE MEXICAN AMERICANS
Joan W. Moore

While the debate continues over whether black Americans are a colonized minority, there is little disagreement on the status of Mexican Americans. After all, many were members of another society in a foreign land that the United States acquired after the Treaty of Guadalupe Hidalgo.

Here, Joan Moore distinguishes between three types of colonialism under which, she argues, Mexican Americans must function: "classic colonialism" in New Mexico, "conflict colonialism" in Texas, and California's "economic colonialism."

Of late a militant ideology has spread across the various regions to unify these "colonial subjects" under a single Chicano banner. This, too, is discussed in the pages that follow.

American social scientists should have realized long ago that American minorities are far from being passive objects of study. They are, on the contrary, quite capable of defining themselves. A clear demonstration of this rather embarrassing lag in conceptualization is the current reassessment of sociological thought. It is now plain that the concepts of "acculturation," of "assimilation," and similar paradigms are inappropriate for groups who entered American society not as volunteer immigrants but through some form of involuntary relationship.[1]

The change in thinking has not come because of changes within sociol-

From *Social Problems* **17**, 4 (Spring 1970), 463–472. Reprinted by permission of the Society for the Study of Social Problems and the author, Joan W. Moore.

ogy itself. Quite the contrary. It has come because the minorities have begun to reject certain academic concepts. The new conceptual structure is not given by any academic establishment but comes within a conceptual structure derived from the situation of the African countries. In the colonial situation, rather than either the conquest or the slave situation, the new generation of black intellectuals is finding parallels to their own reactions to American society.

This exploration of colonialism by minority intellectuals has met a varied reaction, to say the least, but there have been some interesting attempts to translate these new and socially meaningful categories into proper academic sociologese. Blauner's (1969) article in [*Social Problems*] is one of the more ambitious attempts to relate the concept of "colonialism" as developed by Kenneth Clark, Stokely Carmichael and Eldridge Cleaver to sociological analysis. In the process, one kind of blurring is obvious even if not explicit: that is, that "colonialism" was far from uniform in the 19th Century, even in Africa.[2] In addition, Blauner (1969) makes explicit the adaptations he feels are necessary before the concept of colonialism can be meaningfully applied to the American scene. Common to both American internal colonialism of the blacks and European imperial expansion, Blauner argues, were the involuntary nature of the relationship between the two groups, the transformation or destruction of indigenous values, and, finally, racism. But Blauner warns that the situations are really different: "the . . . culture . . . of the (American black) colonized . . . is less developed; it is also less autonomous. In addition, the colonized are a numerical minority, and furthermore, they are ghettoized more totally and are more dispersed than people under classic colonialism."

But such adaptations are not needed in order to apply the concept fruitfully to America's second largest minority—the Mexican Americans.[3] Here the colonial concept need not be analogized and, in fact, it describes and categorizes so accurately that one suspects that earlier "discovery" by sociologists of the Mexican Americans, particularly in New Mexico, might have discouraged uncritical application of the classic paradigms to all minorities. The initial Mexican contact with American society came by conquest, not by choice. Mexican American culture *was* well developed; it *was* autonomous; the colonized *were* a numerical majority. Further, they were—and are—less ghettoized and more dispersed than the American blacks. In fact, their patterns of residence (especially those existing at the turn of the century) are exactly those of "classic colonialism." And they were indigenous to the region and not "imported."[4]

In at least the one state of New Mexico, there was a situation of comparatively "pure" colonialism. Outside of New Mexico, the original conquest colonialism was overlaid, particularly in the 20th century, with a grossly manipulated voluntary immigration. But throughout the American Southwest where the approximately five million Mexican Americans are now concentrated, understanding the Mexican minority requires understanding both conquest colonialism and "voluntary" immigration. It also requires understanding the interaction between colonialism and voluntarism.

In this paper I shall discuss a "culture trait" that is attributed to Mexican Americans both by popular stereotype and by social scientists—that is, a comparatively low degree of formal voluntary organization and hence of organized participation in political life. This is the academic form of the popular question: "What's wrong with the Mexicans? Why can't they organize for political activity?" In fact, as commonly asked both by social scientist and popular stereotype, the question begs the question. There is a great deal of variation in three widely different culture areas in the Southwest. And these culture areas differ most importantly in the particular variety of colonialism to which they were subjected. In the "classically" colonial situation, New Mexico, there has been in fact a relatively high order of political participation, especially by comparison with Texas, which we shall term "conflict colonialism," and California, which we shall term "economic colonialism."[5]

New Mexico.—An area that is now northern New Mexico and parts of southern Colorado was the most successful of the original Spanish colonies. At the beginning of the war between the United States and Mexico, there were more than 50,000 settlers, scattered in villages and cities with a strong upper class as well as a peasantry. There were frontier versions of Spanish colonial institutions that had been developing since 1600. The conquest of New Mexico by the United States was nearly bloodless and thus allowed, as a consequence, an extraordinary continuity between the Mexican period and the United States period.[6] The area became a territory of the United States and statehood was granted in 1912.

Throughout these changes political participation can be followed among the elite and among the masses of people. It can be analyzed in both its traditional manifestations and in contemporary patterns. In all respects it differs greatly in both level and quality from political participation outside this area. The heritage of colonialism helps explain these differences.

On the elite level, Spanish or Mexican leadership remained largely intact through the conquest and was shared with Anglo leadership after the termination of military rule in 1851. The indigenous elite retained considerable strength both in the dominant Republican party and in the state legislature. They were strong enough to ensure a bilingual provision in the 1912 Constitution (the only provision in the region that guarantees Spanish speakers the right to vote and hold office). Sessions of the legislature were—by law—conducted in both languages. Again, this is an extraordinary feature in any part of the continental United States. Just as in many Asian nations controlled by the British in the 19th century, the elite suffered little—either economically or politically.

On the lower-class level, in the villages, there was comparatively little articulation of New Mexican villages with the developing urban centers. What there was, however, was usually channeled through a recognized local authority, a *patrón*. Like the class structure, the *patrón* and the network of relations that sustained him were a normal part of the established local social system and not an ad hoc or temporary recognition of an individual's power. Thus political participation on both the elite and the lower-class levels were outgrowths of the existing social system.

Political participation of the elite and the *patrón* system was clearly a colonial phenomenon. An intact society, rather than a structureless mass of individuals, was taken into a territory of the United States with almost no violence. This truly colonial situation involves a totally different process of relationship between subordinate and superordinate from either the voluntary or the forced immigration of the subordinate—that is, totally different from either the "typical" American immigrant on the eastern seaboard or the slave imported from Africa.

A final point remains to be made not about political participation but about proto-political organization in the past. The villages of New Mexico had strong internal organizations not only of the informal, kinship variety but of the formal variety. These were the *penitente* sects and also the co-operative associations, such as those controlling the use of water and the grazing of livestock.[7] That such organizations were mobilized by New Mexican villages is evidenced by the existence of terrorist groups operating against both Anglo and Spanish landowners. González (1967) mentions two: one functioning in the 1890's and one in the 1920's. Such groups could also act as local police forces.

Let us turn to the present. Political participation of the conventional variety is very high compared to that of Mexican Americans in other states of the Southwest. Presently there is a Spanish American in the United States Senate (Montoya, an "old" name), following the tradition of Dennis Chavez (another "old" name). The state legislature in 1967 was almost one-third Mexican American. (There were no Mexican American legislators in California and no more than six percent in the legislature of any other Southwest state.) This, of course, reflects the fact that it is only in very recent years that Mexican Americans have become a numerical minority in New Mexico, but it also reflects the fact that organized political participation has remained high.

Finally, New Mexico is the locus of the only mass movement among Mexican Americans—the *Alianza Federal de Mercedes,* headed by Reies Tijerina. In theme, the *Alianza,* which attracted tens of thousands of members, relates specifically to the colonial past, protesting the loss of land and its usurpation by Anglo interests (including, most insultingly, those of the United States Forest Service). It is this loss of land which has ultimately been responsible for the destruction of village (Spanish) culture and the large-scale migration to the cities.[8] In the light of the importance of the traditional village as a base for political mobilization, it is not really surprising that the *Alianza* should have appeared where it did. In content the movement continues local terrorism (haystack-burning) but has now extended beyond the local protest as its members have moved to the cities. Rather than being directed against specific Anglo or Spanish landgrabbers, it has lately been challenging the legality of the Treaty of Guadalupe Hidalgo. The broadening of the *Alianza's* base beyond specific local areas probably required the pooled discontent of those immigrants from many villages, many original land grants. It is an ironic feature of the *Alianza* that the generalization of its objectives and of its appeal should be possible only long after most of the alleged land-grabbing has been accomplished.

Texas.—Mexican Americans in Texas had a sharply contrasting historical experience. The Mexican government in Texas was replaced by a revolution of the American settlers. Violence between Anglo-American settlers and Mexican residents continued in south Texas for generations after the annexation of Texas by the United States and the consequent full-scale war. Violence continued in organized fashion well into the 20th Century with armed clashes involving the northern Mexican *guerilleros* and the U.S. Army.

This violence meant a total destruction of Mexican elite political participation by conquest, while such forces as the Texas Rangers were used to suppress Mexican American participation on the lower status or village levels. The ecology of settlement in south Texas remains somewhat reminiscent of that in northern New Mexico: there are many areas that are predominantly Mexican, and even some towns that are still controlled by Mexicans. But there is far more complete Anglo economic and political dominance on the local level. Perhaps most important, Anglo-Americans outnumbered Mexicans by five to one even before the American conquest. By contrast, Mexicans in New Mexico remained the numerical majority for more than 100 years after conquest.

Texas state politics reflect the past just as in New Mexico. Mexican Americans hold some slight representation in the U.S. Congress. There are two Mexican American Congressmen, one from San Antonio and one from Brownsville (at the mouth of the Rio Grande river), one of whom is a political conservative. A minor representation far below the numerical proportion of Mexican Americans is maintained in the Texas legislature.

It is on the local level that the continued suppression is most apparent. As long ago as 1965 Mexican Americans in the small town of Crystal City won political control in a municipal election that electrified all Mexican Americans in Texas and stirred national attention. But this victory was possible only with statewide help from Mexican American organizations and some powerful union groups. Shortly afterward (after some intimidation from the Texas Rangers) the town returned to Anglo control. Some other small towns (Del Rio, Kingsville, Alice) have recently had demonstrations in protest against local suppressions. Small and insignificant as they were, the demonstrations once again would not have been possible without outside support, primarily from San Antonio. (The most significant of these San Antonio groups have been aided by the Ford Foundation. The repercussions in Congress were considerable and may threaten the future of the Ford Foundation as well as the Mexican Americans in Texas.)

More general Mexican American political organizations in Texas have a history that is strikingly reminiscent of Negro political organization. (There is one continuous difference: whites participated in most Negro organizations at the outset. It is only very recently that Anglos have been involved with Mexicans in such a fashion. In the past, Mexicans were almost entirely on their own.) Political organization has been middle class, highly oriented toward traditional expressions of "Americanism," and accommodationist. In fact, the first Mexican American political association refused to call itself a political association for fear that it might be too provocative to the Anglo power structure; it was known as a "civic" organization when it was formed in Texas in the late 1920's. Even the name of this group (LULAC or the League of United Latin American Citizens) evokes an atmosphere of middle-class gentility. The second major group, the Ameircan G.I. Forum, was formed in an atmosphere of greater protest, after a Texas town had refused burial to a Mexican American soldier. In recent years, increasing politicization has been manifested by the formation of such a group as PASSO (Political Association of Spanish Speaking Organizations). But in Texas, throughout the modern period the very act of *ethnic* politics has been controversial, even among Mexican Americans.[9]

California.—The California transition between Mexican and American settlement falls midway between the Texas pattern of violence and the relatively smooth change in New Mexico. In northern California the discovery of gold in 1849 almost immediately swamped the sparse Mexican population in a flood of Anglo-American settlers. Prior to this time an orderly transition was in progress. Thus the effect was very much that of violence in Texas: the indigenous Mexican elite was almost totally excluded from political participation. A generation later when the opening of the railroads repeated this demographic discontinuity in southern California the Mexicans suffered the same effect. They again were almost totally excluded from political participation. The New Mexico pattern of social organization on a village level had almost no counterpart in California. Here the Mexican settlements and the economy were built around very large land holdings rather than around villages. This meant, in essence, that even the settlements that survived the American takeover relatively intact tended to lack internal social organization. Villages (as in the Bandini rancho which became the modern city of Riverside) were more likely to be clusters of ranch employees than an independent, internally coherent community.

In more recent times the peculiar organization of California politics has tended to work against Mexican American participation from the middle and upper status levels. California was quick to adopt the ideas of "direct democracy" of the Progressive era. These tend somewhat to work against ethnic minorities.[10] But this effect is accidental and can hardly be called "internal colonialism," coupled as it was with the anti-establishment ideals of the Progressive era. The concept of "colonialism," in fact, appears most useful with reference to the extreme manipulation of Mexican immigration in the 20th Century. Attracted to the United States by the hundreds of thousands in the 1920's, Mexicans and many of their U.S.-born children were deported ("repatriated") by welfare agencies during the Depression, most notably from California. (Texas had almost no welfare provisions; hence no repatriation.) The economic expansion in World War II required so much labor that Mexican immigration was supplemented by a contract labor arrangement. But, as in the Depression, "too many" were attracted and came to work in the United States without legal status. Again, in 1954, massive sweeps of deportations got rid of Mexicans by the hundreds of thousands in "Operation Wetback." New Mexico was largely spared both waves of deportation; Texas was involved primarily in Operation Wetback rather than in the welfare repatriations. California was deeply involved in both.

This economic manipulation of the nearly bottomless pool of Mexican labor has been quite conscious and enormously useful to the development of California extractive and agricultural enterprises. Only in recent years with increasing—and now overwhelming—proportions of native-born Mexican Americans in the population has the United States been "stuck" with the Mexicans. As one consequence, the naturalization rate of Mexican immigrants has been very low. After all, why relinquish even the partial protection of Mexican citizenship? Furthermore the treatment of Mexicans as economic commodities has greatly reduced both their motivation and their effectiveness as political participants. The motivations that sent Mexican Americans to the United States appear to have been similar to those that sent immigrants from Europe. But the conscious dehumanization of Mexicans in the service of the railroad and citrus industries in California and elsewhere meant an assymmetry in relationship between "host" and immigrant that is less apparent in the European patterns of immigration. Whatever resentment that might have found political voice in the past had no middle class organizational patterns. California was structurally unreceptive and attitudinally hostile.

Thus in California the degree of Mexican political participation remains low. The electoral consequences are even more glaringly below proportional representation than in Texas. There is only one national representative (Congressman Roybal from Los Angeles) and only one in the state legislature. Los Angeles County (with nearly a million Mexican Americans) has no Supervisor of Mexican descent and the city has no

Councilman of Mexican descent. Otherwise, the development of political associations has followed the Texas pattern, although later, with meaningful political organization a post-World War II phenomenon. The G.I. Forum has formed chapters in California. In addition, the Community Service Organization, oriented to local community political mobilization, and the Mexican American Political Association, oriented to statewide political targets, have repeated the themes of Texas' voluntary association on the level of the growing middle class.

How useful, then, is the concept of colonialism when it is applied to these three culture areas? We argue here that both the nature and extent of political participation in the state of New Mexico can be understood with reference to the "classical" colonial past. We noted that a continuity of elite participation in New Mexico from the period of Mexican rule to the period of American rule paved the way for a high level of conventional political participation. The fact that village social structure remained largely intact is in some measure responsible for the appearance of the only mass movement of Mexicans in the Southwest today— the *Alianza*. But even this movement is an outcome of colonialism; the expropriation of the land by large-scale developers and by federal conservation interests led ultimately to the destruction of the village economic base—and to the movement of the dispossessed into the cities. Once living in the cities in a much closer environment than that of the scattered small villages, they could "get together" and respond to the anti-colonialist protests of a charismatic leader.

Again following this idea, we might categorize the Texas experience as "conflict colonialism." This would reflect the violent discontinuity between the Mexican and the American periods of elite participation and the current struggle for the legitimation of ethnic politics on all levels. In this latter aspect, the "conflict colonialism" of Texas is reminiscent of black politics in the Deep South, although it comes from different origins.

To apply the colonial concept to Mexicans in California, we might usefully use the idea of "economic colonialism." The destruction of elite political strength by massive immigration and the comparative absence of local political organization meant a political vacuum for Mexican Americans. Extreme economic manipulation inhibited any attachment to the reality or the ideals of American society and indirectly allowed as much intimidation as was accomplished by the overt repression of such groups as the Texas Rangers.

To return to Blauner's use of the concept of "internal colonialism:" in the case of the Mexicans in the United States, a major segment of this group who live in New Mexico require no significant conceptual adaptation of the classic analyses of European overseas colonialism. Less adaptation is required in fact than in applying the concepts to such countries as Kenya, Burma, Algeria, and Indonesia. Not only was the relationship between the Mexican and the Anglo-American "involuntary," involving "racism" and the "transformation . . . of indigenous values," but the culture of the Spanish American was well developed, autonomous, a majority numerically, and contained a full social system with an upper and middle as well as lower class. The comparatively non-violent conquest was really almost a postscript to nearly a decade of violence between the United States and Mexico which began in Texas.

The Texas pattern, although markedly different, can still be fitted under a colonialist rubric, with a continuous thread of violence, suppression, and adaptations to both in recent political affairs.

The Mexican experience in California is much more complicated. Mexicans lost nearly all trace of participation in California politics. Hence, there was no political tradition of any kind, even the purely negative experience in Texas. Then, too, the relationship between imported labor and employer was "voluntary," at least on the immigrants' side. The relationships were much more assymmetrical than in the "classic colonial" case.

If any further proof of the applicability of the idea of "colonialism" were needed, we have the developing ideology of the new *chicano* militants themselves. Like the black ideologies, *chicanismo* emphasizes colonialism, but in a manner to transcend the enormous disparities in Mexican American experience. Thus one of the latest versions of the ideology reaches out to a time *before* even Spanish colonialism to describe the Southwestern United States as "Aztlán"—an Aztec term. "Aztlán" is a generality so sweeping that it can include all Mexican Americans. Mexican Americans are the products of layer upon layer of colonialism and the overlay of American influence is only the most recent. That the young ideologues or the "cultural nationalists" (as they call themselves) should utilize the symbols of the first of these colonists, the Aztecs (along with Emiliano Zapata, the most "Indian" of Mexican revolutionaries from the past), is unquestionably of great symbolic significance to the participants themselves. But perhaps of more sociological significance (and far more controversial among the participants) is the attempt to legitimate *chicano* culture. This culture comes from the habits, ideas, and speech of the most despised lower-class Mexican American as he has been forced to live in a quasi-legal ghetto culture in large Southwestern cities. These symbols are all indigenous to the United States and are neither Mexican, nor Spanish, nor even Aztec. But they *do* offer symbols to all Mexican Americans, after a widely varying experience with Americans in which, perhaps. the ideologues can agree only that it was "colonialist."

NOTES

1. Oddly enough it now appears that the nature of the introduction into American society matters even more than race, though the two interact. I think this statement can be defended empirically, notwithstanding the emergence of, for

example, Japanese-American *sansei* militancy, with its strong race consciousness (see Kitano, 1968).

2. For a good analysis of the variation, and of today's consequences, see the collection of papers in Kuper and Smith, 1969.

3. Mexican American intellectuals themselves have persistently analyzed the group in the conquest frame of reference. For a significant example, see Sánchez (1940).

4. "Indigenous" by comparison wilh the American blacks. Spanish America itself was a colonial system, in which Indians were exploited. See Olguín (1967), for an angry statement to this effect.

5. Of course, we are not arguing that colonialist domination—or for that matter the peculiar pattern of voluntary immigration—offers a full explanation of this complex population, or even of the three culture areas which are the focus of this paper. Mexican Americans and the history of the region are far too complexly interwoven to pretend that any analytic thread can unravel the full tapestry. For other theses, see the analyses developed in Grebler *et al.* (1970).

6. This account draws on González (1967); Lamar (1966); Holmes (1964); and Donnelly (1947). Paul Fisher prepared a valuable analytic abstract of all but the first of these sources while a research assistant. I have used his document extensively here.

7. González (1967:64) concludes that *moradas,* or *penitente* organizations, "were found in most, if not all, of the northern Spanish settlements during the last half of the 19th Century and the first part of the 20th."

8. González (1967:75) analyzes the *Alianza* as a "nativist" movement, and suggests that its source is partly in the fact that *"for the first time* many elements of Spanish-American culture are in danger of disappearing" (emphasis added).

9. This discussion draws on Guzmán (1967) and Cuéllar (forthcoming).

10. Fogelson (1967) gives a good picture of political practices which had the latent consequence of excluding Mexicans from Los Angeles politics—a fact of great importance given the very large concentrations of Mexican Americans in that city. Political impotence in Los Angeles has affected a very significant fraction of California's Mexican Americans. Harvey (1966) gives a broader picture of California politics.

REFERENCES

Blauner, Robert
1969 "Internal colonialism and ghetto revolt." Social Problems 16 (Spring, 1969): 393-408.

Cuéllar, Alfredo
forthcoming "Perspective on politics." In Joan W. Moore with Alfredo Cuéllar, Mexican Americans. Englewood Cliffs, N.J.: Prentice-Hall, Inc.

Donnelly, Thomas C.
1947 The Government of New Mexico. Albuquerque: The University of New Mexico Press.

Fogelson, Robert M.
1967 The Fragmented Metropolis: Los Angeles, 1850-1960. Cambridge, Mass.: Harvard University Press.

González, Nancie L.
1967 The Spanish Americans of New Mexico: A Distinctive Heritage. Advance Report 9. Los Angeles: University of California, Mexican American Study Project.

Grebler, Leo *et al.*
1970 The Mexican American People. New York: Free Press.

Guzmán, Ralph
1967 "Political socialization." Unpublished manuscript.

Harvey, Richard B.
1966 "California politics: Historical profile." In R. B. Dvorin and D. Misner (eds.), California Politics and Policies. Reading, Mass.: Addison-Wesley, Inc.

Holmes, Jack E.
1964 Party, Legislature and Governor in the Politics of New Mexico, 1911-1963. Ph.D. Dissertation, Chicago: University of Chicago.

Kitano, Harry H. L.
1968 The Japanese Americans. Englewood Cliffs, N.J.: Prentice-Hall, Inc.

Kuper, Leo and M. G. Smith (eds.)
1969 Pluralism in Africa. Berkeley and Los Angeles: University of California Press.

Lamar, Howard Roberts
1966 The Far Southwest, 1845-1912: A Territorial History. New Haven: Yale University Press.

Olguín, John Phillip
1967 "Where does the 'justified' resentment begin?" New Mexico Business offprint, July 1967.

Sánchez, George I.
1940 Forgotten People. Albuquerque: The University of New Mexico Press.

COLONIZED AND IMMIGRANT MINORITIES
Robert Blauner

Robert Blauner suggests that all non-whites (or "Third World" Americans) are victims of colonial exploitation. His essay, the introduction to a new book, *The Third World Within,* offers a sociological critique of what is viewed as the conventional wisdom as presented through the writings of Robert Park, Louis Wirth, Oscar Handlin, Nathan Glazer, and Milton Gordon. In addition to a strong indictment of the tendency to suggest that black Americans are simply the latest immigrants, Blauner argues that most sociologists have ignored or, at best, underplayed the plight of millions of other Americans including the Chicanos, Puerto Ricans, Indians, and Orientals.

Sociological perspectives on racial and ethnic relations have not sufficiently taken into account the distinctive, indeed the unique, experiences of the Third World groups. Models of ethnic process have rather mystified the situation, obscuring the qualitatively different nature of the encounter between people of color and Anglo-American society. The focus has been on assimilation. The careers of immigrants and their children and the adaptations of European ethnic communities have been the yardsticks by which the problems and progress of all ethnic peoples have been analyzed, measured, and evaluated. The assumptions of an inevitable "race relations cycle" ending in assimilation was advanced by Robert Park almost 50 years ago.[1] Park's model has been improved but the same

From *The Third World Within,* edited by Jack Forbes, Octavio Romano, Troy Duster, Isao Fujimoto, Robert Blauner. To be published by Wadsworth Publishing Company, Inc., Belmont, California 94002. All rights reserved.

assumption of a final absorption through "Americanization" is found in
the more recent writings of Oscar Handlin, Nathan Glazer, and Milton
Gordon.[2]

In addition to the immigrants, sociologists have concentrated on "The
American Negro." The blatantly unique dimensions of the Black experience have made problems for the prevailing theoretical models. Even
here attempts are made to force Afro-American realities into the ethnic
group mold. Migration from rural South to urban North is posed as an
analog of European migration. Blacks become the latest "new comers"
to the cities.[3]

As for other peoples of color, they have been largely ignored by social
scientists. In what was perhaps the first expression of Third World unity
on the Berkeley campus, representatives from the four major groups co-
signed letters to the Sociology faculty in 1968, protesting the failure to
treat, in our classes, the experiences of Native Americans, Asians, and
Chicanos. The Third World movement is a recognition that there are
other racial experiences that are unique in America, and that blacks—
central as they are to the nation's system of racial oppression—can also
be viewed as one part of a larger entity.

Of course every human group is unique, forged in its special mold
of history and circumstance. The uniqueness of human groups, a reality
that is inevitably violated by the sociological impulse to generalize and
classify, is particularly salient for ethnic peoples. For out of a distinctiveness of culture and history, ethnic and racial groups define their identities,
their sense of nationality, and their particular relation to the world. Yet
self-contradictory as the question may appear, are not the experiences of
some groups *more unique* than those of others? The stories of the various
immigrant nationalities in the United States contain very similar chapters—despite important differences in cultural background and old country condition, in the social and economic "welcome" received, and in
the character of collective response to the New World. The intensity of
poverty among the Irish was marked; Jews were unusual in their past
experience with quasi-urban occupations; the Scandinavians settled on
farms in the Midwest and thus avoided the slums of the cities. Yet for
all this and other variation, there were still common lines that justify a
socio-historical model of European immigration and assimilation.[4]

Such a common model of American experience is not possible for the
ethnic peoples of non-Western cultures. The parameters of the historical
experiences by which people of color became part of an Anglo-dominant
society are simply more complicated and diverse than in the case of the
European immigrants. Aside from the added element of race and racism
which provides a shared dimension to Third World realities, each of
these groups underwent distinctive experiences on the continent that
were cataclysmic, and which separate their histories *from one another*
as well as from whites. The Indians were the first Americans, only they

have an historic moral claim to the entire hemisphere. The Native Americans are unique in the 300-year war which they fought against white encroachment; only against them did expansion and racism assume policies of genocide and systematic removal. Mexican-Americans underwent some similar experiences, and perhaps this is why there is a special affinity between these two peoples. Like the Indians with whom they shared the land and mutually interpenetrated cultures, they were in the Southwest long before the Anglos. But the Chicano population is the only one which was severed from an ongoing modern nation, becoming subjects of the United States as a result of conquest and annexation. That no others besides blacks were introduced to American democracy through 250 years of apprenticeship in chattel slavery is obvious.[5] The Chinese received the honor of becoming the first people whose presence was limited by exclusion laws. Later other Asians joined in this distinction; the Japanese in addition became the only ethnic group to be declared an internal enemy and to be imprisoned in concentration camps.

But considering the diversity of the experiences that have shaped the unique situations of our racial groups, what justifies their inclusion in the same volume? Once again there is an insight in the Third World concept of the student movement. For the vicissitudes of American race relations and the position of people of color have to be viewed from an international as well as an internal perspective. The economic, social, and political subordination of Third World groups in America is a microcosm of the position of peoples of color in the world order of stratification. This is neither an accident nor the result of some essential racial genius. Racial domination in the U.S. is part of the same historical drama, through which white Western people expanded their culture and economic system, bringing their rule to virtually all of the world. The expansion of the West, particularly Europe's domination over nonwestern people of color, was the major theme in almost 500 years that followed the onset of "The Age of Discovery." The European conquest of Native American peoples, leading to the white settlement of the hemisphere, and the African slave trade, were the major historical events that ushered in the age of colonialism, and incidentally made possible modern industrial capitalism. Colonial subjugation and racial domination began much earlier and have lasted much longer in North America than in Asia and Africa, the continents usually thought of as colonial prototypes. Thus the Third World groups are or have been the colonial subjects of the United States; racial colonies within our national borders whose oppression can only be understood in terms of world-wide patterns of white European hegemony.

In this essay I use the concept of *colonialization* to approach the special situation of Third World groups and to contrast their experiences with those of the non-colonized immigrant minorities. But there are dangers in the introduction of a new catch-all category, such as "colonized minorities." Black, Red, Yellow, and Brown Americans are not all in the same bag. If they are indeed colonized peoples, colonization has taken different forms within individual group histories. Each group itself is strikingly heterogeneous, and the variables of time, place, and manner have affected the forms of colonialism, the character of racial domination, and the responses of each people. Furthermore, the bag of "colonized" invokes comparisons with the situation of Algerians, Kenyans, Indonesians, and other nations who suffered under white European rule. While this terminology is used advisedly, what is different as well as what is common to these disparate contexts most be closely attended. World colonialism was an incredibly diversified system; generalizations about its structure and dynamics do not come easily. Though there are many parallels in the cultural and political developments between colonialized nations and the "internally" colonized groups within America, the differences in land, economy, population composition, and power relations make it impossible to transport wholesale sociopolitical analyses or strategies of liberation from one context to another. The "colonial analogy" has gained great vogue recently among militant nationalists—partly because it is largely valid, partly because its rhetoric appears to aggressively condemn white America, past and present. Yet it may be that the comparison with English, French, and Dutch overseas rule lets our nation off too easily! For in many ways the special versions of colonialism practiced against Americans of color have been more pernicious in quality and more profound in their consequences than the modal European overseas variety. This point will be developed later after Third World and European immigrant groups are first compared.

The Colonial Labor Principle in the United States

At the point of entrance into Anglo-American society, the Third World people and the European immigrants did have some things in common— the overwhelming majority of both groups were poor, and they entered the system to work.[6] The question of how, where, and why newcomers worked in the United States is central, for the differences in the labor systems that introduced Third World and immigrant groups to America may be the fundamental cause of their diverging social realities.

The labor forces that built up the Western hemisphere were structured on the principle of race and color. As already suggested, the European conquest of the Native Americans and the introduction of plantation slavery were crucial beginning points toward the emergence of a world-wide colonial order. These "New World" events established the pattern for labor practices in the colonial regimes of Asia, Africa, and Oceania during the centuries that followed. The key equation was the association of free labor with people of white European stock and the association of unfree labor with nonwestern people of color, a correlation that did not develop all at once but took time to become a more or less fixed pattern.

North American colonists made several attempts to force Indians into dependent labor relationships, including slavery. But the situation and cultures of the native North American tribes, many of which were mobile hunters and warrior peoples, predisposed them to resist agricultural peonage and more importantly to fight directly the theft of their lands. The relative sparsity of Indian populations north of the Rio Grande limited their potential utility for colonial labor requirements. Thus Native American peoples were either massacred or pushed out of the areas of European settlement and enterprise. South of the Rio Grande, where the majority of Native Americans lived in more fixed agricultural societies, they were too numerous to be killed off or pushed aside—though drastic losses were incurred through disease and massacre.[7] In most of Spanish America, the white man wanted both the land and labor of the Indian. Agricultural peonage was established and entire communities were subjugated economically and politically. Either directly or indirectly the Indian worked for the white man.

In the Caribbean region (which may be considered to include the American South[8]), neither Indian nor white labor was available in sufficient supply to meet the demands of large-scale plantation agriculture. African slaves were imported to the West Indies, Brazil, and the colonies that were to become the United States to labor in those industries which promised and produced the greatest profit: sugar, coffee, and cotton. Whereas many lower class Britishers submitted to debt inservitude in the 1600's, by 1700 slavery had crystallized into a condition associated as natural and appropriate only to people of African descent. White men, even if from lowly origin and self-like pasts, were able to own land, property, and to sell their labor in the free market. Though there were always anomalous exceptions such as free and even slave-owning Negroes, people of color within the Americas had become essentially a class of unfree laborers. Afro-Americans were overwhelming bondsmen, Native Americans were serfs or peons in most of the continent.

Colonial conquest and control had been the cutting edge of Western capitalism in its expansion and penetration of the world. Yet capitalism and free labor as Western institutions were not developed for people of color but reserved for white people and white societies. In the colonies European powers also organized systems of work that were noncapitalist and unfree: slavery, serfdom, peonage, etc. Forced labor in a myriad of forms became the province for the colonized and "native" peoples. European whites managed these systems and dominated the segments of the labor force based on "free labor." This has been the general situation in the Western Hemisphere (including the U.S. region) for more than three out of four centuries of European settlement, as well as the pattern in the more "classical" colonial societies. Except that from the labor point of view, the colonial dynamic unfolded more totally within North America, for only here emerged a correlation between color and work status that was almost "perfect." In Asia and Africa as well as much of Central and South America, many if not most of the indigenous peoples remained formally free in their daily work, engaging in traditional subsistence economies rather than in the plantations, fields, and mines established by European capital. Though these economics came within the orbit of imperial control, they helped maintain communities and group life and thus countered the uprooting tendencies and the cultural and psychic penetration of colonialism. Because such "traditional" forms of social existence were viable and preferred, labor could only be moved into the arenas of Western enterprise through some form of coercion. Though the association of color and labor status was not perfect in the classical colonial regimes, the racial principle remained inviolate since white Europeans did not become slaves, coolies, or peons.

Emancipation in the United States was followed shortly by a rapid period of industrialization in the last third of the 19th century. These two events were related. The Civil War and its temporary resolution of sectional division greatly stimulated the economy. More significantly, they provided the opportunity to drastically transform the nation's racial labor principle. But the manpower needs in the new factories and mines of the East and Middle West were filled primarily through immigration from Europe rather than by the proletarianization of the freed men. American captains of industry *and* the native white proletariat preferred the employment of despised, unlettered European peasants to that of the emancipated Negro population of the South. Low as was the condition and income of the factory laborer, his status was that of a free worker. Afro-Americans, on the other hand, became share-croppers and tenant farmers, agricultural serfs little removed from formal slavery, due to Northern capital's encouragement of immigration and the resurgent Southern ruling class which blocked the political and economic democratization movements of Reconstruction.

The 19th century also saw the colonial pattern assert itself in the new Western states and territories. The Texan War of 1836 was followed by the full-scale imperialist conquest of 1846-1848. Anglo-Americans assumed economic as well as political dominance over the Mexican Southwest. As white colonists and speculators gained control (often illegally) over the land and livelihood of the independent Hispano farming and ranching villages, a new pool of dependent labor was produced to work the fields and build the railroads of the region.[9] Later, the United States' economic hegemony over a semi-colonial Mexico and the upheavals that followed the 1910 revolution brought additional mass migrations of Brown workers to the croplands of the region. The Mexicans and Mexican-Americans who literally created the rich agricultural industries of the Southwest were typically bound to contractors, owners, and officials in a status little above peonage.[10] Beginning in the 1850's shipments of Chinese workmen—who had sold themselves or had been forced into debt servitude—were imported to build railroads and to mine gold and other metals. Later other colonized Asian populations, Filipinos, and East Indians, were used as gang laborers for Western farm factories. Among the Third World groups that contributed to this labor stream, only the Japanese came from a nation which had successfully resisted Western domination. This may be one important reason why the Japanese entry into American life and much of the group's subsequent development bears some striking parallels in the European immigrant pattern. But the racial labor principle also confined this Asian people who were viewed as fit only for subservient field employment. When they began to buy land, set up businesses and enter occupations "reserved" for whites, the outcry led to immigration restriction and to exclusion acts.

A tenet central to Marxian theory is the view that work and systems of labor are crucial in shaping larger social forces and relations in society. The orthodox Marxist critique of capitalism, however, often obscures the significance of patterns of labor status. Since capitalism is a system of wage-slavery and the proletariat are "wage-slaves" by definition, varying degrees of freedom within industry and among the working-class have not been given much theoretical attention. Max Weber, on the other hand, while accepting most of Marx' analysis of capitalism, emphasized the difference between the free mobile proletariat and those forms of labor which were more bound to particular masters and work situations. He saw "formally free" labor as an essential condition for modern capitalism. Of course, freedom of labor is always a relative matter and formal freedoms are often limited by informal constraint and the absence of choice. For this reason, the labor situations of Third World and European newcomers to American capitalism cannot be seen as polar opposites. Many European groups entered as contract laborers,[11] and an ethnic stratification (as well as a racial one) prevailed in industry. Particular immigrant groups dominated certain industries and occupations: the Irish built the canal system that linked the East with the Great Lakes in the early 19th century; Italians were concentrated in roadbuilding and other construction; slaves and East Europeans made up a large segment of the labor force in steel and heavy metals; the garment trades for many years was a Jewish enclave. Yet this ethnic stratification had different consequences than the racial labor principle since the white immigrants worked within the wage system whereas the Third World groups tended to be clustered in pre-capitalist employment sectors.

The differences in labor placement between Third World and immigrant can be further broken down. Like European overseas colonialism, America has used African, Asian, Mexican and to a lesser degree Indian workers for the cheapest labor, concentrating people of color in the most unskilled jobs, the least advanced sectors of the economy, and the most industrially backward regions of the nation. In an historical sense, people of color provided much of the hard labor (and also technical skills) that built up the agricultural base and the mineral-transport-communication "infrastructure" necessary for industrialization and modernization, whereas the Europeans worked primarily within the industrialized, modern sectors. The initial position of European ethnic while low, was therefore strategic for movement up the economic and social pyramid. The placement of nonwhite groups however imposed barrier upon barrier on such mobility, freezing them for long periods of times in the least favorable segments of the economy.

1. European immigrants were located primarily in urban centers whereas the colonized minorities have done primarily agricultural labor in rural areas. In the United States, family farming and corporate agriculture have been primarily white industries. Some immigrants, notably Germans, Scandinavians, Italians, and Portuguese have prospered through farming. But with a few exceptions—17th century indentured servants, French, Canadians, Portugese, and "Oakies"—white and European ethnic groups have not been a significant element within the most exploited and low status sector of our industrial economy: agricultural labor.

2. Though European immigrants began usually as unskilled laborers, they worked within manufacturing enterprises or close to centers of industry. Therefore they had a foot in the most dynamic center of the economy and could naturally rise with time to semiskilled and skilled positions.[12] Except for a handful of industrial slaves and Free Negroes, Afro-Americans did not gain substantial entry into manufacturing industry until World War I, and the stereotype has long existed that Asians and Indians were not fit for factory work. For the most part then, Third World groups have been relegated instead to labor in preindustrial sectors of the nonagricultural economy. Thus Chinese and Mexicans were used extensively in mining and railroads, industries that were essential to the early development of a national capitalist economy, but which were primarily prerequisites of industrial development rather than industries with any dynamic future.[13]

3. The Europeans were also more fortunately placed regionally. The dynamic and modern centers of the nation have been the North East and the Middle West, the predominant areas of white immigration. The Third World groups were located away from these centers: Africans in the South, Mexicans in their own Southwest, Asians on the Pacific Coast, the Indians pushed relentlessly "across the frontier" toward the margins of the society. Thus Irish, Italians, and Jews went directly to the Northern cities and its unskilled labor market, whereas Afro-Americans had to take two extra "giant steps" before their large-scale arrival in the same place in the present century: the emancipation from slavery and migration from the underdeveloped semi-colonial Southern region. The result of colonized entry and labor placement is that the racial groups had to go

through major historical dislocations within this country before they could arrive at the point in the economy where the immigrants began!

4. To these "structural" factors must be added the fact of racial discrimination. The argument that Jews, Italians, and Irish also faced prejudice in hiring is at best specious. Herman Bloch's historical study of Afro-Americans in New York provides clear evidence that immigrant groups benefited directly from racism. When blacks began to consolidate in skilled and unskilled jobs that yielded relatively decent wages and some security, Germans, Irish, and Italians came along to usurp occupation after occupation, forcing blacks out and down into the least skilled, marginal reaches of the economy.[14] Bloch's material suggests that it was precisely the European immigrant who blocked the upward economic mobility of Northern black communities. Without this deadly combination of immigration and white racism, the Harlems and the South Chicagos might have become solid working class and middle class communities, with the economic and social resources to absorb and aid the coming masses of Southerners, much as European ethnic groups have been able to do for their newcomers.[15] The mobility of Asians, Mexicans and Indians has been contained by similar discrimination and expulsions from previously gained occupational bases.

Our look at the labor situation of the colonized and the immigrant minorities calls into question the popular sociological idea that there is no fundamental difference in condition and history between the nonwhite poor today and the ethnic poor of past generations. This dangerous myth is used today by the children of the immigrants to rationalize away racial oppression and to oppose the demands of Third World people for special group recognition and economic policies—thus the folk beliefs that all Americans "started at the bottom" and most have been able to "work themselves up through their own efforts." But the racial labor principle has meant in effect that "the bottom" has by no means been the same for all groups. In addition, the cultural experience of Third World and immigrant groups has diverged in America, a matter we take up in the next section.

Culture, Social Organization, and Political Consequences

The racial labor principle which opened the gap in immigrant and Third World group experiences brought in its train a number of social processes which served to widen the breach still further. Status in the labor market above all determined the quality of entrance into Anglo-American life. Because the European groups were responding to the labor demands of a free capitalist market, they were for the most part and in the main *voluntary* immigrants. The existence of industrial development in other societies with labor shortages—Australia, Brazil, Argentina, *etc.*, meant that many people could at least envision alternative destinations for their emigration. Though the Irish were colonized at home and poverty, potato famine, and other disasters made their exodus more of a flight than those of other Europeans, they still had some choice of where to flee.[16] Thus people of Irish descent are found today in the West Indies and Oceania as well as in other former British colonies. Germans and Italians moved in large numbers to South America; Eastern Europeans immigrated to Canada as well as to the United States.

For the European then, entering the American order involved choice and self-direction, both of which were denied Third World groups. Choice is important because it is a necessary condition for commitment. Voluntary immigration predisposed individual Europeans and entire ethnic groups to identify with America, to assimilate the host culture as a positive benefit, rather than as an alien and dominating value system demanding submission. The voluntary nature of their immigration was therefore fateful for the entire career of a white ethnic group in America.

Because the Europeans moved on their own, they had a degree of autonomy within the society that was denied those whose entry followed upon conquest, capture, or involuntary labor contracts. They expected to move freely within the society to the extent that they acquired the economic and cultural means. Though they faced great hardships and even prejudice and discrimination on a scale that must have been disillusioning, the Irish, Italians, Jews, and other groups had the advantage of European ancestry and white skins. When living in New York became too difficult, Jewish families moved on to Chicago. Irish trapped in Boston could get land and farm in the Midwest; Italians with hard luck in the East pushed on to the opposite coast. It is obvious that parallel alternatives were unavailable to the early generations of Afro-Americans, Asians, and Mexican-Americans because they were not part of the free labor force.

Labor status and the quality of entry had its most significant impact on the cultural dynamics of the minority groups. Every new group that entered America experienced cultural conflict, the degree of which varied according to the newcomers' distance from the Western European, Anglo-Saxon Protestant norm. But the divergent situations of colonization and immigration were fateful in determining the ability of minorities to maintain group integrity and autonomous community life in the face of WASP ethnocentrism and cultural hegemony.

Free labor status and voluntary immigration made it possible for European minorities to *regroup* their social relationships and cultural forms after a period of adjustment to the American scene. One feature of the modern labor relationship is the separation of the place of work from the place of residence or community. European ethnics were oppressed on the job, but in the urban ghettoes they had the insulation and freedom to carry on their old country cultures—to speak their language, establish their religion and build other institutions such as newspapers, welfare societies, and political organizations. In fact, because many ethnic groups were oppressed in Europe by such imperial powers as England, Tsarist Russia, and the Hapsburg Monarchy, the Irish, Poles, Jews, and other East Europeans actually had more autonomy for cultural and political development in the New World. Of course there were also pressures toward assimilation and the norm of "Anglo-conformity" has been a dynamic of domination central to American life.[17] With the passage of time, many if not most European ethnics have merged into the larger society and the distinctive Euro-American communities have taken on more and more characteristics of the dominant culture.

The cultural experience of Third World people in America was different. The labor systems through which people of color became Americans tended to destroy or weaken cultures and communal ties. Regrouping and new institutional forms developed, but in situations with extremely limited possibilities. The forced transformation of group life that is the essence of the colonial cultural dynamic took place most totally on the plantation. Slavery in the United States appears to have gone the farthest in eliminating African social and cultural forms; the plantation system also provided the most restricted context for the development of new modes of group integrity.

In New York City, Jews could reconstruct their East European family system, with its distinctive sex roles and interlocking sets of religious rituals and customs. Some of these patterns broke down or changed, in response primarily to economic conditions, but the change took time and occurred within a community of fellow ethnics which had considerable cultural autonomy. The family systems of West Africans, however, could not be reconstructed under plantation slavery since in this labor system the "community" of workers was subordinated to the imperatives of the production process. Africans of the same ethnic group could not gather together because their assignment to plantations and subsequent movements were controlled by slaveholders who were careful to minimize any basis for group solidarity. Even assimilation to American kinship forms was denied as an alternative, since masters freely broke up families when it suited their economic or other interests.[18] In the nonplantation context, the disruption of culture and suppression of the regrouping dynamic was less extreme. But systems of debt servitude and semi-free agricultural labor had similar, if less drastic, effects. The first generations of Chinese in the United States were recruited for gang labor, and they therefore entered without women and children. Had they been free immigrants, the group composition would have normalized in time with the arrival of wives and families. But as bonded laborers without the common law rights of immigrants, the Chinese were powerless to fight the exclusion acts of the late 19th century which left primarily male communities in America's Chinatowns for many decades. In such a skewed social structure, leading features of Chinese culture could not be reconstructed. A similar male-predominant group emerged among mainland Filipinos as a result of colonial labor requirement. The migrant work situation of Mexican-American farm laborers has also operated against stable community life and the building of new institutional forms in politics and education.

The colonial attack on culture cannot be reduced to such economic determinants as labor recruitment and special exploitation, however. The colonial situation differs from the class situation of capitalism precisely in the importance of culture as an instrument of domination.[19] Colonialism depends on conquest, control, and the penetration of new institutions and ways of thought. Culture and social organization are important as the vessels of a people's autonomy and integrity; when cultures are whole and vigorous, conquest, penetration and certain modes of controls are more readily resisted. Thus imperial regimes either consciously or unwittingly attempt to destroy the cultures of colonized people, or when more convenient exploit the social institutions and heritages of conquered nations for the purposes of more efficient *control and economic* profit.[20] Among America's Third World groups, Africans, Indians, and Mexicans are all conquered people whose cultures have been in part destroyed and in part exploited. One key function of racism, defined here as the assumption of the superiority of White Westerners and their cultures and the concomitant denial of the humanity of people of color, is that it "legitimates" cultural oppression in the colonial situation.

For this reason the racism that comes down on Third World people and the ethnic prejudice and persecution that immigrant groups experienced cannot be equated. Compare for example intolerance and discrimination in the sphere of religion. European Jews who followed their orthodox religion were mocked and scorned, but they never lost the freedom to worship in their own way. Bigotry certainly contributed to the Americanization of contemporary Judaism, but the Jewish religious transformation has been a slow and predominately voluntary adaptation to the group's social and economic mobility. In contrast, the U.S. policy against Native American religion in the 19th century was one of all-out attack; the goal was cultural genocide. Various tribal rituals and beliefs were legally proscribed and new religious movements were met by military force and physical extermination. The largest 20th century movement, the Native American Church, remains outlawed allegedly because of its peyote ceremony.[21]

In summary then, the relationship of Third World and immigrant groups to American society has been significantly different. This explains why their collective goals and orientations toward the larger society tend to vary in the present period. The white Europeans could become Americans more or less at their own pace and on their own terms because *their group realities were not systematically violated* in the course of immigration, adaptation, and integration. The cultural dynamic of the immigrants has moved from an initial stage of group consciousness and ethnic pluralism to a present strategy of individual mobility and assimilation. Ethnic identity is by no means dead among the European groups—for some it has asserted itself in a third generation reaction to "over-assimilation" or more recently as a response to Third World movements. But the ethnic groups have basically accepted the overall culture's rules of "making it" within the system, including the patterns of racial oppression that benefit them directly or indirectly.

From the moment of their entry into the Anglo-American system, the Third World peoples have been oppressed as groups and their group realities have been under continuing attack. Unfree and semi-free labor relations as well as the undermining of nonwestern cultures deprived the colonized of the autonomy to regroup their social forms according to their own needs and rhythms. For certain periods in the past, individual assimilation into the dominant society was seen as both a political and a personal solution to this dilemma. As an individual answer it has soured for many in face of the continuing power of racism at all levels of the society. And as a collective strategy assimilation is compromised by the recognition that only a small minority can improve their lot in this way and by the feeling that it implies a denial of group heritage and personal integrity.

Therefore the emphasis among Third World people has shifted strikingly to cultural pluralism and ethnic nationalism. The present-day building of social solidarity and culture is an attempt to complete the long historical project that colonial oppression made so critical and so problematic. It involves a de-emphasis on individual mobility and assimilation since these approaches cannot speak to the condition of the most economically oppressed nor fundamentally affect the realities of colonization. Such issues require group action and political struggle. Thus collective consciousness is growing among Third World people and their efforts to advance economically have a political character that challenges long-standing patterns of racial and cultural domination.

★ ★ ★

Despite the fact that our colonized minorities gain economic benefit from their restricted participation in the world's most industrialized nation, in the long view the "internal colonization" within the U.S. may be more profound and long-lasting. In traditional colonialism, the colonized "natives" have usually been the majority of the population, and their culture, while less prestigeful than the white Europeans', still pervaded the landscape. The Third World within the United States are individually and collectively outnumbered by whites, and Anglo-American cultural imperatives dominate the society, although this has been less true historically in the Southwest where the Mexican-American population has never been a true cultural minority.[22] The oppressed masses of

Asia, and Africa had the relative "advantage" of being colonized in their own land.[23] In the U.S., a more total cultural domination, the process of territorial uprooting, and the fact of numerical minority status have weakened the group integrity of the colonized and their possibilities for cultural and political self-determination.

Many critics of the Third World perspective seize on these differences to question the value of viewing America's racial dynamics within the colonial framework. But all they demonstrate is that colonialisms vary greatly in their structures, so that in our own land political power and group liberation are more problematic outcomes than in the overseas situation. The fact that we have no historical models for decolonization in the American context does not alter the objective realities. Decolonization is an insistent and irreversible project of the Third World groups; however its contents and forms are at present unclear and will be worked out only in the course of an extended period of political and social conflict.

NOTES

1. Robert Park, *Race and Culture* (Glencoe, Ill.: The Free Press, 1950).
2. See Oscar Handlin, *The Uprooted* (New York: Grosset and Dunlap 1951); Nathan Glazer and D. P. Moynihan, *Beyond the Melting Pot,* (Cambridge: M.I.T.-Harvard, 1963); and Milton Gordon, *Assimilation in American Life* (N.Y.: Oxford University Press).
3. For a critical discussion of this thesis and the presentation of contrary demographic data, see Karl E. Taueber and Alma F. Taueber, "The Negro as an Immigrant Group: Recent Trends in Racial and Ethnic Segregation in Chicago," *American Journal of Sociology,* 69 (1964), 374–382. More recent expressions are Irving Kristol, "The Negro Today is like the Immigrant of Yesterday," *New York Times Magazine* (September 11, 1966), and especially Edward Banfield, *The Heavenly City,* 1970. Nathan Glazer in his many articles has tended to subscribe to his notion, though not without some ambivalence—see esp. "Negroes and Ethnic Groups: The Difference, and the Potential Differences it Makes," in Nathaniel Huggins, (ed.), *America's Race Paradox.*
4. For such a model see Handlin, *op. cit.;* W. L. Warner and L. Srole, *The Social Systems of American Ethnic Groups* (New Haven: Yale University Press, 1945); and M. Gordon, *op. cit.*
5. Indians were also enslaved in colonial America, and some Native Americans merged with African bondsmen and colonies of freed men. But slavery of Indians was the exception; it did not characterize the condition of Native American tribes as a whole. W. C. Macleod, *The American Indian Frontier.*
6. In a sense these two points do not apply to American Indians who came to the continent many thousands of years before white men, nor to the Chicano population which was living in the Southwest at the time of the War with Mexico.
7. For a discussion of these differences in ecological and material circumstances,

see Marvin Harris, *Patterns of Race in America* (New York: Walker and Company, 1964), especially chapters 1–4. Compare also John Collier, *The Indians of the Americas* (Mentor Books, 1947), pp. 100–103.

8. Harry Hoetink, *The Two Variants of Race Relations in the Caribbean* (London: Oxford University Press, 1967), on this point present a strong argument.

9. See Carey McWilliams, *The Mexicans in America,* A Student's Guide to Localized History (Teachers College Press, Columbia University, 1968), for a summary discussion.

10. C. McWilliams, *Factories in the Field* (Hampden, Conn.: Shoe String), and *North From Mexico* (Westport, Conn.: Greenwood).

11. John Higham, *Strangers in the Land* (New York: Atheneum, 1969), pp. 45–52.

12. Even in the first generation, immigrants were never as thoroughly clustered in unskilled labor as were blacks, Mexicans, and Chinese in their early years. In 1855, when New York Irishmen dominated the fields of common labor and domestic service, there were sizeable numbers (more than a thousand in each category) working as blacksmiths, carpenters, masons, painters, stonecutters, clerks, shoemakers, tailors, food dealers, and cartmen. Robert Ernst, *Immigrant Life in New York City, 1825–1863* (Port Washington, N.Y.: Ira J. Friedman, Inc., 1965), pp. 214–217.

13. Of course some Europeans did parallel labor in mining and transportation construction. But since they had the freedom of movement that was denied colored laborers, they could transfer the skills and experience gained to other pursuits.

14. Herman Bloch, *The Circle of Discrimination* (New York: New York University Press, 1969), esp. 34–46.

15. The great influx of European immigration to Brazil also followed the abolition of slavery and the new white Brazilians similarly monopolized the occupational opportunities brought on by the industrialization that would have otherwise benefited the black masses. F. Fernandes, "The Weight of the Past" in H. H. Franklin (ed.), *Color and Race* (Boston: Beacon Press, 1969), pp. 283–286.

16. Oscar Handlin, *Boston's Immigrants* (Cambridge: Harvard University Press, 1959), ch. 2.

17. M. Gordon, *op. cit.*

18. I do not imply here that African culture was totally eliminated, nor that Afro-Americans have lived in a cultural vacuum. A distinctive Black culture emerged during slavery. From the complex vicissitudes of their historical experience in the United States, Afro-American culture has continued its development and differentiation up to the present day, providing an ethnic content to Black peoplehood. See R. Blauner, "Black Culture: Myth or Reality," in Peter I. Rose, *Americans from Africa,* Volume II (New York: Atherton Press, 1970), pp. 416–441.

19. As Stokley Carmichael has expressed it, capitalism exploits its own working classes, while racist systems colonize alien peoples of color. Here colonization refers to dehumanization, the tendency toward the destruction of culture and peoplehood, above and beyond exploitation. In a speech given in an Oakland, California, Black Panther rally, February 1968.

20. As Mina Caulfield puts it, imperialism exploits the cultures of the colonized as much as it does their labors. Mina Caulfield, "Culture and Imperialism: Proposing a New Dialectic," mimeographed paper, Berkeley, 1970.

21. John Collier, *op. cit.*, pp. 132–142. The Jewish ghetto is often mentioned as a parallel to the Black ghetto, but in the United States only Third World groups have experienced European-style pogroms. Virtually every Chinatown on the Pacific Coast was burned down or sacked in the early 20th century.

22. C. McWilliams, *North From Mexico, op. cit.*

23. Within the United States, Native Americans and Chicanos in general retain more original culture than blacks and Asians, because they faced European power in their own homelands, rather than being transported to the nation of the colonized. Of course the ecological advantage of colonization at home tends to be undermined to the extent that large European settlement overwhelms numerically the original people—as happened in much of Indo-America. And in much of the Americas a relative cultural integrity among Indian peoples exists at the expense of economic impoverishment and backwardness—this in effect is one of the characteristic colonial contradictions.

RACE RELATIONS MODELS AND EXPLANATIONS OF GHETTO BEHAVIOR
William J. Wilson

William J. Wilson's article is a fitting addition to this section. Here in a few succinct paragraphs, Wilson pulls many threads together.

He reviews and discusses various typologies of racial behavior: the economic-class model, the assimilation model, and the colonial model. Then he offers his own analysis focussing, in particular, on explanations of ghetto riots during the 1960s.

His commentary ends with a discussion of two courses being elected by black Americans—cultural nationalism vs. revolutionary nationalism—and the meaning and implications of these alternatives.

Sociologists have failed to explain adequately the collective responses to racial subjugation in ghetto communities across the United States. In one sense, this problem stems from a lack of empirical and theoretical development in fields such as race relations, urban sociology, social stratification and social movements. However, in another sense it may reflect a predilection among intergroup relations specialists to analyze the experiences of minority groups on the basis of preconceived models or frames of reference that are often unduly selective in their focus. In an insightful paper written in 1962, Harold Cruse (a black scholar who,

Reprinted by permission of the author.

incidentally, is not formally trained in sociology) critically discussed sociological approaches to race. He declared:

> Integration vs. separation has become polarized around two main wings of racial ideology, with fateful implications for the Negro movement and the country at large. Yet we are faced with a problem in racial ideology without any means of properly understanding how to deal with it. The dilemma arises from a lack of comprehension of the historical origins of the conflict.
>
> The problem is complicated by a lack of recognition that the conflict even exists. The fundamental economic and cultural issue at stake in this conflict cannot be dealt with by American sociologists for the simple reason that sociologists never admit that such issues should exist at all in American society. They talk of "Americanizing" all the varied racial elements in the United States: but, when it is clear that certain racial elements are not being "Americanized", socially, economically, or culturally, the sociologists proffer nothing but total evasion or more studies on "the nature of prejudice". Hence the problem remains with us in a neglected state of suspension until they break out in what are considered to be "negative", "antisocial", "antiwhite", "antidemocratic" reactions (Cruse, 1962: 16).

It is true, however, that the aftermath of ghetto riots has witnessed a proliferation of sociological studies denying the Americanization of blacks and stressing the widening gaps in living standards and social contact between the races. The problem today, therefore, is not so much that American sociologists have failed to recognize the existence of racial conflict, as it is that they have failed, as Cruse suggests, to comprehend the basis of the conflict. To repeat, it is my contention that this may, in part, stem from our tendency to analyze problems of race vis à vis preconceived models which are selective in their focus and restrictive in their use. To amplify this point I shall attempt below to show the effectiveness of major sociological models of racial behavior in explaining research data on ghetto revolts, cultural nationalism and revolutionary nationalism. These events represent very recent forms of protest by urban black residents to racial subjugation and ghetto isolation.

I have selected three competing models for this investigation—the economic-class model, the assimilation model, and the colonial model.[1] Each of these models constitutes a major theoretical approach to racial problems in America. Nevertheless, when used separately and independently, each has distinct limitations as I shall endeavor to show. First, however, let us examine briefly the essential features of the three models of racial behavior.

Models of Racial Behavior

The assimilation model, which has held a prominent position in the field of race relations for decades, began sharing the spotlight with the economic-class model during the middle 1960's. Today both of these models are in danger of being overshadowed by the colonial model which, unlike the other two models, was developed and used systematically after the first summer of nationwide ghetto revolts and during the rise of the Black Power movement.[2]

Although the interpretation and use of these models may vary from one study to another or from one writer to another, there are, nonetheless, certain basic features of each model which directly pertain to the experiences of minority groups in urban areas: an outline of these characteristics follows.[3]

THE ECONOMIC-CLASS MODEL

The central thesis of the economic-class model is that economic dislocation rather than racial strife forms the basis of racial tension in America.[4] Increasing automation has created a situation in which more and more blacks are irrelevant to the process of economic growth. Moreover, black people face conditions that are quite different from those encountered earlier by European immigrants. The latter entered urban centers at a time when the economy operated at a local level and when the need for an unskilled labor force was great. However, blacks have migrated to urban centers when the economy was beginning to operate at a national level and when the need for unskilled labor was declining. Under this situation the Negro's feelings of unworthiness *to himself* have increased and thus his motivation to search for identity disposes him to reject moderate civil rights organizations and to accept extremist groups that provide a meaningful identity, a hope and a dream.

THE ASSIMILATION MODEL

Stated in its simplest form, the assimilation model asserts that the migration of blacks from the South to the urban centers of the North and West has much of the character of the migration of European and Asian immigrants to America.[5] Each case represents a *voluntary* move from a condition of destitution and oppression to a situation of some opportunity and of less prejudice and discrimination. Moreover, the patterns of urban residential segregation for both blacks and the immigrant ethnic groups have many elements in common, e.g., a restriction of movement because of economic limitations, and a desire to live among people with a common culture and heritage.[6]

The assimilation model further states that the Negro's experiences with economic and political power is not very different from that of the European immigrant groups. The latter varied in their degree of economic power (e.g., in some cases the creation of local stores was a response to language barriers. On the other hand, the Irish, who spoke English, seem to have, like blacks, experienced difficulty in controlling the stores in their community). Moreover, the rate at which blacks have gained control of the key elected positions in their communities does not seem to differ significantly from the rate at which the immigrant groups

acquired control of the same positions in their neighborhoods. Furthermore, almost every ethnic group has experienced an initial period when
it was administered to, policed and educated by members of other ethnic
groups who had arrived before them. Negroes have had a higher rate of
this type of control but the difference here is not one of kind. Finally,
arguments positing that urban blacks have had a harsher experience in
the economic realm are incorrect because the recent decrease in unskilled
jobs has been accompanied by a decline in the number of persons qualified to work only in such positions.[7]

   In short, the experiences of blacks in urban ghettoes can be analyzed
in ethnic terms.[8] Blacks represent the last of the immigrant groups, and
although presently they are the worst off, over time they are expected to
ascent to positions of greater influence, power and wealth.

THE COLONIAL MODEL

Fundamental to the colonial model is the distinction between colonization as a process and colonialism as a social, political and economic system.[9] It is the process of colonization that defines experiences which are
common to many non-white peoples of the world, including black Americans. Briefly, colonization includes four basic components: (1) The racial
group's entry into the dominant society is forced and involuntary; (2) the
members of the dominant group administer the affairs of the suppressed
or colonized group; (3) the culture and social organization of the suppressed group is destroyed; and (4) racism exists, i.e., "a principle of social domination by which a group seen as inferior or different in terms
of alleged biological characteristics is exploited, controlled and oppressed
socially and psychically by a superordinate group" (Blauner, 1969:396).

   The colonial model asserts that the essential difference between colonized black people and ethnic immigrant groups is that unlike blacks,
European ethnic groups voluntarily came to urban areas seeking a better
life. Their movement was not administratively controlled by the dominant group and they were able to assimilate the American culture at
their own pace. For all of these reasons, they were able to operate more
freely and more competitively than black Americans. Moreover, unlike
ethnic ghettoes, black ghettoes did not develop out of a sense of choice,
and have tended to be of a more permanent nature than the one or two
generation ethnic ghettoes. Furthermore, the ethnic group's experiences
of having their homes, stores and other enterprises owned by outsiders
lasted only a short time, in many cases less than a generation. Black
Americans, on the other hand, are unique in the extent to which their
institutions have remained under the control of whites who live outside
the ghetto community. Finally, the black American population in most
cities is able to exert very little influence on the power structure.

   The colonial status of black Americans has given rise to certain collective responses that cannot be explained by the so-called "assimilation

theories," "caste theories," or "economic-class theories." These responses have been manifested in ghetto revolts, which indicate alienation from the system; the emergence of cultural nationalism, which is similar to the emergence of revitalization movements under classical colonialism; and the move to control schools and the police in the ghetto.

Collective Responses to Racial Subjugation

It is evident from the above summaries that the three models of racial behavior offer different and sometimes contradictory explanations of the experiences of black people in urban ghettoes. Competing models are characteristic of a developing science, but the final test of any model is based on the degree to which it adequately organizes and accounts for data. With this in mind we now may examine the way in which the three models aid in accounting for recent collective responses by black ghetto residents to racial subjugation.[10]

GHETTO RIOTS

The term "race riot" has been used in two ways: first to describe those periodic outbreaks, primarily between 1913 and 1943, where groups of black citizens were attacked by and retaliated against groups of white citizens; and second, to describe the recent outbreaks in black ghettoes where groups of blacks rebelled against symbols or agents of the dominant white group. The major difference between these two interpretations of "race riots" is that, unlike in the earlier forms of racial violence, the white citizenry has very rarely been identified as combatants in the present ghetto uprisings. For conceptual clarity, I have termed the earlier confrontations between black and white citizens "interracial riots" and the more recent outbreaks "ghetto riots" or "ghetto revolts".

Although the first major ghetto riot actually may have occurred in Harlem in 1943 shortly after the last large interracial riot in Detroit, the ghetto riot has emerged clearly as a pattern of racial violence only since 1964. Since that time, however, American cities have experienced hundreds of revolts in which damage has been estimated in the billions of dollars and thousands, mostly blacks, have been injured or killed.

Neither the economic-class model nor the assimilation model provides *explicit* arguments that would suggest possible explanations of ghetto riots. And even though the economic-class model does state that the anonymity of an automated American society will lead blacks increasingly to identify with extremist groups, it does not imply that this type of alienation could be manifested in ghetto revolts. However, findings consistent with some aspects of the economic-class model have been published in various riot studies. For example, a survey of attitudes of Detroit's black residents following the 1967 revolt reported that: "Those who had

been jobless for more than a year were more than three times as likely
to riot as those who were unemployed for only a month" (Meyers, 1967:6).
Commenting on such findings, Lee Rainwater states:

> It seems likely that the starting mechanisms for a riot are fairly dependent
> on the existence of pronounced poverty coupled with very high rates of unem-
> ployment. This, at least, would seem to be important to the extent that young
> men (say men under twenty-five) have a disproportionate influence on getting
> a riot going. (1967:29).

However, Rainwater further points out that "when a riot takes place, a
significant portion even of those above the poverty line may well be
drawn into participation. This should alert us to the fact that rioting is
not exclusively a problem of poverty as currently defined" (1967:29). It
could be, as Rainwater's analysis seems to suggest, that the economic-
class model has its greatest import in attempting to explain the "starting
mechanisms" of a revolt. But once the riot has gotten under way, factors
of a different nature e.g., racial caste position, must be taken into account.

The assimilation model contributes even fewer arguments that would
enhance the explanation and prediction of ghetto riots. If we accept the
assimilationist's argument that the experience of black Americans differs
from the experience of European immigrants only in a matter of degree
and not of kind, then it is à propos to ask why only blacks (and occasionally Puerto Ricans) have revolted thus far, and also, why earlier urban
ethnic groups—the European immigrants—failed to resort to spontaneous
rebellions against the symbols or agents of the dominant group (c.f. Gans,
1968). Unfortunately, the assimilation model contains few insights that
would provide a meaningful response to these questions.

Unlike the other two models, the colonial model attempts to directly
explain ghetto revolts. It postulates that riots are "a preliminary if primitive form of mass rebellion against a colonial status", and that: "The
guiding impulse in most major outbreaks has not been integration with
American society, but an attempt to stake out a sphere of control by
moving against that society and destroying the symbols of its oppression"
(Blauner, 1969:396). Stated in another way, riots seem to attest to the
fact that black community identity has crystallized in the form of a
nationalistic eruption against foreign agents and symbols, and that these
outbursts bear resemblance to the demonstrations of anti-colonial crowds
against alien control, even though both types of protest occur under quite
dissimilar situations.

Evidence for these assertions, however, is sketchy at best. Rioters have
been reported to have said that the items they had looted "really belonged" to them anyway (Blauner, 1969:399). Such attitudes evidence a
certain disrespect for America's "sacred" value of private property. Also,
the findings of the Kerner report disclosed that only 33 percent and 55
percent of the self reported rioters in Newark and Detroit respectively

felt that America was worth fighting for in the event of a world war (Report of the National Advisory Commission on Civil Disorders: 178).

It has been argued that these findings fail to support conclusions that rioters are seeking greater participation in the American system. Rather they suggest that those who rebel are alienated from the system (Blauner, 1969). It is clear, from the available evidence, that rioters tend to express anger and mistrust against politicians, police and governmental institutions (c.f. Feagin and Sheatley, 1968; and Report of the National Advisory Commission on Civil Disorders, 1968). Moreover, there seems to be a stronger antiwhite sentiment among rioters than among nonrioters (c.f. Meyer, 1967, and Kaplan and Paige, 1968). But the nature of this alienation and the extent to which it is indicative of a colonized people is not clear. For example, it was found in the Detroit survey that "most Negroes —rioters and nonrioters alike—said that they would prefer an integrated neighborhood. But the rioters were significantly less likely to express their views than non-rioters" (Meyers, 1967). It is true, however, that the rioters showed little respect for private property, which in itself is a kind of alienation. At the same time it is also true that: "In Watts, Newark, and Detroit, the main businesses affected were groceries, supermarkets, and furniture stores. In contrast, banks, utility stations, industrial plants, and private residences have been generally ignored" (Dynes and Quarantelli, 1968:13).

If indeed the revolts were nationalistic outbreaks against foreign symbols, why then were businesses that handle consumer goods the only ones attacked? Surely, outsiders equally control banks, industrial plants and utility stations. It could be that the tendency of the rioters to attack and loot only businesses that sell consumer goods may not indicate a rejection of the culturally defined goals of the American system so much as it may represent a rejection of the means to attain desired material goods. If rioters do in fact identify with the goals of the larger society, then the colonial argument stating that they have rejected the system is too categorical and hence should be modified.

It cannot be denied, however, that there are similarities between the ghetto riots and the colonial uprisings. In both the riots that have occurred under classical colonialism and those that have occurred in American cities, nonwhite groups revolted in the face of suppressive conditions. Both Africans and Afro-Americans showed little regard for the customary proprieties and treated the pleas for law and order with contempt. Moreover, both groups have been victims of racism and racists' rationalizations (cf. Fogelson, 1968).

But, there are also major differences between the ghetto revolts and the colonial riots. Fogelson has outlined some of these differences.

The recent American riots were spontaneous and unorganized, opposed by the Negro leadership, confined almost entirely to the ghettoes, and quelled with vigor but not without restraint by the authorities. The colonial uprisings, by contrast, developed out of nonviolent demonstrations against colonial exploitation; the African leaders led the demonstrations and then directed the uprisings. The rioters attacked governmental buildings and did other damage outside their districts; and the authorities, relying largely on the military, responded relentlessly and ruthlessly (1968:33).

Robert Blauner, who is credited with systematically developing the colonial model, also stresses points of dissimilarity between the two types of riots, but, in addition, finds a common element in their psychic function. He states:

> It is difficult to forsee how riots in our cities can play a role equivalent to rioting in the colonial situation as an integral phase in a movement for national liberation . . . But despite the differences in objective conditions, the violence of the 1960's seems to serve the same psychic function, assertions of dignity and manhood for young Blacks in urban ghettoes, as it did for colonized of North Africa described by Fanon and Memmi (Blauner, 1969: 399–400).

Although the evidence to support Blauner's arguments is impressionistic, many ghetto residents did appear to have experienced a sense of dignity and manhood during the following revolt. The question is whether this behavior is indeed unique to colonial uprisings and ghetto riots. Similar psychic responses by black Americans have been observed in the interracial riots of the early twentieth century (cf. Waskow, 1966), riots which were, as I indicated above, of an entirely different nature from the current day ghetto revolts. There is nothing in the colonial model which would suggest that the violence between black and white citizens (many of whom were immigrant ethnics), in these earlier riots is unique to colonization process.

What the above analysis suggests then is that a good deal of variance remains unexplained when attempting to account for ghetto riots via the three models. The assimilation model provides little or no insight into explaining and predicting ghetto riots. The economic-class model could be helpful in predicting the probability of a revolt occurring, and the colonial model could aid in focusing on certain aspects of alienation. Accordingly, it appears that a combination of the economic-class model and the colonial model would explain much more of the variance than would the exclusive use of each, but that a comprehensive explanation will have to await the development of more definitive propositions.

CULTURAL NATIONALISM AND REVOLUTIONARY NATIONALISM

In the aftermath of the black power movement, two forms of nationalistic sentiment have begun to take shape in the urban black community—cultural nationalism and revolutionary nationalism. The former is concerned mainly with the development, elaboration and/or perpetuation of cultural and historical matters related to black people, while the latter represents a move to promote effective revolution in order to alter existing social and power arrangements between blacks and whites, and ultimately to improve the status of black Americans (cf. Wilson, 1970).

Cultural nationalism,[11] first of all, was the subject of an excellent article by Blauner. He states:

> In their communities across the nation, Afro-Americans are discussing "black culture." The mystique of "soul" is only the most focused example of this trend in consciousness. What is and what should be the black man's attitude toward American society and American culture has become a central division in the Negro protest movement. The spokesmen for black power celebrate black culture and Negro distinctiveness; the integrationists base their strategy and their appeal on the fundamental "American-ness" of the black man. There are nationalist leaders who see culture building today as equal or more important than political organization. From Harlem to Watts there has been a proliferation of black theater, art, and literary groups; the recent ghetto riots (or revolts, as they are viewed from the nationalistic perspective) are the favored materials of these cultural endeavors. The spread of resistance to the draft and Vietnam war seems to indicate an increasing tendency among blacks to reject certain basic values of American life. But as with so many of these apparent "tendencies," it is difficult to know whether this one portends an actual change in sentiment or instead reflects the new conditions that have lifted some of the past inhibitions against its expression (Blauner, 1970:417–418).

Empirical evidence strongly supports the view that cultural nationalism is increasing among urban black Americans. For example, the Opinion Research Corporation (1968) survey revealed that 86 percent of the blacks in their sample felt that black people should be taught subjects in school that add to their feeling of pride in being black. Only seven percent disapproved of such subjects. Strong supports among Afro-Americans for programs stressing positive black cultural identity were also found in the studies of Campbell and Schuman (1968), and Caplan and Paige (1968).[12]

As Blauner has indicated, however, the unanswered question is whether this mood of cultural nationalism among black Americans reflects an actual change or whether it is an indication that "new conditions have lifted some of the past inhibitions against its expression." Whichever is the case, sociologists and anthropologists have increasingly responded to this manifestation of black pride and cultural identity by focusing their studies on various aspects of ghetto culture and diverse types of cultural expression (cf. Hannerz, 1969; Horton, 1970; Rainwater, 1970; Keil, 1966; and Welleman, 1970). Such studies represent a departure from the once widely held views that black Americans have become totally acculturated because of the destruction of their African heritage through slavery (cf. Glazer and Moynihan, 1963); and that the ghetto subculture represents nothing more than lower class culture (cf. Berger, 1967).

But it is one thing to advance adequate descriptions of the content of ghetto culture and quite another to present explanations of the obvious efforts of black Americans from all walks of life to perpetuate what they take to be an unique cultural experience. On this subject only the colonial model seems to provide a reasonable explanation; I shall now proceed to explain why.

The assimilation model stresses the fact that, in time, black Americans will rise to positions of greater influence, power and wealth. This optimistic view receives some support from recent surveys of the United States Census Bureau which show that, contrary to many expectations, the black migration to the suburbs appears to be increasing sharply while the growth of the Negro population in the central cities seems to be decreasing just as rapidly (Rosenthal, 1970). David Birch has commented on these findings:

> Blacks finally appear to be moving throughout the metropolitan region in something like the way that older immigrants did before them . . . We can anticipate a gradual decline of the younger black generation in the central city, its emergence in the inner suburbs, and, as black income increases still further, its entry in today's outer, wealthier suburbs (Birch, 1970:34).

If one accepts the fairly well founded proposition that cultural pluralism can only exist under conditions of structural pluralism (cf. Gordon, 1964), then the use of the assimilation model would lead to the prediction that the black cultural nationalist movement should decline rather than increase as barriers to structural assimilation are removed. But for black Americans this has not been the case. In fact, increased structural assimilation has been accompanied by a rise in cultural nationalism among all segments of the black population, (especially those who have experienced the greatest opportunities for mobility). Blauner's comments are quite relevant to this point:

> There is a remarkable paradox here in the phenomenon of Negro Americans more actively rejecting the society and its values at the very time when that social order has began to open its doors to their participation. To some degree and in some cases this may be a "defense mechanism", a protection against the anxieties of openness, competition, and new possibilities. But from another point of view, the paradox is resolved if we understand the peculiarities of the Negro cultural experience . . . In contrast with the situation of the immigrants ethnics, the period of integration and potential assimilation for Negroes is coinciding with the upsurge of the group's sense of peoplehood and with the institutionalization of its culture, rather than with the decline of these phenomena. Negro Americans with mobility and integration chances are more profoundly torn than were the children of immigrants, the so-called marginal men (Blauner, 1970:433).

The colonial model suggests some possible answers to this seeming paradox. That is, the current emphasis of cultural nationalism in the black community represents a type of cultural revitalization movement, similar in many respects to the revitalization movements that have occurred under classical colonialism where the colonized group makes an explicit attempt to revive or perpetuate aspects of its culture (cf. Wallace, 1956). Revitalization movements represent a collective response to a situation in which the culture and social organization of the suppressed group has been destroyed by colonization and hence in which personal and group identities have been weakened. Thus, the argument continues, regardless of increasing structural assimilation, black Americans of all economic backgrounds are responding collectively to the historic consequences of colonization.

Crucial to this process has been the influence of racism, a basic component of colonization. Neither the economic-class model nor the assimilation model stresses the role of racism, but Blauner sees it as central to an understanding of black peoples' emphases on culture. He states:

> Racist oppression attacks men and manhood more directly and thoroughly than does class oppression. For these reasons racist and class oppression—while intimately interacting—still have diverse consequences or group formation, and for the salience of identities based on these groups and for individual and group modes of adaptation and resistance (Blauner, 1969:432).

Accordingly, it is on the theme of cultural nationalism that the colonial model seems to have its greatest explanatory import. In short, it suggests that racism is the key factor in producing the current black cultural nationalist movement.

That blacks have been suffering from racism in American society cannot be denied. The question is whether American racism has to be explicated vis à vis domestic colonialism. It may very well be that the quest for cultural identity among blacks could be adequately explained by invoking the concept of "racism" independent of the more general issue of colonization. Obviously more research on this subject is needed.

However, there are additional considerations suggested by the colonial model that must be taken into account, namely that:

> Cultural revitalization movements play a role in anti-colonial movements. They follow an inner necessity and logic of their own that comes from the consequences of colonialism on groups and personal identities; they are also essential to provide the solidarity which the politicial or military phase of the anti-colonial revolution requires (Blauner, 1969: 402).

This is probably the most provocative argument of the colonial model. It asserts that cultural nationalism represents the initial phase of a process of decolonization and that it provides the mechanism and the solidarity needed for a political revolution. The obvious question is whether this analysis is at all applicable to the American scene. Nationalist black leaders are divided on this issue. Ranking members of the Black Panther Party for instance, refuse to acknowledge the connection between cultural nationalism and revolutionary nationalism. In fact, they have observed that the inordinate emphasis on the virtues and roots of black culture tends to conceal the fact that blacks constitute an oppressed colony in the United States, and have stressed that it is revolutionary action that will enable black Americans to gain their dignity and not the revival of African cultural roots (cf. Sheer, 1969). Former S.N.C.C. representative Julius Lester provides an opposing argument. He maintains that:

> It is cultural nationalism that has laid the foundation for revolutionary nationalism. It is cultural nationalism that has, more than any other ideology, brought a common consciousness to blacks.
>
> To oppose cultural nationalism and revolutionary nationalism to each other is to ignore totally the transition from cultural nationalism to revolutionary nationalism which some blacks have made and many are in the process of making. It is unjust to condemn the black youth who yesterday was "Negro" and has just awakened to himself (his blackness). To condemn him for his cultural nationalism will only make him defensive and retard his growth to revolutionary nationalism (Lester, 1969:13).

In one sense, this debate is academic, for despite the black community's sentiments for cultural nationalism, revolutionary nationalism receives little support, except among ghetto youths. But as the history of American race relations has shown, events change rapidly and sometimes quite drastically. And if the colonial model can be applied to aspects of America's racial problem, it warns us not to ignore the possibility of increasing sentiment for revolutionary nationalism in the "decolonization" process.

It is likely that the question of the relationship between cultural nationalism and revolutionary nationalism would be overlooked by the sole use of the economic-class model or the assimilation model in explaining and interpreting data concerning urban racial problems. Neither model includes arguments that would meaningfully address issues concerning the content and character of black liberation movements. On the other hand, race relations analysts who rely exclusively on the colonial model could find themselves in a position wherein they are unable to anticipate not only certain structural changes in the relations between black and white Americans, but also certain alterations in behavior and attitudes resulting from these changes. Specifically, if it is true that the barriers to structural assimilation are being broken, that the gradual movement of blacks from the inner city ghettoes to the suburbs is accompanied by their increasing entry into positions of greater wealth and influence, then what will be the long range effect of these changes on American racism and on black liberation movements?

It could be, that for some time to come, black liberation movements will continue to proliferate in the face of improvements especially if these improvements continue on what is perceived to be a slow, piece-meal process. The effect of racism and historic subjugation have had an indelible effect on black Americans that cannot be easily erased. But since racism is in part dependent on the existence of a social structure which denies the subordinate group access to positions of power, prestige and influence, a social structure which, in short, reinforces racist stereotypes and definitions, it is altogether reasonable to assume that as structural opportunities for black Americans increase, the ideology of racism will be undermined and its nefarious effects reduced.

All of this, however, is cast in hypothetical terms. It could be that the future course of events will bring an indefinite period of polarization between the races; yet in view of the fact that as sociologists we were sadly ill prepared to anticipate or explain the racial explosions of the late 1960's, we should make every effort to free ourselves of positions that tend to be too restrictive in the explanation of racial behavior. In some cases, therefore, it may be necessary to investigate a particular problem with a multi-model approach, in another situation a single model may suffice. Finally, in some instances none of the existing models may apply and hence altogether new propositions have to be constructed to arrive at a satisfactory explanation. In fine, a recognition of the limitations of the existing models of race behavior could be a crucial first step in improving our overall knowledge and in broadening our imagination.

NOTES

1. The term "model" is used loosely here to refer to a theoretical framework that does not have the status of a scientific theory and whose propositions are vaguely and sometimes implicitly formulated. It does, nonetheless, contain certain concepts and hypotheses that could provide direction for empirical research.

2. The models I have selected for investigation represent three of the most recent approaches to race relations in America. They are also relevant to explanations of ghetto behavior. To conserve space, I have chosen not to include a discussion of the racial caste model (or the theory of prejudice as it is often called), which enjoyed considerable status during the 1940's and 1950's but which has since been overshadowed by the more recent frameworks.

   Moreover, I have omitted other possible approaches such as the power model (cf. Schermerhorn, 1956) or the social structural model (cf. van den Berghe, 1967) which, like the colonial model, have a comparative perspective but which are quite abstract and are only indirectly relevant to ghetto behavior.

3. It should be emphasized that this outline of the models represents my own reconstruction of the manner in which they have been discussed in the literature. The identification of certain authors with certain aspects of each model does not necessarily mean that they themselves agree with my designations or with the arguments I have advanced.

4. This synopsis is based principally on Willhelm and Powell (1964). For a widely read popular statement that reflects this view, see Rustin (1965).

5. This synopsis is based primarily on Glazer (1970). Also see Glazer and Moynihan (1963) and Handlin (1951).

6. On this subject, Glazer (1970:15) has stated: "Most Negroes do not want to live only among Negroes—recent surveys make that clear. Nor do most want to live only among whites. This is not very different from immigrant ethnic patterns."

7. Glazer has amplified this point. He states: "Negro migrants have a higher level of education than European immigrants of the beginning of the century and are consequently not as limited in the kinds of jobs they can fill to unskilled jobs. The fact that there are many jobs for the unskilled unfilled shows that there has not been any decline in the ratio of jobs to applicants. Two other things have happened however. There are now more alternatives to unskilled work—there are social programs which mean that less people may be driven to unpleasant and low-paying jobs by the need to feed their families and children. Secondly, there is a change in attitudes toward unskilled and low-paying work. It is not seen as commonly as suitable or appropriate life-long work for men. Expectations have changed, and fewer blacks and whites today will accept a life at menial labor with no hope for advancement, as their fathers and older brothers did, and as European immigrants did" (Glazer, 1970:22).

8. However, an important distinction of the assimilation model should be made here: "If one takes the national view, the view which includes the reality of Negro enslavement, the legally inferior position of Negroes in the Constitution and in State and local law for centuries, the disenfranchisement of Negroes after the Civil War, and the heroic and not yet completed struggle to achieve full legal equality in the South, then it is indeed deceptive to introduce the ethnic comparison. The conservative and optimistic bias of this comparison underestimates what has been and still is necessary to achieve full quality (sic) for the Negroes.

"But if one concentrates on the Northern urban experience, then the elements of continuity are important. There the Negro arrives as a migrant" (Glazer, 1970:23).

9. This synopsis is based principally on Blauner (1969) and (1970). Also see Cruse (1962); Clark (1965); and Carmichael and Hamilton (1967).

10. I recognize of course that the evaluation of any given model could be a consequence of the type of behavior selected for analysis and that different conclusions concerning each model's explanatory and predictive import could be obtained if another problem were adopted for investigation. The areas I have chosen for consideration however represent the themes dominant in the black community today. Thus we are provided with the opportunity to determine at least partially whether or not current working models in sociology are applicable to some of the major experiences of black people in America's urban ghettoes,

11. I have chosen to use the term "cultural nationalism," in favor of the more widely used sociological term "cultural pluralism" to connote a social movement in which black Americans are attempting to revive or perpetuate aspects of their cultural heritage. The term "cultural pluralism" does not necessarily imply a social movement. However, the two terms can often be used interchangeably for purposes of analysis.

The above distinction represents a departure from my previous position in which I attempted to associate the term "cultural nationalism" with blacks who advocate both structural and cultural pluralism as opposed to those who only support cultural pluralism. See Wilson (1970).

12. In their study of black attitudes in 15 American cities, Campbell and Schuman (1968:6) have stated: "There is a strong trend in the data that is related to, but different from and much stronger than, 'separation'. It concerns the positive cultural identity and achievements of Negroes, rather than their political separation from whites. The finding appears most strikingly in the endorsement of 42 percent of the Negro sample of the statement: 'Negro school children should study an African Language': Two out of five Negroes thus subscribe to an emphasis on 'black consciousness' that was almost unthought of a few years ago."

BIBLIOGRAPHY

Berger, Kenneth M.
1967 "Soul Searching, Review of Charles Keil's *Urban Blues," Trans-Action* (June), 44–64.
Birch, David L.
1970 *The Economic Future of City and Suburbs.* Committee for Economic Development.
Blauner, Robert
1970 "Black Culture: Myth or Reality," in Peter Rose, *Americans From Africa: Old Memories, New Moods.* New York: Atherton Press, Inc., 417–442.
Blauner, Robert
1969 "Internal Colonialism and Ghetto Revolts," *Social Problems,* 16 (Spring), 393–408.
Blauner, Robert
1966 "White-wash Over Watts: The Failure of the McCone Report," *Trans-Action* (March–April), 3–9, 54.
Campbell, Angus and Howard Schuman
1968 "Racial Attitudes in Fifteen American Cities," in the *National Advisory Commission on Civil Disorders, Supplemental Studies.* Washington, D.C.: Goverment Printing Office.
Caplan, Nathan S. and Jeffery Paige
1968 "A Study of Ghetto Rioters," *Scientific American,* 219 (August), 15–21.
Carmichael, Stokely and Charles Hamilton
1967 *Black Power.* New York: Random House.
Clark, Kenneth B.
1965 *Dark Ghetto.* New York: Harper and Row.
Cruse, Harold W.
1962 "Revolutionary Nationalism and the Afro-American," *Studies on the Left,* 2, No. 3.
Dynes, Russell and E. L. Quarantelli
1968 "What Looting in Civil Disturbances Really Means," *Trans-Action* (May), 9–14
Feagin, Joe R. and Paul B. Sheatsley
1968 "Ghetto Resident Appraisals of a Riot," *Public Opinion Quarterly,* 32 (Fall), 352–362.

Fogelson, Robert M.
1968 "Violence as Protest," in Robert Hall Connery (ed.), *Urban Riots: Violence and Social Change*. New York: Proceedings of the Academy of Political Science, Vol. 24, No. 1, 25–41.

Gans, Herbert
1968 "The Ghetto Rebellions and Urban Conflict," in Robert Hall Connery (ed.), *Urban Riots: Violence and Social Change*. New York: Proceedings of the Academy of Political Science, Vol. 29, No. 1, 42-51.

Glazer, Nathan and Daniel Moynihan
1963 *Beyond the Melting Pot*. Cambridge Mass: M.I.T. Press.

Glazer, Nathan
1970 "Negroes and Ethnic Groups: The Difference, and The Political Difference It Makes," Paper presented at a *Symposium on Race and Ethnicity in America*, sponsored by the Department of American Studies at Amherst College, Amherst, Massachusetts, May 1.

Gordon, Milton M.
1964 *Assimilation in American Life*. New York: Oxford University Press.

Hannerz, Ulf
1969 *Soulside: Inquiries into Ghetto Culture and Community*. New York: Columbia University Press.

Horton, John
1970 "Time and Cool People," in Lee Rainwater (ed.), *Soul*. Chicago: Aldine Publishing Co. 31–50.

Keil, Charles
1966 *Urban Blues*. Chicago: University of Chicago Press.

Lester, Julius
1969 "From the Other Side of the Tracks," *National Guardian* (April 19), 13–22.

Meyer, Philip
1967 *A Survey of Attitudes of Detroit Negroes After the Riot of 1967*. The Detroit Urban League, 1–15.

Opinion Research Corporation
1968 *White and Negro Attitudes Toward Race Related Issues and Activities*. Research Park. Princeton, New Jersey: July 9.

Rainwater, Lee
1970 "Introduction," in Lee Rainwater (ed.) *Soul*. Chicago: Aldine Publishing Co., 1–14.

Rainwater, Lee
1967 "Open Letter on White Justice and the Riots," *Trans-Action* (May), 22–32.

Report of the National Advisory Commission on Civil Disorders.
1968 New York: Bantam Press.

Rosenthal, Jack
1970 "Black Exodus to Suburbs Found Increasing Sharply," *The New York Times*, 119 (July 12), 1 and 22.

Rustin, Bayard
1965 "From Protest to Politics: The Future of the Civil Rights Movement," *Commentary*, 39, 25–31.

Sheer, Robert
1969 "Introduction," in *Eldridge Cleaver*. New York: Random House. vii–xxxiii.

Schermerhorn, Robert A.
1956 "Power as a Primary Concept in the Study of Minorities," *Social Forces*, 35 (October), 53–56.

van den Berghe, Pierre
1967 *Race and Racism*. New York: Wiley Press.

Wallace, Anthony F. C.
1956 "Revitalization Movements," *American Anthropologists*, 58 (April), 264–281.

Waskow, Arthur I.
1966 *From Race Riot to Sit In*. New York: Doubleday.

Wellman, David
1970 "Putting on the Youth Opportunity Center," in Lee Rainwater (ed.), *Soul*. Chicago: Aldine Publishing Co., 93–116.

Wilson, William J.
1970 "Revolutionary Nationalism 'Versus' Cultural Nationalism: Dimensions of the Black Power Movement," *Sociological Focus*, 3 (Spring), 43–51.

COMPETITION AND CONFLICT

In which current interethnic
tensions are considered and their
implications for the future are
assessed.

IS WHITE RACISM THE PROBLEM?
Murray Friedman

It is commonplace today to argue that the United
States is a racist society and that interethnic conflict
(particularly between whites and others) is a reflection
of "white racism." Murray Friedman takes issue with
this view. While mindful of the extent of discrimination,
he suggests that such a position obscures the complexities of social life in America.

We are a nation of groups more than a nation of individuals says Friedman. And the groups to which we
belong have long competed for space and status.
Change will only come when the interests of all connecting groups are understood and the anxieties of members are dealt with compassionately and
empathetically.

One of the less fortunate results of the black revolution has been the
development of a by now familiar ritual in which the white liberal is
accused of racism and responds by proclaiming himself and the entire
society guilty as charged; the Kerner report was only the official apotheosis
of this type of white response to the black challenge of the 60's. No doubt
the report has performed a service in the short run by focusing the attention of great numbers of Americans on the degree to which simple racism
persists and operates throughout the country, but in the long run its picture of an America pervaded with an undifferentiated disease called
"white racism" is unlikely to prove helpful. And even in the short run,

Reprinted from *Commentary*, by permission. Copyright © 1969 by the American Jewish Committee.

the spread of the attitudes embodied in the report may have had a share in helping to provoke the current backlash.

It is, perhaps, understandable that blacks should take phrases like "white racism" and "white America" as adequate reflections of reality. Nevertheless, these phrases drastically obscure the true complexities of our social situation. For the truth is that there is no such entity as "white America." America is and always has been a nation of diverse ethnic, religious, and racial groups with widely varying characteristics and qualities; and conflict among these groups has been (one might say) "as American as cherry pie." According to the 1960 census, no fewer than 34 million Americans are either immigrants or the children of immigrants from Italy, Poland, Ireland, and a host of other countries. Racially, the population includes not only caucasians and 22 million blacks, but 5 million Mexican-Americans, and smaller numbers of Indians, Chinese, Japanese, and Puerto Ricans. Membership in U.S. religious bodies, finally, breaks down into 69 million Protestants (who themselves break down into 222 denominations and sects), 46 million Roman Catholics, and 5.6 million Jews.

Neither earlier restrictive immigration laws nor the forces working toward the homogenization of American life have rendered these groups obsolete. While it is true that we have carved out for ourselves a collective identity as Americans with certain common goals, values, and styles, we are still influenced in highly significant ways by our ethnic backgrounds. A number of social scientists, including Gerhard Lenski and Samuel Lubell, have even gone so far as to suggest that these factors are often more important than class. And indeed, membership in our various racial, religious, and ethnic groups largely accounts for where we live, the kinds of jobs we aspire to and hold, who our friends are, whom we marry, how we raise our children, how we vote, think, feel, and act. In a paper prepared for the National Consultation on Ethnic America last June, the sociologist Andrew Greeley reported that Germans, regardless of religion, are more likely to choose careers in science and engineering than any other group. Jews overchoose medicine and law. The Irish overchoose law, political science, history, and the diplomatic service. Polish and other Slavic groups are less likely to approve of bond issues. Poles are the most loyal to the Democratic party, while Germans and Italians are the least.

Such ethnic differences are by no means mere survivals of the past, destined to disappear as immigrant memories fade. We seem, in fact, to be moving into a phase of American life in which ethnic self-confidence and self-assertion—stemming from a new recognition of group identity patterns both by the groups themselves and by the general community— are becoming more intense. The "black power" movement is only one manifestation of this. Many alienated Jews suddenly discovered their Jewishness during the Israeli War of Independence and especially the Six-Day War. Italians have recently formed organizations to counteract "Italian jokes" and the gangster image on television and other media, while Mexican-Americans and Indians have been organizing themselves to achieve broadened civil rights and opportunities. At the same time large bureaucracies like the police and the schools are witnessing a growth in racial, religious, and ethnic organization for social purposes and to protect group interests. To some degree, each of us is locked into the particular culture and social system of the group from which we come.

The myth, to be sure, is that we are a nation of individuals rather than of groups. "There are no minorities in the United States," Woodrow Wilson, a Presbyterian, declared in a World War I plea for unity. "There are no national minorities, racial minorities, or religious minorities. The whole concept and basis of the United States precludes them." Thirty years later, the columnist, Dorothy Thompson, warned American Jews in the pages of COMMENTARY that their support of Israel was an act of disloyalty to the United States. "You cannot become true Americans if you think of yourselves in groups. America does not consist of groups. A man who thinks of himself as belonging to a particular national group in America has not become American, and the man who goes among you to trade upon your nationality is not worthy to live under the Stars and Stripes." And more recently the New York *Times* criticized Martin Luther King, Jr., and James Farmer in similar terms after the two Negro leaders had laid claim to a share of the national wealth and economic power for Negroes as a group. Terming this plea "hopelessly utopian," the *Times* declared: "The United States has never honored [such a claim] for any other group. Impoverished Negroes, like all other poor Americans, past and present, will have to achieve success on an individual basis and by individual effort."

The ideology of individualism out of which such statements come may be attractive, but it bears little relation to the American reality. Formally, of course, and to a certain extent in practice, our society lives by the individualistic principle. Universities strive for more diverse student bodies and business organizations are increasingly accepting the principle that, like government civil service, they should be open to all persons qualified for employment. But as Nathan Glazer has suggested:

> These uniform processes of selection for advancement and the pattern of freedom to start a business and make money operate not on a homogeneous mass of individuals, but on individuals as molded by a range of communities of different degrees of organization and self-consciousness with different histories and cultures.

If, however, the idea that we are a nation of individuals is largely a fiction, it has nonetheless served a useful purpose. Fashioned, in part, by older-stock groups as a means of maintaining their power and primacy, it also helped to contain the explosive possibilities of an ethnically heterogeneous society and to muffle racial divisiveness. Yet one symptom of the "demystification" of this idea has been the recognition in recent years that the older stock groups are themselves to be understood in ethnic terms. The very introduction of the term WASP into the language, as Norman Podhoretz has pointed out, signified a new realization that "white Americans of Anglo-Saxon Protestant background are an ethnic group like any other, that their characteristic qualities are by no means self-evidently superior to those of the other groups, and that neither their earlier arrival nor their majority status entitles them to exclusive possession of the national identity." As the earliest arrivals, the WASP's were able to take possession of the choicest land, to organize and control the major businesses and industries, to run the various political institutions, and to set the tone of the national culture. These positions of dominance were in time challenged by other groups, in some cases (the Irish in city politics, the Jews in cultural life) very successfully, in others with only partial success (thus Fletcher Knebel reports that, contrary to the general impression, "the rulers of economic America—the producers, the financiers, the manufacturers, the bankers and insurers—are still overwhelmingly WASP").

But whatever the particular outcome, the pattern of ethnic "outs" pressuring the ethnic "ins" for equal rights, opportunities, and status has been followed since colonial times and has been accompanied by noisy and often violent reaction by the existing ethnic establishment. There was the growth of the Know-Nothing movement when the mid-19th century influx of Irish Catholics and other foreigners posed a challenge to Protestant control; there was the creation and resurgence of the Ku Klux Klan at every stage of the black man's movement toward equal rights; there was the organization of Parents and Taxpayers groups in the North and White Citizens Councils in the South to oppose school desegregation and Negro school gains. Bigotry and racism certainly played a part in these phenomena. Yet they are best understood not as symptoms of social illness but as expressions of the recurring battles that inevitably characterize a heterogeneous society as older and more established groups seek to ward off the demands of newer claimants to a share of position and power.

Even the recent explosions in the black ghettos have a precedent: "In an earlier period," Dennis Clark tells us, "the Irish were the riot makers of America par excellence." They "wrote the script" for American urban violence and "black terrorists have added nothing new." So, too, with some of the educational demands of today's black militants. As late as 1906, the New York *Gaelic American* wanted Irish history taught in the New York City schools!

Racial and ethnic conflict takes its toll, but it has frequently led to beneficial results. When pressures mounted by the "outs" have caused widespread dislocation, the "ins" have often purchased community peace by making political, economic, legal, and cultural concessions. As the Irish, for example, became more fully absorbed into American life through better jobs, more security and recognition—in short, as the existing ethnic establishment made room for them—Irish violence decreased, and the Irish have, in fact, become some of the strongest proponents of the current racial status quo. The hope of achieving a similar result undoubtedly accounts in some measure for concessions which have been made to Negroes in many racially restive cities today. Thus, when white voters in Cleveland helped elect a Negro mayor (Carl Stokes), they were not only recognizing his abilities—which are said to be considerable—but also acting in the belief that he could "cool it" more effectively than a white mayor. Nor is it a coincidence that the Los Angeles city and county school boards are now headed by Negroes.

In the past, a major barrier to the advancement of black people has been their inability to organize themselves as a group for a struggle with the various "ins." Their relative powerlessness has been as crippling as the forces of bigotry arrayed against them. As one Philadelphia militant said, "Impotence corrupts and absolute impotence corrupts absolutely." But some black power leaders have recently emerged with a better understanding than many of their integrationist colleagues of the fact that successful groups in American life must reserve a major portion of their energies for the task of racial or religious separation and communal consolidation. Divorced from posturing and provocative language, the emphasis by certain (though not all) black militants on separatism may be seen as a temporary tactic to build political and economic power in order to overcome the results of discrimination and disadvantage. "Ultimately, the gains of our struggle will be meaningful," Stokely Carmichael and Charles V. Hamilton wrote in *Black Power*, "only when consolidated by viable coalitions between blacks and whites who accept each other as co-equal partners and who identify their goals as politically and economically similar."

This is not to suggest that black power (or Jewish power or Catholic power) is the only factor in achieving group progress, or that "the American creed," of equal rights, as Gunnar Myrdal has called it, is a mere bundle of words. Indeed, the democratic tradition can act as a powerful force in advancing minority claims even when the majority does not accept its implications. Public opinion polls have reported consistently that open-housing laws are unpopular with a majority of Americans, and yet 23 states and 205 cities have enacted such legislation and the Civil Rights Act of 1968 makes it a federal responsibility. Nevertheless, the democratic ideal obviously has never guaranteed full entry into the society to ethnic out-groups. In a pluralistic society, freedom is not handed out; for better or worse, it has to be fought for and won. The "outs" can attain it only by agitation and pressure, utilizing the American creed as one of their weapons.

It is important in all this to recognize that no special virtue or culpability accrues to the position of any group in this pluralistic system. At the moment the American creed sides with Negroes, Puerto Ricans, American Indians, and other minorities who have been discriminated against for so long. But we should not be surprised when Italians, Poles, Irish, or Jews respond to Negro pressures by rushing to protect vital interests which have frequently been purchased through harsh struggles of their own with the ethnic system. Here is how a skilled craftsman replies to the charge of maintaining racial discrimination in his union in a letter to the New York *Times*:

> Some men leave their sons money, some large investments, some business connections, and some a profession. I have only one worthwhile thing to give: my trade. I hope to follow a centuries-old tradition and sponsor my sons for an apprenticeship. For this simple father's wish it is said that I discriminate against Negroes. Don't all of us discriminate? Which of us when it comes to a choice will not choose a son over all others? I believe that an apprenticeship in my union is no more a public-trust, to be shared by all, than a millionaire's money is a public trust.

Surely to dismiss this letter as an expression of white racism is drastically to oversimplify the problem of discrimination. But if the impulse to protect vested interests accounts for the erecting of discriminatory barriers, no less often than simple bigotry or racism, it is also true that Americans are sometimes capable of transcending that impulse—just as they are sometimes capable of setting aside their prejudices—for the sake of greater social justice. E. Digby Baltzell has pointed out in *The Protestant Establishment* that the drive to gain equal rights and opportunities for disadvantaged minorities has frequently been led by members of older-stock groups. On the other hand, members of minority groups are not necessarily ennobled by the experience of persecution and exploitation. As Rabbi Richard Rubenstein has observed, "the extra measure of hatred the victim accumulates may make him an especially vicious victor."

Nor does the position of a given ethnic group remain static; a group can be "in" and "out" at the same time. While Jews, for example, continue to face discrimination in the "executive suite" of major industry and finance, in private clubs and elsewhere, they are in certain respects becoming an economic and cultural in-group. To the degree that they are moving from "out" to "in" (from "good guys" to "bad guys"?), they are joining the existing ethnic establishment and taking on its conservative coloration. Rabbi Rubenstein has frankly defended this change in an article, "Jews, Negroes, and the New Politics," in the *Reconstructionist*:

> After a century of liberalism there is a very strong likelihood that the Jewish community will turn somewhat conservative in the sense that its strategy for social change involves establishment politics rather than revolutionary violence. Jews have much to conserve in America. It is no sin to conserve what one has worked with infinite difficulty to build.

So far so good—though, regrettably, Rubenstein uses this and other arguments to urge Jews to opt out of the Negro struggle. The point, however, is that not all the groups resisting black demands today are "in" groups. Just as in a fraternity initiation the hardest knocks come from the sophomores, the most recently accepted and hence least secure group, so in ethnic struggle the greatest opposition will sometimes come from groups whose interests would seem to make them natural allies.

At the moment some of the hottest group collisions are taking place in the big-city schools. The "outs"—in this case the blacks—see the older order as maintaining and fostering "basic inequities." Hence, we are now witnessing the demand for decentralization or "community control" of big-city school systems. The "ins"—in the case of New York, the Jews; in the case of Boston, the Irish—naturally see these demands as a threat. The blacks claim that the existing system of merit and experience tends to favor educators from older religio-ethnic groups; the latter fear that new and lowered criteria of advancement and promotion will destroy many of their hard-won gains. The result is increasing conflict amid charges of racism from both sides.

The underlying problem, however, is a power struggle involving the decision-making areas controlled by an older educational and ethnic establishment. At the heart of the issue is a group bargaining situation whose handling calls for enormous sensitivity and the development of procedures that will protect the interests of the conflicting groups. A similar confrontation in the 19th century which was badly handled was a major factor in the withdrawal of Catholics from the Protestant-dominated public schools and the creation of their own school system.

In the meantime, struggles among other groups persist, often also involving the schools. Frequently, these result from differences in group values and styles as well as interests. An example is the school board fight in Wayne Township, New Jersey, which attracted national attention in February 1967. The Jewish, and total, population of Wayne, a suburb of Paterson and Newark, had grown sharply since 1958, when it was a homogeneous Christian community with only 15 Jewish families. With a changing community came new pressures—burgeoning school enrollment and school costs, and anxiety over court rulings banning prayer and the reading of the Bible in public schools. There was one Jew on Wayne's nine-member school board in 1967 when two others decided to run. The vice president of the board, Newton Miller, attacked both Jewish candidates, noting, "Most Jewish people are liberals especially when it comes to spending for education." If they were elected, he warned, only two more Jewish members would be required for a Jewish majority. "Two more votes and we lose what is left of Christ in our Christmas celebrations in the schools. Think of it," Miller added.

Subsequently, the Jewish candidates were defeated amid widespread condemnation of the citizens of Wayne. The incident was cited by sociologists Rodney Stark and Stephen Steinberg as raising the "specter of political anti-Semitism in America." In their study, they concluded, "It couldn't happen here, but it did."

Miller's statements may indeed have appealed to existing anti-Semitic sentiment in Wayne. But this was not the whole story. After all, the Jewish member already on the board had been elected by the same constituency that now responded to Miller's warnings. And it must be admitted, furthermore, that by and large Jews *are* "liberals," willing to spend heavily on the education of their children just as they are desirous of eliminating religious practices from the public schools—attitudes shared, of course, by many non-Jews. Miller appealed to group interests above all: to an interest in preserving traditional religious practices in the schools and in holding down education expenditures. There was in this case genuine concern by an older religio-ethnic establishment that its way of life and values were in danger of being swept away. The votes against the Jewish members were of course illiberal votes, but that was just the point. In Wayne, charges of anti-Semitism obscured the real problem: how to reconcile differences in group values in a changing, multigroup society.

All this is not of course meant to deny the existence of racism as a force in American life, nor to underestimate the cruel and pervasive conflicts which it engenders. But it must be recognized that the crucial element in much of inter-group conflict is not how prejudiced the contending parties are, but what kinds of accommodations they are capable of making. For many years, a federal aid to education bill has been tied up in Washington, in part because of a Roman Catholic veto. The Catholic hierarchy, whose schools have been undergoing financial crisis, and a number of Orthodox Jewish groups who also want government assistance for their schools are ranged on one side of the issue. On the other side are most Protestant and Jewish groups, along with civil-liberties and educational organizations, who are suspicious of the motives of the Catholic Church and fear that financial assistance by government to parochial schools will lead to an abandonment of the separation of church and state principle embodied in the federal and state constitutions, with the resultant destruction of the public schools. Debate now ranges in many states over providing free busing of pupils to parochial schools, supplying textbooks, auxiliary services, and equipment to non-public school students, and financing construction of buildings at church-related colleges and universities. The result has been an intensification of religious tensions.

In this controversy, however, the problem is not, as many seem to believe, mainly one of constitutional law. In spite of the First Amendment, American public education throughout our history has reflected the values and goals of a Protestant society—until, that is, Catholics and other groups began to press for, and finally obtained, a more neutral posture. The problem here is rather one of adjusting to the reality of the Catholic parochial school system—to the public service it performs and to the political power it represents. When the Constitution was adopted, Catholics numbered less than 1 per cent of the total population. Today they are the largest single religious group and they support a parochial school system which, in spite of criticism inside and outside the Church, continues to educate large numbers of Americans.

It seems likely that this controversy will be resolved through a redefinition of the American public education system. Thus, secular and other aspects of parochial education that benefit the general community—subjects such as foreign languages, mathematics, physics, chemistry, and gym —will in all probability receive some form of public assistance. Indeed, this is already happening in the form of shared time or dual enrollment (parochial school children spend part of the day in public schools), aid to disadvantaged children under the Elementary and Secondary Education Act of 1965, and various other measures.

It is a tribute to our social system, proof of its workability, that the inexorable pressures of pluralistic confrontation do result in shifts in power and place. WASP control of political life in the nation's cities was displaced first by the Irish and later by other ethnic groups. The newest group moving up the political ladder is the Negro, with mayors now in Gary and Cleveland. The Negro press predicts that by 1977 there may be 21 black mayors.

There are, of course, many real differences between the Negro and other groups in this country, including the Negro's higher visibility and the traumatic impact of slavery. He is, nevertheless, involved in much the same historical process experienced by all groups, with varying success, in attempting to "make it" in American life. The idea that he faces a monolithic white world uniformly intent for racist reasons on denying him his full rights as a man is not only naive but damaging to the development of strategies which can lead to a necessary accommodation. It does no good—it does harm—to keep pointing the finger of guilt either at Americans in general or at special groups, when what is needed are methods for dealing with the real needs and fears of all groups.

As David Danzig has written: "Few people who live in socially separated ethnic communities, as most Americans do, can be persuaded that because their communities are also racially separated they are morally sick. Having come to accept their own social situation as the natural result of their ethnic affinities, mere exhortation is not likely to convince them—or, for that matter, the public at large—that they are thereby imposing upon others a condition of apartheid." Nor is exhortation likely to convince the 20 million families who earn between $5,000 and $10,000 a year that they are wrong in feeling that their own problems are being neglected in favor of the Negro. It is clear that intergroup negotiation, or bargaining, with due regard for protecting the interests of the various groups involved, is one of the major ingredients in working out racial and religious adjustments. In other words, power has to be shared—in the schools, on the job, in politics, and in every aspect of American life.

The time has come to dispense with what Peter Rose has called the "liberal rhetoric . . . of race relations." There can be no effective intergroup negotiation or bargaining unless due regard is paid to the interests of all groups. Nor will effective bargaining take place until we learn to go beyond simplistic slogans and equally simplistic appeals to the American creed.

ALIENATION IN THE WHITE COMMUNITY
Peter H. Rossi

Increasingly, if belatedly, sociologists are turning attention to the study of reactions of white workers to the
upsurge of Black Pride and Black Power movements.
Close scrutiny, as sociologist Peter H. Rossi points out in
this brief interview, belies the notion of blatant racism
and hatred. Fear and anger (and jealousy, too) are
probably more accurate labels for the mounting tensions between black and white communities across the
land. One primary target of white workers is what they
see as a distant "Establishment" that seems to be ever
willing to placate black protesters at their expense.
In the end Rossi calls for the understanding of all parties
to the current American racial crisis. He reminds us, if
not in so many words, that all who are cut, bleed and
all who are frightened, cower.

Q. The conservative trend in the nation, expressed in backlash, in the
support for George Wallace, and in the apparent slowdown in the push
for civil rights, has drawn attention to a substantial number of disaffected white Americans. The white working class—particularly ethnics
of European stock in northern cities and the less affluent WASPs in the
South—are often referred to as prime examples of such alienation. Do
you agree with this characterization? How do you explain their resistance
to the effort for greater equality?

A. The situation, as I read it, is somewhat more complicated. First,

From *Social Action*, May 1970. Copyright © 1970 by the Council for Christian Social
Action of the United Church of Christ.

there has been very little diminution in the trend (evident in the public opinion polls since the start of World War II) for increasingly greater support for the concept of racial equality, including equality of treatment in education, public accommodations, and housing. These trends affect every part of the American population although, as in the case of other liberalizations of traditional society, the trends started sooner among the better educated and the young and have reached the more poorly educated and the old later.

Secondly, there has been very little change in the public attitude towards the Civil Rights Movement. At the time of the "freedom riders" the majority of the population felt that Blacks were pushing too hard for their civil rights and that the "freedom riders" hurt the Black cause more than they helped. The same sentiments have been voiced concerning the civil disorders, Black nationalists, etc. The public seems to be saying *yes* to the principles of equality but *no* to movements in that direction. Or, perhaps, what is going on is that many Americans believe that there is a sufficient measure of equality already, a kind of optimistic denial that there are severe problems facing the American Black population.

Thirdly, there is no reason to believe that these sentiments of opposition to the civil rights movement are more prevalent among ethnics than among working class people in general. The problem is that equality for Blacks is being achieved at costs which are being borne by the working class population of our urban centers. Thus, it is perfectly easy for the liberal, well educated whites in the silk stocking districts of New York to be for integration in the public schools: After all, they send their children to private schools. To integrate the public schools in Manhattan means that working class whites living in Greenwich Village will be sharing their schools with Blacks. Similarly with jobs, public accommodations, transportation, or what have you. The fact of the matter is that the burden of bringing about equality is distributed unevenly among the white population of our large cities, and it is the working class and working class neighborhoods which have to bear the major costs of integration. Note that the middle class can get pretty upset when their jobs are threatened, as in the school teachers' strike in New York over community control.

In short, the backlash seems to be concentrated among working class whites, some of whom are of recent immigrant stock.

Q. Apart from competition for jobs, how is the working class threatened by racial equality?

A. The backlash is not an irrational paranoia: it is a realistic appraisal that without changes in social policy the costs of producing racial equality are going to be borne more heavily by the white working class than by any other group in the society. The working class will have to share jobs, schools, neighborhoods, political posts, influence in city hall, and so on with Blacks—types of sharing which come close to where people really live, in their families, jobs, and neighborhoods.

The sense of deprivation is further heightened by the fact that the Establishment has apparently turned against the white working class in the cities, or at least the Establishment is paying more attention to Blacks and making special attempts to deal with the problems of Blacks. Thus to the white working class man (and his family), whose back is up against the wall financially and who now is threatened with the prospect of unemployment, the special attention given to Blacks can be interpreted as neglect. Further, the snide remarks of intellectuals concerning "rednecks," "bigots," and so on, are additional signals to him that he and his are the stepchildren of our time. The Establishment looks upon him with contempt, caters to the demands of Blacks, at the same time that his job, his schools, and his neighborhood are being threatened by takeovers. Thus in our research on race relations in fifteen major metropolitan areas we find that white militancy rises and black militancy declines when city administrations are seen as responsive to Black demands. A liberal mayor of the Lindsay or D'Alesandro (Baltimore) stripe is seen by working class whites as not their man, as someone who is sensitive to the needs of the very group which is threatening the little that they presently enjoy.

Q. Recognizing that resistance on the part of southern whites was to be expected, what is the outlook in the South?

A. White Southerners differ from their counterparts in the North mainly in that the peculiar Southern customs justified until very recently a perpetual lower position for Blacks. Prejudice in the South was legitimate, while in the North it was regarded as something one had to make excuses for. This makes movement for change a lot more difficult because at the same time one had to change the legitimacy of race prejudice as well as change racially motivated policy and behavior. This is the reason why it is so important for the achievement of racial equality in the South that official institutions, federal and state officials, churches, schools, major industries come out strongly for racial equality. Any sign to the public at large that the major institutions are divided in their ideology or indecisive in applying the equalitarian ideology leads to constant troubles, as the disaffected working class and their leaders attempt to keep the question of racial integration eternally open and eternally ready to be brought up again on the agenda.

In the South, as in the North, it is the working class who will have to bear more than their share of the costs of integration. Note that it is in those cities in which the Establishment has formed a coalition with the Blacks—as in Atlanta or Nashville or Baltimore—that progress towards equality has proceeded the farthest. The price of integration to be paid is obviously heaviest where Blacks are a larger proportion of the population. Hence in Alabama and Mississippi the resistance to integration and equality will be the greatest.

The evidence I have seen in public opinion polls is that Southern whites have become reconciled to the long run integration of Blacks into American society. Thus while in 1942 it was impossible to find any Southern white who thought it was the right thing to do to educate whites and Blacks in the same schools, today a bare majority think that the principle is correct. Southern whites are fighting to keep the long run still at a distance.

Q. You have done much to direct attention to the white ethnic groups. Do they have any special problems? Are their fears justified?

A. Regarding the ethnic groups, I think this is another example of a "putdown." In the South we can sneer at the "rednecks." In the north it is the ethnics—the Poles, Italians, Lithuanians, and so on—who serve the role of being the "bad guys." It happens that the working class of the Northern cities is heavily second-, third-, and fourth-generation stock, but there seems to me to be nothing particularly ethnic about race prejudice: it's as American as apple pie and violence.

The question whether these fears are justified or not is hard to answer. The fears are real enough; and the consequences of school integration, neighborhood integration, and job integration are also real. Integrated schools are not pleasant places to send children to. Integrated neighborhoods are not safe places to live in. Integrated work places have similar, although not as serious, problems. It is not enough to say that these problems will in the long run iron themselves out. In the long run one's children will grow up and not need the schools; in the here and now, to send one's children to a school in which there is so much inter-racial conflict that there is a significant probability that they will be beaten up is not a pleasant prospect to face day after day.

Q. As you look at the current situation with its elements of discrimination and polarization, what should we try to do?

A. It is obvious that for the sake of our souls and our present dignity as human beings we must end segregation as quickly as we possibly can. This is a wrong which has gone on so long it is difficult to understand how our country has managed to hold its head up in the family of man at all. Yet there is no denying that the period of transition will be difficult. The only reasonable path to take is one which will minimize the damage and maximize the speed of the transition. This means concretely that the costs of ending discrimination have to be borne by all elements of the population in a more equitable fashion.

Q. Can you suggest any guidelines as to how we can build the broad base of common concern that will accomplish that aim?

A. Policies can vary somewhat from area to area. Thus, I think it would be wise for the government to make very strong moves in the direction of assuring equal employment opportunities, but at the same time make sure that no one goes unemployed as a consequence. It would not be as intelligent or prudent to move towards the integration of neighborhoods or schools, because it would be difficult to do so without impinging directly on working class neighborhoods and schools. A much more sensible policy would be for the provision of new housing and better housing in small areas outside the central city for Blacks, the establishment of small Black neighborhoods in areas where there are many whites. Thus I would favor very heavily the subsidization of Black sub-suburbs located within white suburbs, closer to new job opportunities, and closer to better schools. Blacks have a right to better housing than the market presently affords them, located in the same areas that whites are. This suggested policy would accomplish that end without inundating areas bordering on the existing main ghettos with Blacks.

These policies and their like can only be accomplished by increasing our expenditures in the public sector. It may mean (and I hope it does) that we divert revenues from the military and military procurement to employment, housing, and education. It may also mean heavier taxes. Yet the American population has never shied away from heavy taxes when the tax burden was equitable and the purposes for which revenues were used were reasonable.

The fact of the matter is that America has committed itself in principle to racial equality. Let's get on with the job.

Thank you, Dr. Rossi.

NEGRO-JEWISH CONFLICT IN NEW YORK
Herbert J. Gans

In recent years, much has been written about the mounting tensions between blacks and Jews, particularly in New York City. Here, in what is perhaps the best sociological analysis of the conflict, urbanologist Herbert Gans describes the relationship between these two American minorities and offers an in-depth evaluation of the school crisis of 1968–1969 which in many ways brought the members of these groups into open opposition—or so it seemed.

I

The conflicts between black advocates of local control and Jewish teachers during the school strikes, the anti-Semitic outbursts of various black militants, and the angry counter-reactions by Jewish leaders and citizens are generally thought to have ended the once seemingly peaceful relationship between Negroes and Jews in New York City. There is no doubt that new tensions have developed in recent months, of course, but instead of dwelling on these—or on further exegeses of public statements to determine whether the Ocean Hill-Brownsville Governing Board is anti-Semitic or the United Federation of Teachers racist—it is more useful to look at the Negro-Jewish relationship from a longer sociological perspective. From that perspective, the recent incidents are only more visible instances in a long series of primarily economic conflicts between blacks, Jews (and other ethnic groups) which are endemic to New York and to several other large American cities, and which can only be dealt with through economic solutions.

From *Midstream*, March 1969. Reprinted by permission of the author and publisher.

To a considerable extent, these conflicts have been about what sociologists call *succession,* the process by which members of one ethnic or racial group (the departing group) move up a notch on the socio-economic ladder and are succeeded in their old position by a less affluent group (the successors). The history of professional boxing, an occupation of low status and uncertain reward, offers a typical example of the process. The initial American pugilists were mainly poor white Protestants, who were succeeded first by Central Europeans, then by a predominantly Irish contingent, then by Italians, and some Jews, and since World War II, by Negroes, Puerto Ricans and other Latins, as young men in each of the earlier groups found more secure and respectable jobs.

In this instance, the succession process has been tranquil, but conflict can develop, especially if the departing group is not leaving quickly enough to make room for the successors. When the economy is not expanding sufficiently or when the departing group lacks the skill or inclination to take better jobs, large remnants will stay put and block the upward move of the successors. Thus, the underworld went through the succession process from Protestant to Irish to Italian and Jewish, but while most Jews departed two generations ago, many Italians did not, preventing the entry of Negroes and others. Similarly, when the Jewish captains of the New York City Police Department thought the time had come for one of their men to head the department, the Irish portion of the force put its foot down, and an Irish commissioner was brought in from Philadelphia.

It should be emphasized that succession is neither automatic, universal, nor inevitable. Sometimes a poor group will remain in an occupation because it is unable or unwilling to depart or because no successors are knocking at the door. As a result, the Chinese still dominate New York's hand laundries. Moreover, all departing groups try to hold on to the most profitable sources of income in the old occupation. Thus, New York's slums were originally owned and managed by WASPs, but while they eventually passed into ethnic hands, the mortgages are often still held by WASP-run institutions. And because of racial discrimination, Negroes have usually been excluded from succession until the courts have stepped in. In fact, the only jobs which blacks have been able to enter and to move up in relatively freely from the lowest-paid levels are in government, where civil service has, with some notable exceptions, allowed them to compete on the basis of skill.

II

In American cities, the succession process has generally reflected the order in which ethnic and racial groups have arrived in the city, and the succession from English Protestants to Northern European Protestants and Catholics to Irish to Italians and Jews (and Greeks and Poles, etc.) to

Negroes and Latins can be traced for many occupations—except that Negroes have often been pushed out of jobs by new white immigrants. In New York, the succession relationship between Jews and Negroes, and more recently Puerto Ricans, has been particularly close, if only because the three groups constitute a major portion of the city's population. Although good data on ethnic succession is scarce, it seems clear that as Jews moved up the economic ladder, their places were often taken by blacks and Puerto Ricans, with many Jews holding on to the more profitable sources of income in the occupations from which they departed. For example, Puerto Ricans and blacks now hold many of the low-wage jobs in the garment industry, while Jews have kept many ownership and managerial posts as well as union officerships. (Several generations earlier, German Jews had been the owners and managers of garment industry firms, until they were succeeded by Eastern Europeans.)

Similarly, when the Jews moved out of the slum neighborhoods in which they began life in America, they were frequently succeeded by Negroes, but retained ownership of many tenements and stores in these areas. For example, a recent study by Hunter College Professor Naomi Levine showed that 37 per cent of the stores in a 20 block area of Central Harlem were owned by whites, and 80 per cent of these, by Jews.[1] Since the study limited itself to "neighborhood stores" and excluded the large shops on 125th Street and other major business streets, it underestimates the proportion of Jewish ownership, however. This is suggested by the report of a 1968 Mayor's Task Force, which showed that 47 per cent of all stores in Central Harlem are owned by whites.[2] (Negro ownership is concentrated in service establishments, particularly barbershops and beauty shops, dry cleaning stores and restaurants; whites, however, own 74 per cent of the food stores, 72 per cent of the apparel stores, 89 per cent of the hardware, furniture and appliance stores, and over 60 per cent of liquor and drug stores.) Assuming that clothing stores in Harlem are, as they are everywhere else, more likely to be owned by Jews than by other whites, the Task Force Report data would suggest that Jews own at least two-thirds of these stores. Consequently, if the results of the Levine study are extrapolated to all of Harlem, it seems likely that Jews own about 40 per cent of the stores—as many as 40 per cent, or only 40 per cent, depending on one's values. This figure is similar to a Kerner Commission study of 15 cities which found that 39 per cent of the ghetto storeowners were Jewish.[3] Moreover, although most Harlem stores, white or black owned, are small, the Task Force study indicated that whites owned the larger stores, and concluded that "non-whites would be shown to own about 10 per cent or less of the capital invested in the community. A similar pattern would also be obtained if a comparison of gross sales were to be made."[4]

Beginning with the Depression, Negroes often became clients of Jewish professionals, for at that time Jews began to find jobs in the public schools and in the social work agencies. Today, it is estimated that about 60 per cent of New York City's school teachers are Jews. They came into "municipal professions" during the 1930's partly because of the workings of the succession process, the Jews replacing the Irish who had previously dominated the school system, and partly because jobs were now scarce in the private professions. For example, a number of Jewish men who had planned to become lawyers joined the Police Department in the Depression, and today they account for some of the high-ranking Jews on the force.

During the prosperous years after World War II, many—but not all—Jews continued to move up in the economic hierarchy, and today young Jews rarely replace their parents as slum store-owners, tenement managers or cabbies. Blacks (and Puerto Ricans) are succeeding to many of the jobs now being given up by Jews. For example, Levine found that among Harlem stores in business from 5 to 10 years, two-thirds were Negro owned. While the *number* of black owners, white collar workers and professionals is still far too low, the *rate of growth* of Negro white collar and professional employment in the country is now higher than among whites.

Jews continue to enter public school teaching, however, at least in New York. A generation ago, the city still had sizeable Jewish blue collar and poor white collar worker populations and their children presumably saw teaching as an attractive opportunity for upward mobility. Although the one available study showed that the proportion of Jews among teachers entering the city's public schools declined in 1960 after a peak in 1950, the percentage of Jews among the 1960 entrants was still 59 per cent.[5]

For many of New York's poor blacks, then, a large proportion of regular economic and professional contacts—as employees, tenants, customers and clients—are with whites, and although no conclusive figures are available, it seems likely that more of these contacts—but by no means all, as some black militants suggest—are with Jews than with other ethnics. Consequently, when blacks seek to obtain better jobs, the succession process frequently involves Jews, just as generations earlier, Jews competed with other ethnic groups for better jobs.

The reason for this Negro-Jewish relationship, and for the lesser economic involvement of blacks with the Irish, Italians, and other ethnics is a by-product of rapid Jewish upward mobility. Jews moved into white collar and professional jobs, and into ownership of factories and stores more quickly than other ethnics, so that they not only hired more employees, but were less likely to find fellow-Jews, at least for the low-wage jobs. In recent decades, they seem to have hired blacks and Puerto Ricans more often than Irish or Italian workers, partly because they were easier to hire, but perhaps also because Jews always discriminated less against them than did other whites. Moreover, Jews left the slums more quickly than the other ethnics, so that at the time when most Irish, Italians, Poles, Hungarians, etc., were still too poor to move to middle class neighborhoods, Negroes could often find housing only in a Jewish neighborhood in which an exodus was taking place. Thus, Negroes replaced the Jews in Central Harlem, and today they and Puerto Ricans are replacing them on the Upper West Side, in Washington Heights, the South Bronx, the Grand Concourse and elsewhere.

While the Negro-Jewish relationship may have appeared to be peaceful in the past, it has always been tense below the surface, at least in the slums. Owners of tenements and stores, whatever their race and religion, often exploit the slum dwellers, whatever *their* race and religion, if not always intentionally. The poor pay more, partly because insurance rates and other costs of doing business are higher in the slums, and partly because they are a captive market, particularly when they are segregated. Frequently, the poor also suffer in their contacts with professionals, for when ghetto schools are inadequate and welfare payments insufficient, the professionals cannot help their clients very much. Also, some professionals are trained only to work with middle class clients—or with poor people who have taken on middle class ways. When the poor do not behave in these ways, and professionals find that their techniques of teaching or counseling do not work, they may "put down" their poor clients, often without being aware of doing so.

The tension in Negro-Jewish relations is probably heightened because the majority of Jews whom blacks (and Puerto Ricans) deal with are of middle age, and many of the businessmen among them are engaged in small or declining enterprises. Thus, the Kerner Commission study cited previously reported that "our typical merchant was a man about fifty years old with a high school education, . . . most likely Jewish [and] if he belonged to any groups or organizations, he belonged to only one." Such businessmen and perhaps even the professionals are the remaining lower-middle class members of an ethnic group which is rapidly becoming upper-middle class in its choice of occupations. Many Jews who work in the ghetto therefore are, or feel they are, being left behind in the mobility race, and such feelings do not foster tolerance or empathy with the problems of a poor population. The lack of empathy often develops into hostility as militants demand that blacks be allowed to move up in the succession process and to take over the ghetto properties and positions held by Jews and other whites.

III

Although the current tensions in the Negro-Jewish relationship are to some extent instances of the "normal" (historically speaking) conflict between the remnants of a departing group and the upwardly mobile successors, some new elements have also changed the nature of the succession process, and are now overturning all kinds of historical precedents.

We have long known that the succession process has broken down at the bottom of the economic ladder, for the unskilled jobs by which European immigrants made their way into the mainstream are not as often available for the rural in-migrants, black and white, who have come to the city in the last two decades. The process seems to be breaking down at higher economic levels as well, however, for in these days of chain stores and corporate mergers, it is more difficult than ever to become a store owner or small entrepreneur. Some children of blue-collar workers cannot move out of the working class because they failed to obtain the schooling or diplomas now required for white collar jobs, and as automation proceeds, it is not at all clear whether the supply of technical and semi-professional jobs will be sufficient for the millions currently attending college. And now as in the past, the succession process is complicated by both blue and white collar workers who, satisfied with their jobs, do not want to move up to a higher status, thus blocking the way of their successors.

At the same time, many young blacks—although not as many as fearful whites think—are less willing than their parents to repeat the traditionally slow, step-by-step climb up the economic ladder. Having been held back by discrimination for so long, they are now asking that they be allowed to succeed to the profitable or prestigious jobs which whites have not been willing to give up. For example, Negroes employed in the Italian-dominated numbers game of New York have demanded, without much success so far, that they be given their fair share of the better jobs, and black as well as Puerto Rican teachers are demanding principalships in the city school system. In cities all over the country, upwardly mobile elements in the black community are demanding more jobs as teachers (in New York City, only about 10 per cent of teachers are black or Latin), college professors—and students—policemen and firemen, anti-poverty officials, and in other municipal and public service positions.

To achieve these demands, the organized ghetto and its mobile young leaders are turning to political means for speeding up the succession process. As a result, this process is now being politicized, making it more visible than it was in the private economic sphere, and more important, transforming succession conflicts into public issues. When Negroes fought for better jobs in the numbers racket, no one, other than the underworld or the ghetto, paid much attention, but the struggle between the teachers and the decentralized ghetto schools is a public conflict between organized groups, with government firmly in the middle and ultimately required to find a solution. The conflict thus becomes raw material for newspaper headlines and TV leads, which in turn draws in previously uninvolved citizens who then side with their own ethnic or racial group.

As a result, both sides in the school strikes employed the politically potent weapons of ethnic and racial loyalty to influence public opinion. Blacks who resent the Jewish role in the ghetto economy and the U.F.T.'s attacks on local control occasionally resorted to widely publicized outbursts against the Jews, Jewish teachers occasionally made less publicized antiblack remarks, and the U.F.T. appealed to New York Jewry for support by intimating that the anti-Jewish rhetoric of black militants constituted the re-emergence of organized anti-Semitism.

In the heat of political battle, each side saw its opponent as more cohesive and unified than it actually is. Thus, despite the union's efforts, many Jews and other whites began to believe that the entire ghetto was in favor of local control, whereas in reality, many blacks still believe strongly in the desirability of integration. Some black advocates of local control argued that all Jews were against them, when in fact the city's Jewish population is not homogeneous, and on this issue, as on others, was divided along class lines. Lower-middle class Jews seemed to be solidly behind the U.F.T., for while they had supported the civil rights movement in the past, they became edgy when Negroes began to ask for local control, and thus for some of their jobs and properties as well. The latest phase of the succession process is threatening their income and status, making them react with the same "backlash" previously expressed by other ethnics of the same socio-economic level.

The smaller but influential upper-middle class Jewish population, the highly educated professionals, managers and intellectuals of Manhattan and the expensive suburbs who provided a significant proportion of the funds for the national civil rights movement seem to be more sympathetic to local control.[6] Since this population has little to fear—or to lose—from school decentralization, it has not responded to the U.F.T.'s appeals to fear of anti-Semitism, and this is presumably why major Jewish organizations dominated by upper-middle class Jews did not take a stand on the union cause.

Yet another change has taken place to increase the visibility and bitterness of succession conflict: the breakup of the traditional ethnic-Negro alliance in the Democratic party. Before the black community began to demand its rights of succession, the ethnics in the Democratic party were usually able to maintain their power by granting a few concessions to the ghetto or buying off its leaders. Today, however, as Negroes are seeking their fair share of public jobs and political power from the ethnics, the party has become a warring camp. Although it was barely able to preserve the traditional coalition in the last national elections, at the local level, the party is split in almost every city. A Democratic mayor cannot continue to favor the ethnics without angering the ghetto, and he cannot often grant the demands of the blacks without enraging the ethnics.

In New York City, where the Democratic split and the availability of a liberal Republican candidate led to the election of John Lindsay, the black-ethnic conflict has moved beyond the confines of the Democratic party and thus into the public arena. Indeed, one of the major reasons for Lindsay's failure to settle the school strikes was his inability to use party loyalty as a tool in negotiating with the U.F.T. or with the ethnic labor unions in the Central Labor Board who stood behind the teachers' union.

IV

While anti-Semitism and anti-Negro prejudice were very visible in the school strikes, neither played a major causal role in the strikes, however. The strikes were, I believe, largely an economic and political struggle over the succession process, and a class conflict, primarily over jobs, between the upwardly mobile black poor and a coalition of unions and other organizations representing white working class and lower-middle class New Yorkers, people who might be described as "sub-affluent."

The U.F.T., which has always worked for the improvement of ghetto schools and even supports some form of decentralization, turned against local control the moment when Ocean Hill-Brownsville demanded the right to transfer or fire teachers, and to hire its own. The union seems to have reacted less against this demand than against an assumption about the future, that in a totally decentralized school system, and with the proportion of Negroes in the city and in the public schools rising, many white teachers might someday find themselves rejected by black (or Puerto Rican) school districts. Indeed, the union membership perceived the strike as being concerned first and foremost with job security, and implicitly with the succession process, for as one much quoted union member put it, "We don't deny their equality but they shouldn't get it by pulling down others who have just come up."[7] The U.F.T.'s feelings about the future were shared by other predominantly white ethnic unions, for example the electricians and plumbers who feared that under local control, their members would lose their jobs, not only in decentralized schools but also in the Model Cities programs and whatever other ghetto municipal programs might be decentralized in the years to come.

Nevertheless, the contested issues are over the economic positions of the participants, not their ethnic characteristics. When Negroes express their anger in anti-Semitic terms, it is only because many of the whites who affect their lives are Jewish; if the ghetto storeowners, landlords and teachers were Chinese, Negro hostility would surely be anti-Chinese. Similarly, when Jews resort to overt racism, they do so primarily because they feel their economic and social position is threatened by blacks, just as they sometimes make racist remarks about "the goyim" when their economic progress is held back by non-Jews.

Still, ethnic and racial considerations have been raised, and therefore become part of the issue and even of the succession conflict. The fact is that the school strike was perceived as setting Jewish teachers against blacks, whereas neither the struggle of the Welfare Rights movement against the Department of Welfare, nor that of the ghetto against the Police Department has involved ethnic hostility. Of course, these municipal agencies are ethnically more heterogeneous; policemen these days are no longer just Irish and the department includes a sizeable proportion of Italians and even white Protestants. Moreover, it is entirely possible that if and when ghetto demands for decentralization extend to police and fire protection and garbage removal, and jobs will be at issue, the political rhetoric of the succession conflict will include anti-Irish and anti-Italian outbursts.

Why black leaders have so far resorted to public expressions of anti-Semitism while not deprecating the ethnic origins of policemen or social workers, at least in public, is probably a result of the greater ethnic homogeneity in the city's public schools. When this is combined with the large number of Jewish landlords and storeowners in the ghetto, racially hyper-conscious blacks may easily if inaccurately conclude that they are being held back by *the* Jews. Undoubtedly, some militant leaders believe this to be the case, while others are reflecting sentiments among their followers, making statements they do not believe but must make—or be replaced by other leaders. But then, leaders of every race, religion or political affiliation sometimes make statements they do not believe but which express the sentiments of their followers.

Some black leaders may also be reacting against the reduction of Jewish support that took place after the civil rights movement turned toward Black Power, for people are always angrier at rejections from old friends than from traditional enemies. It is unlikely, however, that the rank-and-file ghetto resident was disappointed; he has had little contact, after all, with the liberalism of organized Jewry, and the Jews he sees regularly often call him "the schwarze" behind his back. And finally, one cannot ignore the habitual anti-Semitism that exists within the Christian culture shared by Negroes.

Nevertheless, when all is said and done, the crucial issues are more economic than ethnic, and if these issues which are polarizing New York and much of American society generally are to be dealt with, it is high time to find appropriate solutions—and to refrain from the politics of ethnic and racial labeling.

The black militants who have resorted to anti-Semitic attacks should realize that they are criticizing practices which have nothing to do with ethnicity. However much some Jewish businessmen or professionals have exploited black customers and clients, Negroes in the same occupational position have done exactly the same—or worse, because usually their insurance rates and other costs of doing business are even higher. Moreover, black businessmen are often no more a part of the ghetto than whites; Levine found that only a little more than half of the black storeowners her students interviewed lived in Harlem. The militants must also understand that Jews, more than other whites, have supported not only integration but Black Power. But most important, the militants must realize that they are pursuing an immoral as well as dangerous tactic. If they fan the flames of anti-Semitism, either in anger or to please their constituents, they will encourage the fascist and other anti-Semitic groups that still exist in America, who, if they obtain power, will deal as ruthlessly with blacks as with Jews.

Conversely, Jews should refrain from anti-black attacks, especially when they are really objecting to the militancy rather than the racial characteristics of their target. They should also beware of what Roy Innis has called "the double standard that characterizes much of the dialogue on black anti-Semitism." As he points out, and rightly so, "Jews can and have criticized black leaders, especially those considered to be militant or nationalistic, with impunity. If a Jewish organization issues a statement tomorrow harshly criticizing a black leader, it will not be accused of anti-black sentiments. But let a black leader criticize Israel or a Jewish group, and he automatically becomes anti-Semitic."[8]

At the same time, Jews should be careful not to over-react, and to interpret all attacks on them as instances of one undifferentiated entity called anti-Semitism. There is a difference of degree between attacks on Jewish individuals and on the Jews as a group, and a difference in quality between attacks on Jews who behave unethically as businessmen, professionals or politicians, and attacks on Jews as persons. There are also differences in the content of the attacks; describing Jews as greedy is a calumny; calling them clannish is closer to the truth—and a truth that is celebrated by Jews themselves when the word cohesive is substituted.

Attacks on the Jews as a group, on behavior that is attributed to Jews as persons, and on personal qualities that are attributed to being Jewish are clearly instances of anti-Semitism; attacks on individual Jews or on the unethical behavior of individuals and quasi-accurate statements about Jews as a group are no more justifiable, but they are not quite the same. Of course, ascribing any behavior or attitude to a person because he is Jewish—or because he is black—is racist, but as long as television entertainers can tell "Polish" or "Italian" jokes without blinking, Jewish leaders should not rush to the mimeograph machine every time a black militant points out that most school teachers in New York are Jewish.

Obviously there are many—and tragic—justifications for the Jewish sensitivity to any attack that bears even the slight resemblance to anti-Semitism, and as Earl Raab pointed out in the January, 1969 *Commentary,* enough anti-Semitism is still buried in the American psyche to put Jews perpetually on their guard. But in responding to the outbursts of black militants, Jews should also realize that the use of demagogic rhetoric is frequent among political organizations of the poor, black or white, just as pentecostal preaching is in their churches. There is a danger that Jews will develop the same over-reaction to the black rhetoric and the black demands for equal rights that has emerged among poor and sub-affluent whites in recent years: for example, the panicky demands for law and order after the ghetto rebellions even though these rebellions did not touch white areas; and the exaggerated fears that the federal government and the Lindsay administration are favoring the blacks and ignoring white demands, when in fact precious little money or power has flowed into the ghetto since the federal civil rights efforts and the War on Poverty began.

The U.F.T.'s reprinting of anti-Semitic literature spawned by the school strikes surely encouraged white over-reaction to ghetto demands and rhetoric, as did the union's too-easy assumption that the Ocean Hill Brownsville Governing Board was responsible both for initiating and not repressing the anti-Semitic outbursts in the school district. The union not only exaggerated the power of the Board over its community, but forgot that Rhody McCoy was hiring mainly white teachers, many of them Jewish, to replace the union teachers who had walked out.

Since the end of the last strike, both sides have been over-reacting dangerously. Jews are justified in attacking radio poetry that preaches Jewish extermination, but they should not make a fuss over every streetcorner slur about the Jewish role in the ghetto. Blacks are justified in objecting to exploitation, but they have no right to describe it as a Jewish practice, and not even the most intense black anger can justify comparisons of Jews with Nazis. In the present political climate, in which every over-reaction by one side leads to an over-reaction from the other, the resultant spiral can only increase racial polarization. Jews and other whites will feel that their anti-Negro prejudices are now more reasonable, and the many ghetto residents who still retain deep faith in racial integration will begin to think that maybe the militants are right after all.

Clearly, both Jews and blacks should think about the consequences before they attack each other. Blacks must understand that any program of Black Power or local control that does not involve some cooperation with whites is bound to fail, for whites are the political majority in the city, and they control the purse-strings here and in Washington. Jews and other whites must understand that traditional integration policies have helped the middle class Negro but not the rank-and-file ghetto resident, and that the Black Power movement emerged precisely because of this reason. Whites need to realize that the movement is a serious striving for dignity and self-respect, seeking to exorcise the unconscious rejection and depersonalization of the poor, black or white, which more affluent people and their institutions, black or white, often express in dealing with groups they consider inferior. Thus, for ghetto residents, at least, the demand for local control of the schools is principally an attempt to find teachers, curricula and school infra-structures which do not put down their children as culturally disadvantaged or "hard-core."

Moreover, while Black Capitalism cannot upgrade ghetto incomes by itself, and local control may not improve the educational performance of poor black children significantly, Black Power is a social movement, and social movements are militant, quasi-religious (and somewhat paranoid) bodies which are not deterred by logical critiques of their fundamental beliefs or their political irrationalities. They lose their supporters' allegiance only if society as a whole does something about the deprivations that give rise to social movements in the first place.

Unfortunately, political organizations rarely think about the consequences before they attack each other. Such groups think first and foremost about their own survival; how to retain their members and followers and to prevent their departure to a more militant competitor. If the constituents of Jewish defense organizations and black militant groups urge their organizations to attack and counterattack, a skirmish of speeches and press releases can easily escalate into a full-scale war of words and political acts. Of course, no one knows how much pressure black and Jewish constituencies are putting on their organizations, and it might therefore well be worth calling a summit meeting of leaders of all Jewish defense organizations and black groups to see if a joint moratorium on attacks and counter-attacks can be declared in order to prevent further escalation of the war.

V

Above all, Jews, other whites and Negroes must start to deal with the fundamental economic issue which underlies all of the recent conflicts: that technological change and other economic and social trends are creating a post-industrial society in which the policies of both private enterprise and government tend to favor first and foremost the college-educated professional and technical population. These days, the best jobs, public and private, and the highest government subsidies go to the middle and upper-middle classes, leaving the sub-affluent population and the poor to divide the economic leftovers. When automation comes to the factory or a computer is installed in the office, they eliminate jobs among sub-affluent and poor workers while increasing the need for educated technical and professional workers. Indeed, that portion of the economy in which the sub-affluents and the poor play a major role is constantly decreasing in size and importance, so that the two groups are fighting each other for an ever-smaller share of the economic pie. Similarly, with suburbanites having a clear majority of the votes in the nation—or in metropolitan government if it ever comes to be—if they choose to vote in unison, the urban sub-affluents and the poor are also fighting over their share of a constantly decreasing amount of political power.

In short, national economic and political changes have so altered the urban succession process, in New York and elsewhere, that many sub-affluent and poor cannot move up, or make sure that their children will be able to improve their position. As a result, the sub-affluents are opposing the poor in order to maintain their present status and to prevent succession from taking place. And since education is one of the basic ingredients to success in the post-industrial society, it is no coincidence that a major locus of the current conflict, in New York and other cities, is in the schools.

My description of the basic class-conflict in the post-industrial society might suggest that the sub-affluent population should join with the poor to fight the common enemy, but such a coalition is highly unlikely. Given the heterogeneity and conflicting interests within each of these aggregates, there can probably be no organized union of the poor, or of the sub-affluent, or of both, and there is not even a united affluent enemy. Indeed, radical and liberal segments among the affluent often side with the poor against the sub-affluent, if only because the latter are a numerical majority in the country and can outvote radicals, liberals and the poor. Also, in the short-run world of politics, sub-affluent people find it easier and more effective to attack those below them in income and status than to fight the affluent sector which they are themselves trying to enter.

The competition between the subaffluents and the poor is of course interlaced with ethnic and racial considerations, and some observers are already fearful that Jews and blacks will be fighting each other on many fronts—or will be urged to do battle by affluent WASPs. Although evidence for a WASP conspiracy is hard to find, there is no doubt that sub-affluent Jews will continue to fight with poor blacks over succession, and that affluent Americans will not do much to ameliorate the conflict unless it begins to hurt them. Affluent Jews (and blacks) will probably also remain on the sidelines, making it unlikely that the conflict will ever involve *all* Jews and *all* blacks. Indeed, economic interests may instead create a wider split within the Jewish population between affluents and sub-affluents, just as these interests have split the affluent and the poor in the black community.

Nevertheless, even if the conflict between sub-affluents and the poor—and its ethnic and racial spinoffs—increases, it is unlikely that the kind of class-consciousness postulated by Marx or ethnic and racial consciousness based on economic considerations will ever develop to the point that Americans, rich or poor, act only on their so-called class-interest. The modern economy is just too diverse for lower-middle class employees of a national corporation to feel much communality of interests with lower-middle class shopkeepers. Nor are ethnic and racial allegiances strong enough for all members of an ethnic or racial group to unite politically when their economic and status interests diverge.

The solution, then, is not to be found in a 20th century doctrine of the class struggle, and it may even be too late for the coalition of the poor, the working class and the democratic radicals which Bayard Rustin, Michael Harrington and their associates have been urging. The working class is not only shrinking in size but is finding that it often has more in common with the lower-middle class than with the poor, and it is entirely possible that the organizations of the sub-affluents might try to build an alliance against both the poor and the affluent. Still, there is something to be said for the Rustin-Harrington coalition model, particularly if it can overcome its animus against all forms of Black Power and New Left thought, and admit the democratic and programmatically oriented among these two movements, and if it can attract the disaffected among the lower middle class as well.

Planning or predicting coalitions is always risky, however, and it is probably more realistic to think in terms of programs and policies that will attract various sectors of the total population than to begin with hypothetical coalitions and then find programs on which they can agree.

Such programs can be described only briefly here, but in addition to anti-poverty efforts, the elimination of unemployment and underemployment, and the establishment of a guaranteed income policy and a higher minimum wage, the time has come also to reinvigorate the succession process. This reinvigoration should use public funds and public power to create jobs in the professional, semi-professional, and technical occupations that would allow both the sub-affluent and the poor to move up in the economic hierarchy. What I have in mind is a massive federally-aided job development scheme in those occupations which are most likely to grow anyway in the post-industrial economy: teachers and teachers aides, and a variety of other professionals, semi-professionals and para-professionals in the public services. For example, the expansion and improvement of educational institutions—from nursery schools to post-graduate university departments—would create the kinds of jobs to which both the poor and the sub-affluent are aspiring, and would at the same time provide citizens with the schooling they need to enjoy life in post-industrial modernity. Such a program would enable many people to move up to new occupational slots, and others to succeed to the vacancies so created. If federal funds could be used to make public school teaching a less strenuous and better-paid profession, it would attract people now working in or preparing themselves for various blue and white collar jobs, and these jobs could then be taken by less skilled workers who are not yet ready, for one reason or another, to enter the professions. Their jobs could be upgraded by yet other means, for example, by increasing the worker's autonomy and providing for the application of his craftsmanship in mass production, and by the automation of "dirty" elements of work.

A publicly stimulated succession process would not eliminate all conflict over succession, but it would go far to reduce the insoluble elements of the conflict by providing new resources. Suppose the federal government had been able to provide funds to New York City last fall to create a few hundred new teaching positions. These funds could have produced additional slots in Ocean Hill-Brownsville, or offered new job possibilities to the union members who were removed from or who wanted to leave the Brooklyn school district, thus reducing the job security fears of the U.F.T. membership. The two strikes might have been avoided and the current Negro-Jewish animosity might not have become so heated. Ethnic and racial conflicts are part of American life, but there is nothing like an infusion of new economic opportunities to erode the sharp edges of these conflicts.

NOTES

1. Naomi Levine, "Who Owns the Stores in Harlem?," *Congress Bi-Weekly*, September 16, 1968, pp. 10–12.
2. *The Mayor's Task Force Report on the Economic Redevelopment of Harlem*, January 15, 1968, Table IV-3.
3. *Supplemental Studies for the National Advisory Commission on Civil Disorders*, July 1968, p. 126.
4. Mayor's Task Force Report, p. IV-17.
5. The study, based on judgments about religion from names on lists of entering teachers, showed that in 1920, Jews made up 26 per cent of entrants. The percentage rose to 44 in 1930; 56 in 1940; and 65 in 1950. (Stephen Cole, "The Unionization of Teachers," *Sociology of Education*, Vol. 41, Winter 1968, Table 13, p. 85.) Needless to say, findings gathered by judging names are not very reliable, but this method tends to underestimate the number of Jews because of the 2nd and 3rd generation tendency to Americanize Jewish-sounding names.
6. An earlier and similar split between lower-middle class and upper-middle class Jews over a New York City school issue, the attempt to pair schools in Queens, is described by Kurt Lang and Gladys Engel Lang, "Resistance to School Desegregation: A Case Study of Backlash among Jews," *Sociological Inquiry*, Vol. 35, Winter 1965, pp. 94–106.
7. The succession process was also alluded to in the recently controversial statement of the Metropolitan Museum's "Harlem on my Mind" catalogue, that "behind every hurdle that the Afro-American has yet to jump stands the Jew who has already cleared it." Needless to say, neither all Jews nor *the* Jew stand behind every hurdle, and if some Jews stand behind some hurdles, Jews also have some hurdles yet to clear.
8. *Manhattan Tribune,* November 30, 1968.

THE RED AND THE BLACK
Vine Deloria, Jr.

Several authors suggested in the previous section that
when social scientists look beyond the situation of white
immigrants, they tend to see only as far as black Americans, viewing them through ethnocentric prisms or lumping them with all colored minorities under a single "third
world" label.

Vine Deloria, spokesman for the Indians, notes this,
too. Indeed, he argues that Indians either have been
systematically excluded from consideration of social
scientists and most civil rights activists, or have been
seen by both groups as people who are somehow "red-
dish black."

Deloria is not at all satisfied with either tendency. He
explains his position by recounting the special problems
faced by the multifarious Indian peoples who seek to
recapture their traditional values.

Civil rights has been the most important and least understood movement
of our generation. To some it has seemed to be a simple matter of fulfilling
rights outlined by the Constitutional amendments after the Civil War.
To others, particularly church people, Civil Rights has appeared to be a
fulfillment of the brotherhood of man and the determination of humanity's relationship to God. To those opposing the movement, Civil Rights
has been a foreign conspiracy which has threatened the fabric of our
society.

For many years the movement to give the black people rights equal to those of their white neighbors was called Race Relations. The preoccupation with race obscured the real issues that were developing and meant that programs devised to explore the area of race always had a black orientation.

To the Indian people it has seemed quite unfair that churches and government agencies concentrated their efforts primarily on the blacks. By defining the problem as one of race and making race refer solely to black, Indians were systematically excluded from consideration. National church groups have particularly used race as a means of exploring minority-group relations. Whatever programs or policies outlined from national churches to their affiliates and parishes were generally black-oriented programs which had been adapted to include Indians.

There was probably a historical basis for this type of thinking. In many states in the last century, Indians were classified as white by laws passed to exclude blacks. So there was a connotation that Indians might in some way be like whites. But in other areas, particularly marriage laws, Indians were classified as blacks and this connotation really determined the role into which the white man forced the red man. Consequently, as far as most Race Relations were concerned, Indians were classified as nonwhites.

There has been no way to positively determine in which category Indians belong when it comes to federal agencies. The Bureau of Indian Affairs consistently defined Indians as good guys who have too much dignity to demonstrate, hoping to keep the Indian people separate from the ongoing Civil Rights movement. Other agencies generally adopted a semi-black orientation. Sometimes Indians were treated as if they were blacks and other times not.

The Civil Rights Commission and the Community Relations Service always gave only lip service to Indians until it was necessary for them to write an annual report. At that time they always sought out some means of including Indians as a group with which they had worked the previous fiscal year. That was the extent of Indian relationship with the agency: a paragraph in the annual report and a promise to do something next year.

Older Indians, as a rule, have been content to play the passive role outlined for them by the bureau. They have wanted to avoid the rejection and bad publicity given activists.

The Indian people have generally avoided confrontations between the different minority groups and confrontations with the American public at large. They have felt that any publicity would inevitably have bad results and since the press seemed dedicated to the perpetuation of sensationalism rather than straight reporting of the facts, great care has been taken to avoid the spotlight. Because of this attitude, Indian people have not become well known in the field of inter-group and race relations. Consequently they have suffered from the attitudes of people who have only a superficial knowledge of minority groups and have attached a certain stigma to them.

The most common attitude Indians have faced has been the unthoughtful Johnny-come-lately liberal who equates certain goals with a dark skin. This type of individual generally defines the goals of all groups by the way he understands what he wants for the blacks. Foremost in this category have been younger social workers and clergymen entering the field directly out of college or seminary. For the most part they have been book-fed and lack experience in life. They depend primarily upon labels and categories of academic import rather than on any direct experience. Too often they have achieved positions of prominence as programs have been expanded to meet needs of people. In exercising their discretionary powers administratively, they have run roughshod over Indian people. They have not wanted to show their ignorance about Indians. Instead, they prefer to place all people with darker skin in the same category of basic goals, then develop their programs to fit these preconceived ideas.

Since the most numerous group has been the blacks, programs designed for blacks were thought adequate for all needs of all groups. When one asks a liberal about minority groups, he unconsciously seems to categorize them all together for purposes of problem solving. Hence, dark-skinned and minority group as categorical concepts have brought about the same basic results—the Indian is defined as a subcategory of black.

Cultural differences have only seemed to emphasize the white liberal's point of view in lumping the different communities together. When Indians have pointed out real differences that do exist, liberals have tended to dismiss the differences as only minor aberrations which distinguish different racial groups.

At one conference on education of minority groups, I once mentioned the existence of some three hundred Indian languages which made bicultural and bilingual education a necessity. I was immediately challenged by several white educators who attempted to prove that blacks also have a language problem. I was never able to make the difference real to them. For the conference people the point had again been established that minority groups all had the same basic problems.

Recently, blacks and some Indians have defined racial problems as having one focal point—the White Man. This concept is a vast oversimplification of the real problem, as it centers on a racial theme rather than on specific facts. And it is simply the reversal of the old prejudicial attitude of the white who continues to define minority groups as problems of his —that is, Indian problem, Negro problem, and so on.

Rather than race or minority grouping, non-whites have often been defined according to their function within the American society. Negroes, as we have said, were considered draft animals, Indians wild animals. So too, Orientals were considered domestic animals and Mexicans humorous lazy animals. The white world has responded to the non-white groups in

a number of ways, but primarily according to the manner in which it believed the non-whites could be rescued from their situation.

Thus Orientals were left alone once whites were convinced that they
preferred to remain together and presented no basic threat to white social
mores. Mexicans were similarly discarded and neglected when whites felt
that they preferred to remain by themselves. In both cases there was no
direct confrontation between whites and the two groups because there
was no way that a significant number of them could be exploited. They
owned little; they provided little which the white world coveted.

With the black and the Indian, however, tensions increased over the
years. Both groups had been defined as animals with which the white had
to have some relation and around whom some attitude must be formed.
Blacks were ex-draft animals who somehow were required to become non-
black. Indeed, respectability was possible for a black only by emphasizing
characteristics and features that were non-black. Indians were the ex-wild
animals who had provided the constant danger for the civilizing tendencies of the invading white. They always presented a foreign aspect to
whites unfamiliar with the western hemisphere.

The white man adopted two basic approaches in handling blacks and
Indians. He systematically excluded blacks from all programs, policies,
social events, and economic schemes. He could not allow blacks to rise
from their position because it would mean that the evolutionary scheme
had superseded the Christian scheme and that man had perhaps truly
descended from the ape.

With the Indian the process was simply reversed. The white man had
been forced to deal with the Indian in treaties and agreements. It was
difficult, therefore, to completely overlook the historical antecedents such
as Thanksgiving, the plight of the early Pilgrims, and the desperate straits
from which various Indian tribes had often rescued the whites. Indians
were therefore subjected to the most intense pressure to become white.
Laws passed by Congress had but one goal—the Anglo-Saxonization of the
Indian. The antelope had to become a white man.

Between these two basic attitudes, the apelike draft animal and the wild
free-running antelope, the white man was impaled on the horns of a
dilemma he had created within himself.

It is well to keep these distinctions clearly in mind when talking about
Indians and blacks. When the liberals equate the two they are overlook-
ing obvious historical facts. Never did the white man systematically exclude Indians from his schools and meeting places. Nor did the white man
ever kidnap black children from their homes and take them off to a
government boarding school to be educated as whites. The white man
signed no treaties with the black. Nor did he pass any amendments to the
Constitution to guarantee the treaties of the Indian.

The basic problem which has existed between the various racial groups
has not been one of race but of culture and legal status. The white man

systematically destroyed Indian culture where it existed, but separated blacks from his midst so that they were forced to attempt the creation of their own culture.

The white man forbade the black to enter his own social and economic system and at the same time force-fed the Indian what he was denying the black. Yet the white man demanded that the black conform to white standards and insisted that the Indian don feathers and beads periodically to perform for him.

The white man presented the *problem* of each group in contradictory ways so that neither black nor Indian could understand exactly where the problem existed or how to solve it. The Indian was always told that his problem was one of conflicting cultures. Yet, when solutions were offered by the white man, they turned out to be a reordering of the legal' relationship between red and white. There was never a time when the white man said he was trying to help the Indian get into the mainstream of American life that he did not also demand that the Indian give up land, water, minerals, timber, and other resources which would enrich the white men.

The black also suffered the same basic lie. Time after time legislation was introduced which purported to give the black equal rights with the white but which ultimately restricted his life and opportunities, even his acceptance by white people. The initial Civil Rights Act following the thirteenth, fourteenth, and fifteenth amendments was assumed to give the black equal rights with "white citizens." In fact, it was so twisted that it took nearly a century to bring about additional legislation to confirm black rights.

In June of 1968 the Supreme Court finally interpreted an ancient statute in favor of blacks in the matter of purchasing a house. Had the right existed for nearly a century without anyone knowing it? Of course not, the white had simply been unwilling to give in to the black. Can one blame the black athletes at the recent Olympic Games for their rebellion against the role cast for them by white society? Should they be considered as specially trained athletic animals suitable only for hauling away tons of gold medals for the United States every four years while equality remains as distant as it ever was?

It is time for both black and red to understand the ways of the white man. The white is after Indian lands and resources. He always has been and always will be. For Indians to continue to think of their basic conflict with the white man as cultural is the height of folly. The problem is and always has been the adjustment of the legal relationship between the Indian tribes and the federal government, between the true owners of the land and the usurpers.

The black must understand that whites are determined to keep him out of their society. No matter how many Civil Rights laws are passed or how many are on the drawing board, the basic thrust is to keep the black out of society and harmless. The problem, therefore, is not one of legal status, it is one of culture and social and economic mobility. It is foolish for a black to depend upon a law to make acceptance of him by the white possible. Nor should he react to the rejection. His problem is social, and economic, and cultural, not one of adjusting the legal relationship between the two groups.

When the black seeks to change his role by adjusting the laws of the nation, he merely raises the hope that progress is being made. But for the majority of blacks progress is not being made. Simply because a middle-class black can eat at the Holiday Inn is not a gain. People who can afford the best generally get it. A socio-economic, rather than legal adjustment must consequently be the goal.

★   ★   ★

It was more than religious intolerance that drove the early colonists across the ocean. More than a thousand years before Columbus, the barbaric tribes destroyed the Roman Empire. With utter lack of grace, they ignorantly obliterated classical civilization. Christianity swept across the conquerors like the white man later swept across North America, destroying native religions and leaving paralyzed groups of disoriented individuals in its wake. Then the combination of Christian theology, superstition, and forms of the old Roman civil government began to control the tamed barbaric tribes. Gone were the religious rites of the white tribesmen. Only the Gothic arches in the great cathedrals, symbolizing the oaks under which their ancestors worshiped, remained to remind them of the glories that had been.

Not only did the European tribes lose their religion, they were subjected to a new form of economics which totally destroyed them: feudalism. The freedom that had formerly been theirs became only the freedom to toil on the massive estates. Even their efforts to maintain their ancient ways fell to the requirements of the feudal state as power centered in a few royal houses.

Feudalism saw man as a function of land and not as something in himself. The European tribes, unable to withstand the chaos of medieval social and political forces, were eliminated as power consolidated in a few hands. Far easier than the Indian tribes of this continent, the Europeans gave up the ghost and accepted their fate without questioning it. And they remained in subjection for nearly a millenium.

The religious monolith which Christianity had deviously constructed over the Indo-European peasants eventually showed cracks in its foundations. The revolution in religious thought triggered by Martin Luther's challenge to Papal authority was merely an afterthought. It did no more than acknowledge that the gates had been opened a long time and that it was perfectly natural to walk through them into the new era.

In the sixteenth century Europe opened up the can of worms which had been carefully laid to rest a millenium earlier. The Reformation again brought up the question of the place of Western man in God's scheme of events. Because there was no way the individual could relate to the past, he was told to relate to the other world, leaving this world free for nationalistic exploitation—the real forger of identity.

Because tribes and groups had been unable to survive, the common denominator, the individual, became the focal point of the revolt. Instead of socially oriented individuals, the Reformation produced self-centered individuals. Social and economic Darwinism, the survival of the fittest at any cost, replaced the insipid brotherhood of Christianity not because Christianity's basic thrust was invalid, but because it had been corrupted for so long that it was no longer recognizable.

The centuries following the Reformation were marked with incredible turmoil. But the turmoil was not so much over religious issues as it was over interpretation of religious doctrines. Correctness of belief was preferred over truth itself. Man charged back into the historical mists to devise systems of thought which would connect him with the greats of the past. Fear of the unfamiliar became standard operating procedure.

Today Europe is still feeling the effects of the submersion of its original tribes following the demise of the Roman Empire. Western man smashes that which he does not understand because he never had the opportunity to evolve his own culture. Instead ancient cultures were thrust upon him while he was yet unprepared for them.

There lingers still the unsolved question of the primacy of the Roman Empire as contrasted with the simpler more relaxed life of the Goths, Celts, Franks, and Vikings.

Where feudalism conceived man as a function of land, the early colonists reversed the situation in their efforts to create "new" versions of their motherlands. Early settlers made land a function of man, and with a plentitude of land, democracy appeared to be the inevitable desire of God. It was relatively simple, once they had made this juxtaposition, to define Indians, blacks, and other groups in relation to land.

The first organizing efforts of the new immigrants were directed toward the process of transplanting European social and political systems in the new areas they settled. Thus New England, New France, New Spain, New Sweden, New Haven, New London, New York, New Jersey, Troy, Ithaca, and other names expressed their desire to relive the life they had known on the other side of the Atlantic—but to relive it on their own terms. No one seriously wanted to return to the status of peasant, but people certainly entertained the idea of indigenous royalty. If your ancestor got off the boat, you were one step up the ladder of respectability. Many Indians, of course, believe it would have been better if Plymouth Rock had landed on the Pilgrims than the Pilgrims on Plymouth Rock.

The early colonists did not flee religious persecution so much as they wished to perpetuate religious persecution under circumstances more favorable to them. They wanted to be the persecutors. The rigorous the-ocracies which quickly originated in New England certainly belie the myth that the first settlers wanted only religious freedom. Nothing was more destructive of man than the early settlements on this continent.

It would have been far better for the development of this continent had the first settlers had no illusions as to their motives. We have seen nearly five centuries of white settlement on this continent, yet the problems brought over from Europe remain unsolved and grow in basic intensity daily. And violence as an answer to the problem of identity has only covered discussion of the problem.

In transplanting Europe to these peaceful shores, the colonists violated the most basic principle of man's history: certain lands are given to certain peoples. It is these peoples only who can flourish, thrive, and survive on the land. Intruders may hold sway for centuries but they will eventually be pushed from the land or the land itself will destroy them. The Holy Land, having been periodically conquered and beaten into submission by a multitude of invaders, today remains the land which God gave to Abraham and his descendants. So will America return to the red man.

The message of the Old Testament, the Hebrew-Jewish conception of the Homeland, has been completely overlooked. Culture, if any exists, is a function of the homeland, not a function of the economic system that appears to hold temporary sway over a region.

Thus the fundamental error of believing a transplant possible prac-tically canceled any chances for significant evolution of a homogeneous people. Even more so, it canceled the potentiality of making the new set-tlements the land of the free and the home of the brave—not when it was already the home of the Indian brave.

There never really was a transplant. There was only a three-hundred-year orgy of exploitation. The most feverish activity in America has been land speculation. Nearly all transactions between Indian and white have been land transactions. With Emancipation, the first program offered the black was one hundred dollars, forty acres, and a mule! But when it appeared the black might be able to create something on the land, that was immediately taken away from him.

Land has been the basis on which racial relations have been defined ever since the first settlers got off the boat. Minority groups, denominated as such, have always been victims of economic forces rather than beneficiaries of the lofty ideals proclaimed in the Constitution and elsewere. One hun-dred years of persecution after Emancipation, the Civil Rights laws of the 1950's and 1960's were all passed by use of the Interstate Commerce Clause of the Constitution. Humanity, at least on this continent, has been subject to the whims of the marketplace.

When we began to talk of Civil Rights, therefore, it greatly confuses the issue and lessens our chances of understanding the forces involved in the rights of human beings. Rather, we should begin talking about actual economic problems; and in realistic terms we are talking about land.

No movement can sustain itself, no people can continue, no government can function, and no religion can become a reality except it be bound to a land area of its own. The Jews have managed to sustain themselves in the Diaspora for over two thousand years, but in the expectation of their homeland's restoration. So-called *power* movements are primarily the urge of peoples to find their homeland and to channel their psychic energies through their land into social and economic reality. Without land and a homeland no movement can survive. And any movement attempting to build without clarifying its goals usually ends in violence, the energy from which could have been channeled toward sinking the necessary roots for the movement's existence.

★   ★   ★

In 1963, when the Civil Rights drive was at its peak, many of us who occupied positions of influence in Indian Affairs were severely chastised by the more militant churchmen for not having participated in the March on Washington. One churchman told me rather harshly that unless Indians *got with it* there would be no place for us in America's future. Equality, he assured me, was going to be given to us whether we want it or not.

We knew, of course, that he had equality confused with sameness but there was no way to make him understand. In the minds of most people in 1963, legal equality and cultural conformity were identical.

We refused to participate in the Washington March. In our hearts and minds we could not believe that blacks wanted to be the same as whites. And we knew that even if they did want that, the whites would never allow it to happen. As far as we could determine, white culture, if it existed, depended primarily upon the exploitation of land, people, and life itself. It relied upon novelties and fads to provide an appearance of change but it was basically an economic Darwinism that destroyed rather than created.

It was therefore no surprise to us when Stokely Carmichael began his black power escapade. We only wondered why it had taken so long to articulate and why blacks had not been able to understand their situation better at the beginning.

A year earlier, during the Selma March, Abernathy introduced Martin Luther King with a stirring speech. He reminded his audience that "God never leaves His people without a leader." When we heard those words we knew where the Civil Rights movement was heading. It was then merely a question of waiting until the blacks began to explore *peoplehood,* toy with that idea for awhile, and then consider tribalism and nationalism.

Peoplehood is impossible without cultural independence, which in turn is impossible without a land base. Civil Rights as a movement for legal equality ended when the blacks dug beneath the equality fictions which white liberals had used to justify their great crusade. Black power, as a communications phenomenon, was a godsend to other groups. It clarified the intellectual concepts which had kept Indians and Mexicans confused and allowed the concept of self-determination suddenly to become valid.

In 1954, when the tribes were faced with the threat of termination as outlined in House Concurrent Resolution 108, the National Congress of American Indians had developed a Point Four Program aimed at creating self-determinative Indian communities. This program was ignored by Congress, bitterly opposed by the national church bodies and government agencies, undercut by white interest groups, and derided by the Uncle Tomahawks who had found security in being the household pets of the white establishment.

So, for many people, particularly those Indian people who had supported self-determination a decade earlier, Stokley Carmichael was the first black who said anything significant. Indian leadership quickly took the initiative, certain that with pressures developing from many points the goal of Indian development on the basis of tribal integrity could be realized. Using political leverage, the NCAI painstakingly began to apply itself to force change within the Bureau of Indian Affairs.

In April of 1966, following the forced resignation of Philleo Nash as Commissioner of Indian Affairs, Stewart Udall, Secretary of the Interior, held a conference to determine what "they" could do for "their" Indians. The tribes balked at the idea of bureaucrats planning the future of Indian people without so much as a polite bow in their direction. So sixty-two tribes arrived at Santa Fe for their own meeting and forced Interior to realize that the days of casually making Indian policy at two-day conferences was officially over. It took, unfortunately, another two years for Udall to get the message that the Indian people meant business.

All through 1966 and 1967 Interior tried one scheme after another in an effort to sell an incredibly bad piece of legislation the Omnibus Bill, to the tribes. In May of 1966 an embryo bill was conceived within Interior, which purported to solve all existing Indian problems. September of that year saw the Commissioner of Indian Affairs embark on a tour of the West to gather tribal suggestions "in case the Interior Department wanted to suggest some legislation"—coincidentally the bill of May, 1966.

In July of 1966, however, the National Congress of American Indians obtained a copy of the Interior bill. By September all of the tribes had versions of the proposed legislation—the same legislation which Interior claimed wouldn't even be on the drawing boards until after the regional meetings to gather tribal opinions on legislative needs.

Commissioner Bennett's task of presenting the facade of consultation while Udall rammed the bill down the Indians' throats later that year dissolved in smoke as irate tribal chairmen shot down the proposal before it left the launching pad.

As success followed success, Indians began to talk playfully of *red power* in terms similar to what SNCC was saying. The bureaucrats became confused as to which path the tribes would take next. After all, a two-year skirmish with the Secretary of the Interior and achievement of a standoff is enough to whet one's appetite for combat.

As 1968 opened, national Indian Affairs appeared to be heading faster and faster toward real involvement with other minority groups. In January, twenty-six urban centers met at Seattle, Washington, to begin to plan for participation of urban Indians in national Indian affairs. Seattle was the high point of the red power movement. But Indians quickly veered away from "power" as a movement. We knew we had a certain amount of power developing. There was no need to advocate it. The task was now to use it.

Too, black power, as many Indian people began to understand it, was not so much an affirmation of black people as it was an anti-white reaction. Blacks, many Indian people felt, had fallen into the legal-cultural trap. They obviously had power in many respects. In some instances, publicity for example, blacks had much more power than anyone dreamed possible. Indians began to question why blacks did not use their impetus in decisive ways within the current administration, which was then sympathetic to the different minority groups.

As spring came Martin Luther King had begun to organize the Poor People's Campaign. The thesis of the movement, as many of us understood it, was to be built around the existing poverty among the minority groups.

Indians had understood when Carmichael talked about racial and national integrity and the need for fine distinctions to be made between white and black. But when King began to indiscriminately lump together as one all minority communities on the basis of their economic status, Indians became extremely suspicious. The real issue for Indians—tribal existence within the homeland reservation—appeared to have been completely ignored. So where Indians could possibly have come into the continuing social movement of the 1960's, the Poor People's Campaign was too radical a departure from Indian thinking for the tribes to bridge.

Some Indians, under the name of Coalition of Indian Citizens, did attend the Washington encampment, but they remained by themselves, away from Resurrection City. By and large they did not have the support of the Indian community and were largely the creation of some national churches who wished to get Indians involved in the Poor People's Campaign. With church funding, these individuals wandered around Washington vainly trying to bring about a "confrontation" with Interior officials. They were sitting ducks for the pros of Interior, however, and the effects of their visits were negligible.

The remainder of 1968 was a traumatic experience for Indian tribes. Ideology shifted rapidly from topic to topic and dared not solidify itself in any one place for fear of rejection. National leaders trod softly when discussing issues. No one seemed to know which direction the country would take. Return to the old integration movement seemed out of the question. Continuing to push power movements against the whole of society seemed just as senseless.

Cautiously the subject of capital began to come into discussion. Too many Indian people realized the gulf that existed between the various groups in American society. A tremendous undefined need for consolidation, capitalization, and withdrawal took hold of Indian Affairs. Many tribal chairmen began to withdraw from conferences and others began to hedge their bets by remaining close to the reservation.

Tribal leaders became concerned about ongoing economic development which would be aimed at eventual economic independence for their tribes, rather than accepting every grant they could squeeze out of government agencies.

The National Congress of American Indians refused to join the Poor People's March because the goals were too generalized. Instead the NCAI began a systematic national program aimed at upgrading tribal financial independence.

In 1968 Indian leadership finally accepted the thesis that they would have to match dollar for dollar in income and program to fight the great clash between white and non-white that was coming in the months ahead. And Indian leaders began to realize that they had a fair chance of winning.

Many tribes began to shift their funds from the U.S. Treasury into the stock market. Mutual funds and stocks and bonds became the primary interest of the tribal councils. Those tribes with funds available put them into high-paying investment programs. Other tribes ordered a general cutback on overhead to give them additional funds for programming and investment.

In the move toward capitalization the tribes followed the basic ideas outlined years before by Clyde Warrior and others when the National Indian Youth Council first began to concentrate on building viable Indian communities. But it was too late for the National Indian Youth Council to take advantage of their success. Warrior died in July of 1968, some say of alcohol, most say of a broken heart.

Warrior had already been a rebel in 1964 when the majority of the tribes had lined up to support the Johnson-Humphrey ticket in the general election. Clyde supported Goldwater. His basic thesis in supporting Goldwater was that emotional reliance on a Civil Rights bill to solve the black's particular cultural question was the way to inter-group disaster. Warrior had been right.

What the different racial and minority groups had needed was not a new legal device for obliterating differences but mutual respect with economic and political independence. By not encouraging any change in the status quo, Goldwater had offered the chance for consolidation of gains at a time when the Indian people had great need to consolidate. Now consolidation was a move that may have started too late.

When a person understands the basic position developed by Warrior in 1964, one comes to realize the horror with which the Indian people contemplated their situation in 1968.

All the white man could offer, all that Johnson offered, was a minor adjustment in the massive legal machinery that had been created over a period of three hundred years. Rights of minority groups and reactions of the white majority depended solely on which parts of the machinery were being adjusted.

For many Indians the white had no culture other than one of continual exploitation. How then, they wondered, could an adjustment in methods of exploitation which had prevented formation of a culture solve their cultural problem? Thoughtful Indians, young and old, began to withdraw as they saw America building up toward a period of violent conflict. The basic problems which the colonists had brought over from Europe had not been solved and many felt there was a great danger that they would be solved violently in the future.

Culture, as Indian people understood it, was basically a lifestyle by which a people acted. It was self-expression, but not a conscious self-expression. Rather, it was an expression of the essence of a people.

SPLITTING APART:
THE THREE CULTURES OF TAOS
Jon Stewart

Another case of intercultural conflict is that described
by Jon Stewart who went to Taos, New Mexico in search
of hippies. He found them. He also found that the flower
people are not always welcomed with equanimity either
by those they often seek to emulate in dress or by those
whose land they wish to camp on.
Many local Indians and Chicanos deeply resent the encroachment on their lands of these seekers of com-
munalism and freedom. For the Indians life is not one
continuous party but a struggle for survival. For the
Chicanos, more fully imbued with Anglo values and
aspirations but also barred from easy access, the hippies may represent a convenient scapegoat for displaced aggression.

This pictures a time when inferior people are pushing forward and are
about to crowd out the few remaining strong and superior men. . . . The upper
trigram stands for the mountain, whose attribute is stillness. This suggests that
one should submit to the bad time and remain quiet. . . . It is impossible to
counteract these conditions of the time. Hence it is not cowardice but wisdom
to submit and avoid action.

— Po, "Splitting Apart," the *I Ching*

On April 3, near Penasco, New Mexico, a VW van belonging to a small
hippie "family" is dynamited during the night. A week later, the home
of the same family is invaded late at night by Chicanos; windows are
broken, and a building on the property is burned to the ground.

From *Scanlan's,* September 1970. Reprinted by permission.

On April 8, at Arroyo Seca, four men, two of whom are respected businessmen in Taos, stumble out of a bar and brutally beat several longhairs on the street. Charges are finally pressed, despite considerable reluctance to do so on the part of the police and court officials; the four men are apprehended and fined $5 each, plus court costs. The next night the Craft House, owned by Rachel Brown who pressed the charges against the four men, is shot up.

The same night, in Valdez, the home of a longhair is stoned by 10 or 11 men. When the resident comes out to defend his home he is beaten; the resulting injuries require a doctor's care.

On April 26, in Taos, a longhair photographer is accosted in the plaza in the middle of town by six Chicanos who ask him if he is a hippie. He replies, "No," but is nonetheless beaten to the ground and kicked, receiving multiple fractures to the jaw. State and local police are decidedly uncooperative, and no arrests are made.

The same day, Steve Durkee, founder of the Lama Foundation commune, is attacked while sitting in his truck at the A&W in Taos. The windows are smashed and Steve had his nose broken in two places. Steve assessed the situation for the Foundation of Light newspaper: "It is not the people who hit us who are to blame but everything which has produced this terrible situation. All one can do is to pray, 'Father forgive them, for they know not what they do.'"

A longhair is busted for hitching through the town of Taos. He's searched, and police discover a "concealed weapon" for which he receives a jail sentence. The weapon: a two-inch penknife.

An occupied bus parked in front of Taos' General Store is laced by a ribbon of bullets fired by Pete Sahd, a local resident. Sahd is apprehended and charged with "negligent use of firearms." He is fined $25 by local Judge Guintana.

Everywhere in Taos County cars and houses have been burned, windows smashed and late-night phone calls threaten arson and murder. So far, no one has actually been murdered. But the people are waiting. About 25 per cent of the communalists have left the area—mostly those with children.

The foregoing selected excerpts from the program of events represent only the smoke from the volcano. Taos seethes with bigotry and prejudice —you can feel it in the air. Taos County is an in-depth study in radical change and opposition to that change, of the clash of radically different cultures trying to coexist; of poverty, and of ignorance.

The stable population of Taos County is about 75 per cent Spanish-American, or Chicano. Several thousand Taos Indians also reside in the county, where their ancestral roots reach back over 2000 years. Longhairs, living mostly in communes, number only 500–600—a negligible percentage of the population, especially since few of them are registered voters. However, for a variety of reasons, they've made an impact on the county that far exceeds their numerical proportion.

The most controversial manifestation of the hippies' impact on northern New Mexico came in the form of a bastard child bred by an assortment of media men, show biz personalities, and rock festival promoters: Earth People's Park. Spawned (quite appropriately) on Halloween weekend of 1969, the notion that a piece of Mother Earth should be liberated from the throes of capitalism and returned to "the people" caught the imaginations of countless underground media men and counterrevolutionary visionaries. The plan was to raise $1,000,000 to purchase a piece of northern New Mexico where the biggest rock festival in history would be held, after which the land would be turned over to the people: any and all people, freely, to live on it as they pleased. A new nation would evolve, Aquarius would arrive, growing naturally out of the principles of open land, love, brotherhood, and natural (ecological) religion.

Of course it wasn't long before the inherent contradictions of Utopian society became apparent to some people. Gradually it was realized that the principal people who contrived the plan were businessmen, promoters who had no intention of living on the land beyond the five-day festival. They'd take the profit and split back to Hollywood or New York. Then too, the realization of the potential ecological disaster became apparent, and it was clear that the promoters of the plan didn't really give a shit. Questioned by a Berkeley ecologist as to what kind of ecological example it was to drop half a million people on 70,000 acres of wilderness, the promoters replied, "We need flamboyance!" They added: "There is no way to predict or prevent improper use of the land." So much for the bullshit artists.

Another problem arose. The New Mexican Chicanos, already up in arms over the hippie influx into Taos, were adamantly against the plan. They saw it in terms of another white, middle-class rip-off of the land they felt was rightfully theirs and had already been ripped off once by the state. The *Alianza,* a militant Chicano organization fighting (literally) for restoration of lands deeded to Chicanos by ancient land grants, swore that they would "commit murder" to keep the hippies off the land they'd been fighting for. "These lands are ours. They have been stolen from us once, and will not be stolen again," they promised. Governor Cargo swore to fence off Taos County with state police if the festival tried to settle in. He boasted, in a personal interview, "They're gonna meet some *resistance,* yessiree boy. Just keep watching."

By the time of the Spring Equinox 1970, Earth People's Park was a dead issue in New Mexico. The idea—fantastic, absurd, beautiful, awful —was done in chiefly by ecologists and the already tense scene in New Mexico.

★   ★   ★

The "three cultures of Taos" are about as different as any three cultures can be. The hippies may emulate the life-style of the Indians, but they will remain hippies, not Indians. That's OK, because they manage to get along incredibly well as it is. Even the Indians and the Chicanos, though no love is lost between them, manage to coexist fairly peaceably. The major friction in Taos is between the Chicanos and the hippies, with the local rednecks siding with the Chicanos. (Lest these generalities be too easily accepted, I must emphasize that many exceptions exist, as the communalists eagerly point out. Numerous instances of goodwill have transpired between the communes and the neighboring Chicano farmers.)

Many factors conspire to cause the hostility between the longhairs and the Chicanos—including poverty, the schools' middle-class standards, and the Chicanos' own confused cultural identity. Roughly 25 per cent of the Chicanos in Taos are unemployed. Consequently, many are dependent on welfare and food stamps for survival. Their poverty is generations old —stretching back even to the Mexican rule—and for many of them dependency on the government for survival is simply a bitter fact of life.

Combined with the Chicanos' low economic status is an education— or, rather, an indoctrination—which teaches them to value and respect, to honor and emulate, the American Middle-Class Way of Life, where success and happiness are measured in terms of greenbacks, two-car garages, college educations, and barbeque pits in manicured backyards. At the same time, they are reportedly taught that hippies are disease-ridden, sex-crazed dope fiends, communist conspirators who are out to rip off the Great White American Way. The result—frustrating to say the least —is that the Chicanos in Taos (whose children comprise 87 per cent of the county's students) are taught to value a life-style which they haven't a beggar's chance of attaining.

The issue of the Chicano's cultural identity is crucial to his economic and social development. In Taos, one is warned to avoid any suggestion that the Chicanos are of Mexican descent. Presumably, they prefer to trace their ancestry directly to the invading Spanish, ignoring their Indian and Mexican heritage. This gap in their cultural past leaves them in a condition which might be described as "cultureless." Yet the Chicanos do constitute a visible ethnic group and are subject to every form of economic and social oppression that America has to offer its minority peoples. To overcome those oppressions, they need the strength of cultural pride—but without a cohesive and recognized cultural heritage, how does one begin to muster ethnic pride? Beginnings along these lines are evident elsewhere in the country, especially in California, but the winds of change are not yet blowing through the dry air of Taos County.

★   ★   ★

Enter the hippies. They come, many of them, with enough money to buy or lease land for farming. They come with college educations. They come with *city* educations, which is even more important. They come, too, with the technical know-how of middle-class America, from which they sprung. They know how to make a buck, how to hustle, how to operate a business, even how to farm. And though they may not have a cultural past, they're rapidly developing a cultural form in which they find a great deal of strength and security.

But worst of all, from the Chicano's point of view, they squat over middle-class values, empty their bowels, and wipe their asses with the dollar. They've been through the purgatory of the middle class, they've walked the great golden highway to the stars, and they've rejected it. They've elected to live outside the "laws" of America, those iconographic boundaries of society, and to create their own society, with their own rules.

So the friction between the Chicanos and the hippies in Taos is caused largely by the disparity between their ideals, beliefs, life-styles—their gods. Still, while this situation understandably engenders resentment, it needn't have come to violence. The impetus for violent action, for active repression, comes from quite another quarter: the small middle class of Taos—the merchants, businessmen and town and county officials.

The establishment has a very genuine stake in the disruptive atmosphere in Taos. The hippies provide the very scapegoat that America's system of oppression depends upon. The formula is simple: if you keep enough smoke in the air, the people will never know who's stabbing them in the back. The commune hippies are perfect scapegoats; they're physically recognizable, concentrated, and "different." Tag them with a dirty name (pinko, sex-freak, drug-freak) and let it be known that it's open season on them. Then the establishment can continue to rip off the land and the people while senseless war rages. Take, for instance, the case of Taos real estate agent, banker and Town Council member Jim Brandenburg. From reliable reports, Brandenburg is in the forefront of the repressive movement, actively stirring up hatred for the hippies among local Anglos and Chicanos. Yet, inside of one year Brandenburg sold well over a half-million dollars' worth of Taos land to longhairs.

The manager of the Taos Chamber of Commerce, Colonel Fay, recently sent a series of letters to the local conservative weekly newspaper decrying the hippies as harmful to the community and suggesting that they should be discouraged from staying in the county. Fay's bad-mouthing eventually led to a full-page ad in the Taos News—a petition signed by 425 citizens which called for an "increase in police protection" and "stiffer penalties to be enforced against offenders." In addition, it called upon the Chamber of Commerce to assist the town and county officials in establishing a climate of law and order.

Which brings us to the issue of law and order in Taos County. Police laxity toward local crimes against the longhairs is matched only by the severity of penalties dealt out to the hippies for the slightest infractions. One incident involved a young girl who was picked up for hitching.

When she was unable to present identification, she was handed a ten-day sentence in a jail which has no facilities for females.

It's easy to imagine a huge coalition in Taos composed of the Chamber of Commerce, the Town Council, the Police Department, the School Board and perhaps even the Catholic Church. Just how much actual organization exists among the establishment powers is impossible to determine, but the fact that incidents of harassment can be begun or canceled on a moment's notice suggests that some powerful country-wide network of repression does exist. A very reliable source told me that he believes the Minutemen in Texas are at the decision-making peak of the network, with orders filtering down through the various state, county and town officials to the young Chicanos who carry out the actual acts of terrorism.

There is surprisingly little organization among the longhairs themselves. The communes, each of which has a different philosophy and style of organization, show little interest in forming any kind of coalition for mutual protection. The only real effort in this direction has come from Lorien Enterprises—which operates the Fountain of Light newspaper, the Taos Switchboard, La Clínica (free medical aid) and the General Store, and offers free legal aid to longhairs. Bill Quinn, the head of Lorien, is keeping a file on confirmed reports of repression throughout the county and is trying to register resident hippies to vote in county and state elections. Besides keeping pressure on police and court officials, he is trying to discourage an increase in the hip population of Taos.

The communes' lack of interest in cooperative protection stems from the fact that very little violence has occurred on the communes themselves. Most acts of violence have taken place in town, or on the smaller communal farms, and have been directed against no more than two or three hippies at a time.

The real harassment of the communes comes from a much more impersonal source: county and state authorities. As in California, the health officials of New Mexico have threatened to close down most of the communes for failing to meet minimum standards of health and sanitation. However, since the communes are officially registered as farming enterprises, a loophole is provided through the state laws which exempt farms from the sanitary code. Efforts to change the law so as to include the communes under the code were an issue in a recent election. It is estimated that if the communes were closed for sanitary reasons, three-quarters of the dwellings in the state of New Mexico could also be condemned.

Another tactic in its efforts to drive out the hippies is the state's recent decision to withdraw from the federal food stamp program. The official reason is that the administration of the program is too costly. Though there may be some truth in this, it is apparent that officials believe that if the hippies stop receiving free food they'll leave. They couldn't be more wrong. In point of fact, several communes have voluntarily gone off food stamps, and most others welcome the end of the program. The feeling is that reliance on the establishment for any kind of help fosters an unwanted dependence, hindering the communes from becoming self-reliant. The real effects of the demise of the food stamp program will be felt among the poor and elderly Indians and Chicanos, who really need the stamps for survival. If the establishment formula for repression works as it should, the Chicanos will blame the hippies for ending the program, and the legislature will have saved itself about $400,000 a year.

THE EVE OF
THE BLUING OF AMERICA
Peter and Brigitte Berger

The "greening of America" means opting out of the system for many upper and upper-middle class (WASP and Jewish) radicals. As more and more young rebels seek new pastures removed from the mainstream, others will come in and fill the leadership void. Some might be black, but most will be white and working class.

According to Peter and Brigitte Berger, those farthest removed ideologically from the rhetoric of revolution, indeed, those most opposed, may stand to gain the most from its curious course. They suggest that many may be on the threshold of something far removed from Consciousness III: the "bluing of America."

A considerable number of American intellectuals have been on a kick of revolution talk for the last few years. It began in a left mood, with fantasies of political revolution colored red or black. The mood now appears to have shifted somewhat. The fantasies have shifted to cultural revolution, which, we are told, will color America green.

What the two varieties of revolution talk have in common is a sublime disregard for the requirements of technological society and for the realities of power and class in America. To be sure, drastic (if you like, "revolutionary") things are happening in this society, but the currently fashionable interpretations only serve to obfuscate them.

It is conceivable that technological society will collapse in America. In that case, as grass grows over the computers, we would revert to the ways of an underdeveloped country. Conceivable, yes; probable, no. The more likely assumption is that technological society will continue. If so, who will run it? We would venture, first a negative answer: It will *not* be the people engaged in the currently celebrated cultural revolutions.

The "greening" revolution is not taking place in a sociological vacuum, but has a specific location in a society that is organized in social classes. There are enough data now to pinpoint this location. The cadres of the revolution are, in overwhelming proportions, the college-educated children of the upper middle class. Ethnically, they tend to be Wasps and Jews. Ideologically, they are in revolt against the values of this class—which is precisely the class that has been running the technological society so far. But the essentially bucolic rhetoric of this rebellion goes far beyond a radical (in the leftist sense) rejection of American class society and its allegedly evil ways. The rhetoric intends a dropping out of technological society as such.

The matrix of this revolution has been the youth culture. What are the prospects for the children of the people of the emerging counter-culture? We don't want to speculate in detail about the probable career of the son of a dropped-out sandal maker in Bella Vista—except for the suggestion that he is unlikely to make it to the upper-middle-class status of his grandfather. In sociological parlance, he is probably headed for downward social mobility.

The black revolution, for quite different reasons, is also headed for a counter or subculture, segregated from the opportunity system of technological society and subsidized through political patronage. The prospects here are for segregated social mobility. This may have its own cultural or ideological satisfactions. But upward mobility in a black ("community controlled") educational bureaucracy is unlikely to lead to positions of power and privilege in the enveloping technological society.

If the "greening" revolution will in fact continue to lure sizable numbers of upper-middle-class individuals out of "the system," and if the black revolution will succeed in arresting outward mobility among its adherents, a simple but decisively important development will take place: There will be new "room at the top." Who is most likely to take advantage of this sociological windfall? It will be the newly college-educated children of the white lower middle and working classes (and possibly those nonwhites who will refuse to stay within the resegregated racial subcultures). In other words, precisely those classes that remain most untouched by what is considered to be the revolutionary tide in contemporary America face new prospects of upward social mobility.

A technological society, given a climate of reasonable tolerance, can afford sizable regiments of sandal makers and Swahili teachers. It must have quite different people, though, to occupy its command posts and to keep its engines running. These will have to be people retaining the essentials of the old Protestant ethnic—discipline, achievement orientation and, last not least, a measure of freedom from gnawing self-doubt.

If such people are no longer available in one population reservoir, another reservoir will have to be tapped. There is no reason to think that "the system" will be unable to make the necessary accommodations. Should Yale become hopelessly "greened," Wall Street will get used to recruits from Fordham or Wichita State, Italians or Southern Baptists will have no trouble running the Rand Corporation. It is even possible that the White House may soon have its first Polish occupant (or, in a slightly different scenario, its first Greek).

There is one proviso—namely, that the children of these classes remain relatively unbitten by the "greening" bug. If they, too, should drop out, there would literally be no one left to mind the technological store. So far, the evidence does not point in this direction.

Indeed, what evidence we have of the dynamics of class in a number of European countries would indicate that the American case is not all that unique. Both England and West Germany have undergone very similar changes in their class structures, with new reservoirs of lower-middle-class and working-class populations supplying the personnel requirements of a technological society no longer serviced by the old élites.

The aforementioned process is not new in history. It is what Vilfredo Pareto (that most neglected of classical sociologists) called the "circulation of élites." Even Marx, albeit in the most ironical manner, may be proved right in the end. It may, indeed, be the blue-collar masses that are, at last, coming into their own. "Power to the people!"—nothing less than that. The class struggle may be approaching a decisive new phase, with the children of the working class victorious—under the sign of the American flag. In that perspective, alas, the peace emblem represents the decline of the bourgeois enemy class, aptly symbolizing its defeat before a more robust adversary. This would not be the first time in history that the principals in the societal drama are unaware of the consequences of their actions.

"Revolutionary" America? Perhaps. We may be on the eve of its bluing.

ENDING
NOTES

Two very different, and very personal, reflections on
the immigrant experience and the racial crisis.

LEFT BEHIND IN BROOKLYN
Ralph Levine

Sometimes people are trapped in a social matrix over which they have little control. Such is the plight of many poor white immigrants who, like the blacks with whom they find themselves in competition, are trying to survive in the urban jungle. Two such people are the parents of Ralph Levine, a political scientist lucky enough to have been able to leave the ghetto behind. Still he is troubled by the extent to which his middle-class colleagues who support black aspirations are blind to the sufferings of others.

Levine's story was not easy to tell. It is difficult to admit one is a racist at heart. In certain circles it is equally difficult not to.

My mother is now seventy years old. Given the state of her health, she probably has no more than a short time to live. Her life has been marked by a series of tragedies, although the relative success of her oldest son is a source of real pride. The last ten years have been especially difficult. The world bewilders and frightens her. Having fled from one neighborhood in Brooklyn, she is now preparing to flee again. A life-long instinctive "liberal" and once a strong backer of John Lindsay, she voted for Procaccino in the last New York mayorality race. She is opposed to busing school children and is an ardent supporter of "law and order." Indeed, in 1968, she considered voting for George Wallace but finally decided not to on the grounds that he was probably anti-semitic.

In the current sociological literature and in the journals read by upper middle class New York intellectuals, and by upper middle class suburban

Ralph Levine is a pseudonym for a well known political scientist. Reprinted by permission of the author.

students, she is part of that white racist "silent majority" which refuses to act justly toward black people. I wonder. To me she does not fit into this category at all. Indeed, like many others who are lumped together in this fashion, she is the victim of forces beyond her control—a victim whose sufferings have gone largely unrecorded, and whose plight seems unable to capture the imagination of those who specialize in doing good. But let me tell her story from the beginning.

My mother was born in 1900 to immigrant parents who had come to the United States from Austria and Russia. Her childhood years were spent in a five story, walk-up, rat-infested tenement house with five younger brothers and sisters, a tenement in which the bathroom in the hall was shared by four families. She remembers that the apartment, heated by a coal stove in the winter, was so hot in the summer that people used to sleep on the fire escape or in the street.

When she completed the eighth grade of public school, she went to work to help support the family. (She considers herself lucky to have had that much schooling—many of her friends had less.) She did attend night school for several years and eventually became a bookkeeper. In 1925, she married my father, a young man of much the same background as hers. They set up housekeeping and eventually moved to a three room apartment in the East Flatbush section of Brooklyn. I was born in 1927.

My father was a taxi driver. With the depression his earnings dropped off sharply, and, indeed, were not sufficient to provide for his family, especially after the birth of a second child in 1932. My mother had accumulated some savings, and these were used to supplement his income. Late in 1935 my father died. During his illness, my mother spent the remainder of her savings in frantic attempts to save his life, and with his death she was left with nothing except a rather meager widow's pension.

Unable to afford the apartment in which she was living, she moved the family to the Crown Heights section of Brooklyn, an area bordering on Bedford Stuyvesant and East New York, and it was here that I grew up. From 1935 to 1938 we lived in a three room apartment infested by roaches and bedbugs, insects against whom my mother fought a never-ending and largely unsuccessful battle. In 1938, she re-married. Her second husband had come to the United States from a small village in Russia in the wake of the Revolution. He was little more than a child when he spent over a year wandering semi-starved through Europe with a younger brother and sister in tow. He was finally brought to the United States by Jewish philanthropic organizations.

Once in this country, he went to work almost immediately some 10–12 hours a day for six days a week. He was to spend the rest of his life working at about the same rate. As a result, he never learned to read or write English, although he could sign his name and could make out street signs.

When my mother married him, he owned a small candy store in the neighborhood in partnership with his brother, and, in celebration of our new affluence we moved across the street to a four-room apartment. In 1941, a third child was born, my half-brother. My sister and I shared the same bedroom until I was 18 and she was 13.

World War II created opportunities for a number of small Jewish businessmen. For my step-father, however, it was disaster. After his brother left for the army, the economic position of the candy store rapidly deteriorated, and he was forced to abandon it. Out of either ignorance or pride, he did not go into bankruptcy, and with substantial debts hanging over him, he started looking for a new job. He eventually obtained one in the Brooklyn Navy Yard, where he remained until the end of the war. His wages were not substantial and a goodly portion of them went to repaying his obligations.

I had matriculated at C.C.N.Y. in the fall of 1944 and returned to college after a short stint in the U.S. Navy. Using the GI Bill of Rights and money which I earned at part-time jobs during the school year, and as a bus boy or waiter during the summer months, I moved out of the house and into a dormitory which had been set up near the college in what had once been an orphan asylum. When I graduated from City in 1949, a combination of the GI Bill and various scholarships enabled me to go to Harvard University, where I obtained a Ph.D. I never returned to New York after leaving, except for relatively short visits. Most of my contemporaries at City who had academic ambitions entered the New York public school system as high school teachers.

In the meantime, my father and others like him had been discharged from the Navy Yard. In the years immediately following the war, he tried a number of unskilled jobs, before settling down to working for a dry cleaning plant in the neighborhood. Essentially he picked up and delivered clothing to various tailor shops and dry cleaning stores for a combination salary and commission. He continued to work a ten or eleven hour day six days a week for relatively little, although his income improved somewhat in the late 1950's and early 1960's. He hoped someday to open a store for himself again. However, the hope was never to be realized.

During these years my sister graduated from high school and married a semi-skilled worker. With the aid of a loan from the Federal Housing Administration, she and her husband moved to a small box-like house on Long Island where they still live. After graduation from high school, my brother tried a number of jobs, finally settling down as a bank clerk. Still unmarried, he lives with my mother.

Between 1949 and 1959 the nature of the neighborhood in which my parents lived began to change, as the black community to the north expanded, and a new generation of Jews began their trek to the suburbs. The change, gradual at first, accelerated as the remaining Jews began to flee. My parents remained in the neighborhood in part because I (a far away Harvard "liberal") urged them to do so, in part because of inertia and, in part, because they felt that they could not afford to move.

In time, however, their desire to leave grew. In part they simply wanted to live among their own kind, that is with Jewish people. While a large measure of ethnocentrism was involved in their attitudes, they were hardly "racists," a term which has become a loosely used epithet without empirical content. They did not regard blacks as inherently inferior. In fact, they were quite deferential toward those of my black friends (all academics) whom they met briefly, regarding them primarily as "professors," i.e., learned men. They also developed reasonably cordial relations with some of their black neighbors, and my father was on friendly terms with most of his black co-workers. Nevertheless, they were uncomfortable in what was becoming a predominently black neighborhood.

Their attitudes were far from unique. The self-identity of most working class and even lower middle class people is defined in primordial terms. They are most comfortable among those who share their cultural experience and look like themselves. Here the question of color plays a key role. Intellectuals and professionals are less caught up with such parochial ties, although they, too, relate more easily to those who share their life style and are not "narrow minded bigots living in ticky tacky houses." Thus, I can talk more easily to black academics than I can to most of my relatives. Like almost all "cosmopolitan liberal" intellectuals, I look forward to the erosion of narrowly defined ethnic ties. However, I find it hard to hate people whose life style is bound up with them.

There is some evidence that, given time, the barriers of color and background can be breached. A young black couple had bought the house next door to the one in which my parents lived and in an amazingly short time they adopted my mother and father as parent (or, perhaps, grandparent) surrogates. My parents liked them because they were "clean, quiet, hard-working young people," and because of the concern the wife, especially, demonstrated for their well-being.

Unfortunately, however, time was not available, for the composition of the black community in the neighborhood was changing. The new immigrants were increasingly multi-problem families of the black underclass, and as their numbers increased the neighborhood deteriorated physically. Five, six and seven children crowded into three and four room apartments; vandals broke windows, toilets, mailboxes and front doors; garbage began to be thrown from windows onto the streets, and the area rapidly became a slum.

It has become fashionable to blame the rapid deterioration of such neighborhoods on "slumlords." While these may have played a role elsewhere in the city, and, to a limited extent in this neighborhood, the root cause of the problem did not lie in the machinations of evil men. Most of the buildings on the block were rent controlled. In many cases the landlords were small property owners, living in the houses they rented. Their profit had been marginal, and they had managed to survive only by skimping on services. With the advent of increasing numbers of the black poor, and the increasing destruction of property, as well as the increasing refusal to pay rent, their margin of profit evaporated. Most tried desperately to sell. Some succeeded, and the houses may have been bought by slumlords—Jewish and Christian, white and black, too. Others just walked away from the houses, because they were impoverished by trying to maintain them, and eventually the neighborhood became dotted with abandoned buildings, which were still relatively sound structurally. Interestingly enough, when the city took over most of these buildings, it was unable to break even on them, as indeed it has found it difficult to do with some public housing.

Finally, there was fear—fear of being robbed, beaten or knifed any evening or even during the day. Younger women feared rape; mothers feared for their children in school. My mother's letters were full of stories of violence, including attacks on relatives or people I had known since childhood. In the schools young hoodlums regularly extorted money from white (and black) children, children who, for the first time, were being introduced to the world of drugs. My mother knew that only a minority of the black community was actually violent, but the proportion was large enough to make living in the neighborhood increasingly intolerable.

Those who suffered most were the small Jewish store owners in the neighborhood. Most of the stores were marginal enterprises at best, which had always charged more than supermarkets, because they were marginal. Despite my urgings, my mother continued to patronize them. They often stocked foods unobtainable elsewhere and she felt a certain loyalty to the owners, who were her neighbors and who invariably advanced credit in time of stress.

By the middle 1950's most of the Jewish shopkeepers in the neighborhood were closing their stores. Some had been stabbed or shot; others had been merely beaten; almost all had been robbed on a number of occasions, and all were finding it increasingly difficult to make ends meet. Those whom I knew were desperately and unsuccessfully trying to sell. In the end, a good many of these "exploiters" lost what little savings they had managed to accumulate and became completely dependent upon social security or their children. There is little question but that some of them had long held stereotypes about the "Schvartzes" or about non-Jews in general and dealt unfairly with the black patrons from the beginning. It is also true that others probably generalized from their experiences and became increasingly anti-black with time. However, the boarded-up stores that began to line Ralph Avenue long before the beginnings of large-scale riots testified to the fact that store keeping in the ghetto was not a particularly profitable enterprise.

For my parents and many of their neighbors, fear was the major factor influencing their decision to move. In an essay in *The New York Times,* Andrew Hacker notes, somewhat sardonically, that the white middle class is no longer able to cope with violence. Aside from his snide tone, which is altogether appropriate for a professor living in Ithaca, New York, he is unquestionably right. There had been little or no violence in the ghetto in which my mother grew up and the same had been true of my neighborhood. My parents and their friends were and are gentle, timid people. They cannot cope with violence. By the late 1950's the elite papers were already full of stories of police brutality and police "oppression." Of more concern to my mother and her neighbors, however, was the inability or unwillingness of the police to protect them. Time and time again, she would report that the police were, themselves, afraid to get involved.

Topping all of these was an increasing sense of injustice. My father did not resent working 10 or 11 hours a day, six days a week to earn ninety or a hundred dollars. So did many of his black co-workers. What angered him was that some black women on welfare were receiving what appeared to be a comparable income, while they entertained a series of male friends, spent a good deal of the money on alcohol, and left their children on the street until all hours of the night. It was his theory that black adolescents behaved badly because their parents did not bring them up in the right way.

In 1963 my parents finally decided to move. Their friends urged them to stay, pointing out that the rent they would have to pay would be much higher, and arguing that, since they were getting on in years, they should try to save their money. The pressures, however, were too great, and, in the late spring of that year, my mother and father settled in a section of East Flatbush about two miles from the old neighborhood. The apartment they rented was a small one—they could not afford any better. However, the neighborhood was reasonably clean and predominantly Jewish. Once again, they could walk the streets in safety.

The dry cleaning plant for which my father worked finally moved from the old neighborhood, too, as a result, primarily, of constant thefts and threats of violence. Thus the situation eased somewhat for my father— but only somewhat. He still had to go into the old neighborhood to deliver and pick up clothes and to risk being robbed or worse. He remained on good terms with his black co-workers and with those black store owners he serviced, many of whom, incidentally, earned considerably more money than he. While some of them used "revolutionary" language in talking of the future, they always excluded him from their threats of dire consequences. Indeed, during the riots of the mid-sixties, a number of them went out of their way to protect him, escorting him to the edge of the neighborhood, and actually attacking some black adolescents who threatened him. On one occasion he was approached by a lush who tried to extort money from him. One of his black co-workers knocked the man down, and threatened to kill him if he ever bothered my father again. "That damn nigger works hard for his money," he said, referring to my father. "You leave him alone." He used to tell me of the difficulties they were having trying to raise their own children, and of their feeling of hopelessness in the face of the violence and disorder which characterized the ghetto. Most of them hoped and prayed for the day when they could somehow find a "decent" neighborhood.

My step-father was, at this time, in his early 60's. Some years before, he had had a fairly serious heart attack, and had been warned to give up smoking, to watch his diet, and to try to cut down on his work. He could not even think of seeking another job at this time of his life, although he was looking forward to opportunities for a greater relaxation once he became eligible for social security. Of course, I continued to urge him to try something else. I knew that every day produced new anxieties because of his fear of being molested by young hoods.

For a time at least, the new neighborhood and neighborhood life were such as to provide a source of real satisfaction. My parents joined the local temple, which was partly a social center, and began to participate actively in its life. They made new friends, became reacquainted with old friends, and began to enjoy life together in a way they had not been able to for a number of years.

However, a general anxiety pervaded the neighborhood; an anxiety based on fears that it would change, as well as on the feeling that the city as a whole was deteriorating. Some of the people in the neighborhood were workers; others held white collar jobs. On one visit I remember talking to a man whom I had not seen for many years. He and my first father had worked a cab as partners in the 1930's, and he lived not too far from my parents' apartment. He was on the verge of retiring, and the dominant theme of his conversation was his constant fear of being robbed or mugged while working. He admitted that he would not stop for black customers at night, especially, because of these fears, and recounted stories of friends who had been robbed, beaten, or killed. He readily admitted that many blacks were "nice" people, but even then he was afraid of what might happen if he dropped a customer off in a predominantly black neighborhood.

In the middle 1960's, the neighborhood began to change, repeating an earlier pattern. The first big shift came with a decision on the part of the Board of Education to bus black students into the local public school, and white students into a school in the old neighborhood. Local parents were in a panic. They had fled the old neighborhood to escape violence and now they felt trapped again. My mother was horrified. She simply could not understand. *The New Republic* carried an essay by Murray Kempton describing some of the parents who opposed busing. To him, the women he interviewed were all obviously irrational racists. His characterization did not fit the people I knew. I also remember discussing the matter with some of my middle class Jewish friends who lived on the upper west side (and east side) of Manhattan. People like my parents shocked them. Most of them, of course, sent their own children to private schools which had been "integrated" only recently by the addition of a few *middle class* black children.

I, in turn, was struck by their simplistic moralism. I was in favor of busing under certain circumstances, but felt that some attempt, at least, should be made to deal with the realistic fears of white parents who were being asked to send their children to schools which contained a sizeable portion of *lower class* black children. Name calling would not deal with the real problems. Those upper middle class professionals who condemn working class whites for refusing to make educational guinea pigs of their children, a sacrifice *few* of us would make willingly, seem to me blatantly hypocritical. For one thing, busing a child from the upper east side of Manhattan into Harlem would make far more sense—and cost less—than stocking the ghetto schools of Manhattan with Brooklyn or Bronx recruits.

More to the point, though, the subscribers to *The New York Review of Books* can absorb the psychological costs of such laudable endeavors with greater ease than can ordinary readers of *The Daily News*. For the latter, people like my mother and her neighbors, the normal demands of daily living in New York exhaust most of their energy. They have little sense of available options and their social horizons are quite limited. Situations which my professional friends might dismiss as minor crises often overwhelm marginal working class people—black as well as white.

Comparable to the attitude of my friends is that of many of my students. Those who appear most willing to sacrifice time and effort in a "good" cause, whatever the cause, prove invariably to be those who can retreat to upper middle class sanctuary and rejoin the "establishment" whenever the need arises. Such students seem either unable or unwilling to recognize a simple truth; that people considerably lower (although not the lowest) in the class structure, lack a similar sense of mastery and freedom, but rather are fighting desperately to achieve the sense of economic and social security which these students accept as their birthright.[1]

These same friends were quite virulent in their denunciation of teachers in the school system who, they argued, were engaged in educational genocide, because they didn't want to make the effort to reach black students. The charge did not square with my own experience. My classmates who had entered the New York system were, on the whole, anxious to help black students. They had begun their careers as committed radicals and were far superior to the teachers who had educated me. Many of them, however, found themselves unable to deal effectively with the violence and disorder which characterized their classrooms. Some of those who remained in the system were drained at a fairly early age. Others left New York for suburban schools. They may have lacked the skills for dealing with the new kinds of problems the school system faced, although

I am skeptical at many of the magical solutions which have been proposed by the new educational alchemists. The will, however, was there. They were, of course by and large, fairly ordinary lower middle class types, caught up with financial worries and family problems, and it is possible that a new generation will do better. However, to set standards for a school system that only a few extraordinarily dedicated and talented people can hope to meet only occasionally has always seemed to me to be both unrealistic and unfair.

If, as some critics charged, the "horrible" school bureaucracy had really gotten worse (it is always the "bureaucracy" or the "establishment" that is the source of our problems) it was largely because school administrators were unable to meet the excessive demands placed upon them, and had become increasingly demoralized. People often begin to emphasize rigid adherence to rules when faced with a situation which doesn't respond to reasonable efforts. At least some of my friends had become administrators. They did not seem, to me at least, excessively rigid; nor did the system seem more centralized or bureaucratic than when I had attended school. Many of my friends were unquestionably demoralized and their sense of futility was only heightened by what they considered unfair attacks upon them, attacks which, they felt, were only reducing the effectiveness of the school system by contributing to the complete breakdown of the authority of both teachers and administrators.

The plans for busing white students into the black ghetto were not consummated, although the local school was rezoned and black students bused in to achieve a better racial balance. The threat of busing, however, and fears of what would happen to neighborhood schools contributed to a new outmigration. This was by no means the only factor. As the black community to the north continued to expand, gangs of black youths began to rob stores and attack people on the streets. Gradual' , the streets emptied at night. Stores began to close earlier; to take various complicated security measures, and then to go out of business. An article in *The New York Times* called the neighborhood "transitional." It spoke of efforts which would be made to save it, and of the mayor's determination to curb the evil "blockbusters" who were causing people to panic. Blockbusters there may have been, although I never came across any evidence of them during my visits. However, if they accelerated the movement, they did not cause it, and it most certainly would have occurred without them.

Thus, life began to deteriorate for my parents once again. In the late spring of 1969 my father turned 62 and applied for social security. He could now, at least, work fewer hours. Here was a bonus. The joy was to be short-lived. On a hot July day in that year, he complained of a chest pain to one of his co-workers just before starting on his route. At his first stop he collapsed while carrying a bundle of clothing to his truck. He was dead on arrival at the hospital. The constant fear which accompanied him on the job may not have killed him. It certainly contributed to his death.

He left hardly anything, and, aside from social security, my mother's income consists of contributions from my brother and myself. There is some possibility of a workman's compensation award. However the case is still pending. Money, though, is not the most important element in the tragedy. My mother feels but half a person. She does not drive, and there is no one to take her to the temple or shopping now. Also, her friends are leaving the neighborhood and she feels increasingly isolated. She finds it difficult to think clearly about anything, and is almost constantly depressed. Once again the first migrants to the area have been "decent working people." However, this time my mother doesn't want to wait; the youthful gangs which are already roaming the neighborhood are, for her, proof that the old pattern is being repeated.

Late last spring she and my brother came for a visit. Although she does not, she says, like to talk about such matters, she recounted story after story of a kind of oppression in our society which is not covered by television, the elite press, or the elite magazines, and certainly does not rouse the moral fervor of upper middle class radicals—adults or students. One very recent incident had particularly depressed her. There are, it seems, still men in Brooklyn who deliver seltzer water. The man who delivered to her house is sixty-five and worked part-time to supplement his social security. A few weeks earlier he had been attacked in broad daylight by some black adolescents while delivering seltzer just a few doors away. They took the few dollars he had, and, although he did not resist, they beat him and cut him badly with a knife. The women who saw it, including my mother, did nothing (that inability to cope with violence, as Andrew Hacker notes). The police, they feel, will do nothing. The old man has decided to quit work and join his children on Long Island, although he feels that there is nowhere left to run.

The experiences of a number of her friends were roughly comparable, and some were becoming increasingly "anti-black." One of them, an old time Socialist, had told me, some months before, how he dreaded to go to work. He had been with the post office since the 1930's, and would soon retire, having advanced to a minor administrative position. He had worked with black colleagues for many years, and his relationship with them had been, on the whole, satisfactory. In recent years, however, the work situation had sharply deteriorated. Either because it was difficult to hire people for the post office, or because of a desire to use the post office as a mechanism for "rehabilitating" hard core unemployed blacks, there had been an influx of what he called "lower types." They smoked pot and took other drugs, refused to work, physically attacked supervisors who tried to discipline them, and were demanding more rapid advancement than men who had been on the job for many years.

Many of "the better element" among the black employees, he said, were as cowed as he was. Others were demonstrating a hostility to whites he had never known existed and still others, he felt, were being corrupted and going along for the ride (even as whites might in a comparable situation), or were silent because of the feeling that they must maintain "black unity."

While he was talking, I had been thinking of how I might respond. I would explain to him that the sources of the behavior of these black people lay in past injustices. I would add that this was only a temporary phase, through which our society had to go in order to become a better place in which to live. When he finished, however, I had remained silent. Who was I to explain away his sacrifices? It was not I, after all, who, in the late afternoon of my life, was being forced to pay for the sins of Englishmen I had never known. Nor was I really convinced that charging him for their sins would necessarily produce a better world.

As always, during her visits my mother asked me to explain why so many black people seem to behave in this way. I tried. She found it difficult to understand. She and her friends had been poor, and had worked hard. Neither she nor those she knew had ever stolen. I talked of raising expectations and of the scars left by racism. But why, she asked, must she pay for this? She had done nothing. She had not brought the slaves to this country, and, as far as she knew, she had never harmed a black person.

A few days before she arrived, she had read of a mass rally by Yale students in support of the Black Panthers. She asked why the students supported such violent people and had so little sympathy for ordinary working people like her, black and white. I told her that students knew very little about her problems. I might have added that student activism of this type has become a puberty rite during which many of the young and not so young members of the establishment pretend they are attacking the establishment. Thus they can shift most of the cost of dealing with the race problem to those, like herself who can least afford it, while they get cheap moral thrills. She understood that students might be ignorant but what about the professors (she still has a good deal of respect for "learned" men) and what about politicians like Mayor Lindsay? Surely they knew. I have some ideas on the subject, but I could not explain my theories to her. They rest on assumptions which are completely outside her experience. I mumbled some reply. She said that she thought many of those professors and politicians must really be "very wicked men," even though they are always telling everyone how moral they are. At times, I am inclined to agree with her.

NOTES

1. The most ardent white student supporters of a 10 percent or larger "minimum" for black students in the elite college at which I teach are students who are already here and who, in any event, would not be affected were a

quota established, because of their financial resources and very high S.A.T's. I have suggested to some of them that they might do a service to everyone by transferring to a state university and asking their parents to contribute the money saved to scholarships for black students. If they did so, they would be placing themselves in a position somewhat comparable to white students who will not be able to come to this school because of a lack of finances or because their scores are somewhat lower (although often higher than those of the black students admitted). Not one of the students to whom I have spoken has seriously considered the suggestion. Of course, their sacrifice would be only roughly comparable to the one they are asking others to make. Given their backgrounds they have far less to lose than those white students who will be excluded.

AN OPEN LETTER TO MY SISTER, MISS ANGELA DAVIS
James Baldwin

The insights of James Baldwin stirred a nation when his *Letter from a Region in My Mind* was published a decade ago. In that "letter" Baldwin tried to explain why things were as they were, what he thought needed to be done, and what might happen if they were not. Presaging the future, he wrote of "the fire next time."

And we came to see the flames.

Baldwin has again taken to letter writing. This time it is addressed to Angela Davis, a symbol to Baldwin and many blacks (and many whites, too) of strident rebellion. Says Brother James of his "sister" who is standing trial for murder and conspiracy, "If they take you in the morning, they will be coming for us that night."

One wonders how prophetic he remains.

November 19, 1970

Dear Sister:

One might have hoped that, by this hour, the very sight of chains on black flesh, or the very sight of chains, would be so intolerable a sight for the American people, and so unbearable a memory, that they would themselves spontaneously rise up and strike off the manacles. But, no, they appear to glory in their chains; now, more than ever, they appear to measure their safety in chains and corpses. And so, *Newsweek*, civilized defender of the indefensible, attempts to drown you in a sea of crocodile tears ("it remained to be seen what sort of personal liberation she had achieved") and puts you on its cover, chained.

You look exceedingly alone—as alone, say, as the Jewish housewife in the boxcar headed for Dachau, or as any one of our ancestors, chained together in the name of Jesus, headed for a Christian land.

Well. Since we live in an age in which silence is not only criminal but suicidal, I have been making as much noise as I can, here in Europe, on radio and television—in fact, have just returned from a land, Germany, which was made notorious by a silent majority not so very long ago. I was asked to speak on the case of Miss Angela Davis, and did so. Very probably an exercise in futility, but one must let no opportunity slide.

I am something like twenty years older than you, of that generation, therefore, of which George Jackson ventures that "there are no healthy brothers—*none at all*." I am in no way equipped to dispute this speculation (not, anyway, without descending into what, at the moment, would be irrelevant subtleties) for I know too well what he means. My own state of health is certainly precarious enough. In considering you, and Huey, and George and (especially) Jonathan Jackson, I began to apprehend what you may have had in mind when you spoke of the uses to which we could put the experience of the slave. What has happened, it seems to me, and to put it far too simply, is that a whole new generation of people have assessed and absorbed their history, and, in that tremendous action, have freed themselves of it and will never be victims again. This may seem an odd, indefensibly impertinent and insensitive thing to say to a sister in prison, battling for her life—for all our lives. Yet, I dare to say, for I think that you will perhaps not misunderstand me, and I do not say it, after all, from the position of a spectator.

I am trying to suggest that you—for example—do not appear to be your father's daughter in the same way that I am my father's son. At bottom, my father's expectations and mine were the same, the expectations of his generation and mine were the same; and neither the immense difference in our ages nor the move from the South to the North could alter these expectations or make our lives more viable. For, in fact, to use the brutal parlance of that hour, the interior language of that despair, he was just a nigger—a nigger laborer preacher, and so was I. I jumped the track but that's of no more importance here, in itself, than the fact that *some* poor Spaniards become rich bull fighters, or that *some* poor black boys become rich—boxers, for example. That's rarely, if ever, afforded the people more than a great emotional catharsis, though I don't mean to be condescending about that, either. But when Cassius Clay became Muhammed Ali and refused to put on that uniform (and sacrificed all that money!) a very different impact was made on the people and a very different kind of instruction had begun.

The American triumph—in which the American tragedy has always been implicit—was to make black people despise themselves. When I was little I despised myself, I did not know any better. And this meant, albeit unconsciously, or against my will, or in great pain, that I also despised my father. *And* my mother. *And* my brothers. *And* my sisters. Black people were killing each other every Saturday night out on Lenox Avenue, when I was growing up; and no one explained to them, or to me, that it was *intended* that they should; that they were penned where they were like animals, in order that they should consider themselves no better than animals. Everything supported this sense of reality, nothing denied it: and so one was ready, when it came time to go to work, to be treated as a slave. So one was ready, when human terrors came, to bow before a white God and beg Jesus for salvation—this same white God who was unable to raise a finger to do so little as to help you pay your rent, unable to be awakened in time to help you save your child!

There is always, of course, more to any picture than can speedily be perceived and in all of this—groaning and moaning, watching, calculating, clowning, surviving, and outwitting, some tremendous strength was nevertheless being forged, which is part of our legacy today. But that particular aspect of our journey now begins to be behind us. The secret is out: we are men!

But the blunt, open articulation of this secret has frightened the nation to death. I wish I could say, "to life," but that is much to demand of a disparate collection of displaced people still cowering in their wagon trains and singing "Onward Christian Soldiers." The nation, *if* America is a nation, is not in the least prepared for this day. It is a day which the Americans never expected or desired to see, however piously they may declare their belief in "progress and democracy." These words, now, on American lips, have become a kind of universal obscenity: for this most unhappy people, strong believers in arithmetic, never expected to be confronted with the algebra of their history.

One way of gauging a nation's health, or of discerning what it really considers to be its interests—or to what extent it can be considered as a nation as distinguished from a coalition of special interests—is to examine those people it elects to represent or protect it. One glance at the American leaders (or figure-heads) conveys that America is on the edge of absolute chaos, and also suggests the future to which American interests, if not the bulk of the American people, appear willing to consign the blacks. (Indeed, one look at our past conveys that.) It is clear that for the bulk of our (nominal) countrymen, we are all expendable. And Messrs. Nixon, Agnew, Mitchell, and Hoover, to say nothing, of course, of the *Kings' Row* basket case, the winning Ronnie Reagan, will not hesitate for an instant to carry out what they insist is the will of the people.

But what, in America, is the will of the people? And who, for the above-named, *are* the people? The people, whoever they may be, know as much about the forces which have placed the above-named gentlemen in power as they do about the forces responsible for the slaughter in Vietnam. The will of the people, in America, has always been at the mercy of an ignorance not merely phenomenal, but sacred, and sacredly cultivated: the better to be used by a carnivorous economy which democratically slaughters and victimizes whites and blacks alike. But most white Americans do not dare admit this (though they suspect it) and this fact contains mortal danger for the blacks and tragedy for the nation.

Or, to put it another way, as long as white Americans take refuge in their whiteness—for so long as they are unable to walk out of this most monstrous of traps—they will allow millions of people to be slaughtered in their name, and will be manipulated into and surrender themselves to what they will think of—and justify—as a racial war. They will never, so long as their whiteness puts so sinister a distance between themselves and their own experience and the experience of others, feel themselves sufficiently human, *sufficiently worthwhile,* to become responsible for themselves, their leaders, their country, their children, or their fate. They will perish (as we once put it in our black church) in their sins—that is, in their delusions. And this is happening, needless to say, already, all around us.

Only a handful of the millions of people in this vast place are aware that the fate intended for you, Sister Angela, and for George Jackson, and for the numberless prisoners in our concentration camps—for that is what they are—is a fate which is about to engulf them, too. White lives, for the forces which rule in this country, are no more sacred than black ones, as many and many a student is discovering, as the white American corpses in Vietnam prove. If the American people are unable to contend with their elected leaders for the redemption of their own honor and the lives of their own children, we, the blacks, the most rejected of the Western children, can expect very little help at their hands: which, after all, is nothing new. What the Americans do not realize is that a war between brothers, in the same cities, on the same soil, is not a *racial* war but a *civil* war. But the American delusion is not only that their brothers all are white but that the whites are all their brothers.

So be it. We cannot awaken this sleeper, and God knows we have tried. We must do what we can do, and fortify and save each other—*we* are not drowning in an apathetic self-contempt, we *do* feel ourselves sufficiently worthwhile to contend even with inexorable forces in order to change our fate and the fate of our children and the condition of the world! We know that a man is not a thing and is not to be placed at the mercy of things. We know that air and water belong to all mankind and not merely to industrialists. We know that a baby does not come into the world merely to be the instrument of someone else's profit. We know that democracy does not mean the coercion of all into a deadly—and, finally, wicked—mediocrity but the liberty for all to aspire to the best that is in him, or that has ever been.

We know that we, the blacks, and not only we, the blacks, have been, and are, the victims of a system whose only fuel is greed, whose only god is profit. We know that the fruits of this system have been ignorance, despair, and death, and we know that the system is doomed because the world can no longer afford it—if, indeed, it ever could have. And we know that, for the perpetuation of this system, we have all been mercilessly brutalized, and have been told nothing but lies, lies about ourselves and our kinsmen and our past, and about love, life, and death, so that both soul and body have been bound in hell.

The enormous revolution in black consciousness which has occurred in your generation, my dear sister, means the beginning or the end of America. Some of us, white and black, know how great a price has already been paid to bring into existence a new consciousness, a new people, an unprecedented nation. If we know and do nothing, we are worse than the murderers hired in our name.

If we know, then we must fight for your life as though it were our own —which it is—and render impassable with our bodies the corridor to the gas chamber. For, if they take you in the morning, they will be coming for us that night.

Therefore: peace.

Brother James